Great Naval Battles
of the Pacific War

Great Naval Battles of the Pacific War

The Official Admiralty Accounts: Midway, Coral Sea, Java Sea, Guadalcanal and Leyte Gulf

Compiled by John Grehan

FRONTLINE BOOKS

First published in Great Britain in 2022 by
Frontline Books
An imprint of
Pen & Sword Books Ltd
Yorkshire – Philadelphia

ISBN 978 1 39900 116 86

Typeset by Mac Style

Printed and bound by CPI Group (UK) Ltd, Croydon CR0 4YY

Pen & Sword Books Limited incorporates the imprints of Atlas,
Archaeology, Aviation, Discovery, Family History, Fiction, History,
Maritime, Military, Military Classics, Politics, Select, Transport,
True Crime, Air World, Frontline Publishing, Leo Cooper, Remember
When, Seaforth Publishing, The Praetorian Press, Wharncliffe
Local History, Wharncliffe Transport, Wharncliffe True Crime
and White Owl.

For a complete list of Pen & Sword titles please contact

PEN & SWORD BOOKS LIMITED
47 Church Street, Barnsley, South Yorkshire, S70 2AS, England
E-mail: enquiries@pen-and-sword.co.uk
Website: www.pen-and-sword.co.uk

Or

PEN AND SWORD BOOKS
1950 Lawrence Rd, Havertown, PA 19083, USA
E-mail: Uspen-and-sword@casematepublishers.com
Website: www.penandswordbooks.com

Contents

Note

The following narratives have been drawn exclusively from Naval Staff Histories Battle Summaries 23, 28, 40, 45 and 46. It has not been possible to reproduce all the diagrams found in those studies nor all the appendices, most of the latter being orders of battle which are freely available on the internet. Some of the references have also been omitted as they have no modern traceable equivalents. Readers will observe a degree of inconsistency across the five documents, indicating that they were written by different authors and at different dates. A plate section and index not with the original summaries have been added.

Part One

The Battle of the Coral Sea

Chapter I

The Strategic Situation in April 1942

1. Decision by Japan to expand the Defensive Perimeter

The advance of the Japanese to the South and East after the attack on Pearl Harbor on 7 December 1941 was so rapid that in the space of four months they practically completed phase one of the basic plan for the greater East Asia war, namely the occupation of the Philippines, Guam, Hong Kong, Burma, and the rich British and Dutch lands in the South, possession of which was to render Japan self-sufficient.

By the middle of April 1942, a point had been reached at which phase two, the consolidation and strengthening of a defensive perimeter for the southern resources area and the Japanese mainland should have been put into effect. As originally conceived this perimeter consisted of the Kuriles, Wake Island, the Marshall Islands, Bismarcks, Timor, Java, Sumatra, Malaya and Burma.

The unexpected ease with which the first part of the war plan had been carried out caused the Japanese to underestimate the present strength of the United States in the Pacific, just as, when deciding upon war, they had overestimated their own war making capacity and under-estimated the huge Allied potential. Many of the leaders were persuaded that advantage should be taken of the present situation to embark on further expansion. The argument received reinforcement on 18 April 1942 when US Army bombers, flown from the aircraft carrier *Hornet*, raided Tokyo. Though no more than a token raid, it was used as an argument to point the need for additional bases to the East; and it was eventually decided that the defensive perimeter should be moved outward to include the western Aleutians, Midway, Samoa, Fiji, New Caledonia, and Port Moresby in south-eastern New Guinea.

The decision proved an irretrievable mistake. The strategic sphere was already too large. Neither military strength, shipping, nor the Japanese military economy, were of a calibre capable of supporting further expansion; and the attempt used up resources which should have been employed in consolidating the already huge gains.

Vital areas were perforce left insufficiently organized for defence whilst operations were set in train for the capture of Port Moresby, Midway, and the Aleutians. The strategy that inspired these operations might be defensive, but it entailed a tactical offensive and resulted in a situation the opposite of that which it was intended to bring about; instead of strengthening the Japanese position, the attempt at expansion actually weakened it. Losses were incurred which could not be made good and consequently hampered future operations, and the eventual return to the original plan found the Japanese with insufficient strength remaining to carry it through successfully.

The first operation in the expansionist plan was the capture of Port Moresby to form a southern outpost in the Japanese defensive system. The Japanese were already established on the north-eastern shore of New Guinea. Establishment on the Gulf of Papua would deprive the Allies of a potential base within air range of the main Japanese base at Rabaul (New Britain) and would place the Japanese in a position to dominate the entire island of New Guinea, and if they desired, to threaten northern Australia, though even in their present mood of inflated morale, they apparently did not contemplate this latter eventuality.

Whilst en route to Port Moresby the expedition was to seize Tulagi in Florida Island, South Solomons, and establish a seaplane base at Tulagi, which was lightly held by Australian forces, and was a strategically important point from which the main line of communications from the USA to Australia and New Zealand could be attacked. It had one of the best harbours in the South Solomons.

2. Japanese Naval Forces

The great conquests already made by the Japanese found them with their naval military and air strength unimpaired, and that of the Allies severely reduced. In the air and on the ground the Japanese losses were insignificant; shipping sunk to date amounted to less than 300,000 tons; and losses of major vessels were no more than five destroyers being sunk.

On the other hand, the attempt of the Allies to withstand the Japanese advance in Malaya and the Netherlands East Indies had resulted in the piecemeal destruction of the Dutch and British forces in the south-west Pacific and the withdrawal of the United States Asiatic Fleet to Australian and South Pacific bases, whilst even in the more distant waters of the Indian Ocean the British Eastern Fleet had been compelled to withdraw from the Ceylon area, thus enabling the Japanese to proceed with their war plan in the Pacific unhampered by a vulnerable western flank.

A feature of the Japanese operations, which was to set the pattern for the Pacific, was the spearhead employment of carrier-borne aircraft with battleship and cruiser support. Japanese carrier-borne aircraft had caused the most important Allied losses of warships to date and had also sunk thousands of tons of auxiliaries and merchant ships and destroyed hundreds of Allied aircraft, as well as docks, hangars and base facilities, all with complete immunity to the carrier striking force; in fact, it had seldom been sighted. The Battle of the Coral Sea was the first occasion on which it was effectively attacked.

The Japanese Carriers Striking Force which wrought this havoc was made up from the First Air Fleet (six fleet carriers, four light carriers) a cruiser squadron (two cruisers), and screen. Behind it stood the main body of the Second Fleet, two battleships, four heavy cruisers and destroyers, which supported the lighter forces – cruisers, light destroyers, seaplane carriers, destroyers and ancillary vessels – engaged in carrying out the operations in the Philippines, Malaya and the Netherlands East Indies. This powerful striking force of fast battleships, aircraft carriers and several cruisers and destroyers returned to Japanese home waters from operating across a third of the globe, from Hawaii to Ceylon, on 18 April, the day of the US air raid on Tokyo,[1] and a squadron was formed without delay for the attack on Port Moresby, known as the MO Operation.

The forces for the Port Moresby expedition were under the command of Vice Admiral S. Inouye, who flew his flag on board the light cruiser *Kashima* at Rabaul (New Britain). Only one of the three squadrons of the carrier force was available to operate in general support of the expedition, so heavy had been the drain of war on the air groups. This was Carrier Squadron 5, consisting of the *Zuikaku*, flagship of Rear Admiral K. Hara, and the *Shokaku*. Their aircraft complement comprised fighters, bombers and torpedo aircraft to the number of 63 and 72 respectively. The remainder of the 6th Squadron, as the supporting force was termed, consisted of the 5th Cruiser Squadron (the 8-inch cruisers *Myoko*, *Haguro* and *Ashigara*) under Vice Admiral T. Takagi, two destroyer divisions (six destroyers in all), a minelayer, the seaplane carrier *Kiyokawa Maru* and an oiler. Had the expedition gone according to plan, the force would subsequently have carried out an attack on Townsville, in Queensland, where the Japanese had information that there were American and Australian ships and that aircraft were being delivered. The presence and near composition of this force in the area was known to the Americans.[2]

The Occupation Force for Port Moresby and Tulagi consisted of two cruiser squadrons, the 6th with four 8-inch cruisers and the 18th consisting

1. This is the Doolittle Raid, see John Grehan & Alexander Nicoll, *The Doolittle Raid, The First Air Attacks Against Japan April 1942* (Air World Books, Barnsley, 2020).
2. British and US cryptographers had been able to read a percentage of encrypted Japanese communications, which included the Japanese Navy's JN-25 scheme, by 1941.

of two light cruisers, the *Shoho* (one of the two light carriers of the 4th Carrier Squadron) carrying 12 fighters and 9–12 torpedo aircraft, and a destroyer; the 6th Destroyer Flotilla (light cruiser and six destroyers); an auxiliary seaplane tender and a minelayer. Five transports carried the troops.[3] The task of the *Shoho* and her supporting cruisers was purely defensive, to guard the transports in the Occupation Force against submarine air and attack.

The organization also included six submarines of the 8th Flotilla. The Battle of the Coral Sea developed whilst these submarines were off the east coast of Australia. Tey concentrated south of the Solomon Islands to attack the Allied task force, but although there appeared to be close co-ordination between the Japanese air reconnaissance and the submarines, the latter obtained no results.

The Occupation Force and its escort sailed from Rabaul on 30 April, part of the escort being provided from Truk.[4]

At Truk the Japanese had a naval base which, since the Caroline Islands were under their mandate, they had been enabled to develop in peace time, directly contrary though this was to the provisions of the Washington Conference of 1922. Their main base for operations in the Solomons, Bismarcks, and New Guinea was Simpson Harbour (Rabaul) in New Britain, though there were numerous anchorages in the area which could be used by naval ships, e.g. Gasmata (New Britain); Kavieng (New Ireland); Salamoa and Lae (New Guinea); Wantom, Ulu, and Dyaul Islands (Northern Bismarcks). Manus Island in the Admiralty Islands was occupied by the Japanese on 4 April 1942, but the Allies had no information whether they were using the great Sea Eagle Harbour. For the most part, however, naval units remained at sea at this date.

3. Japanese Air Forces

In addition to their carrier-based aircraft, the Japanese had in the Bismarcks a naval air flotilla, the 25th, shore-based at Rabaul, and estimated by the Allies to number 12 fighters, 20 bombers, 17 patrol aircraft, and four small seaplanes, total 53. American intelligence indicated that air reinforcements to Rabaul from the Marianas and Marshall Islands were being hastened. The airfield at Kavieng, in the adjacent island of New Ireland, was known to be used by enemy bombers. The only airfield known to be used by the enemy in New Guinea was Lae, at the head of Huon Gulf, where it was estimated

---

3. The 144th Infantry Regiment, 1 Battalion Mountain Artillery, with attached cavalry, engineer, transport and anti-aircraft companies, under the command of Major General Horii.
4. Truk Lagoon was the Empire of Japan's main base in the South Pacific theatre at this stage of the war.

that 15 heavy bombers, 30 fighters and four patrol aircraft were based. Patrol seaplanes used Salamua on Huon Gulf, and were also based at Shortland Island, south of Bougainville in the Solomons, long range aircraft of this type being employed by the Japanese for reconnaissance, thus relieving the carriers of this task. There were no other land-based naval air forces nearer than Kendari in the Celebes, where the 23rd Air Flotilla was established in February 1942; and no Army air forces nearer than the Philippines (Fifth Air Army) and Malaya-Burma (Third Air Army).

4. Allied Forces

The concentration of Japanese ships near Truk and Palau (West Caroline Is.) at the end of April was reported by Allied intelligence in sufficient time for the Americans to assemble a strong force to oppose the expected move through the Solomons. Admiral C. W. Nimitz, Commander-in-Chief, US Pacific Fleet, had operating under him in the central and south Pacific areas three American task forces, two of them, Nos. 17 and 11, each containing one fleet carrier and the third, No. 16, two carriers. Task Force 17 (Rear-Adm. F. J. Fletcher) consisted of the carrier *Yorktown* (flag), the three 8-inch cruisers *Astoria*, *Portland* and *Chester*, and six destroyers. The ships had been at sea continuously since leaving Pearl Harbor on 14 February, operating against Wake, Marcus and Lae-Salamua, and were returning to the Coral Sea after a week spent in maintenance and replenishment at Tongatabu in the Tonga Islands. Task Force 11, consisting of the carrier *Lexington*, the 8-inch cruisers *Minneapolis* and *New Orleans*, and seven destroyers, under Rear-Admiral A.W. Fitch, had proceeded to Pearl Harbor after the raid on Lae-Salamua on 10 March, and sailed from there on 16 April for Christmas Island. The third carrier force, Task Force 16, which included the two carriers *Enterprise* and *Hornet*, did not return to Pearl Harbor until 25 April after the air raid on Tokyo. The Australian Squadron, including the 8-inch cruiser *Australia*, which had taken part in the Lae-Salamua operation, and the light cruiser *Hobart*, under the British Rear-Admiral J.G. Crace, was at Sidney, Australia.

The aircraft complement of the US carriers was some ten less than that of the Japanese, the difference being accounted for by the greater number of fighters, 27 against an average of 17, borne aboard the Japanese carriers. Both the Japanese fighters and torpedo aircraft were obsolescent, and their low performance reduced the effectiveness of their attacks. The Commander-in-Chief US Pacific Fleet was not satisfied with the effectiveness of the US bombs and torpedoes; the speed of the latter was so low that the Japanese stated they could turn and run from them.

There were at this date the following Allied advanced bases in the area, outside Australia:

(a) Tongatabu in the Friendly Is., a limited monarchy under British protection, was in process of development as an intermediate operating base. The anchorage could accommodate 12 deep draft and 36 medium and light draft vessels but pending the installation of minefields it was insecure. The shore defences were not strong but were being increased. There was an airfield.

(b) Numea in New Caledonia (French) had an excellent anchorage for ships of any draft, but until the defences were completed it was not considered a secure anchorage for carriers.

(c) Efate in the New Hebrides, an Anglo-French condominium, was being organized as a defended base. There was known to be a landing field, but the report on its condition and suitability was still awaited.

(d) Suva and Nandi in Fiji, and Tutuila, a US Protectorate, south-east of Samoa, were considered suitable for ships of any draft and their entrances were mined and their defences well organized. They were considered secure anchorages for other than carriers.

The Allied task forces operated in strategical co-ordination with aircraft of the South-west Pacific area, at Port Moresby and at Tulagi, Florida Island (Solomon Is.) until evacuation of the latter by the Australian forces on 1 May, two days before the Japanese began to move into the island. At Numea in New Caledonia there were fleet patrol aircraft and army pursuit squadrons.

These shore-based air forces obtained information of the enemy which was of much value and their almost daily attacks on shipping were of cumulative assistance, but they did not cooperate tactically, for this problem had not at that date been solved. Numbers of aircraft were inadequate, and the Australian bases were remote. Difficulties of communication were being overcome but there was still much to be done in providing for the readiness and training of shore-based aircraft to co-ordinate their operations tactically with fleet units to relieve carrier-based aircraft of long range reconnaissance as did the Japanese, and to be ready to attack, with full groups, any targets located.

Chapter II

The Action at Tulagi, 4 May 1942

5. Allied Forces concentrate, 1–4 May

US intelligence reports indicated that a Japanese airborne attack on Port Moresby might occur in the first week of May, and a concentration of the available Allied forces in the Coral Sea, Task Forces 17, 11, 16 and the Australian Squadron to oppose it, was accordingly ordered. Task Force 11 had left Pearl Harbor on 16 April for Christmas Island; it was now diverted to the Coral Sea, where the Australian Squadron was also to join up. Task Force 16 at Pearl Harbor was unable, in the event, to arrive before battle was joined.

Task Forces 17 and 11 made rendezvous as arranged at 0545 on 1 May in latitude 16° 16′ S., 162° 20′ E., some 300 miles west of the New Hebrides. Two of the three oilers used for servicing the fleet, the *Neosho* and *Tippecanoe*, were in the area; Rear-Admiral Fletcher directed Rear-Admiral Fitch to meet the *Tippecanoe* with her escort the *Chicago* and *Perkins* in latitude 16° 00′ S., longitude 161° 43′ E and fuel, steering to re-join Task Force 17 next morning, the intention being to retain the *Neosho* as a reserve and to send the *Tippecanoe* back empty to Efate (New Hebrides). Task Force 17 completed fuelling from the *Neosho* on 2 May, but Rear-Admiral Fitch reported that he did not expect to finish until noon on 4th. With enemy action now reported imminent, Commander Task Force 17 could not contemplate remaining so far to the south-eastward; he set course to the north-westward, directing Rear-Admiral Fitch to fuel his destroyers, if practicable, at night, on the same course and re-join Task Force 17 at daylight on 4 May in latitude 15° 00′ S., longitude 157° 00′ E., the position in which Rear-Admiral Crace had been directed to rendezvous with the *Australia* and *Hobart* from Australia.

At 1515 on the 2nd, shortly before the two task forces separated, one of the *Yorktown*'s reconnaissance aircraft sighted a submarine on the surface in latitude 16° 04′ S., longitude 162° 18′ E., 32 miles to the northward, but in spite of being closely depth charged by three aircraft sent out to attack it, the enemy escaped. The Americans thought that they had been sighted and that wireless signals intercepted subsequently pointed to the probability of their position having been reported, but actually this was not so.

Rear-Admiral Fletcher continued to the north-westward during the night 2nd–3rd May and topped up his destroyers from the *Neosho* next day; it was his consistent practice to top up his light craft from tankers, cruisers or carriers whenever they could take 70 tons. He intended to fuel the remainder of his ships after effecting concentration next day with Task Forces 11 and 44. The latter consisted of the Australian Squadron reinforced by the cruiser *Chicago* and two US destroyers. Before this could take place, however, news came in which completely altered the situation.

6. Japanese occupy Tulagi, 2 May

On 30 April the Japanese occupation force with its escort of six cruisers, the light carrier *Shoho*, and a screen of destroyers and submarines, sailed from Rabaul to the southward. Part of the expedition was sighted by aircraft of South-west Pacific Forces at 1700 on 2 May off the southern end of Santa Isabel Island, possibly heading for Tulagi in Florida Island. This strategically important point in the South Solomons, from which the main line of communications from the USA to Australia and New Zealand could be attacked, had been evacuated by the Australians on 1 May. Two transports were reported unloading troops into barges in the harbour, though no indication was given of the time at which the occupation commenced.

The intelligence reached Commander Task Force 17 at 1900 on the 3rd and Rear-Admiral Fletcher at once headed for Tulagi (2000) and worked up to 27 knots to reach a position for an air strike at daylight. With his flagship, the *Yorktown*, were the heavy cruisers *Astoria, Chester, Portland* and *Chicago* and the destroyers *Hammann, Anderson, Perkins, Walke, Morris,* and *Sims.* To wait for the *Lexington* and Task Force 11 might have jeopardized the success of the operation; he detached the *Neosho*, with the destroyer *Russell* as escort, with orders to proceed to the rendezvous in latitude 15° 00′ S., 157° 00′ E., arranged for 4 May, and inform all ships that a new rendezvous would be made in latitude 15° 00′ S., 160° 00′ E.

7. First air strike at Tulagi, 0815 4 May

By 0631 on the 4th Task Force 17 had reached a suitable position for launching strikes, in latitude 11° 18′ S., longitude 158° 49′ E., about 100 miles south-west of Guadalcanal Island. A wide zone of bad flying weather covered Guadalcanal and extended southward for a distance of 70 miles. Visibility was limited by showers from cumulo-nimbus and strato-cumulus clouds in the morning, which gave way to scattered squalls in the afternoon. In the launching area, the wind gusts varied in force from 17 to 35 knots. At Tulagi harbour, however, conditions were somewhat better, with broken to scattered cumulus at 3,000 feet and winds between 10 and 15 knots from the south-east.

Launching now began of a combat air patrol of six fighters and an attack group made up of 12 torpedo aircraft under Lieut.-Commander J. Taylor, 13 reconnaissance aircraft led by Lieut.-Commander W. O. Burch, and 15 bombers under Lieut. W.C. Short. Torpedoes were set to 10 feet, and both the reconnaissance aircraft and the bombers were armed with 1,000-pound bombs. Similar armament was used in all attacks that day. A combat air patrol of six fighters was kept overhead throughout 4 May, and the cruisers maintained inner air patrol. Task Force 17 remained south of Guadalcanal Island, the general course steered during the action being easterly.

Torpedo, reconnaissance and bomber aircraft respectively proceeded independently, with instructions to co-ordinate their attacks. Co-ordination was not, however, achieved. They found Tulagi off guard. In the inner harbour and adjacent Gavutu Harbour they reported there were two large transports or cargo ships of 8,000 tons, one 5,000-ton cargo ship, four gunboats, two destroyers, a light cruiser (the *Okinoshima*, an old ship used as a minelayer), the seaplane carrier *Kiyokawa Maru*, as well as a number of small patrol boats and launches, and five seaplanes moored off Makambo Island where the Japanese had established a seaplane base for the operation against Port Moresby. There was no sign of the carrier *Shoho* or the powerful cruiser escort of the transports, whilst the carriers *Zuikaku* and *Shokaku* with the Moresby Task Force, covering the operation, were still far away to the northward of Tulagi.

The scouts arrived first and commenced their attacks at 0815, taking as their target the *Okinoshima* and two destroyers which were moored together. Altitude of bomb release was 2,500 feet, angle of dive 70 degrees. Heavy but ineffective AA fire was encountered from the ships in harbour and from the shore. Four bomb hits were claimed. At 0931 the first of the scouts returned to the *Yorktown* and commenced landing. Re-arming began at once.

The torpedo aircraft attacked five minutes after the scouts, seven of the 12 attacking the same target, though one aircraft failed to release its torpedo. Three hits were reported. Three aircraft attacked a large cargo ship but made no hits. The remaining two each reported making a hit on another cargo ship. All torpedo releases were made individually from a reported altitude of about 50 feet, at ranges of 400–500 yards.

The 15 bombers attacked in three divisions of five aircraft each, coming at 0830. Only one certain hit was reported on the seaplane carrier. All dives were made downwind from about 10,000–11,000 feet, dive angle 70 degrees, altitude of release 2,500 feet.

8. Second air strike at Tulagi, 1115 4 May

By 1036 all aircraft were back on board the *Yorktown* and the serviceable machines had been rearmed and refuelled and a second group was despatched to attack. This group comprised 14 bombers, 13 reconnaissance and 11 torpedo aircraft, the squadrons proceeding independently as before. The bombers attacked first. About five miles east-north-east of Savo Island they sighted what were taken for three gunboats but were probably landing barges, making the best of their way from Tulagi, for every ship that could steam was now getting out of harbour. The 14 bombers attacked (1115) in three sections of 5, 5, and 4, each section taking one landing barge, two of which they blew to pieces with direct hits. The third escaped for the moment by manoeuvring but was shortly afterwards reduced to a sinking condition by strafing and was later seen beached.

The reconnaissance aircraft covered the area to the west and north-west of Florida Island, sighting the seaplane carrier and a destroyer steering north-westward between Tulagi and Savo Island, and a cargo ship standing out of Tulagi Harbour. The first of these was attacked (1210), two hits being claimed. The torpedo aircraft were divided tactically into two divisions, both of which attacked the same target, at 1245. Six of them made their releases from ranges of 2,000 to 3,000 yards, target angle from about 10 degrees on the starboard bow to broad on the port bow, the remainder attacking five minutes later, from 1,000 to 1,500 yards range, target angle being abaft the beam. The seaplane carrier increased speed from 10 to 25 knots on being attacked and manoeuvred under full helm. None of the 11 torpedoes hit, the length of range at which they were released enabling the seaplane carrier to avoid them.

9. Third air strike launched at Tulagi, 1310 4 May

Before sending off the third air strike to Tulagi, the *Yorktown* at 1310 launched four fighters to destroy enemy seaplanes which had attacked bombers and reconnaissance aircraft engaged in the second strike. Three of the *Kiyokawa Maru*'s fighters were encountered and shot down, and a destroyer heading away from Tulagi was strafed. Two of the American fighters became lost and were forced to land on the south coast of Guadalcanal Island, while the destroyer *Hammann* with difficulty rescued the pilots that night. All attempts to set fire to the two aircraft failed and the Americans had to be content with destroying papers and secret equipment.

The third and last group of aircraft, 12 reconnaissance and nine bombers, was launched at 1400. Apart from launches, there was only one cargo ship in

Tulagi harbour. This was attacked by dive bombing at 1500; it put up light AA fire and got under way. One bomb hit was reported by the reconnaissance aircraft, which also reported sinking several launches and the beached landing barge after the earlier attack. The nine bombers attacked at 1515 in two divisions, one from the westward and the other from the southward, the seaplane carrier that had been the target of previous attacks, which they located by following up an oil streak left by a destroyer in its company. Both ships increased speed on sighting the aircraft, and the seaplane carrier manoeuvred to avoid bombs. No hits were made. By 1632 the last aircraft had landed aboard the *Yorktown*.

10. Results of the operation

Ammunition expenditure in the attack at Tulagi was high compared with results achieved; more particularly, since there was practically no air opposition and very little anti-aircraft fire. In the light of subsequent knowledge, the results were even smaller than was believed at the time.

Damage to the enemy:

	Estimated	Actual
Sunk:	2 destroyers	1 destroyer (*Kikuzuki*)
	1 cargo ship	4 landing barges
	4 gunboats	
	Several small barges	
Damaged:	1 seaplane carrier	1 minelayer (*Okinoshima*)
	1 cargo ship	1 destroyer (*Yuzuki*)[1]

Total expenditure was 22 torpedoes; 76 1,000-lb. bombs; 82,665 rounds of machine gun ammunition. Five Japanese single-float seaplanes operating from the *Kiyokawa Maru* were shot down. The Americans lost three aircraft; in addition to the two fighters lost on Guadalcanal, one torpedo aircraft was forced to land in the sea and was lost, the crew being recovered later.

Admiral C. W. Nimitz, C-in-C US Pacific Fleet, cited the performance as an example of the manner in which proficiency drops off in wartime and of the necessity for target practices at every opportunity. The first strike, in which the reconnaissance aircraft commenced their dives at 19,000 feet and the bombers from 10,000–11,000 feet, was adversely affected by fogging of sights and windshields, to such an extent that the sights could not be used, a condition which did not occur in dives commenced at lower altitudes.

---

1. Personnel casualties only, from strafing.

Chapter III

The Action off Misima and Japanese Air Attacks, 7 May

11. Allied forces reorganized, 6 May

After landing-on the *Yorktown*'s aircraft Rear-Admiral Fletcher ran to the southward during the night 4–5 May for the rendezvous previously arranged with Task Force 11 and the Australian Squadron in 15° S., 160° E. The destroyer *Perkins* was left behind to search for the crew of the lost torpedo aircraft, and the *Hammann* recovered the pilots from the two fighters forced to land on Guadalcanal: both destroyers re-joined on the morning of the 5th.

Rear-Admiral Fitch (Task Force 11) was making for the rendezvous from the southward on an almost opposite course. Rear-Adm. Crace was bringing the Australian Squadron from Sydney. At 0755 on the 5th the *Yorktown* launched four fighters to investigate radar contact on an aircraft bearing 252 degrees, distance 30 miles; they found an enemy four-engine flying boat which they shot down at 0820 in position 15 miles from the *Lexington* and 27 from the *Yorktown*. One of the latter's reconnaissance aircraft had reported an enemy submarine at 0738, bearing 285 degrees, distance 150 miles, course 105 degrees, and it was thought the aircraft was directing the submarine on to one of the US task forces. Three torpedo aircraft searched for the submarine without success.

Task Forces 17, 11 and 44 (the Australian Squadron plus the *Chicago* and two destroyers) made rendezvous at 0846 on the 5th. Task Force 17 fuelled from the *Neosho* on that and the following day and combined with Task Forces 11 and 22 as Task Force 17 and at 0700 on the 6th the operation orders issued by Rear-Admiral Fletcher at sea on 1 May were put into effect. The role of the combined task force was to 'destroy enemy ships, shipping and aircraft at favourable opportunities in order to assist in checking further advance by enemy in the New Guinea-Solomon area'.

Task Force 17 was organized into five groups. An attack group of five cruisers and seven destroyers under Rear-Admiral T. C. Kinkaid, had the dual role of operating against the Japanese forces reported advancing southward in the New Guinea-Solomons area and defending the carriers against air and submarine attack whilst in company. A support group under Rear-Admiral Crace, consisting of Task Force 44, also had a dual role of defending the carriers against air, surface and submarine attack and supporting or operating tactically with the attack group. Rear Adm. Fitch in the *Lexington* commanded the Air Group; two destroyers were assigned to the fuelling group, and Rear-Admiral Fletcher had also under his orders a search group consisting of the seaplane tender *Tangier* with 12 patrol aircraft which operated from Numea in New Caledonia.

12. Japanese movements, 4–6 May

The orders specified that the force was to operate generally in the Coral Sea about 700 miles south of Rabaul (i.e., outside the range of Japanese shore-based reconnaissance aircraft) until word was received of an enemy advance, the anticipated date of which was given by the Commander-in-Chief, Pacific Fleet, as 7 or 8 May. On the 5th reports began to come in from the C-in-C Pacific Fleet and the Commander South-west Pacific Area of the sighting of numerous enemy ships in the New Guinea-New Britain Solomon Islands area. It was fairly definitely established that three aircraft carriers were amongst them, but although almost every type of ship was reported, including (incorrectly) a battleship, the forces were scattered and there seemed to be no common direction of movement.

Actually, the Japanese occupation force was engaged on the 4–5 May in effecting its final rendezvous in the Shortland Islands, in the north-west part of the Solomons, in preparation for the advance on Port Moresby. On the morning of the 6th, it was sighted and attacked by a division of some five US long-range bombers (B.17s), about 150 miles south-west of Buin, but no hits or damage occurred. The course of the enemy indicated that the invasion fleet would pass through the Jomard Passage, in the Louisiade Archipelago, the south-eastward prolongation of New Guinea, with Port Moresby as its probable objective, and establish a base in the Deboyne Islands in the Louisiades.

By the morning of 6 May, however, the Japanese came to the conclusion that the Allied air reconnaissance had been sufficiently thorough to discover their intentions. When, therefore, on this same morning one of their reconnaissance aircraft sighted the Allied task force, the Occupation Force transports were ordered to retire towards Rabaul and orders went out for the escorting naval units to concentrate with the support force for attack on the Allied force. The order to retire seems to have been rescinded during the afternoon, and the transports steered once more for the Jomard Passage.

13. Support Group detached, 0530 7 May

During the forenoon of 6 May the wind and sea had made it necessary to fuel Task Force 17 on a south-easterly course; at 1130, however, course was altered to the north-westward in order to reach a position for a strike on the invasion fleet at daylight on the 7th. Fuelling was discontinued and the *Neosho* was detached to the southward with the destroyer *Sims* as escort, at 1725 on the 6th.

Task Force 17 continued north-westward at 20 knots during the night, and at 0530 on the 7th was in latitude 13° 25.5′ S., longitude 154° 48′ E. Rear-Admiral Fletcher now detached the support group (17.3), under Rear-Admiral Crace, reinforcing him with a third destroyer, the *Farragut*, to proceed ahead to attack the enemy transports and light cruisers which has been reported heading for the Jomard Passage during the night. Rear-Admiral Crace increased speed to 25 knots and steered for a position off the southern exit of the passage.

14. Enemy occupation force sighted off Misima, 0815

Meanwhile there had been no information of the movements of the Japanese carriers, the most important target for air attack, since the previous afternoon, when two of this type, correctly estimated by the Americans as the *Zuikaku* and *Shokaku* of the 5th Carrier Squadron, and therefore additional to the unidentified carrier reported with the Occupation Force, had been sighted near Bougainville Island. Morning air searches by the *Yorktown*'s reconnaissance aircraft were planned to cover two areas, namely the neighbourhood of Deboyne İsland and also to locate the 5th Carrier Squadron, which was expected to run southward from Bougainville and to be within striking distance on the morning of the 7th.

At 0619 the *Yorktown* launched a search group of 10 scout bombers to conduct a single plane search for a distance of 250 miles over a 120 degrees arc, on a median bearing of 025 degrees, limiting bearings 325 degrees and 085 degrees. One scout, having the sector with median 067 degrees, went out only some 150 to 165 miles and returned on account of bad weather, and it is probable that the *Zuihaku* and *Shokaku* were in this unsearched bad weather area to the east-north-eastward. At 0735 another scout made contact with two heavy cruisers in latitude 10° 40′ S, longitude 153° 15′ E., 25 miles cast of Misima Island, in the Louisiades; the enemy ships sighted and challenged him. Two other scouts each shot down one twin float torpedo bomber, one near Misima Island and one in latitude 11° 35′ S., latitude 156° 43′ E.

Two hours after launching, the first anxiously awaited report of the Japanese carriers came in. At 0815 a sighting report was received of two aircraft carriers and four heavy cruisers in latitude 10° 03′ S., longitude 152° 27′ E about 40 miles north of Misima Island, steering 140 degrees, speed 18 to 20 knots.

On receipt of this report, orders were given to launch the attack groups at the enemy carriers, which were estimated, not unnaturally, to be the *Zuihaku* and *Shokaku*. The *Lexington* began launching at about 0855 a group of 10 fighters, 28 scout bombers and 12 torpedo aircraft, retaining eight scout bombers at the ship for anti-torpedo aircraft patrol. Ten of the bombers were armed with one 500-lb and two 100-lb. bombs each, the remainder with 1,000-lb. bombs. The *Yorktown* launched, nearly an hour later, from 0944 to 1013, a total of 25 scout bombers, 10 torpedo aircraft, and five escort fighters;[1] the bombers carried 1,000-lb. bombs, and the depth setting of the torpedoes was 10 feet. The distance to the enemy was about 160 miles.

At 1022 a message was received in *Yorktown* from shore-based aircraft of the Australian Command, that a force consisting of an aircraft carrier (*Shoho*) 16 warships and 10[2] transports was in latitude 10° 34′ S., longitude 152° 26′ E., a few miles north of Misima Island, course 285 degrees. A few minutes later, at 1030, the *Yorktown*'s search group began to land, and it was discovered that, owing to a fault in the reporting mechanism, the report of two carriers at 0815 was in error; the pilot had sighted, and imagined he was reporting cruisers. The *Lexington* was informed (1123), and the attack group was re-directed to the enemy reported by shore-based aircraft an hour earlier, in latitude 10° 34′ S., longitude 152° 26′ E. There was little difference in the two positions. The message was apparently sent by voice transmission though the element of surprise does not seem to have been lost thereby, and no harm seems to have been done: on the contrary, some hours had been saved in sending off the strike, though it must have been a disappointment that the *Zuikaku* and *Shokaku* were still unlocated and that instead of two carriers the powerful attack group would have only one as its target.

15. Sinking of the Shoho

The *Lexington*'s group made contact with the *Shoho* about 1100. The Japanese Occupation Force was in an area of fine weather, with unlimited ceiling and

1. These are the figures given in the *Lexington*'s Report. The US Combat Narrative *The Battle of the Coral Sea*, p. 15, says that there were 10 SDBs (Douglas Dauntless Scout Bombers) armed with 1 × 500 and 2 × 100 bombs each, and 16 dive-bombers armed with 1,000lb bombs.
2. This appears to have been a case of mistaken identity since there were only six transports in the Occupation Force.

visibility 20 miles or more. The *Lexington's* more lightly armed bombers attacked at once. The attack apparently came as a complete surprise to the enemy. One or perhaps two hits were made by this first wave, causing a small fire and possibly damaging the *Shoho's* steering gear. This did not, however, prevent the enemy carrier from turning into the wind, directly a lull came, to launch her aircraft, 10 to 20 of which were seen on her flight deck. She had however chosen her moment for launching aircraft with bad judgment, for just as she was turning into the wind, about 1115, the *Lexington's* dive bombers (i.e. scout bombers, carrying 1,000-lb. bombs) and her 12 torpedo aircraft made a co-ordinated attack, followed almost simultaneously by the *Yorktown's* bombers. The target was a perfect one. The *Shoho* was steaming into the wind, making no attempt to manoeuvre. The four or five cruisers of her screen were on a 5,000 to 6,000-yard circle, a formation too loose to afford effective anti-aircraft gun support. The enemy fighters were drawn off by the *Lexington's* first wave, giving the *Yorktown's* aircraft a clear field. Dives were made from 18,000 feet, very steeply, bomb releases at about 2,500 feet.

The *Shoho* was completely overwhelmed by this mass attack. By the time the *Yorktown's* slow torpedo aircraft arrived and made their attack, the enemy carrier was listing to starboard and burning furiously. The torpedo aircraft, however, were unaware that the ship was already a wreck, for they had approached at less than 1,000 feet altitude, insufficient to enable the objective to be seen before deploying. The leader of the escort fighters for the torpedo aircraft, who was coaching the latter from a position above them, made an attempt to divert part of the group to another target, but was unsuccessful, for they were already in their approach. This was made from the starboard bow of the Japanese formation between the two leading cruisers whose fire the aircraft encountered, then circling out and launching their attack on the starboard beam of the carrier, making use of the smoke which almost completely shrouded her and releasing their torpedoes at very close range. The *Shoho* was only a light carrier, and no unarmoured ship could have hoped to stand up to this terrible bombardment.

Approximately three minutes after the attacks were completed the ship capsized and sank in lat. 10° 29' S., long. 152° 55' E., taking with her some 500 of her crew. None of the American air crews had been able to identify her.

There was no officer in tactical command at the scene to divert the attack groups when it was apparent that the *Shoho* was a wreck, and consequently with one exception every bomb and every torpedo was aimed at the carrier, and the other Japanese ships escaped unscathed. The sole exception was the last *Yorktown's* bomber, who, seeing the carrier enveloped in flames, attacked a cruiser, unsuccessfully. The Americans reported 21 bomb and 19 torpedo hits on the *Shoho*. The official Japanese figures were 13 bomb and seven torpedo hits. Of the latter three were on the port and four on the starboard side.

Air cover from Rabaul had been arranged for the Japanese Occupation Force, but all the aircraft encountered during the battle were apparently launched by the *Shoho*, which had a fighter patrol of 10 or 12 aircraft overhead. Several of the *Lexington*'s attack group had encounters with them during the attack and withdrawal. One American scout bomber was shot down, and another made a forced landing on Roussel Island, in the Louisiade Archipelago, friendly territory when the crew was later rescued by the Australians. Four Japanese fighters and a torpedo aircraft were shot down by the *Lexington*'s aircraft.

The enemy protective aircraft having been apparently drawn off by the *Lexington*'s attack group, the *Yorktown*'s aircraft encountered no opposition before the attack. After it was completed, however, some six Japanese fighters and three scout bomber types attacked the *Yorktown*'s dive bombers and torpedo aircraft. The escorting American fighters shot down three of the enemy fighters. The ruse new to the American pilots of emitting smoke when heavily attacked, saved some Japanese aircraft. One *Yorktown* dive bomber was lost, last seen on the return flight when it broke off to attack an enemy aircraft.

16. Japanese attempts to locate US carriers, 7 May

Whilst the attack on the *Shoho* was in progress evidence of the efforts of the enemy's aircraft to locate the American carriers was continually seen on the radar screen. The Japanese aircraft operated, however, under the handicap of not being fitted with radar. At 0833, before the launch of the attack groups, the first enemy aircraft was picked up by radar, 30 miles to the north-westward, but *Yorktown* fighters were unable to make contact. The *Lexington*, when launching her attack group, retained at the ship eight scout bombers for anti-torpedo aircraft patrol; and at 1019 the *Yorktown* launched a combat air patrol, maintaining one throughout the day. All aircraft in the combat air patrol were controlled by the fighter director on board the *Lexington*.

Weather favoured Task Force 17. The ships were in an area of unsettled weather extending east and west. The wind was east to south-east, force 12 to 22 knots, and up to 30 knots in gusts. There were sufficient breaks in the clouds to allow aircraft to be launched and landed without undue difficulty. But visibility was generally limited to 10 or 15 miles, reduced during the day by frequent rain squalls to less than a mile and at sunset to 4 miles by pronounced haze. Actually, Rear-Admiral Fletcher's force was sighted by Japanese aircraft from Tulagi early in the forenoon of the 7th, and had he been attacked by the air groups of the *Zuikaku* and *Shokaku* before his strike groups had returned and been rearmed his situation would have been serious. The Commander of the Japanese Covering Force, Rear-Admiral Goto, ordered the *Shoho* to attack, but she was overwhelmed and sunk before she could do so.

Meanwhile, enemy aircraft were about continually. At 1044 an unidentified aircraft was picked up coming in on bearing 045 degrees, distance 41 miles. Four of *Yorktown's* fighters, vectored out, made contact with a Japanese four-engine patrol bomber and shot it down. Radio interceptions indicated that the position of Task Force 17 was known to the enemy. On the other hand, the position of the Japanese 5th Carrier Squadron was still not known to the Americans, and there was little likelihood of finding a suitable objective near the scene of this morning's attack. Rear-Admiral Fletcher decided to launch no further strike against the Japanese Occupation Force. The *Neosho* at 1021 had reported being bombed by three aircraft in lat. 16° 50′ S., long. 159° 08′ E., but the signal did not specify whether the attackers were carrier-borne type. With the probability that the Japanese 5th Carrier Squadron was in the neighbourhood it was considered the air striking force should not be squandered on any lesser target but should be held in readiness to counter-attack. Commander Task Force 17 therefore decided to rely upon shore-based aircraft to locate the *Zuikaku* and *Shokaku*. The day wore on. At 1308 the attack groups returned from sinking the *Shoho*. Still there was no news of the enemy carriers. Fighters were continually being sent out to investigate contacts which proved to be the *Yorktown's* fighters, who did not use radar identification. Rear-Admiral Fletcher decided to take his force westward during the night, in the expectation that the enemy would pass through the Jomard Passage by morning, making for Port Moresby, probably accompanied by carriers.

However, as night was coming on, a succession of events occurred, which rendered necessary a fresh appreciation of the situation. At 1629 an enemy seaplane came in sight of the *Yorktown* bearing 315 degrees, distance 9 miles, and escaped in the failing light despite the efforts of two sections of fighters to intercept it. At 1747 radar showed a large group of enemy aircraft to the south-eastward on a westerly course. The *Lexington's* fighters in the air were vectored out, and the *Yorktown* launched 11 more in support. Some of the latter were kept over the ships, but seven went out and made contact in the haze and falling darkness with a group of Japanese Navy dive bombers, one of which they shot down. This was apparently a force of about 27 bombers and torpedo aircraft from the *Zuikaku* and *Shokaku* which Rear-Admiral Hara sent out during the afternoon to make a dusk attack on the American force. They searched for 300 miles but failed to find the US carriers and finally they jettisoned their bombs and were now making towards their own ships.

Meanwhile, the *Lexington*'s fighters were engaging successfully a formation of nine Zero fighters, part, no doubt, of the bombers' escort. When the *Yorktown*'s fighters arrived, they saw four or five oil patches on the sea, marking aircraft which had been shot down. The *Yorktown*'s fighters also claimed to have destroyed three of the enemy. One *Lexington* and two *Yorktown* fighters were lost.

It was deep dusk, or as some say, after dark, when the American fighters returned to their ships and commenced landing. At 1850, whilst they were in the landing circle, three enemy aircraft, apparently mistaking the carriers for their own, flew past on the starboard side with their running lights on and blinking in Morse code on an Aldis lamp. One of them gave an incorrect response to the landing signal and took a wave off. He was recognized as hostile, and as the group crossed over the bow to port, one of the *Yorktown*'s fighters opened fire on them, but without visible effect. At 1910, again, three enemy aircraft appeared, whilst the combat air patrol was still landing. Some ships opened fire, accidentally damaging one of the *Yorktown*'s fighters and possibly shooting down one of the enemy.

Twenty minutes later the *Lexington*'s radar showed aircraft circling and apparently landing on a carrier 30 miles to the eastward. The Japanese carriers at this time had neither radar nor homing devices, and the American radio telephone inadvertently jammed the frequency used by their aircraft, preventing the pilots from getting a bearing on their carriers. Admiral Hara switched on searchlights to aid the night recovery, but eleven aircraft came down in the sea.

The *Yorktown*'s radar gave somewhat similar indications to the *Lexington*'s, of a single aircraft circling at 25 to 30 miles on bearing 60 degrees, but later plotted on course 310 degrees and believed to be one of her own fighters. On the other hand, radio interception on the homing of lost Japanese aircraft indicated that the enemy carriers were probably within 150 miles either to the eastward or westward; the aircraft were quite close to Task Force 17, but none of the American ships were equipped for taking bearings of the transmissions on the frequency employed.

It was now dark, and in the uncertainty of being able to locate the enemy carriers Rear-Admiral Fletcher dismissed the idea of sending a surface force to attack them. A force despatched during the night might fail to make contact with the enemy or to re-join by daylight. He detached the destroyer *Monaghan* (0055 8 May) to search for survivors of the *Sims*, the oiler *Neosho*'s escort, which the Commander-in-Chief Pacific Fleet reported sunk; but apart from this, he decided to keep his ships concentrated and to prepare for a battle with the enemy carriers next morning. The Japanese, too, had decided against a night attack, for although they believed the American force to be only 40 miles to the southward, they were uncertain of its size. The Port Moresby landing was postponed for two days and the invasion transports headed for Rabaul. The Japanese retreat had begun although nobody yet admitted the fact.

17. Attack on the *Neosho* and *Sims*, 7 May

Unfortunately, the *Monaghan*'s search was vain, for the position in which the *Sims* had been sunk was incorrectly worked out by the *Neosho*'s people.

During the attack on the *Shoho*, and in fact ever since the raid on Tulagi had revealed to the Japanese the presence of American carriers in the Coral Sea, land planes and seaplanes from Rabaul and Shortland Island had been searching without success to locate the Allied task force. Finally, on the morning of the 7th, their reconnaissance aircraft sighted what they took to be the American carriers and directed to the attack the bombers from the *Zuikaku* and *Shokaku* which with the remainder of the Moresby task force were to the north-eastward of the Occupation Force and still undiscovered by the Americans.

Unfortunately for the enemy, the identification of their reconnaissance aircraft was wrong, though this was not discovered until too late. The ships sighted were not the *Lexington* and *Yorktown*, but the oiler *Neosho* and her escort *Sims*.

After being detached from Task Force 17 at 1725 on 6 May these two ships had proceeded southward in accordance with the arrangements for fuelling and by about 0730 on the 7th reached a position in latitude 16° 01′ S., longitude 158° 01′ E., when radar and visual contact with aircraft began to be made. It was at first thought the aircraft were American, but at 0859 a bomb suddenly fell about 100 yards from the *Sims*, released by an aircraft which came over at a height of 15,000 feet and was not seen before the bomb fell.

Both ships increased speed and ran south-eastwards, and after one or more radar contacts two groups of 15 and seven aircraft respectively, coming from the northward in succession, examined without molesting the ships, and disappeared to the north-eastward, fired on without effect.

At 1003 another group of 10 aircraft approached from a bearing 140 degrees, and three of them, twin-engine bombers, made a horizontal run on the *Neosho* and dropped three bombs to starboard from a high altitude, two of which fell within 25 yards of the ship. Both ships opened fire, but the enemy made off to the north-eastward.

For an hour and a half no further attack took place, though aircraft continued to show on the radar screen, until 1131, when approximately 24 enemy dive bombers were sighted at a considerable height, apparently manoeuvring into position to attack. The *Sims* thereupon took station on the port quarter of the *Neosho*. Of the actual attack which took place during the next quarter of an hour or more no clear picture was retained of the two doomed ships. The enemy aircraft dived from all directions and the sequence of events was lost in the ensuing confusion and destruction.

In a few minutes, the destroyer *Sims* was a wreck, struck by at least three bombs, estimated at 500 pounds, released by four enemy aircraft who pulled out of their dives at altitude so low that survivors of the *Neosho* averred that those which were not shot down were destroyed by the blast of their own bombs. Bombs exploded in both the forward and after engine rooms and wrecked the *Sims*. The ship lost all power and stopped. Her topside was a shambles. An effort to keep the vessel afloat was made by jettisoning all possible weight. A motor boat and two life rafts were launched, and the former was ordered to go aft and try to extinguish a fire in the after deck house and flood the after magazine. But before this could be done the *Sims* seemed to break amidships. She went down slowly, stern first. All hands began leaping into the sea and swimming clear, but as the water reached the top of the funnel a very heavy explosion occurred, followed a moment later by a second, causing heavy loss of life amongst the men in the water. Only 15 men, two of whom later died, reached the *Neosho* in the motor boat, during the early afternoon. The Commanding Officer, Lieut.-Comdr. Willford M. Hyman, was last seen on the bridge of the *Sims* giving orders in an attempt to save the ship.

Meanwhile, the *Neosho* was also in trouble. The majority of the Japanese bombers had concentrated on her, and although the crews of the 20mm guns are reported to have shot down three of the enemy and damaged others, the oiler received seven direct hits and a number of near misses. One of the three enemy bombers that was shot down, crashed in flames into No. 4 gun enclosure; intense fires broke out at once and spread aft over the stack deck. The time was about 1144.

Soon after the attack ended the Commanding Officer, Commander John S. Phillips, ordered all hands to prepare to abandon ship but not to do so until word was passed. Unfortunately, several men on the after deck began leaping into the sea without orders, and seven life rafts were cut adrift. Motor whaleboats were sent to pick up and bring back the men, but many were lost.[3]

---

3. The US Combat Narrative, *The Battle of the Coral Sea*, p.51 states: 'A muster upon return to ship of the whaleboats shows 16 officers and 94 men accounted for; 1 officer and 19 men known dead, and 4 officers and 154 men missing, besides the 15 from the *Sims*. Many were wounded and several later died '.

Wind and sea increased, and darkness came on before any of the rafts could be towed back to the oiler.

The latter was obviously doomed, for although the fires had been brought under control the pumps were unable to keep down the rising water, and the main deck was buckling and seemed likely to break in two at any time. Nevertheless, the ship remained afloat all night, though by the morning of the 8th she had developed a list to starboard of 26 degrees and the utmost endeavours could only reduce this by some 3 degrees.

The 8th and 9th passed with the men employed in making rafts and rigging masts and sails for all available boats. At 1012 on the 9th the *Neosho's* position was taken as latitude 15° 35′ S., 156° 55′ E. The signal codes had been destroyed, but wireless transmission in plain language was possible on the auxiliary transmitter.

At 1230 on the 10th an Australian Hudson bomber appeared, inquired if the ship was in distress, and on receiving an affirmative answer flew off to the southward after circling the ships several times. The *Neosho* gave her position but received no reply. By the 11th it was apparent that the ship had settled appreciably during the night and the distortion of her plates had increased alarmingly. About 1130, when the question of abandoning ship and making for the Australian coast was being considered, a Navy Catalina patrol bomber from the *Tangier* appeared from the east and within an hour and a half the US destroyer *Henley* which had been despatched from Numea, was sighted approaching. By 1412 all survivors were taken off, and at 1522, at Commander Phillips request, the doomed Neosho was sunk by two torpedoes and several rounds of 5-inch gunfire in lat. 15° 35′ S, long. 155° 36′ E.

The *Henley* searched the area until dark without finding any of the men who had abandoned ship, then headed for Brisbane, in order to get the wounded to hospital. Ordered at 0100 on the 12th to return to the scene of the bombing, she went and made a wider, but still fruitless, search.

Meanwhile, it was discovered that the position of the *Neosho* at the time of attack had been incorrectly plotted and transmitted, and the US destroyer *Helm* was sent from Numea, on the 14th, to make a search in the corrected position. On the 17th, in lat. 15° 16′ S, long. 155° 07′ 3″ E, four of the *Neosho's* survivors were rescued from a life raft: all were in a critical condition from exposure, and one man died soon after being taken aboard. They were the sole survivors of 68 men from four rafts lashed together, and they told a grim story of food and water becoming exhausted because neither was rationed, of men being crazed and leaping into the sea or dying on the rafts. The *Helm* searched until sunset on 17th and aircraft from the *Tangier* maintained a search until the 2nd, but no further survivors were found.

18. Attacks on the support group, 7 May

The support group of cruisers and destroyers under Rear-Admiral Crace which had been detached at 0530 on 7 May, did not long remain undiscovered by the enemy. At 0810 radar indicated that three aircraft were shadowing the force, and one of the enemy, a twin-float monoplane, was sighted to the north-eastward by the *Chicago*, at a range of some 20,000 yards, and remained in view for about half an hour, circling well out of gun range.

No further enemy aircraft approached until the afternoon. At 1345, when the force was approximately 12° S., 151° 30′ E., 60 miles south of the Jomard Passage, radar contact was made with a group of aircraft bearing 135 degrees, range 56,000 yards, and 12 minutes later a formation of some 12 single-engine monoplanes was seen coming up from astern on a parallel course and was taken under fire at ranges of 6,000–12,000 yards. The enemy quickly retired unhit.

Half an hour later there was radar contact at 150,000 yards with a group of aircraft closing on a bearing 250 degrees. The weather was fine, wind eight knots from 120 degrees, sea slight, sun bearing 318 degrees, altitude 52 degrees, when at 1432 sunlight flashing on their wings revealed a group of aircraft, range 25,000 yards, approaching from right ahead. These were 13-14 Type 97 (Navy) Mitsubishi twin-engine torpedo aircraft, with fighter protection, from the 25th Air Flotilla at Rabaul.

Task Force 17.3 was steering 275 degrees, speed 25 knots at the time, in V Formation, with the flagship *Australia* as guide, the *Chicago* and *Hobart* bearing 135 degrees and 225 degrees respectively, distance 1,600 yards, and the destroyers *Farragut*, *Perkins*, and *Walke* disposed as anti-submarine screen.

Within three minutes the enemy began their attack. Gliding down at 12 miles from 5,000 feet to 100 feet at eight miles they started their approach from the starboard quarter. The ships opened fire and almost immediately two of the enemy, including their leader, were seen to crash about 1,000 yards ahead, whereupon the remainder separated into groups. The larger group continued on their bearing, whilst one small group swung to the left to come in from the starboard bow and another group swung right to come in slightly later from the port quarter. With the exception of one of the enemy, which released its torpedo at a height of 100–150 feet, all the aircraft made their release at 40 feet, range 1,000–2,000 yards.

The next few minutes were crowded, torpedoes coming from all angles and enemy aircraft machine gunning the ships. The latter put up a heavy curtain of fire and manoeuvred to avoid torpedoes. At least two more of the enemy were shot down by the ships' fire. Only five torpedo tracks were seen, all of which were successfully avoided by every ship, and at 1442 the engagement was at an end. The only damage suffered was by the *Chicago*, which had seven men wounded by machine gun fire, two of whom died later.

There was, however, no respite for Rear Admiral Crace's ships, for almost immediately they came under attack by Navy Type Mitsubishi high level heavy bombers which approached from astern and were sighted at 1443 at 14,000 feet after being picked up by radar at 45 miles. The ships opened fire, but none of the enemy was hit. Although observers reported the group to number 25 aircraft only one salvo of bombs was dropped near the ships. This straddled the *Australia* with a pattern 500 yards long, but all bombs missed and only two of the nearer ones shook the ship slightly. At 1501 the attack was over; the task group reduced speed to 20 knots and steered a southerly course until 2000 when Rear-Admiral Crace altered to the westward and proceeded on a course parallel to the New Guinea coast.

It was reported that a few minutes after the high level bombing attack three aircraft, subsequently identified as United States Army B.26 bombers, passed over and dropped a salvo of bombs close to one of the destroyers of the task group. However, not all of the ships witnessed the incident. Although shadowed by enemy aircraft, the support group was not further molested; and the successful air battles in which Rear-Admiral Fletcher's attack group engaged next day, to the westward, destroyed any opportunity the force might have had of engaging the Japanese in a surface encounter.

Chapter IV

Air Battles of 8 May

19. Japanese carriers sighted, 08.20

After the decision to defer action against the *Zuikaku* and *Shokahu* until daylight Rear-Admiral Fletcher continued to the southward during the night of the 7th–8th and at 0800 on the 8th was in lat. 14° 25′ S long. 154° 31′ E., course 125 degrees, speed 14 knots, the composition of his force being the carriers *Yorktown* (flagship) and *Lexington*, the five cruisers *Astoria, Chester, Portland, Minneapolis* and *New Orleans*, and seven destroyers *Phelps, Dewey, Aylwin, Morris, Anderson, Hammann* and *Russell*.

The weather was fine, clouds few, wind from 085 degrees to 112 degrees, 16–20 knots, sea smooth, ceiling almost unlimited, but horizontal visibility somewhat restricted through haze. These conditions held, with slight variations, throughout the entire day.

Intelligence reports received during the night had indicated that the enemy invasion force was retiring northward, but there was no news of the *Zuikaku* and *Shokahu*. Because of the uncertainty over whether the Japanese carriers were to the eastward or westward it was necessary to carry out a 360 degrees search, and at 0652, about half an hour before sunrise, the *Lexington* launched a scouting group of 22 aircraft to cover a radius of 20 miles in the northern and 150 miles in the southern semicircle.

The enemy were located almost by chance. At 0820, just as one of the scouts was turning for home he sighted a carrier hidden in rain squalls.[1] The scout keyed the report to his ship on voice frequency, but a slipping generator clutch prevented receipt. However, the scout of the adjoining sector, to whom he had made a voice report relayed the message to the *Lexington*, and also found the enemy himself, and reported their subsequent movements; and at 0828, the news was received on board the *Lexington* that a force of two carriers, four heavy cruisers and some destroyers had been sighted. Position was given at 0835, lat. 11° 51′ S., long. 156° 04′ E.,

---

1. In view of the general impression that the American forces were lavishly equipped it is of interest that at this date apparently only the Commanders of scouting squadrons were equipped with binoculars, an item of equipment very difficult to obtain in USA as in the U.K.

bearing 28 degrees distant 175 miles from Task Force 17. The enemy carriers were standing south at high speed, and an intercepted radio transmission indicated that the Japanese, in their turn, had sighted Task Force 17 almost simultaneously.

The force sighted was the Japanese Sixth Squadron, the so-called Port Moresby Task Force, containing, in addition to the *Zuikaku* (flagship of Rear-Admiral Hara) and *Shokaku*, the cruisers *Myoko* and *Haguro* reinforced by two of the Occupation Force cruisers, and six destroyers. The seaplane carrier *Kiyokawa Maru* which had been encountered at Tulagi on 4 May belonged to this force, but if she was in company with the force on the 8th she was not sighted.

Launching of attack groups by the carriers commenced at 0900, the *Lexington* launching 24 scout bombers, ten fighters, and 12 torpedo aircraft, and the *Yorktown* seven scouts and 17 bombers, all with 1,000-lb. bombs, six escort fighters, and nine torpedo aircraft with torpedoes set to run at 10 feet.

20. The *Yorktown*'s group attacks

The *Yorktown*'s group went first, the scouts and dive bombers going ahead of the torpedo aircraft at 17,000 feet, escorted by two fighters. The bombers sighted the enemy at about 1032, steering course 190 degrees at 20 knots. The Japanese force had the protection of the area of bad weather that had concealed Task Force 17 on the previous day. The weather in the neighbourhood of the enemy was unsettled, intermittent rain squalls; and a broken lower layer of clouds covered the area at 2,000 to 3,000 feet. Visibility varied from 2 to 15 miles.

At 1049 the bombers were near the enemy and commenced circling whilst waiting for the slower torpedo aircraft to arrive and take up position for attack. One enemy carrier, apparently the *Zuikaku*, now headed for a large rain squall, but the *Shokaku* turned into the east-south-easterly wind and began to launch her aircraft. Some of the enemy opened fire.

Nine minutes elapsed before the torpedo aircraft were in position and a co-ordinated attack by dive bombers and torpedo aircraft began on the *Shokaku*. The bombers attacked down-wind, from 17,000 feet, altitude of release 2,500 feet, and as on 4 May, they were handicapped by the fogging of their telescopes and wind shields, which greatly reduced their bombing accuracy. They encountered considerable anti-aircraft fire and were attacked, both in the dive and the pull-out, by Zero fighters, some 15 to 18 of which were over the Japanese formation, outnumbering the American fighters. The *Yorktown*'s scouts shot down four and the bombers seven of the enemy, besides damaging others. The Americans made good use of the low cloud cover and had no losses. The fighters also attacked unsuccessfully two Japanese dive bombers on the return trip, but the engagement had taken place near their extreme range and they were hampered by shortage of fuel, having had to climb to altitude with the bombers. The *Yorktown*'s bombers claimed six certain hits, three further possible hits, and several near misses; actually they made two hits.

Meanwhile, the torpedo squadron made its approach from the south-east, the four escorting fighters driving off an attack by six Zero fighters, and thus permitting the torpedo aircraft to make their releases unmolested. As the dive bombers made their attack the carrier had commenced a turn to port and then put her helm over and turned sharply to starboard; and it was during this turn that the *Yorktown*'s torpedo aircraft made their releases, under very heavy fire from the carrier and her four escorting cruisers, though the latter were on so wide a circle that the range was too great to be effective. As on 7 May, the Japanese ships escorting the carrier scattered, either in order to obtain sea room for themselves or to give the carrier plenty of sea room, although they materially reduced the effectiveness of their supporting anti-aircraft by doing so. This was the more fortunate for the American torpedo aircraft, compelled as they were by the slow speed and low altitude of drop of their Mark 13 torpedoes, to come in low and slow. They reported that three or possibly four

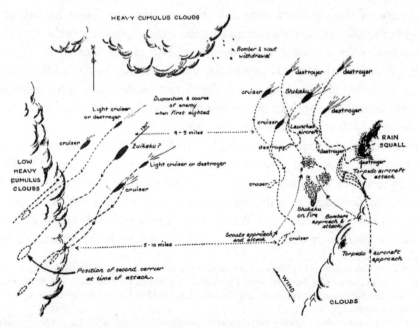

Fig. 1. Attack by *Yorktown*'s aircraft on Japanese carriers, 8 May.

torpedoes hit, though all apparently made erratic runs.[2] The Japanese stated, however, that all were released at a range which permitted the *Shokaku* to avoid them.[3] Three Japanese Zero fighters and one scout were shot down during the torpedo attack; and during the return to the *Yorktown* one enemy torpedo aircraft was shot down.

21. Attack by the *Lexington*'s group

The *Lexington*'s attack group had difficulty in prevailing very poor visibility. The three fighters escorting the dive bombers lost contact with the latter en route and returned to the carrier. Eighteen bombers also returned without finding the enemy, and one torpedo aircraft turned back on account of engine trouble.

Four scouts and two fighters joined up with the 11 remaining torpedo aircraft and their four escorting fighters.

After flying to the end of their navigational leg without sighting the enemy, they began flying around a square. A few minutes later they entered a clear area, on the far side of which, some 20 miles away, were enemy ships. An unsuccessful attempt was now made to call up the lost bombers. Japanese fighters, Zeros and Me.109s appeared. The American fighters engaged them, losing at least three of their number, without being successful, however, in shooting down any of the enemy.

As one of the survivors came out of cloud cover, he found himself at a height of 1,000 feet, directly above a Japanese carrier, presumably the *Zuikaku*, accompanied by a cruiser and a destroyer. The carrier showed no sign of damage, and the fighter was presumably undetected, for he circled the carrier twice, unmolested by aircraft or AA fire. Fifteen miles away to the eastward another large group of ships was visible one large ship of which, apparently a carrier and no doubt the *Zuikaku*, was on fire.

Meanwhile, the four scouts and 11 torpedo aircraft, leaving the fighters engaged in combat, had gone on and attacked a carrier, together. The time was given in the radio logs at 1057, i.e. approximately simultaneously with that by the *Yorktown*'s aircraft, but it is not known whether the clocks of the two groups were synchronized. Whether this attack was made on the *Zuikaku* or on the *Shokaku* is uncertain. The *Zuikaku*, although she reported being

---

2. The *Yorktown*'s Report, p.87 says that three torpedoes were seen to make erratic runs. On p.100 the report states that all nine Mark 13. Mod 1 torpedoes fired during the operations of 4–8 May made erratic runs; but the report also shows that the only Mark 13. Mod 1 torpedoes fired were those nine fired in this attack.

3. We do not know at what range the torpedoes were released in this attack as this has not been revealed by the Americans.

attacked at this time, was not hit or damaged; all bombs missed her and, owing to the long range at which the torpedoes were fired, the ship was able to avoid them. The *Lexington*'s attack group reported that their target, when last seen, was on fire, and they claimed two 1,000 lb. bomb and five torpedo hits. Actually, they made one bomb hit and no torpedo hits.

No less than seven of the *Lexington*'s fighters were shot down in this engagement and one torpedo aircraft and three scout bombers ran out of fuel on the return journey and were lost. Two enemy scouts were shot down by the fighters, and four enemy fighters were probably destroyed, two over the carrier by the fighters and two by torpedo aircraft on the return from the attack. The *Shokaku* sustained in all three bomb hits, causing severe damage. Her position at the end of the engagement was reported by CTF 17 [Commander Task Force 17] as lat. 12° 00′ N., long. 155° 50′ E.

22. Preparations to meet Japanese air attack

The Americans became aware that they had been sighted by the enemy almost simultaneously with the sighting of the *Zuikaku* and *Shokaku* by the *Lexington*'s scouts, for at 0832 a Japanese plain language wireless transmission was intercepted, giving the position, course and speed of Task Force 17, apparently sent by a 4-engine patrol aircraft which was sighted and shot down by the *Yorktown*'s combat air patrol.

Preparations were made to meet the attack which it was estimated would come about 1100. The *Yorktown* had launched first combat air patrol and eight scout bombers as anti-torpedo aircraft patrol about 0724; the fighters were brought in and at 0941 second combat air patrol was launched. The *Lexington* launched her returning scouts as anti-torpedo aircraft patrol and additional fighters were launched by both carriers up to 1102-04, at which time all serviceable aircraft were in the air, the fighters as combat air patrol, with scout bombers as anti-torpedo aircraft patrol. The cruisers' aircraft, which had been up as an inner air patrol, were recalled when the enemy attack appeared imminent.

In order to reduce signalling between carriers and to allow Commander Air (Rear-Admiral A. W. Fitch, USS *Lexington*) freedom of action for his carriers and air groups, CTF 17 at 0908 ordered him to assume tactical command of the Fleet. The ships were in circular disposition with the carriers as centre, axis 350 degrees, cruisers on 3,000-yard circle, destroyers on 4,000-yard circle. An even tighter formation was subsequently adopted by the US Pacific Fleet as the result of experience in the battle which took place on this day. Various courses were steered in launching and recovering aircraft, but the general course was south-easterly and just before the commencement of the action was 125 degrees, speed 20 knots; speed varied up to 30 knots after the attack began. Before the action began the *Yorktown* adjusted her position on the *Lexington* so that the latter would not be between her and the sun and thus mask her fire should the enemy approach from that direction. The circular formation was not maintained, however, as the enemy attack developed, for in consequence of high speed manoeuvring to avoid torpedoes and bombs the two carriers gradually drew apart, and several miles separated them at the conclusion of the action. Five ships accompanied the *Lexington*, while seven remained with the *Yorktown*. Apart from her smaller escort the *Lexington* was handicapped by the fact that her new light guns (12 × 1-1-inch and 20 × 20 mm) had only just been received and the guns' crews were not yet fully trained.

At 1000 the enemy's disposition and 0900 position were reported to Commander South-west Pacific Force in the hope of shore-based aircraft being available to attack and shadow; but although Army bombers of General MacArthur's Australian Command were actively engaged during 2–12 May in reconnoitring and bombing enemy bases in the area, weather conditions apparently prevented them from locating the Japanese carriers, though they attacked the retiring transport force.

23. Combat air patrol goes out, 1102

THE FIGHTERS

At 1008 an enemy four-engine patrol bomber was sighted by the *Yorktown*'s lookouts and was shot down by a section of fighters at 1015.

About three-quarters of an hour later ships' radar indicated a large group of enemy aircraft approaching from the northward, distance 68–75 miles. The exact height of the enemy was uncertain, but was known to be over 10,000 feet. They approached on a steady bearing. All aircraft on combat air patrol were recalled to the vicinity of the carriers (1059) and at 1103 the *Yorktown* launched four additional fighters, making a total of eight fighters from that ship and nine from the *Lexington* on combat air patrol. Only three of these 17 fighters intercepted the enemy prior to delivery of his attack, 15 to 20 miles from the Fleet. Fighter direction for the aircraft of both carriers was carried out by the *Lexington*.[4]

---

4. The US *Combat Narrative* states: 'The failure of a large number of our fighters to intercept the enemy planes, despite the fact that ample radar warning of their approach was available, has resulted in criticism of the tactics of the Task Force fighter director … It should be noted, however, that no criticism of the *Lexington* fighter director was contained in any of the official action reports …' The U.S. Secret Information Bulletin No. 1, *Battle Experience from Pearl Harbor to Midway*, p. 8. seems to ascribe the failure fully to exploit the radar and fighter director system to failure to train in peacetime with equipment to be used during war.

At 1102 five of the *Lexington*'s fighters were vectored out on bearing 020 degrees, distance 30 miles, height 10,000 feet. Two of the aircraft were subsequently diverted to intercept torpedo aircraft coming in at a low altitude. The remaining three made contact with the enemy about 20 miles out but were some 1,000 to 2,000 feet below the Japanese who apparently numbered about 60–70, disposed in layers extending from about 10,000 feet upwards. At the lowest level were the torpedo aircraft, then fighters, then dive bombers stated to be at about 17,000 feet or higher, then more fighters. Approximately a third of the force were fighters, and the comparatively small number of fighters borne on board the American carriers, having to protect both their groups and their ships simultaneously, were outnumbered. At 15–20 miles the three *Lexington* fighters attacked the enemy bombers, but their performance was insufficient to enable them to gain enough altitude to prevent the enemy from making their bombing dives.

No other of the 17 fighters was in position to attack the enemy until after the latter had commenced or completed their attacks. The two *Lexington* fighters who were diverted to intercept torpedo aircraft attacked the latter at 1116, about four to five miles from the Fleet. Two more *Lexington* fighters were told to orbit overhead, climbed to 12,000 feet, and attacked the tail end of the enemy formation. What the remaining two *Lexington* fighters did, was not reported.

At 1108 four of the *Yorktown*'s fighters had been vectored out on bearing 020 degrees, distance 15 miles, height 1,000 feet, but they sighted nothing. By this time, the American carriers were under attack, and the four fighters were ordered to return; climbing to 10,000 feet, they were able to shoot down one Zero fighter after the attack was over. The four remaining *Yorktown* fighters were kept over the ship at about 8,000 to 10,000 feet. One section was not able to intercept the enemy before they attacked, though they shot down one Zero fighter and one dive bomber who had already released his bomb. The other section attacked a formation of dive bombers as they commenced their dive, and went down with them, shooting down one dive bomber before it dropped its bomb and another after release. In all, the *Yorktown*'s fighters shot down four Zero fighters and three dive bombers, besides damaging others, without loss to themselves. Two of the *Lexington*'s fighters were shot down, but both pilots were picked up.

THE SCOUT BOMBERS

The eight *Yorktown*'s scout bombers launched at 0724 were still in the air and the *Lexington* had also eight scouts out as anti-torpedo aircraft when the attack came. In default of sufficient fighters, bombers were employed as two-seater fighters, without bombs, at low altitudes against the Japanese torpedo aircraft, being disposed in a protective screen at 3,000 feet outside the cruiser screen. This was recognized as a makeshift arrangement.

The enemy torpedo aircraft were already making their diving approach when sighted by *Yorktown*'s scout bombers. These made a great effort to break up the attack, but the Japanese were high and too fast for them. The patrol was then attacked by a large number of Type 97 and Zero fighters, and a mêlée followed in which the scout bombers, though outnumbered by faster and more manoeuvrable machines, and losing four of their number almost at once, shot down at least four of the enemy fighters and damaged or destroyed several more. The four *Yorktown* aircraft which returned were all badly damaged.

The *Lexington*'s anti-torpedo aircraft patrol (eight scout bombers) was at 2,000 feet, about 6,000 yards out, i.e. somewhat further than its proper station, when the Japanese torpedo aircraft came in over them at high speed. The scout bombers, inferior in performance to the enemy fighters and faced with large numbers of the enemy, were unable to do more than hamper the attacks. One American scout bomber was shot down by enemy fighters and one went over the side on landing.

24. The attack opens

At 1112–1113 the Japanese torpedo aircraft were sighted 15 miles off, approaching in a fast power glide from about 5,000 feet from the port beam. Some ships opened fire at once, but many were slow in starting, and throughout the earlier part of the action at least, AA fire particularly the 5-inch, was extremely erratic and relatively ineffective. There was no arrangement for controlled, co-ordinated fire of the screening ships' anti-aircraft batteries.

The attack began out of range of any guns smaller than 5-inch, and although it was reported that in the course of the action gunfire destroyed at least 17 of the enemy, most of them were apparently shot down after releasing torpedo or bomb, though American doctrine laid stress on the necessity of destruction before release. The American secondary AA armament consisted of 20 mm and 1.1-inch guns. The former were not effective at ranges greater than 1,000 yards, which was insufficient against torpedo attacks and just barely effective against dive bombers. As regards the 1.1-inch gun, there was a lack of directors, and the rate of training with the gears then fitted was slow, and during the early stages of the action there was a tendency to give insufficient lead and to shoot under the target. The Americans at this date did not possess an automatic lead computer, in fact the problem of AA protection had not advanced very far. The *Chester* estimated that 30 per cent.

to 40 per cent. of the US 5-inch shells fired were blind. The executive officer of the *New Orleans* reported that the ship was more seriously 'under fire' from the American ships than from the enemy.

The Japanese attacks appeared to be directed against the two American carriers, though in the circumstances of the moment one or two torpedoes and a few bombs appeared as if aimed at the screening ships. When the enemy were about 8,000 to 10,000 yards away it became clear that they intended to attack both the US carriers simultaneously with torpedo and dive bombers. The numbers, both of torpedo aircraft and dive bombers, that attacked each carrier, were approximately equal.

It quickly became apparent that the American makeshift anti-torpedo aircraft patrol would be unable to prevent the enemy's torpedo attack from getting in. Their approach differed greatly from that employed in the attack on the *Prince of Wales* and *Repulse* a few months earlier, the only precedent on which the Americans could base their tactics. The approach against the British ships was made in squadron formation. Against Task Force 17, however, squadrons broke up into small groups which attacked from various directions. The standard procedure appeared to be a fast relatively shallow power glide from 5,000 feet to altitude of release, ranging from 100 to 200 or 300 feet, release being at relatively high speed. Some torpedo aircraft, however, delivered their torpedoes from heights of as much as 500 feet, either designedly or in consequence of being fired at.

25. Attack on the *Yorktown* 1118

The violent avoiding manoeuvres made by the American carriers soon caused them to draw apart, and the screening ships nearest to each carrier also separated into two groups without signal, to protect them. The cruisers *Astoria*, *Portland* and *Chester*, with four destroyers including the *Russell*, *Hammann*, *Aylwyn* and one other, formed a circular screen around the *Yorktown* at about 2,000–3,000 yards away.[5]

During the engagement the *Astoria* kept the *Yorktown* as nearly as possible on bearing 073 degrees, distance 1,700–2,200 yards, and the *Chester* maintained an approximate bearing 350 degrees from the *Yorktown*, distance 2,300–3,000 yards. The *Portland* was stationed 045 degrees, 2,300 yards from the *Yorktown*, but the first eight point turn to starboard by the latter, at the beginning of the engagement, left her on the carrier's port side, a position in which she

---

5. It is not possible to give, with certainty, the name of the fourth destroyer, though the *Yorktown* reported it was probably the *Dewey*.

remained throughout. The latter, in her efforts to avoid torpedoes and bombs, steered an irregular zigzag course, using full helm; but in spite of the difficulty of keeping station without signals the screening ships maintained throughout positions from which they were able to keep up heavy fire.

One group of Japanese torpedo aircraft attacked the *Yorktown* from the port quarter. Four of them were reported shot down, but three released their torpedoes; their attack was closely followed by that of four aircraft on the port beam, one of which was set on fire and crashed after making his release, two others completed their release successfully, and one dived into the water without dropping a torpedo. The position of release was reported to vary from 500 to 3,000 yards from the *Yorktown*. As the first three torpedoes struck the water the *Yorktown* applied full starboard helm and orders were given to the engine room for emergency full speed.

The three torpedoes dropped on the port quarter were soon lost to sight, and the *Yorktown*, having turned about ten points, was steadied on a course parallel to the second three until these had run past her to port, close aboard.

The remaining group of torpedo aircraft, making sharp left turns, rounded the *Yorktown*'s stern at a distance of about 8,000 to 10,000 yards. They were under heavy fire and released their torpedoes well out, from ranges varying between 1,500 and 4,000 yards, on the starboard quarter of the *Yorktown*. The ship at the time was steering about 215 degrees, and she turned to port and steadied with her stern to the point of release. Two of the torpedoes only were seen, both of which ran past on the starboard side. One of the attackers crashed.

After the torpedo aircraft began their high-speed glide, the dive bombers continued at altitude for some minutes. At 1124 the dive-bombing attack commenced, the enemy, 10 or 12 in number, coming out of the sun and peeling off at about 6,000 feet, making their dives across the deck, generally from port to starboard with the bridge or island structure as point of aim. Dives were reported to be relatively shallow, perhaps not more than 45 degrees. Reports as to the bomb release point vary, some putting it at 2,000–3,000 feet, others no higher than 500–1,000 feet. The attackers were kept under heavy fire and course was changed under full helm, generally under the dive or towards the direction from which it started. The *Yorktown* received one bomb hit and a total of ten or 11 near misses; six on the starboard side, two very close (one touched the edge of the catwalk) between the bow and the bridge: at least two very near on the port quarter; and two or three on the starboard quarter which lifted the propellers clear of the water. All the bombs appeared to be of the same size and type as that which struck the ship, with two exceptions which were thought to approximate to the US 1,000-lb. bomb.

The single direct bomb hit (at 1127) struck the flight deck about 23 feet before No. 2 lift and about 15 feet from the island. Fragments recovered indicated that it was probably a 12-inch projectile converted to an armour piercing bomb, similar to those used at the attack on Pearl Harbor in December 1941. It pierced the flight deck, making a hole 14 inches in diameter, passed through No. 3 ready room, the hangar deck, and second deck at an angle towards the starboard side, and after hitting a beam and a stanchion turned to port and pierced the third deck. Damage was not great, but the ship's speed was reduced to 24 knots through concussion damage necessitating the temporary securing of three boilers.

At 1131 the ship's radar went out of action but began to function again without attention at 1222; the cause, namely action damage, was not discovered until the next day. The YE homing transmitter[6] was put out of action by damage at 1150, and as a result, there was a period of several hours following the loss of communications in the *Lexington*, when no YE homing means was available to either air group.

In the final phase of the attack which occurred about 1140, a single torpedo aircraft maintained its course parallel to the *Yorktown* on her starboard side under continuous 5-inch and 1.1-inch fire until it was before the carrier's beam, when it turned towards the ship. Faced with the fire of every gun on that side, he released his torpedo at about 2,000 yards and escaped by a violent manoeuvre, apparently untouched. As he turned towards the *Yorktown*, the latter turned to starboard, and the torpedo passed harmlessly across her bows. The ship continued her turn through a complete circle, and resumed the approximate course she had been steering at the commencement of the engagement.

There is little doubt that brilliant manoeuvring was largely responsible for saving the ship from all but a single bomb hit and the avoidance of every torpedo fired at her; whilst the considerable volume of AA put up by the carrier and her screening ships, erratic though it was, attributed to her immunity by making the enemy hurry their torpedo bomb releases. Expenditure of AA ammunition by the *Yorktown* was as follows:

8 × 5-inch / 38 cal. Guns	404 rounds
4 × 1.1-inch mounts	2906 rounds
24 × 20 mm. guns	7900 rounds
18 × 0.5-inch guns	15800 rounds

---

6. The YE-ZB was the primary aircraft-to-carrier radio homing system used by all US carriers and aircraft during the war.

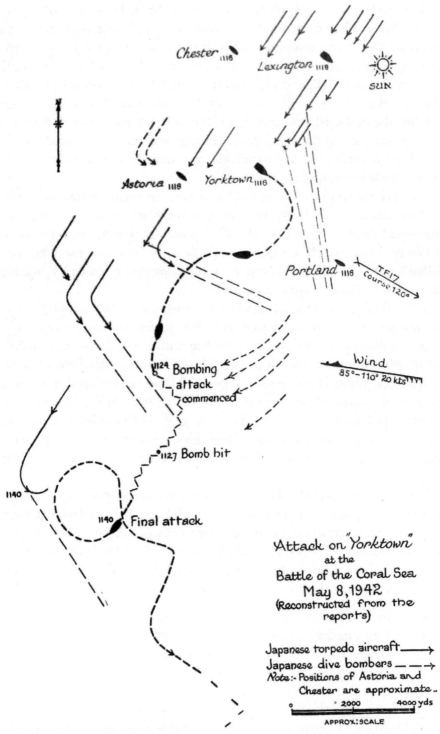

Chester ₁₁₁₈

Lexington ₁₁₁₈

SUN

Astoria ₁₁₁₈   Yorktown ₁₁₁₈

Portland ₁₁₁₈   TF17 Course 120°

1124 Bombing
attack
commenced

Wind
85°–110° 20 kts

1127 Bomb hit

1140

1140 Final attack

Attack on "Yorktown"
at the
Battle of the Coral Sea
May 8, 1942
(Reconstructed from the
reports)

Japanese torpedo aircraft ⟶
Japanese dive bombers – – –⟶
Note:- Positions of Astoria and
Chester are approximate.

0   2000   4000 yds

APPROX: SCALE

Fig. 2. Attack on *Yorktown*, 8 May 1942.

The attack was then over, and the *Yorktown* reduced speed to 18kn and came into the wind (course 085 degrees) to land aircraft. She had sustained little damage and in less than two hours was capable of 30 knots. Her casualties were 40 killed (37 by the bomb hit) and 26 serious wounded. None of her screening ships had been hit or damaged.

26. Attack on the *Lexington*

The attack on the *Lexington* was practically simultaneous with that on the *Yorktown*, or perhaps a minute or two earlier, since the former, being to northward of the Fleet flagship was nearer to the approaching enemy aircraft. AA fire was opened by the *Lexington* at 1113, and raggedly within the next few minutes by the ships near her, some delays being caused by the difficulty of aircraft identification. Her screening ships were both fewer and in general further out than the *Yorktown*'s; the *New Orleans*, for example, owing to the *Lexington*'s abrupt alterations of course and speed, found herself as much as 4,300 yards away from her at the start of the dive bombers' attack. This was too far away to render effective AA fire support. The *Lexington* was, moreover, a less manoeuvrable ship than the *Yorktown*. The five ships which screened the *Lexington* were the cruisers *Minneapolis*, and *New Orleans* and the destroyers *Morris*, *Anderson*, and one other, probably the *Phelps*.

The first attacks were made by torpedo aircraft from two directions, port beam and starboard bow. The *Lexington* turned to port under full helm, to bring the first torpedoes ahead, but torpedoes soon began to arrive from both starboard and port, and though Captain [Frederick C.] Sherman manoeuvred as best he could to avoid them, the ship was struck just before the port forward gun gallery by a torpedo, released by an aircraft which reached a position a few hundred yards on the *Lexington*'s port beam without being taken under fire. At the time, the carrier had not long completed launching aircraft, which were still near, and the identity of the enemy machine remained undiscovered until it was on the point of releasing its torpedo, upon which firing commenced from all directions. One minute later a second torpedo struck the ship on the port side, abaft the first level with the bridge.

In all, eleven torpedo tracks were seen; some from the starboard crossed the *Lexington*'s bows; two were combed, one on each side; some from port ran ahead; and two ran under the ship without detonating. The *Lexington* reported four torpedo aircraft shot down by their gunfire.

Meanwhile, the dive-bombing attack, synchronized with the torpedo attack, had begun. Dive angles were reported to be about 70 degrees, much steeper, that is, than those of the aircraft attacking the *Yorktown*, and commencing at the high altitude of 17,000 feet. Making their approach, as they did, high in the sun and aided by a cloud, the enemy were not visible until in the final stages of their dive. The first bomb, estimated at 1,000 pounds, struck the ready ammunition locker at the after end of the port forward gun gallery about the same time as the first torpedo. The explosion put out of action the entire battery, killed all the crew of one gun and caused a number of other casualties both in the battery and inboard, and started extensive fires. Two other very near misses on the port quarter which tore holes in the hull were at first mistaken for torpedo hits. Another bomb, estimated at 500 pounds, struck the superstructure on the port side; and a much smaller bomb exploded inside the funnel. Fragments from near misses on the starboard quarter killed and injured a number of men. One apparent incendiary bomb was seen flaming as it fell, though it was not seen to hit.

The end of the action, which lasted only about 15 minutes, found the *Lexington* on fire in four places, and listing 6 degrees to port with three stoke holds partially flooded. But the fires were manageable, the list was already in process of being corrected by transfer of oil fuel, the pumps were keeping the water down, the steering gear was intact, and the ship was making 25 knots under good control.

No ship of the *Lexington*'s screen had received any damage, though the destroyer *Dewey* had six men wounded by machine-gun fire from torpedo aircraft, apparently whilst screening the *Yorktown*.

27. Sinking of the *Lexington*, 1952 8 May

The attackers had gone, and the American force was apparently in good shape. About 1230 the attack group began to return from the attack on the *Shokaku* and *Zuikaku* and commenced landing. In the case of the *Yorktown* this was completed at 1300 and she steered to close the *Lexington* which was some six to eight miles distant from her at the conclusion of the Japanese attack. Both the *Lexington*'s lifts were jammed, but as they were in the up position she was able to land her aircraft. There was at this time no doctrine in the US fleet for obtaining maximum flexibility of handling returning aircraft by diverting them from one carrier to another. In any event, the ship was now on an even keel and all fires were either out or well under control, all damage was being cleared up, and so normal did she appear that many of the returning aircraft were unaware the ship had been hit. Certainly, nobody foresaw the dreadful denouement which was about to occur.

Suddenly at 1247 a heavy explosion shook the ship. The explosion appeared to come from amidships, well down in the bowels of the carrier; the cause was not apparent, and it was at first thought to be a 1,000 pound bomb detonating after delay, though it was subsequently found to have been due to an accumulation of gasoline vapor near the central station. The primary explosion occurred in the motor generator room; the resulting damage to bulkheads enabled the fire to spread up through the ventilating system to the third and second decks. From this violent start the fire spread rapidly, above and below the armoured deck, constantly fed by oil, gasoline and other inflammables, and it was never actually got under control. At first her ability to operate was unaffected and she was able to land-on her air group about 1400. Seven of the torpedo aircraft were so short of fuel that they could not afford to spend time in recognition procedure and were fired on by the *Yorktown* for a short time, fortunately without result.

By 1422 all aircraft of both attack groups had either returned or been given up for lost. Consideration was now given to making another air attack or sending in the attack group of cruisers and destroyers for surface action. A returning *Lexington* pilot had reported that one enemy carrier was undamaged; and CTF 17 informed the Commander-in-Chief Pacific Fleet and Commander South-west Pacific Forces that there were strong indications that an additional carrier had joined the enemy forces. Although the *Shokaku* was erroneously believed sunk, wireless interceptions indicated that at least some of her aircraft had been landed on board the *Zuikaku*. The *Yorktown* had only eight fighters, 12 bombers, and eight torpedo aircraft (with seven torpedoes) serviceable; and the idea of making another air attack was consequently rejected. The idea of surface attack was also rejected on account of the force of being detected and subjected to strong carrier air attack before dark. CTF 17 decided to retire southward to investigate further the damage to the carriers and get aircraft in condition to renew the air attack next day. At 1510 Rear-Admiral Fletcher resumed tactical command. He intended to take the *Lexington*'s serviceable aircraft aboard the *Yorktown* and despatch the *Lexington* to Pearl Harbor.

However, the decision had no sooner been taken than events compelled a reversal. For some reason, no report of the internal explosion had been made from the *Lexington* until 1445, nearly two hours after its occurrence, and throughout the afternoon matters had gone from bad to worse with the ship. The fire gradually put out of action more and more communications. All lights forward went out. The fire main pressure dropped to 30 or 40 pounds. Steering control was lost, and about 1630 the order had to be given to evacuate the engine and boiler rooms, and preparations were made to abandon ship. Fire-fighting was no longer possible with all pressure gone, but at Captain Sherman's request Rear-Admiral Fitch directed the destroyer *Morris* to go alongside, pass over fire hoses and also take on board the *Lexington*'s superfluous personnel. But the fire was beyond control, additional explosions were occurring and there was danger of the ship blowing up at any moment. Rear-Admiral Fitch ordered Captain Sherman to abandon ship.

Rear-Admiral Kinkaid was put in charge of the rescue operations which were carried out by the cruisers *Minneapolis* and *New Orleans*, and destroyers *Phelps*, *Morris*, *Anderson* and *Hammann*. Owing to the carrier's heavy list to port, destroyers could not lie alongside and most of the crew had to take to the water or to life rafts; and with the ship in the trough of the sea, drifting to leeward with the wind, the men in the water on her lee side found difficulty in getting clear. Nevertheless, the rescuing destroyers worked with skill and care in the growing darkness, and thanks to this and a high state of discipline on board it is believed that no man was lost by drowning when the ship was abandoned. Out of the *Lexington*'s total complement of 2,951 a preliminary check accounted for all but 26 officers and 190 men.

At 1750 a heavy explosion rocked the listing and burning carrier and threw aircraft from her deck high in the air. A final inspection by Captain Sherman and the executive officer, Commander M. T. Seligman, who both escaped injury in this explosion, showed that no man was left on board and the destroyer *Phelps* was detailed at 1853 to sink the ship by torpedoes; and after five torpedoes had been fired at her singly the *Lexington* sank suddenly at 1952 in 2,400 fathoms of water in Lat. 15° 12' S., Long. 155° 27' E. With her she took 35 of her aircraft. The remaining survivors of the day's battles, five fighters, eight scouts, and six bombers, were landed aboard the *Yorktown*, which with the remainder of Task Force 17 withdrew southward.

28. Japanese plan abandoned

The Battle of the Coral Sea was the first set-back suffered by the Japanese since the raid on Pearl Harbor. And this set-back can be attributed directly to the escape of the carriers which were at sea when the raid took place. The outcome of the battle completely disorganized the Port Moresby expedition. One carrier was sunk, and one was put out of action and had to withdraw to Kure for repairs, heavy losses had been incurred by both carrier- and land-based air groups, and there was a shortage of fuel for aircraft on board the *Zuikaku*, the only carrier remaining operational. The Japanese support force was no longer capable of fulfilling its function, and although the approaches to Port Moresby now lay open, the invasion force retired and the date of the projected operation was postponed until July. In June, however, the door to expansion shut by the Allies at the Battle of the Coral Sea, was finally bolted by the Battle of Midway, and the plan to invade Port Moresby by sea was abandoned.

The turning back of the Port Moresby expedition at the Battle of the Coral Sea put an end to Japanese southward expansion by sea and saved for the Allies a base on which their subsequent progress to the final recapture of New Guinea was founded.

29. Lessons of the battle

The Battle of the Coral Sea showed the aircraft to be the principal offensive weapon of both the US and Japanese fleets. At the same time, it was clear that some method must be found of increasing the capacity of aircraft carriers for sustained operations. The answer was found in the development of the technique of fuelling, rearming, and storing at sea.

The Americans gained in the battle some valuable experience, of which they took immediate advantage.

On the tactical side, the outnumbering of the US fighters resulted in the complements of the carriers being increased from an average of about 17 to 27, bringing them to numerical equality with the Japanese. As a protection for carriers against torpedo air attack a very tight disposal was in future adopted in the Pacific Fleet, the screening ships being stationed on a 1,500 to 2,500-yard circle. The desirability of close co-ordination between torpedo aircraft and dive-bombing attacks was considered to have been demonstrated.

Certain faults in materiel were brought to light. Fogging of sights and windshields received attention; and Admiral Nimitz pressed for more effective aircraft bombs, and for torpedoes of a longer range, as too many hits were required at present to destroy an enemy carrier. Steps were taken to replace the existing torpedo aircraft by machines of greater speed and longer range.

Part Two

Battle of the Java Sea

Chapter I

Japan Enters the War

1. Events in the Far East

Japan opened the war in the Far East on 7 December 1941, with the attack on Pearl Harbor, followed by the commencement of attacks on Malaya and the Philippines[1] which formed separate parts of a single strategic plan that was to culminate in the conquest of the Netherlands East Indies.[2]

By the end of December 1941, the Japanese had compelled the Americans to abandon the Philippines as a naval base.[3]

On 11 January, 1942, Japan declared war on the Dutch,[4] and commenced the systematic bombing and successful invasion of Borneo, Celebes and other Dutch islands which commanded the northern approaches to the Java Sea.

Singapore dockyard was closed down on 30 January, and on the 31st the British forces in Malaya commenced to retire towards Singapore Island. By this time also, the Japanese had established control of the sea and air routes to the Philippines; in Borneo, they had seized the oil centres of Tarakan and Balikpapan and the ports of Miri, Pemangkat and Pontianak; in Celebes they had captured Menado and Kendari and were already extending their conquests to the south.[5]

On 3 February, Surabaya (east Java) and Malang (with its airfield) 50 miles south of it, were bombed. This was the first bombing of Java, and the first indication of a move south of the enemy air strength. By mid-February, the Japanese had completed the occupation of British and Dutch Borneo, of the Dutch islands of Celebes and Ceram, the latter with its airfield, and of the Dutch island naval base of Amboina (Ambon). These conquests gave them

---

1. Japan also attacked the strategically important islands, Guam and Wake, in the Central Pacific, and occupied Shanghai.
2. During December, the Japanese captured Guam and Wake islands, Hong Kong, and the islands of Makin and Tarawa in the Gilbert and Ellice group. In the political sphere they entered into an alliance with Siam.
3. The United States Army, however, held on to the Bataan peninsula until April, 1942.
4. The Japanese had hitherto taken no action on the Dutch declaration of war on 10 December, 1941, preferring to wait until their troops were well established in Malaya, and the fall of Singapore seemed assured.
5. They had captured Rabaul (New Britain) and Kavieng (New Ireland) in the Bismarck Archipelago, and Kieta on Bougainville Island, in the Solomons.

sea and air control of Makassar Strait and of the Molucca Passage, comprising the northern approaches to the Netherlands East Indies. Vice-Admiral Sir Geoffrey Layton says, 'The forces at the disposal of the Allies in the ABDA [American-British-Dutch-Australian] Area (outside Singapore) were never likely to be able to stop the Japanese advance, as Japan could easily allocate stronger naval and forces without incurring undue risks elsewhere. In the circumstances the only possible course for the Allies was to hold on with what forces they could muster in order to deny the Netherlands East Indies to the enemy as long as possible. It was inevitable in so doing that we should expose ourselves to having our weak forces in the area overwhelmed, but this result was on the whole preferable to abandoning it without firing a shot.'

Singapore with its great naval base fell on 15 February, 70 days after Japan entered the war. That very day the Japanese landed on south-east Sumatra and captured the important oil centre of Palembang. As all the available Dutch troops in Sumatra (some three weak divisions) were involved in the fall of Palembang, the Allied command ordered the withdrawal of all its forces from Sumatra to Java. The Japanese now had complete sea and air control of Karimata Channel and Gaspar Strait, comprising the north-western approaches to the Java Sea, and also in great measure, control of the Sunda Strait, the south-western exit from the Java Sea. During these extensive operations the Japanese did not have to contend with any serious Allied attacks on their sea communications.

On 25 February, the Japanese captured Bali Island (east of Java), with its airfield, which gravely impaired the security of the Dutch naval base at Surabaya, 150 miles distant, and gave them air control over the eastern exits, southward, from the Java Sea. They also landed and set up a W/T installation on Bawean Island, 85 miles north of Surabaya.

On 25 February also, an expeditionary force of nearly 100 Japanese ships was reported by General MacArthur to have assembled on 20 February off Jolo island (Philippines) in the Celebes Sea. This was the force which later did in fact proceed south through the Strait of Makassar with Java as its objective.

The Allied attempt to stem the progress southwards of the Japanese expeditionary force culminated in the disastrous battle of the Java Sea, which took place off Surabaya, on 27 February 1942, between an Allied striking force of 5 cruisers and 9 destroyers and a Japanese force of 7 cruisers and 17 destroyers. On this day and the two days following, the Allied striking force was practically annihilated, except for four American destroyers which succeeded in reaching Australia. Some damage was sustained by the enemy, but none of his ships was sunk. Java was invaded during the night of

28 February/1 March, and on 9 March the Netherlands East Indies formally surrendered.

The calamitous outcome of the battle of the Java Sea was due to several factors. Primarily, it was due to the ability of the Japanese to concentrate greatly superior forces of all arms in the areas aimed at. Equally significant, however, was the insufficiency of Allied reconnaissance and fighter planes, which left the enemy fleet free to make full use of its air arm for reconnaissance and spotting, while the Allied naval forces were left without any air assistance whatsoever.

A third handicap was the constitution of the Allied striking force which was composed of American, British, Australian and Dutch ships, which had been assembled only 24 to 48 hours before the battle was joined. Apart from the language difficulty, the striking force had never worked together as a fleet; plans had to be hastily made, and consequently, the efficiency of signal communications was a matter of much greater importance than it would normally have been in a well-organized, trained fleet. Unfortunately, the signalling system was inadequate, the flagship's signalling apparatus was rendered useless by the vibration of her own gunfire, and she was reduced to the primitive method of hand signal lamps.

Last but not least, the Allied command was the outcome of a staff organization, conceived perforce in haste, and never fully developed, the outstanding feature of which was an almost complete lack of co-operation between the air and the naval services. This led to delay in reporting vital information, to the absence of fighter planes which were being used for the protection of bombers carrying out independent and uncoordinated attacks, and to the lack of any co-operation between the air command and the naval command, either ashore or afloat. On no occasion throughout this campaign for the defence of the Netherlands East Indies did any naval operation have the support of a single fighter plane.

A brief account of the evolution of the short-lived Allied command in the South West Pacific, an area which came to be known as the ABDA Area, is therefore essential to an understanding of the battle of the Java Sea.

2. A Unified Command in SW Pacific

In mid-December 1941, there were five different authorities controlling naval dispositions in the Far East – British, American, Dutch, Australian and New Zealand. Each nation controlled its own forces, the strategic control of United States forces being exercised from Washington. The Dutch Naval Command (Vice-Admiral C. E. L. Helfrich) was in Batavia (Java), and on 2 January 1942, the British Commander-in-Chief Eastern Fleet (Vice-Admiral Sir Geoffrey Layton) decided to join him there. The United States Commander-in-Chief Asiatic Fleet (Admiral Thomas C. Hart) arrived at Surabaya on 4 January 1942, having left the Philippines on 26 December 1941, in the United States' submarine *Shark*. He declined Vice-Admiral Helfrich's urgent invitation to join him at Batavia, considering that Surabaya was better suited to American naval needs being nearer to Port Darwin which had been designated as the major American base.[6]

3. General Sir Archibald Wavell, Supreme Commander

For the purpose of establishing a unified command, General Sir Archibald Wavell was appointed on 3 January 1942 as Supreme Commander of the 'ABDA' Area, which stretched for over 5,000 miles from the north of Burma to the Gulf of Carpentaria (in northern Australia) and for nearly 2,500 miles from north to south. General Wavell arrived in Batavia on 10 January 1942, and formally took over the Supreme Command in the ABDA area on 15 January, with the title of 'Abdacom'. He set up his headquarters at Lembang in west Java, about 7 miles north of Bandoeng, and about 100 miles inland, by road and rail, from Batavia.

4. Difficulties of ABDA Command

The attempt to unify the command in the ABDA Area was not successful. The difficulties encountered are summarized by the Allied Commanders-in-Chief as follows:

Vice-Admiral Sir Geoffrey Layton, KCB, DSO: 'Although the formation of the Abda organization produced a settled system in that area, it unfortunately did not put an end to the difficulties experienced. Chief among these, as had been expected, was a great delay and congestion in communications. It was mainly due to this, and not to any laxity on the part of the Abda authorities, that I found during this period, it was almost impossible to get an up-to-date picture of the situation in the Abda area. Very few of Abdacom's operational summaries or appreciations reached me, and intercepted W/T signals were my most effective source of information. Our communications organization for the Far East revolved around Singapore, and once we began to lose the full

---

6. Port Darwin was subsequently found to be too far removed from the scene of operations and proved unsuitable as a base in other respects. Consequently, on 29 January, Admiral Hart ordered American auxiliaries to move to Netherlands East Indies harbours.

use of that, improvised channels became rapidly choked, in spite of every effort to produce a fresh organization. Messages to and from Java took anything up to 10 to 15 days before they found their way from their originator in Supreme Headquarters to the addressees in Colombo or vice versa, and many did not arrive at all.'

Admiral Thomas C. Hart, USN: 'Abdacom had a very complicated command involving four navy, four army and six air organizations, consequently there was a great deal to do in organizing and equipping a GHQ, which naturally required time. In the face of an advancing enemy there was of course, not time. We never reached a condition under which … there would be certainty that information and clear directives would be transmitted with despatch.'

Vice-Admiral C. E. L. Helfrich, RNethN, remarks that in his opinion the operational command was too complicated to ensure real co-operation and rapid communication. He says, 'Abdafloat [the Naval Command] was at Lembang, Abdair [the Air Command] at Bandoeng [7 miles distant]. The Rec-group by whom the reconnaissance flights were operated and who received the reconnaissance reports direct, was also at Bandoeng, but separate from Abdair. After General Wavell … left Java [on 25 February 1942] Abdafloat moved to Bandoeng but we did not succeed in time in improving the co-operation. Abdafloat was still too separate from Abdair and from the Rec-group. There was not one Central War Room, where everything converged and where the officers in command of the forces were together to make immediate decisions after mutual consideration.'

5. Dissolution of ABDA Command

On 25 February 1942, General Wavell, in accordance with orders received, left Java. The Abdacom organization ceased to exist, and Vice-Admiral Helfrich assumed command of the Allied naval forces defending the Netherlands East Indies. The situation that faced him was almost desperate. Singapore had fallen; the Japanese were in the islands of Sumatra and Bali, west and east of Java; their presence in the Dutch port, Koepang (Timor), constituted an increasing threat to Darwin; a Japanese expeditionary force was moving south from Makassar Strait, threatening Java from the north-east, and another was assembling near Banka Island, threatening it from the north-west.

Meanwhile the Allied naval forces had been striving to stem the gathering flood. During the previous five weeks, they had been carrying out raids on the enemy's convoys, in a vain endeavour to stave off the inevitable invasion of Java. They worked under the grave disadvantage of having no port which was free from daily bombings; Surabaya was exposed to air attack and indeed, the fuel lines to the docks there had been ruptured by bombs. Allied ships therefore had to keep at sea during the day, while at night there was always the possibility of the enemy effecting a landing. In such conditions of stress and strain it is not surprising that on 27th February, a few hours before the first shot was fired in the Battle of the Java Sea, Rear-Admiral K. W. F. M. Doorman, RNethN, commanding the Allied fleet at sea, felt called upon to inform Vice-Admiral Helfrich that, 'This day the personnel reached the limit of endurance; to-morrow the limit will be exceeded.'

Chapter II

The Japanese Close In on Java

6 (i). Engagement off Balikpapan, 23–24 January

On 20 January, a large enemy fleet was reported in Makassar Strait, heading towards Balikpapan on the east coast of Borneo. Six American submarines were sent off to meet it, three being stationed in Makassar Strait, and three off Balikpapan. On 22 January, one of the American submarines in Makassar Strait (the *Sturgeon*, Lt-Cdr. William L. Wright, USN) probably damaged or sank a carrier; and on 24 January, a submarine on patrol near Balikpapan HNMS *K-18*, sank a destroyer.[1]

An American force under Rear-Admiral Glassford, USN also set out from Koepang (Timor) to raid the enemy convoy. It consisted of two light cruisers, the *Boise* (flag) and the *Marblehead* (Capt. Arthur G. Robinson), and four destroyers, the *Ford*, the *Pope*, the *Parrott* and the *Paul Jones*. Commander Paul H. Talbot, USN commanded the destroyers.

On the way through Sape Strait, the *Boise* (Capt. Edward J. Moran) struck an uncharted pinnacle rock and had to fall out. She subsequently went to India for repairs and took no further part in the campaign. Rear-Admiral Glassford transferred his flag to the *Marblehead*, whose speed was unfortunately reduced to 15 knots through turbine trouble. The destroyers were therefore ordered on ahead, to carry out the raid on the convoy.

Air reconnaissance on 22 January had reported the enemy force as consisting of four cruisers, fourteen destroyers and nine transports, moving towards Balikpapan in small groups. Dutch bombers attacked this force on the afternoon of 23rd, and claimed hits on two cruisers, one destroyer and four transports.

Meanwhile, on the morning of the 23rd, when the American destroyers were just south of the Postillon (Postiljon) Islands, they were ordered to move northward to attack. At 0245 on 24 January, a column of several enemy destroyers was sighted by the American destroyers off Balikpapan. 'It is difficult to form an entirely accurate picture of the events of the following

---

1. This apparent, though uncorroborated, Dutch success is not mentioned in the *Japanese Report*, though this might be due to a lack of information.

hour ... [the] little column (of 4 destroyers) steamed back and forth among the enemy vessels, firing first their torpedoes and then their guns at dim outlines of ships, spreading havoc and confusion among the Japanese [2]... It seems fairly certain that we sank at least 5 or 6 ships. Two of ... [them], because of the nature of the explosion and of their burning, were thought to have been fuel ships. One was a destroyer, which was completely demolished, and at least 2 merchantmen were sunk ... The whole action took place within an area of only 4 or 5 miles radius, with its centre about 4 or 5 miles north-east of Balikpapan lightship.'[3]

This Allied raid however, successful as it was, did not prevent the Japanese from taking Balikpapan, which they claimed to have done on 24 January.

6 (ii). Action of Madura Strait, 4 February

On 1 February, Allied air reconnaissance reported an enemy force off Balikpapan, consisting of three cruisers, ten destroyers and twenty transports.

Rear-Admiral Doorman thereupon issued a directive stating that enemy transports would be attacked and destroyed in a night attack. His striking force consisted of four cruisers, the *De Ruyter* (flag), the *Houston*, the *Marblehead* and the *Tromp*; the American Destroyer Division 58 (led by Cdr. Thomas H. Binford, USN, in the *Stewart*), consisting of the *Edwards*, the *Barker* and the *Bulmer*; and a Dutch Destroyer Division (commanded by Lt. Cdr. F. J. E. Krips, RNethN, in the *Van Ghent*), consisting of the *Piet Hein* and the *Banckert*. This Allied force was at anchor in Bounder Roads, Madura Island, when enemy planes passed over to bomb Surabaya on 3 February, and sighted it.

On 4 February, it assembled at 0500, at the east end of Madura Strait, and proceeded on an easterly course preparatory to starting a run up Makassar Strait. At 0949, when this striking force was approximately between Kangean Islands and Bali Island, the *Marblehead* sighted Japanese high-level bombing planes at about 17,000 ft., consisting of five groups of nine planes each. After power-gliding down to 14,000 ft. they released their bombs in salvoes on signal from the leader. The attack was successful. The *Marblehead* was so severely damaged that she had to go to Simonstown, and later to the United States for repairs, taking no further part in the campaign. The *Houston*'s after

---

2. 'When the American [destroyer division] attacked our convoy at Balikpapan at night, the patrol ship which first sighted them mistakenly reported them as cruisers.' (*Japanese Report*, p. 8). 'When the *Naka* was attacked by enemy destroyers at Balikpapan, a long time was needed to make preparations for firing torpedoes.' *Japanese Report*, p.11.
3. *United States Combat Narrative*, p.19

triple 8 in. turret was demolished, and out of action for the remainder of the campaign. The striking force had to retire south through Lombok Strait, the American cruisers putting in to Tjilatjap (south Java), while the remainder returned to Batavia via Sunda Strait.

On the same day (4 February), 500 miles away, the Japanese, in their turn, suffered losses. The destroyer *Suzukaze*, while on patrol at 6 knots outside Staring Bay (south of Kendari, on the east coast of Celebes), at 1700, 'received a torpedo attack from starboard.' One torpedo exploded off the port bow, which left her disabled, unable either to fight or steer, though she escaped sinking. This was apparently the work of a US submarine, as there is no report of the incident at Dutch Naval Headquarters in London. Four days later, another attack got home; on 8 February 1942, at 2045, the Japanese destroyer *Natsushio*, off Makassar, was attacked by an Allied, probably a US submarine on the port side. She was split open from the forward part of the port bow to underneath the engine room, and on the morning of the 9th, broke in two amidships.

6 (iii). The Gaspar Strait Action, 14–15 February

On the night of 12–13 February a Japanese expeditionary force moved southward from the Anambas Islands, with Palembang (south-east Sumatra) as its objective. It consisted of 2 heavy cruisers, 4 other cruisers, 14 destroyers, 23 transports (or 22 and one aircraft carrier), one auxiliary and 6 unidentified vessels. Nine enemy flying boats were on the water at Sungeiliat (Banka Island), at dawn, 13 February. On 14 February, Japanese parachutists attacked Palembang.

By direction of Abdafloat, a striking force, operating under the orders of Rear-Admiral Doorman, was ordered to seek out and engage the above Japanese expeditionary force, preferably by night. This striking force consisted of five cruisers, the *De Ruyter* (flag), the *Java*, the *Tromp*, the *Hobart* and the *Exeter*; four Dutch destroyers, the *Piet Hein*, the *Banckert*, the *Van Ghent* and the *Kortenaer*; and six American destroyers, the *Stewart*, the *Barker*, the *Bulmer*, the *Pillsbury*, the *Parrott* and the *John D. Edwards*. No British destroyers were with this force.

Rear-Admiral Doorman's force proceeded northward, from the vicinity of North Watcher Light, about dusk on 14th February. The destroyer *Van Ghent* struck a reef in Stolze Straits (east of Banka) during the night, and she was destroyed by her crew, who were taken off by the *Banckert*. The force proceeded through Gaspar Strait to the north of Banka, but failed to make contact with enemy surface forces, as the Japanese expeditionary force had already reached Banka Strait. Moreover, from 1100 to 1800 on 15 February, the Allied force was subjected to an intense and continuous bombing attack. The *Hobart* was heavily bombed at 1234, 15 February, and though none of the ships was directly hit, damage was sustained from near misses, and two American destroyers, the *Barker* and the *Bulmer* were so badly shaken that they had subsequently (20 February) to sail to Australia for repairs.

The operation ended when the Japanese captured Palembang on 15 February. Rear-Admiral Doorman's force returned to harbour on 16 February, and because of the likelihood of air attack, the force was split up, part going to Tanjong Priok and part to Oosthaven (southern Sumatra).

6 (iv). Sunda Strait Auxiliary Patrol

After the Gaspar Strait action, and in order to deal with the possibility of Japanese attempts to infiltrate across Sunda Strait into Java, the Sunda Strait Auxiliary Patrol was formed on 17 February. Four ships of the 21st Minesweeping Flotilla patrolled the western portion of Sunda Strait by night and anchored off Merak (north-west Java) during the daytime, while six Dutch patrol craft patrolled the north-eastern approach to Sunda Strait.

6 (v). Air attack on Port Darwin, 19 February

On 19 February, the airport, warehouses, docks and practically every ship in Darwin harbour, were destroyed by an attack by about 72 high-level bombers and 18 dive bombers. Dive bombers sank the American destroyer *Peary* (which was under orders to join Rear-Admiral Doorman's striking force), three troop transports, a tanker and two merchantmen. High-level bombers sank two ammunition ships.

Five enemy aircraft were shot down for certain, five probable; the Allies lost eight in the air, and ten on the ground.

The size of the enemy heavy bombers indicated that they were based on carriers or seaplane tenders.

6 (vi). Action off Bali, 19–20 February

On 18 February, a Japanese force of four cruisers and two transports had seized the airfield in the south-east of Bali Island, off east Java. Thereupon, on the night of 19–20 February, Rear-Admiral Doorman attacked an enemy force estimated at two cruisers, four or five destroyers and four transports, off the south-east of Bali.

The Allied force was in two groups. The first group, which lay at Tjilatjap, consisted of the *De Ruyter* (flag), the *Java*, the Dutch destroyer *Piet Hein* and two US destroyers, the *Ford* and the *Pope*. The second group at Surabaya consisted of the Dutch flotilla leader *Tromp*, and four US destroyers, the *Stewart*, the *Parrott*, the *Edwards* and the *Pillsbury*. The group from Tjilatjap arrived off the south coast of Bali about 2130. They found the enemy ships stationed as if our forces had been expected from the north. The group from Surabaya proceeded through Bali Strait, and went into action about 0134.

The Japanese were disposed in two groups, which enabled the Allied force in single column to pass between them. This led to the enemy firing on his own ships.[4] The accounts of the action are not very clear, and the movements on both sides remain obscure.[5]

According to Allied reports, one enemy cruiser and one destroyer were hit by torpedoes, and another cruiser by gunfire. The only Japanese warships mentioned in the *Japanese Report* as being present on this occasion were the three destroyers of the 8th Destroyer Division, viz the *Oshio*, the *Asashio* and the *Michishio*.

The torpedo attacks carried out by these ships were, according to Japanese sources as follows:

0150	*Oshio*	4 torpedoes	target *Java*	running range 1,650 yards, no damage
0212	*Asahio*	4 torpedoes	target *Tromp*	running range 1,650 yards, great damage[6]
0213	*Oshio*	4 torpedoes	target *Tromp*	running range 1,650 yards, great damage
0215	*Asahio*	1 torpedo	target *Tromp*	running range 1,650 yards, great damage
0220	*Michishio*	4 torpedoes	target two U.S. destroyers	1,900 yards, uncertain results

---

4. 'Much difficulty was encountered in identifying types of enemy vessels and estimating the situation. There was considerable error in observation (of types of ships).' (*Japanese Report*, page 17).

5. 'Understanding between the Captain and the Torpedo Firing Control Officer was lacking, and they were unable to respond to the conditions of the moment that the *Oshio* was late in firing and the *Michiskio* was late in training tubes to the opposite side for firing.' *Japanese Report*, p. 18).

6. Speaking of the 'number of torpedoes to be fired against a cruiser,' the CO of the 8th Destroyer Division says: 'Except when an extremely good firing position is gained it is difficult to destroy even a cruiser unless the entire firing line fires (simultaneously). In the engagement off the Island of Bali, even though a torpedo attack consisting of two salvoes of 4 torpedoes each from the *Oshio* and one salvo of 4 torpedoes from the *Asashio* was carried out against an enemy cruiser, successful results were not achieved.' (*Japanese Report*, p.17).

The *Japanese Report* further states that the three destroyers were hit by 4-in. gunfire.[7] The *Michishio* was severely damaged and, being hit in the engine room, stopped dead. Referring to the need for training in emergency measures against heavy damage in action, the *Japanese Report* on the *Michishio*'s torpedo firing in this action states that, 'immediately after giving the order for an "opposite course" torpedo engagement to starboard with a ship 45° to starboard, an enemy torpedo track was sighted, and in turning inside to evade, a sight angle of 30° was exceeded. At the same time, an enemy cruiser was sighted close by, 30° to port, and the order was given for a torpedo engagement to port on opposing courses. Then the compressed air used to operate the training gear … failed and the generators were put out of action by a shell hit in the after engine room, so that the entire communications equipment was useless. Personnel were stationed on the hand training gear and the emergency communications equipment.

'Then a shell struck a tube mount, killing the chief torpedo man and the … follow-the-pointer man. The war heads of torpedoes in No.3 tube mount were damaged; their charges were scattered and caught fire. The determination was maintained to fire torpedoes at the enemy to starboard and also at the enemy to port, as well as to endeavour to extinguish the blaze, but the command station caught fire … from a shell hit on the port side of the bridge, and finally the opportunity for firing was lost because the re-adjusting of the depth setting and the training of the tube mount was accomplished too late.'[8]

Subsequently, the *Oshio* was bombed on 20 February in Batan Strait, by three Allied light bombers, and as a result of near misses, her 'fighting power was for the most part lost'. By near misses on 20 February damage was also done to the *Michishio*, by three Allied heavy bombers while she was being towed in Batan Strait.[9]

Allied losses in the action off Bali were the *Piet Hein* sunk, probably by gunfire, for the *Ford* noted that she did not settle as if holed below the water line, nor does the enemy claim to have torpedoed her: the *Tromp* was so badly damaged by gunfire, that she subsequently had to go to Australia for repairs; the *Java* and the *Stewart* were also hit by shells, and the latter had to be dry-docked at Surabaya, where, owing to faulty blocking she rolled over and damaged both herself and the dock (she was bombed on 24 February, and

7. 'In ordinary drill it is easy to rely on assistants for calculation of the track angle, but in the engagement off the Island of Bali where there was continual damage from a rain of shells, this was not feasible, and the Torpedo Firing Control Officer was compelled to order the torpedo track angle himself.' *Japanese Report*, p. 17.

8. *Japanese Report*, p.52.

9. Other Japanese losses not mentioned in the *Japanese Report* are claimed by the Dutch Naval authorities: 24/12/41, a destroyer of the *Amagiri* class, sunk by the submarine HNMS *K-16*; 10/1/42, a destroyer sunk by the shore batteries at Tarakan (Borneo); 1/2/42, a destroyer, which struck a mine, at Ambon.

destroyed): the *Pillsbury* and the *Parrott* were subsequently withdrawn from the Allied force in urgent need of overhaul.

6 (vii). Sinking of USS *Langley*, 27 February

These actions did little to arrest the Japanese advance and, to meet the serious deficiency in aircraft of the Allied Fleet, on 22 February the American seaplane tender *Langley* (Cdr. Robert P. McConnell, USN) with 32 assembled P-40 Es on deck, and with pilots and flight personnel on board, and the *Seawitch* with 27 crated P-40 Es in her hold, were detached from a Fremantle-Ceylon convoy, and diverted to Java. The *Langley* left the convoy several hours before the *Seawitch*.

On the morning of 27 February, the *Langley* met two US destroyers, the *Whipple* and the *Edsall*, and proceeded with them towards Tjilatjap (south Java). At 0900/27, when within 100 miles of that port, they were sighted by an enemy plane. The *Langley*, having only a small flight deck, was unable to launch the fighters she carried, and no help could be given her, as there were not 15 fighter planes in the whole of Java.

At 1140, when within 74 miles of Tjilatjap, nine enemy bombers arrived and attacked. On their third and last bombing run, the *Langley* received five direct hits and three near misses. She was heavily damaged, and although the fires were got under control, at 1352, the order was given to abandon ship, and the *Whipple* sank her with nine 4-in. shells and two torpedoes. Casualties were six killed and five missing.

The *Seawitch* arrived at Tjilatjap on the forenoon of 28th. There was no time, however, to assemble the crated planes, in view of the imminent landing of the enemy on Java, and they were apparently destroyed in their crates when Tjilatjap was abandoned.

7. Allied Naval losses prior to battle of Java Sea

Thus, in the five weeks preceding the battle of the Java Sea, the Allied Naval Command in Java lost the services, through enemy action or by misadventure, of no less than thirteen ships, viz., one Dutch 5.9-in. cruiser, the *Tromp*; two American 6-in. cruisers, the *Boise* and the *Marblehead*; four Dutch destroyers, the *Van Ghent*, the *Piet Hein*, the *Banckert*[10] and the *Van Nes*,[11] and

---

10. The *Banckert* was damaged by bombs at Surabaya on February 24th. She was further damaged by bombs at Surabaya on 1 March and had to be destroyed by her crew.

11. The *Van Nes* was sunk on 17 February by Japanese bombers south of Banka, while escorting the MV *Sloet Van Der Beele* carrying evacuees from Billiton. No trace of survivors was found.

six American destroyers, the *Barker*, the *Bulmer*, the *Peary*, the *Stewart*, the *Pillsbury*, and the *Parrott*.

Three other destroyers, making altogether nine out of the original 13 American destroyers in the ABDA Area, were not available for Rear-Admiral Doorman's striking force at the battle of the Java Sea, viz., the *Whipple*, which had been damaged in collision with the *De Ruyter*; the *Edsall*, which had been damaged by a depth-charge dropped at too slow a speed; and the *Pope* which was leaking badly. The Australian cruiser *Hobart* was also unable to join Rear-Admiral Doorman's striking force on 27 February, having to refuel at Batavia on 26 February from the RFA *War Sirdar*, which owing to bomb damage received that day, could not fuel her in time to sail for the scene of action.

8. Vice-Admiral Helfrich, Commander Naval Forces

At 1200, on 25 February 1942, General Wavell handed over the command of the ABDA Area to the Dutch, and the ABDACOM command ceased to exist. Vice-Admiral C.E.L.H Helfrich assumed command of the Allied Naval Forces defending the Netherlands East Indies, with the title *Commandant der Zeemacht* (Commander of Naval Forces, short title 'CZM') in place of his previous title of ABDAFLOAT.

9. Formation of Combined Striking Force

Intelligence had been received on 24 February of an enemy transport fleet, carrying an invading force of approximately two divisions, with strong escorting forces, which was proceeding south in the Makassar Strait, and might be off Java by dawn on 27 February. This threat became more acute on 25 February, when the Japanese landed on Bawean Island, 85 miles north of Surabaya, and set up a W/T installation.[12] At 1125 on the 25th, Vice-Admiral Helfrich therefore gave orders that the Eastern Striking Force under Rear-Admiral K.W.F.M. Doorman, RNethN, which was based on Surabaya, was to be reinforced by all available fleet cruisers and destroyers then at Tanjong Priok.

In pursuance of this order, Commodore J.A. Collins, RAN, Commodore Commanding China Force (short title 'CCCF') ordered HMS *Exeter* (HMAS *Hobart* not being available), to proceed at 1500 on 25 February, to

---

12. This installation was bombarded by the US submarine *S.38* (Lt. Henry G. Munson, USN), with her entire supply of 4-in. ammunition, though with what result is not known.

the east Java Sea with HMAS *Perth* and three British destroyers, the *Electra*, the *Jupiter* and the *Encounter*.

On the night of 25 February, Rear-Admiral Doorman with two Dutch cruisers, the *De Ruyter* and the *Java*, two Dutch destroyers, the *Witte de With* and the *Kortenaer*, the American cruiser *Houston* and five American destroyers, the *Edwards*, the *Alden*, the *Ford*, the *Pope* and the *Paul Jones*, made a sweep east along the coast of Madura, in the hope of intercepting the transports reported near the Bawean Islands. No contact was made, and the Allied force returned to Surabaya the following morning. At 0148 on 26 February the *Exeter* while on passage received instructions from Rear-Admiral Doorman to rendezvous in Surabaya harbour about noon. From noon onwards, therefore, the Eastern Striking Force, with the *Exeter*'s detachment from Tanjong Priok, constituted a new force known as the Combined Striking Force (short title 'CSF'), with Rear-Admiral Doorman as its Commander (short title 'CCSF').

10. Formation of Western Striking Force

Following the departure of the *Exeter* from Tanjong Priok, further reports on 26 February confirmed the presence of large numbers of Japanese warships and transports in the east Java Sea, and reports of a convoy of enemy transports at Muntok (Banka Island), in the west, were received which strengthened the belief that an invasion of Java was imminent. A Western Striking Force was therefore formed at Batavia, consisting of three cruisers and two destroyers which sailed at 2200/26 to seek out and attack the Muntok convoy.

11. Orders for Combined Striking Force

About 1615 on 26 February, when Rear-Admiral Doorman was in the operations room at the headquarters of Rear-Admiral Koenraad, the Commander of the Naval Base at Surabaya (Commandant of the Navy, short title 'CMR'), he received the following signal from Vice-Admiral Helfrich, who was at his Naval Headquarters at Bandoeng:

'CZM to E.C., (R) C.C.C.F., Comsowespac.
'Most Immediate
'At 1155 Java time, 26th February, 30 transports were in position lat. 04° 50′ south, long. 114° 20′ east [i.e., about 25 miles north-west of the Arends Islands, and 180 miles north-east of Surabaya.] Course 245°, speed 10 knots. Two cruisers and four destroyers in company with transports. Striking force is to proceed to sea in order to attack enemy

after dark. After attack, striking force is to proceed towards Tanjong Priok. Acknowledge.'[13]

These directions were supplemented by the following signal:

'28th Feb. received at 2055/26: –

'Most Immediate

'My 0533Z/26 you must continue attacks, until enemy is destroyed. 1033Z/26.'

12. Lack of Allied aircraft

During the afternoon of 26 February, Rear-Admirals Doorman and Koenraad endeavoured to procure US Army bombers to carry out a reconnaissance, but none were available for this purpose. Thereupon, in order to minimize the delay attendant on the centralized system adopted by Reconnaissance Group at Bandoeng, Rear-Admiral Doorman urgently requested the Naval Seaplane Base at Moro-Krambagan, Surabaya (*Marine Vliegkamp*, Moro-Krambagan, short title 'MVKM'), to repeat to him immediately all reports made by Reconnaissance Group flying boat pilots to their headquarters at Bandoeng.[14]

All sources agree that the Combined Striking Force had no aircraft whatsoever co-operating with them, although normally the *Houston* carried four planes, the *De Ruyter*, the *Exeter* and the *Java* two each, and the *Perth* one.

13. Allied plans

Rear-Admiral Doorman then considered two possible measures for making contact with the Japanese convoy:

i. By a sweep east, along the north coast of Madura, followed by a sweep west, as far as Toeban.

ii. By a sweep north, to the west of Bawean, continuing north-eastwards towards the Arends Islands.

He decided on the first route, as the second involved the risk of missing the convoy (whose objective appeared to be Madura or the Java coast) through lack of air reconnaissance. This decision probably accounted for his subsequent

---

13. *Dutch Account*, pp.23 & 34.

14. According to Admiral Helfrich: 'The number of planes was insufficient. The Dutch and American naval flying boats had suffered heavy losses; the number of remaining flying boats to be used for reconnaissance was rather limited.' *Dutch Account*, p.28.

omission to seek out the convoy reported in Rear-Admiral Koenraad's 2220/26 to be north-east of Bawean.

14. Allied plan of attack

Later in the afternoon of 26 February, Rear-Admiral Doorman called a conference of all his commanding officers, where the following decisions were taken:

(i)   The Combined Striking Force was at all costs, to prevent a Japanese landing on Java or Madura.

(ii) The Japanese transports were to be attacked, preferably by night.

(iii) After the attack, the Combined Striking Force was to proceed to Tanjong Priok.

(iv) Formation for night. A formation for the night (full moon was on 3 March) was ordered as follows: a screen of British and Dutch destroyers ahead, five cruisers in line, and four US destroyers in rear.[15]

(v)   Plan for night attack:

a. The Dutch and British destroyers were to carry out a torpedo attack as soon as the enemy was sighted and were to follow it up by an attempt to run right into the convoy and cause as much damage as possible. The cruisers were to remain out of the convoy and fire upon it. Finally, the US destroyers were to carry out a torpedo attack.

The Allied destroyers were to be permitted to show distinguishing coloured lights after delivering their torpedo attack, in order to avoid being shelled by their own cruisers.

b. If contact was made near the coast, special precautions were to be taken because Dutch mines had been laid off the north coast of Madura within the 20 metre line, and in the Toeban [Toban] bight within the 10 metre line. Consequently, after the attack, Allied ships would have to turn to the north. If the Combined Striking Force's course was east, and contact was made with enemy transports on the port bow, the Allied cruisers were to

---

15. The reason for the US destroyers being placed in rear was because 'they [had] a rather heavy torpedo armament (12 tubes) but the max. speed of the torpedoes ... [was] very low (27 knots). Owing to this, the US Divl. Comr. wanted to get information from the ships ahead about the targets he ... [had] to attack (type, course and speed).' (*Dutch Account*, p. 5.)

proceed at least 5 miles on course east after passing the enemy's line to avoid US torpedoes.

c. After the night attack the formation would be broken up and it was not considered possible to make definite plans for any subsequent action. In the actual event, the orders for a night formation did not affect the issue, for contact was made with the enemy in daylight and, on receipt of an enemy report on 27 February the dispositions to be taken up by the Allied ships had to be passed by signal.

Chapter III

The Battle of the Java Sea, 27 February 1942

15. Opposing naval forces

The Allied naval force, known as the Combined Striking Force, engaged in the Battle of the Java Sea, consisted of five cruisers and nine destroyers. This was composed of one US[1] and one British 8-inch cruisers and two Dutch and one Australian 6-inch cruiser, with four US, three British and two Dutch destroyers.

The Japanese naval force confronting Rear-Admiral Doorman on 27 February is estimated to have been four 7.8-in. cruisers, three 5-5-in, cruisers, and 17 destroyers.

16. Departure from Surabaya, 1830

Rear-Admiral Doorman having decided to make a sweep to the east along the north coast of Madura as far as Sapoedi Strait, and, if the enemy were not sighted, to sweep west and search the bight of Toeban, sailed from Surabay at 1830 on 26 February, through the *Westervaarwater* (Western Channel), towards the Java Sea. His ships were disposed in line ahead (in succession) as follows: two Dutch destroyers, the *Witte de With* and the *Kortenaer*. Three British destroyers, the *Electra*, the *Encounter* and the *Jupiter*. Five Allied cruisers, the *De Ruyter*, the *Exeter*, the *Houston*, the *Perth* and the *Java*. Four US destroyers, the *Edwards*, the *Alden*, the *Ford* and the *Paul Jones*.

17. Lack of information

Just about the time that the Combined Striking Force was sailing from Surabaya at 1830/26, US Army bombers found and attacked a Japanese convoy in position 05° 30′ S., 113° 00′ E. (about 25 miles north-east of Bawean Island). No report of this was made to Rear-Admiral Doorman until, at 2220/26, twenty minutes after the GOC, 3rd Army Division (East Java Command) had informed Rear-Admiral Koenraad (Commander of the

---

1. After triple turret out of action from a bomb hit on 4 February.

Dutch Naval Base at Surabaya), in the course of conversation, of the attack and of the convoy's position, Admiral Koenraad signalled Admiral Doorman as follows: 'One convoy, course unknown, 05° 30' S., 113° 00' E., T. 1100Z.'

This 'Bawean' convoy, it should be noted, was evidently the same convoy that Vice-Admiral Helfrich had reported to Rear-Admiral Doorman about 1615/26 to be some 25 miles to the north-west of the Arends Islands. It subsequently transpired that this convoy remained in the vicinity of Bawean for two days before proceeding to Java. It was protected by fighter planes, for at 1900, a Y-flying boat reported its inability to reconnoitre round Bawean Island because of the presence of two catapult fighter planes.

18. First report, Bawean convoy

The exact time that Rear-Admiral Doorman received Rear-Admiral Koenraad's signal, 2220/26, is not known, but by 2235 on 26 February, Vice-Admiral Helfrich, having received the US Army bombers' full report, signalled it; he added to his signal a report made by a Dutch Navy plane at 1440/26. Rear-Admiral Doorman probably received Vice-Admiral Helfrich's signal at the same time as Commodore Collins, i.e. at 0255/27, eight hours after the US Army bombers' attack had been made. The signal was as follows:

> 'Reported by two B.17, 1100Z / 26, convoy at 05° 30' S., 113° 00' E., consisting of 18 ships, probably more. One ship possible aircraft carrier or battleship. Six fighters protecting convoy. Reported by Dutch Navy plane 0710Z 26 [i.e.1440 GH] two cruisers *Isuzu* class, two destroyers, position 06° 25' S., 117° 13' E., course 315°, speed 10–20 knots.'
>
> *Time of origin*: 1505Z /26.
> *Time* of receipt: 0255GH /27.

This delay in communicating information no doubt accounts for Rear-Admiral Doorman's subsequent representation, by W/T to Vice-Admiral Helfrich, of a delay of six to eight hours in the receipt of reconnaissance signals.

19. Lack of co-operation

Speaking of the regrettable delay in reporting the position of the Bawean convoy, Vice-Admiral Helfrich says: 'I did not know that the US bombers were to make an attack. It must have been ordered by Vice-Admiral Helfrich [Abdair] and passed to Malang where these bombers were based. This shows the lack of co-operation in the command. It should have been a matter of routine for these bombers to report the position of the convoy immediately.' Vice-Admiral

Helfrich continues: 'CMR [Admiral Koenraad] passed the message to CCSF [Admiral Doorman] at 2220. Apparently CCSF did not think it necessary to search for the convoy, even after my later signal at 0255 on 27 February. I do not know what his motives were; probably he kept to his intention to cover that night, the expected landing places from Madura to Toeban, which would exclude searching for the convoy far away to northward.'[2]

20. Allied Force on patrol

It is possible however that Rear-Admiral Doorman did not receive any signals about the Bawean convoy until too late, because at 1200/27 he informed Vice-Admiral Helfrich that 'good reconnaissance information ... last night failed me.' In any case, after leaving Surabaya at 1830/26 he patrolled eastward, and did not go after the convoy which lay to the north.

21. Allied Force, night formation

At about 2200/26, the Combined Striking Force was through and clear of the eastern passage of the minefield in Surabaya Strait, and after proceeding 8 miles to the north altered course to the east. The force was now in its night formation proceeding at 20 knots, and continuing on an eastward course to Sapoedi Strait, which was reached at 0108 on 27 February. Rear-Admiral Doorman then altered course to 284° and maintained a westerly course throughout the remainder of the night.

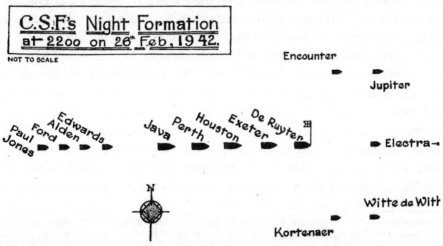

Fig. 3. The Combined Striking Force's night formation, 26 February, 1942.

---

2. *Dutch Account*, p.25.

In the meantime, at about 2200/26, six Dutch MTBs had left Surabaya and by about 2317 had taken up stations off the coast, three near Toeban in 06° 50′ S., 112° 05′ E., and three near the north coast of Madura in 06° 52′ S., 113° 20′ E.

22. Allied submarines, disposition

At 0325/27, Vice-Admiral Helfrich informed Rear-Admiral Doorman that 'at 2330/26, a US submarine had reported that cruisers and three destroyers [were] about 25 miles south-east of Sepandjang Island [south-easternmost of the Kangean group] heading towards Lombok Strait, speed 15 knots.' The Allied submarines took little part in the final phase of the Java Sea campaign.

23. Japanese aircraft attack

At dawn on 27 February, the Allied force was approximately 10 miles north-west of Surabaya and had not yet sighted the enemy. Day formation was assumed.

At 0700, the *Exeter* obtained an RDF bearing of planes in a south-westerly direction. Rear-Admiral Doorman hoped they might be Allied craft, but an hour later he informed his force that the promised fighter protection would not be forthcoming.[3] At 0855, aircraft were heard overhead, and shortly afterwards three 100-lb. bombs fell close to the *Jupiter*; five minutes later a stick of four bombs fell about three cables on her starboard quarter. All these bombs were tumbling and at least three failed to explode. The *Houston* opened fire on the planes, which retreated behind clouds. From this time on, planes continued to shadow the Allied fleet, but remained out of range.

Rear-Admiral Doorman reported this incident to Vice-Admiral Helfrich, and at 0930 altered course from 270° to 115°. At 1000 the latter signalled, 'Notwithstanding air attack you are to proceed eastwards to search for and attack enemy', to which Rear-Admiral Doorman replied at 1200, 'was proceeding eastwards, after search from Sapoedi to Rembang. Success of action depends absolutely on receiving good reconnaissance information in time, which last night failed me.[4] Destroyers will have to refuel tomorrow.' The lack of adequate air protection imposed a constant strain on the crews, and

---

3. According to the Commander Air Defence, Surabaya (Commandant Luchtverdediging), the 4 Brewster Buffalo fighters could not fly higher than 4,000 metres because they had no oxygen apparatus. Moreover, their flying range was so low that they would have only been able to remain 10 minutes above the Allied fleet for the purpose of protection. (*Dutch Account*, p. 7.)

4. Possibly Admiral Doorman meant that had the US Army bombers report of 1100Z /26 (see Section 18) reached him promptly, he could have made direct for the Bawean convoy shortly after leaving harbour, instead of sweeping eastward to Sapoedi Strait, away from the convoy.

at 1240 on 27th, Rear-Admiral Doorman reported, 'This day the personnel reach the limit of endurance; to-morrow, the limit will be exceeded.'

24. Japanese force located

At 1200, the wind was blowing from the east, force 4. At 1400/2 the Combined Striking Force was steering towards Westervaarwater to return to Surabaya. The force passed through the channel in the minefields in the following order: the Dutch destroyers, the British destroyers, the US destroyers, the cruisers.

At 1427 as the fleet was entering harbour, Rear-Admiral Doorman received the following important information from Vice-Admiral Helfrich:

(a) At 1340 GMT, 20 ships, with an unknown number of destroyers were in position 04° 45′ S., 112° 15′ E. (approx. 65 miles north-west of Bawean), course 180°.

(b) At 1345 GMT, one cruiser was in position 04° 40′ S., 111° 07′ E. (approx. 135 miles north-west of Bawean), course 220°.

(c) At 1350 GMT, two cruisers, six destroyers, 25 transports, were 20 miles west of Bawean, course south. Of this force, one cruiser and four destroyers proceeded south at full speed, the transports staying behind.

25. Allied Fleet proceeds to intercept

Rear-Admiral Doorman immediately (i.e., about 1430), turned and proceeded to sea again, with the intention of intercepting the enemy force reported to be 20 miles west of Bawean. After leaving the minefield, the British destroyers were ordered to proceed at full speed to form a screen for the line of cruisers. The *Jupiter* took station at visibility distance, 270° from the *De Ruyter*; the *Electra* searched right ahead, the *Encounter* to starboard. The Dutch and American destroyers were not told to take up any special positions, but the former were on the port quarter, and the latter[5] astern. The cruisers took station in line ahead, in the following order: the *De Ruyter*, the *Exeter*, the *Houston*, the *Perth*, the *Java*, speed 20 knots, later increased to 25 (the maximum speed of the *Kortenaer*). Course 315°.

---

5. *U.S.C.N.*, p. 57, says: 'Their [the American destroyers] assigned position was on the disengaged bow of the cruisers, but at the same time they were under orders not to pass ahead of the Dutch destroyers.' There appears, however, to be some misapprehension here, if the report of the arrangement made by Admiral Doorman at the Surabaya conference on 26 February (see Section 14. (iv)) be accepted as correct.

At 1500, an order came from Vice-Admiral Helfrich to attack the enemy reported 'west of Bawean'.[6] At this time, too, the Commander Air Defence at Surabaya, asked Rear-Admiral Koenraad, Commander of the Naval Base at Surabaya, where and when the Combined Striking Force would attack, because of a projected dive-bombing attack on Japanese transports by the Air Force of the Royal Netherlands Indian Army.[7]

At 1529, enemy aircraft appeared, and dropped a few bombs at random; the *Houston* fired on the planes, and the fleet scattered. By 1550, it had reformed, and was again on course 315°, speed 24 knots.

The *Dutch Account* records a reconnaissance report sent by Vice-Admiral Helfrich at 1555. This report (which was of three cruisers and five transports, 30 miles south-west of Bawean, course 190°), was not apparently sent, however, until 1655, nor was it received until 1830.

26. Request for air protection

At 1600, Rear-Admiral Doorman asked for fighter protection, but the Commander Air Defence Surabaya did not comply, because he needed his eight remaining Brewster Buffalo fighters to protect the four dive-bombers in the projected dive-bombing attack on Japanese transports.

27. Contact

About 1602, three float planes were sighted to the northward, and some minutes later smoke was sighted, bearing 358°. At 1612, in approximate position 06° 28' S., 112° 26' E., on course 315° the Combined Striking Force sighted the enemy. The first report, which came from the *Electra*, was, 'One cruiser, unknown number large destroyers, bearing 330°, speed 18, course, 220°'. At 1614, the Allied fleet, then about 30 miles north-west of Surabaya, increased speed to 26 knots, and the *Perth* sighted a cruiser on the starboard bow. At 1616, the *Exeter* reported a cruiser and four destroyers, bearing 330°, 14 miles distant. Records of the contact reports are scanty, but by about 1626 a report from the *Jupiter* enabled the enemy's force to be identified with fair accuracy. According to the *Japanese Report* it consisted of the 5th Cruiser Division, viz, two 7–8-in. cruisers, the *Nachi* and the *Haguro*; a 5.5 in. cruiser, the *Jintsu*,

---

6. Admiral Helfrich remarks: 'To be sure that my point of view would be quite clear to C.C.S.F. [Admiral Doorman]. I signalled the order to attack, after C.M.R. [Admiral Koenraad] had informed me that C.S.F. was entering Westervaarwater. In no circumstances was the risk to be taken of the enemy preventing the C.S.F. from putting to sea again.' (ibid)
7. This attack was ordered by Abdair. Admiral Helfrich says: 'I did not know anything about the attack.'

leading the 2nd Destroyer Flotilla, i.e., eight destroyers and a 5.5-in. cruiser, the *Naka*, leading the 4th Destroyer Flotilla, i.e., six destroyers. The Allied force of five cruisers (two of them heavy) and nine destroyers was confronted with an enemy force of four cruisers (two of them heavy) and 14 destroyers.

28. Action commences, 1616

At 1616, the *Nachi* and the *Haguro* opened fire at 30,000 yards, directing it mostly at the *Exeter* and the *Houston*. The *Naka* opened fire about the same time on the *Electra*, straddling her with the first and second salvoes which fell roughly abreast of the torpedo tubes; later salvos fell close astern, short or over, but she was not hit. The *Electra* and *Jupiter* fired ranging salvoes at the western (i.e. leading) enemy force, at a maximum range of 15,700 yards, but they fell short.

The Allied force was still on course 315°, and closing the enemy, when the *De Ruyter* altered course to 20° to port (i.e. to 295°) to bring the starboard broadsides to bear; this brought the Allied fleet on an approximately parallel course with the enemy 7.8-in. cruisers. The Allied cruisers were in line ahead, with the *Electra* and the *Jupiter* 280°, four miles from the *De Ruyter*. The US destroyers were astern of the cruiser line, and the Dutch destroyers were about 2 miles to port of them. The *Encounter*'s position is not mentioned in any of the reports, but she appears to have been ahead of the Dutch destroyers and abeam of the *Perth*.

The *Exeter* opened fire at 1617 and the *Houston* at 1618, at a range of from 26,000 to 28,000 yards; this range was maintained for some time, so that at this stage the enemy was under fire only from the two heavy cruisers. Shortly after the action commenced the US destroyers took station about 3,000 yards on the disengaged quarter of the *Java* and maintained this relative position throughout most of the action.

Salvoes almost continuously straddled the *De Ruyter*. The *Exeter* was straddled by every salvo after the third; some splashes were not more than 3 yards from her on the disengaged side, indicating the steepness of the angle of descent. All the time, three float planes were spotting for the enemy. The Captain of the *Perth* says, 'Enemy long range fire was extremely accurate, mostly pitching very close short or over.[8] The spread was incredibly small,

---

8. In spite of the reported accuracy of enemy gunfire, in the four hours of daylight only three hits were scored, one each on the *De Ruyter*, the *Java* and the *Exeter*. The *Houston* reported to have received two 8-in. hits which caused no casualties and little damage but does not say when they were received. No other report mentions them.

never more than 150 yards for elevation and much less for line. They were 10-gun salvoes with very small splashes.'[9]

29. First Japanese torpedo attack, 1833–52

At about 1625, the rear enemy destroyer flotilla, i.e. the 4th Flotilla, appeared from the Allied line to be moving in preparatory to attack. The *Perth* opened fire on the right-hand destroyer, the rear ship the 9th Destroyer Division, the *Asagumo*, and hit her with the second salvo just before she fired torpedoes. The *Asagumo*'s steering was temporarily affected, and she was able to fire only three torpedoes.

30. This first enemy torpedo attack was a co-ordinate attack made by the two heavy cruisers, the two flotilla leaders and six destroyers of the 4th Flotilla. As the attack was developing, the Allied fleet, at 1629, altered course from 295° to 245°, speed 25 knots, and at 1631, the *De Ruyter* was hit by an 8-in. shell in the auxiliary motor room, on the starboard side. A petrol fire was started but was extinguished. One man was killed and six wounded. The enemy account of the torpedo attack is as follows: 'About 18 minutes after the beginning of the (gunnery) engagement, the *Naka*, then the *Jintsu* fired torpedoes. The enemy gradually showed signs of drawing near. The 9th and 2nd Destroyer Divisions fired in succession … About 40 minutes after the opening of the engagement *Haguro* fired [torpedoes].' The *Nachi* also intended to fire torpedoes but through lack of 'liaison between the Torpedo Battery Commander and the Torpedo Fire Control Officer', failed to do so.

The following summarises the attack, the time of firing being that recorded by the Japanese:

1633	*Naka* (leading 4th Flotilla), torpedoes fired 4, target *Exeter*, range 8,200 yards
1635	*Jintsu* (leading 2nd Flotilla), torpedoes fired 4, target *Exeter*, range 15,500 yards
1640–42	9th Division (2 destroyers), torpedoes fired 11, target *Exeter* and *Houston*, 7,100 yards
1645	2nd Division (4 destroyers), torpedoes fired 16, target, *De Ruyter*, *Exeter* and *Houston*, 8,200 yards
1652	*Haguro*, torpedoes fired 8, target *Exeter*, range, 12,500 yards

---

9. Very small splashes are usual at extreme ranges.

Thus in 19 minutes, 43 torpedoes were fired at the Allied cruiser line. That there were no hits is considered by the Commander of the 4th Flotilla to have been due to the long range.

31. Enemy makes smoke

The Japanese 4th Destroyer Flotilla made smoke immediately after its torpedo attack and, after the *Perth*'s second salvo hit, retired behind the smoke, which also concealed the enemy heavy cruisers from view. The *Perth* fired several 'follow-up' salvoes into the smoke screen, which became so dense that the Japanese temporarily lost sight of the Allied fleet.[10]

The *Electra* and the *Jupiter* had closed the US destroyers, and taken by this time position approximately abeam the Allied cruiser line on the disengaged side, with the *Jupiter* about 800 yards on the port bow of the leading US destroyer, *Edwards*.

32. *Haguro* hit

At 1635, the *De Ruyter* led in again towards the enemy on course 267° and about this time, the *Haguro*, the rear enemy heavy cruiser, was apparently hit in the boiler room, as she emitted billowing clouds of black smoke, though continued to fire her guns.

33. Enemy destroyer on fire

As the enemy smoke screen cleared, a Japanese destroyer was seen to be on fire. This may have been the *Minegumo*, which is not mentioned in the Japanese torpedo firing records after the first torpedo attack. The *Nachi* was then, 1635, firing at the *Exeter*, and the *Haguro* at the *Houston* and the *Perth*.

34. Allied air attack

About 1645, splashes of heavy bombs were seen in the vicinity of the enemy ships, though no hits were observed. The nationality of the planes could not

---

10. The Commander of the Japanese 4th Flotilla remarked: 'Thorough consideration must be given to the conditions of battle at the time of laying down smoke screens. They are easily put to advantage by the enemy and ... sometime obstruct the battle activity of our own vessels. An example of this is our use of a smoke screen at the time of our withdrawal, after having fired torpedoes, in the naval engagement off Surabaya, and... our losing sight of the enemy because of this smoke screen.' (*Japanese Report*, p. 8)

be identified, but this may have been the dive-bombing attack ordered by the Allied Air Command without the knowledge of the Allied Naval command.

35. *Haguro* on fire

The *Nachi* and the *Haguro* were still apparently in line ahead, about half a mile apart, at over 26,000 yards, a range attainable only by the two heavy cruisers of the Allies. At 1645, the *Haguro* was observed to be on fire. The Captain of the *Perth* says, 'I found a long period of being 'Aunt Sally' very trying, without being able to return the fire ... The Dutch cruisers all this while were firing occasionally.'

At 1651, the *Exeter* signalled, 'My position course and speed 06° 27' S., 112° 13' E., course 300°, speed 27. No change.' About 1655, Lt.-Cdr. J.E. Cooper of the *Ford* thought he saw the *Java* hit by gunfire, but this report is not confirmed from other sources.

36. A delayed report

At 1700, a US Army bomber attacked a large Japanese convoy west of Bawean, but there was delay in passing the report[11] and Rear Admiral Doorman apparently never received it.

37. Second Japanese torpedo attack, 1700–14

Shortly after 1700, the Japanese delivered a second torpedo attack. It was made by the two heavy cruisers, the flotilla leader *Jintsu* and six of the eight destroyers of the 2nd Destroyer Flotilla. At 1700, the enemy heavy cruisers checked fire but at 1702 they opened up again, although the *Nachi* appeared to have been hit aft. The 2nd Flotilla's attack was inspired by its commanding officer's 'determination to protect a Japanese convoy, which had come into sight from the northwest'.

Between 1700 and 1706, the enemy heavy cruisers commenced, unobserved by the Allied ships, the second torpedo attack. At 1707, the foremost enemy flotilla, i.e., the 2nd, led by the *Jintsu*, on approximately opposite course, was

---

11. It was not until 1930/27 that Admiral Koenraad, Commander of Surabaya Naval Base (who at that time, presumably unofficially, asked the Commander Air Defence, Surabaya, for information), was given the US Army bombers' report, which read: '45 transports, 3 cruisers, 12 destroyers, course west, 20 miles west of Bawean. Time 1700.' Admiral Koenraad passed this on to Admiral Doorman; *officially*, the report was not received by Admiral Koenraad until 2125/27. (*Dutch Account*, p. 13.) Admiral Helfrich states that 'this signal did not reach Admiral Doorman.' (*Dutch Account*, p. 27.).

seen to launch a long range attack, and the Allied cruisers turned away to avoid torpedoes.

Commenting on the attack, the destroyer *Yukikaze*'s torpedo officer says, 'during the execution of the attack the enemy's shells almost never scored a hit until a distance of about 8,000 metres had been reached'. The enemy report further refers to this phase of the battle as follows: 'Fifty minutes after the opening of the engagement, the order "All forces attack" was given. An enemy ship blew up and sank, their formation fell into confusion, and they gradually began to reverse [their] course and retreat under cover of a heavy smoke screen.' Sixty-eight[12] torpedoes were fired in this attack in 14 minutes; they were aimed at the *De Ruyter*, the *Exeter* and the *Houston*, but the only hit scored was on the Dutch destroyer *Kortenaer*, which was torpedoed at 1715. Allowing for a discrepancy of about 48 minutes between Japanese and Allied times, the details of this second enemy torpedo attack are as follows:

1700	*Haguro*, torpedoes fired 8, target *Exeter*, range 13,500 yards
1706	*Nachi*, torpedoes fired 8, target *Exeter*, range 13,500 yards
1706	*Jintsu* (leading 2nd Flotilla) fired 4, target *Houston*, 9,900 yards
1709–10	16th Division (4 destroyers), torpedoes fired 32, target *Exeter* and *Houston*, 5,000 yards
1712–14	14th Division (2 destroyers), torpedoes fired 16, target *De Ruyter* and *Exeter*, range, 7,100 yards

38. Exeter hit, 1708

In the meantime, the Allied cruisers had ceased fire at 1707, when they turned away to avoid enemy torpedoes. The enemy was still firing, but his shots had been falling short, when at 1708, the *Exeter* was hit by an 8-in. shell from the *Nachi*, and her speed rapidly decreased. She turned away to port, hauling out of the line, and the cruisers astern apparently turned with her. The *De Ruyter* continued on her course for a short time, but then turned to port as well. The Dutch and American destroyers also turned to port, thus taking up a position ahead of the cruisers, with the mean course of the fleet about 180°.

---

12. Only 44 torpedoes should have been fired, but owing to a change of plan, the six destroyers of the 16th and 24th Divisions fired 8 torpedoes each instead of 4. The destroyer *Yamakaze* reports this incident as follows: 'Although it had been determined to fire 4 torpedoes each in the first and second rounds of torpedo fire, in the middle of the torpedo firing action the plan was changed to a plan of firing along the entire line, whereupon, because of an error in the command station, the first and second torpedo tube mounts fired at the same time. Fortunately, these torpedoes did not hit any friendly ships.' (*Japanese Report*, p. 44)

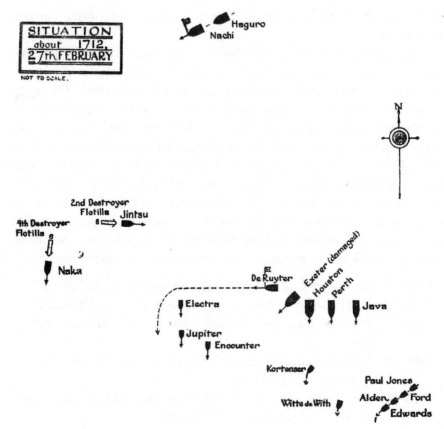

Fig. 4. Situation about 1712, 27 February 1942.

'As a result of this manoeuvre,' says Vice-Admiral Helfrich, 'the Combined Striking Force was in disorder.'

At 1714 *Exeter* stopped, and reported that she had been hit in the boiler room.[13]

39. *Kortenaer* torpedoed, 1715

By this time, the torpedoes fired in the second Japanese attack had reached the vicinity of the Allied fleet and, at 1715, the *Kortenaer*, in approx. position 06° 25′ S., 112° 08′ E., was torpedoed on the starboard side amidships, and immediately blew up, and broke in two. The fore part remained afloat

---

13. The shell passed through the 4-in. AA mounting, killing 6 of the gun's crew, through No. 1 boiler-room ventilator, through the boiler-room, destroying the main steam pipe and putting 2 out of 4 boilers out of action. It then passed through a superheater and boiler in No. 2 boiler-room and exploded in the bottom of the ship, killing 8 stokers. Of the boilers in No. 2 boiler room, only one was put out of action. But there were no stokers available to keep steam in the other three.

for about five minutes, the bow in a vertical position; five hours later, 113 survivors were picked up by the *Encounter*.

At 1715, a torpedo track passed close ahead of the *Jupiter*, and a moment later one was seen astern of the *Exeter*; the *Ford* and the *Edwards* both had to use helm to avoid torpedoes, and several torpedoes surfaced in the vicinity of the American destroyers.

The Captain of the *Kortenaer*, Lt.-Cdr. A. Kroese, RNethN, asserts that his ship was torpedoed by a submarine, on the grounds that at the time, all the enemy ships that he could see were hull down, and beyond torpedo range. He is supported in this view by the 1st Lieut. of the *Witte de With*, Lt.-Cdr. H.T. Koppen, RNethN. Against this assertion, however, stands the fact that none of the reports of periscopes sighted has been substantiated by conclusive evidence. Furthermore, there is the Japanese statement that fifty minutes after the opening of the engagement, the order was given (presumably to the surface craft) 'All forces attack', and an enemy ship blew up; and the more specific claim of the Commander of the Japanese 2nd Destroyer Flotilla, that 'after 45 minutes of shell fire an enemy destroyer was sunk by our torpedoes'.[14] Finally, although the *Japanese Report* refers to the activities of Japanese submarines 'during extended operations,' with the Sixth Fleet, it does not mention the presence of any submarines at the battle of the Java Sea.

40. Enemy shaken

The disablement of the *Exeter*, and the loss of the *Kortenaer* were heavy blows to the Allied fleet which up till then appears to have had the best of the gunnery engagement. That it had done more than hold its own is confirmed by the Commander of the Japanese 2nd Destroyer Flotilla, who, unaware that it was not the sinking of the *Kortenaer*, but the unlucky hit in the *Exeter*'s boiler-room, which had been the prime cause of the Allied fleet's disorder and retirement, says, 'If the enemy admiral had gone ahead with the attack in spite of the loss of one or two destroyers, it is believed that *our fleet would not have escaped a bitter struggle*.'[15]

41. Enemy closes

By 1718, the battle area was covered with dense smoke, in spite of which, the enemy, assisted by his aircraft, maintained an accurate fire. The *Perth* fired at

---

14. *Japanese Report*, pp.4 & 6.
15. The last sentence is not italicised in the *Japanese Report*.

the enemy aircraft, and also at a 'reported' periscope. The *Naka*, leading the 4th Destroyer Flotilla, was now closing the Allied fleet.

42. *Exeter* screened by smoke

Soon after the *Exeter* had stopped, it was found that she was able to proceed at 15 knots, and the *Perth* closed her, and screened her with funnel smoke and all available smoke floats, augmented by screens from the British destroyers. 'While doing this', says the Captain of the *Perth*, 'the Admiral made, "All ships follow me", but I continued to smoke-screen *Exeter*, and reported her damage to the Admiral, who told me by V/S to follow him, when I proceeded to do so.'

43. Allied Fleet reforms

At 1720, in accordance with the above-mentioned signal, and under cover of more smoke which the US destroyers had started to lay, the *De Ruyter* proceeded on a course south-east. Altering almost immediately to north-east, at 1725, the *De Ruyter* led the Allied cruisers between the *Exeter* and the enemy, presumably to draw the latter's fire and to cover the *Exeter*'s retreat, for that, in effect, was the result of the manoeuvre. About this time, an air attack developed on the Allied cruisers which opened fire with their AA guns; a stick of bombs fell 1,000 yards to port of the US destroyers, and two more sticks near them a few minutes later, without doing any damage. The Allied cruisers then proceeded on course east, with the four US destroyers following them.

While this was going on, the *Witte de With* sighted many torpedo tracks, and several torpedoes exploding at the end of their runs. One torpedo exploded to port, and a second to starboard of her; the track of a third torpedo which passed under the ship was also seen. To meet the possibility of the presence of enemy submarines (though actually there were none in the vicinity of the action) the *Witte de With* fired some depth charges at random.

44. Allied submarines

At 1725, Vice-Admiral Helfrich signalled Rear-Admiral Glassford Commander South-West Pacific (short title 'Comsowespac'), 'Confirming oral instructions, request you interpose all submarines possible on east-west line between enemy reported 0620 [Z] position [i.e. 20 west of Bawean] and north coast of Java.'

45. British destroyers attack, 1725

It was just about 1725 that Rear-Admiral Doorman signalled, 'British destroyers counter-attack', whereupon the *Electra* ordered the *Jupiter* and the *Encounter* to follow. Circumstances were not favourable for the smoke was still very thick, and visibility over the battle area was not more than a mile. Moreover, as the three British destroyers were too far apart to make a divisional attack, the *Electra* and the *Encounter* attacked independently. The *Encounter* attacked through a clearing in the smoke; whether she fired torpedoes, or with what result, is not known. The *Jupiter*, finding no suitable target for torpedoes, remained in the vicinity of the *Exeter*, and drove off by gunfire two destroyers which came out of the smoke screen with the intention of making a torpedo attack on the *Exeter*. When the *Encounter* retired from her attack, she was ordered astern of the *Jupiter*, and both destroyers remained ahead of the *Exeter* as a covering force.[16]

46. *Electra* sunk, 1800

In the meantime, the *Electra* had attacked through the smoke astern of the *Exeter*. As she cleared the smoke, a formation of three enemy destroyers from the 4th Destroyer Flotilla was sighted on an opposite course entering the smoke, at a range of about 6,000 yards. The *Electra* immediately engaged and claimed hits with 4 salvoes on the leading ship. She did not fire her torpedoes, although Mr. T. J. Cain, her Gunner (T), thought that 'conditions seemed fairly favourable from the tubes.' As the three enemy destroyers disappeared into the smoke a shell hit the *Electra*. Two of the enemy destroyers proceeded through the smoke, and attempted a torpedo attack on the *Exeter*, which was repelled by gunfire from the *Jupiter* (see Section 45). The third destroyer returned to re-engage the *Electra* which had been hit in No. 2 boiler room, port side, shattering the boiler, and carrying away the telemotor pipes to the steering gear. Steam dropped and then was lost, owing to water from No. 3 boiler running through the damaged one. The *Electra* stopped with a slight list to port. The third enemy destroyer, emerging from the smoke, was immediately engaged by the guns in local control, as communication with the bridge was dead. The enemy commenced hitting with the second salvo, silencing the *Electra*'s guns one by one, causing heavy fires forward, and an

---

16. Admiral Helfrich remarks: '*Jupiter* and *Encounter* manoeuvred so as to cover the withdrawal of *Exeter*. Evidently, they did not take much notice of *Electra*. It does not appear in the [Dutch] report whether they were ordered to protect *Exeter*. Later (1740) the report states that *Witte de With* was ordered to escort *Exeter* to Surabaya.' (*Dutch Account*, p. 26.)

increased list to port. With only 'Y' gun left firing, the order was given to abandon ship. The enemy continued to fire, and closed, so that he could use his machine guns. The *Electra* listed heavily to port and settled by the bows. Mr. Cain says, 'There were no live men left in the after part of the ship ... Once clear of the ship, I saw someone, presumably the captain [Cdr. C. W. May), come to the starboard side of the bridge and wave to the men in the water, who cheered lustily. The captain then appeared to leave by the port side. The *Electra* then ... turned over and slowly sank until her screws and about 6 ft. of the Q.D. were showing ... finally sinking slowly out of sight, about 1800 ... The *Electra* and her ship's company stood up to the punishment in the best traditional manner. She was a grand ship, and I am proud to have served in her with such a fine crowd of men.'[17]

Later, at about 0315 on 28 February, 54 survivors, of whom one subsequently died, were picked up by US submarine *S.38* (Lt. Henry G. Munson, USN).

47. Smoke screens

Of the progress of the action between about 1730 and 1830, the accounts are conflicting. It is particularly difficult to synchronize the varying times at which events were reported by different authorities. Ships on both sides were emerging from, or disappearing into, smoke screens; sunset was at 1821, and by 1812 the light had begun to fail. There was undoubtedly uncertainty as to the situation. The enemy had aircraft which continuously reported Allied movements. Rear-Admiral Doorman had no aircraft to assist him and did not even know the positions of all the Allied ships; at least, he does not seem to have known that the *Electra* was sunk or sinking because, at 2000, he signalled the *Electra*, the *Jupiter* and the *Encounter* to report their position and speed. The *Perth* too, did not know that the *Kortenaer* had been sunk, for at 2217 Captain H.M.L. Waller said: 'I do not yet know if any Dutch ships were sunk.' Again, at 1814 when the US destroyers counter-attacked, one of them, the *Edwards*, thought that the enemy lay to the north-east, while another, the *Alden*, thought that he lay to the north-west; incidentally (according to the *U.S. Combat Narrative*, page 70) it seems that it is not certain whether the American destroyers were on a westerly or northerly course when they set off to make their torpedo attack. At 1812 the *Perth* says she was on opposite course to the two enemy 8-in. cruisers, and was firing at the right-hand one, while the *Houston* engaged the left-hand one; the *Dutch Account* on the other hand, times this incident at 1745, and reverses the order of the targets. These

---

17. Gunnery Officer T.J. Cain was the senior surviving officer.

inconsistencies not only increase the difficulty of giving an accurate account of the action but serve to illustrate that a smoke screen is not an unmixed blessing and may handicap its users. The Japanese experienced the same difficulty, when smoke caused them to lose sight of the Allied fleet, after their first torpedo attack, and when on account of the 'many smoke screens … the enemy bow and stern waves could not be seen'.

48. *Exeter* retires

In the meantime, at 1729, the *De Ruyter* which had been on course east, led away to the southward; enemy cruisers were still firing accurately, but just failing to hit. At 1736, Rear-Admiral Doorman asked the *Exeter*: 'What is the matter with you?" and, at 1740, ordered her to proceed to Surabaya, at the same time instructing the *Witte de With* to escort her there. At 1745, the *Witte de With* saw an enemy destroyer [of the 4th Destroyer Flotilla] astern to starboard, bearing about 300°, 10,000 yards, coming out of the smoke screen, and apparently engaged with a British destroyer (see Section 46). The *Witte de With* opened fire at 9,300 yards; the enemy replied, and both ships fired eight or nine rounds. The enemy was hit twice, turned off to starboard, and disappeared into the smoke. A hit on the *Witte de With* destroyed her aerial, and she then joined the *Exeter.* They reached the entrance of the Surabaya minefield at 2000.

49. Allied fleet reforms

Meanwhile, by 1745, the Allied cruisers, less the *Exeter*, had reformed in single line ahead in the order, the *De Ruyter, Perth, Houston* and *Java*, and had emerged from the smoke screen on an opposite course to the *Nachi* and the *Haguro*, which were about 19,500 yards distant.

50. Third Japanese torpedo attack, 1738-55

Also in sight, having emerged from the north-west out of the smoke, on approximately a parallel course, was the *Naka*, leading five destroyers of the Japanese 4th Destroyer Flotilla. At 1750, the *Exeter* fired a salvo at the *Naka*, and at 1752, the five enemy destroyers moved in to attack. The *Perth* opened fire on them as they came into view in gaps in the smoke; they returned the gunfire and turned away. The 24 torpedoes they fired all missed their targets. Allowing for a discrepancy of about 12 minutes between Japanese recorded times and Allied observation, the details of this third torpedo attack are as follows, the time of firing being given in terms of equivalent Allied time:

- 1738   *Naka* (leading the 4th Flotilla), torpedoes fired 4, target *Houston*, 6,600 yards
- 1752   2nd Division, torpedoes fired 16, target *Houston* and *De Ruyter*, range 4,400 yards
- 1755   9th Division (*Asagumo* only), torpedoes fired 4, target *Perth*, 3,300 yards

51. Allied signal communications

About 1752 Rear-Admiral Doorman signalled Vice-Admiral Helfrich, '*Kortenaer* sunk. *Exeter* damaged. Position 06° 15′ S., 112° 17′ E.' The fight goes on. By then the fleet was severely handicapped by difficulties of communication; the *De Ruyter*'s short-wave radio had been damaged, and hand signal lamps were her only means of communication with ships of the Combined Striking Force. The short-wave voice radio in the *Houston*, on which the US destroyers had been relying for communication, had also broken down. Communications ashore were far from satisfactory. At 1805, Vice- Admiral Helfrich sent the following signal to all ships:

At 1027 [Z] 27, 35 unknown ships course 170°, 05° 10′ S., 111° 35′ E [70 miles north-west of Bawean]. One cruiser. Four destroyers. 05° 45′ S., 111° 35′ E. [60 miles west of Bawean].

At 0900 [GH]/27, five big ships, several smaller, 06° 20′ S., 115° 30′ E. [30 miles north of Kangean Island], course 315°. As result of bomb attack,[18] one cruiser stopped with four destroyers standing by.

This signal was subsequently seriously misquoted, so that the one cruiser and the four destroyers (60 miles west of Bawean), became four cruisers and four destroyers; errors of time and place also crept in, and were promulgated.

52. US destroyers attack

About 1758, when the fleet was on course 190°, Rear-Admiral Doorman ordered the US destroyers to counter-attack. Almost immediately, for what reason is not known, the *De Ruyter* cancelled the order, and signalled them

---

18. Admiral Helfrich says: 'Probably there was a bomb attack but apparently I was not informed about it.' (Dutch Account, p.26)

to make smoke. While the US destroyers were laying smoke, Rear-Admiral Doorman altered course to 090°, and signalled, 'Cover my retirement'. When they received this order, the four US destroyers were between the Allied cruiser line and the enemy; it was growing dark, and visibility had decreased to about 15 miles. Commander Thomas H. Binford, USN, commanding the US 58th Destroyer Division, decided that the most effective way to cover the Allied fleet's retirement was to deliver a torpedo attack. Thereupon the US destroyers altered course to starboard, in order to break clear of the smoke they had just laid. The enemy heavy cruisers were about 20,000 yards away to the north-west on a westerly course. The US destroyers closed the range to about 14,000 yards and fired their starboard torpedoes at about 1814. As these first torpedoes hit the water there was a large explosion on 'the right-hand enemy ship'. Both enemy heavy cruisers then made smoke; before they were hidden by the smoke, however, the US destroyers altered course 180° and, at about 1819, fired their port torpedoes. Shortly after this, the enemy cruisers, under cover of smoke which they made, altered course to the north.

At 1831 the *De Ruyter* signalled, 'Follow me.' The US destroyers turned under cover of smoke, crossed under the stern of the Allied cruiser column and took up a position on its disengaged quarter on a course between east and north-east. Comdr. Binford reported to Vice-Admiral Helfrich that all the US destroyers' torpedoes had been fired.

53. *Haguro* hit

Meanwhile, at 1810, Captain Waller in the *Perth* had observed that 'no Allied cruisers were firing, but there were several destroyer duels going on.' Captain Waller then says, 'At 1812 ... I found myself on opposite course to the two 8-in. cruisers at a range of 21,000 yards and engaged the right-hand ship [the *Haguro*]. After getting ... [on] for line, the target was found and, after several rapid salvoes, got in on the target, two of which hit. One of these hits caused a very big explosion aft in the target, with volumes of bright lava-like emissions and a pink smoke.[19] Both enemy cruisers then retired behind this smoke and a funnel smoke screen ... When the smoke cleared away, our target appeared to be stopped, the bow rose in the air and then seemed to settle back, we then lost sight of her, whether because she sank[20] or whether the light failed I do not know.'

---

19. According to *U.S.C.N.*, p. 71, 'An American plane which saw this portion of the battle reported that one of the burning 8-in. enemy cruisers succeeded in controlling its fires and resumed its place in line. The same plane also reported that 3 enemy destroyers were on fire and were left behind'.
20. No enemy ship was sunk in this battle.

'During this engagement', continues Captain Waller, *Houston* was engaged with the left-hand cruiser [the *Nachi*]. *Java* and *De Ruyter* were both firing at something. *Houston* reported to me that she had very little 8-in. ammunition left, and I informed the Admiral'.[21]

Sunset was at 1821.

54. Enemy retreats, 1830

About 1830, Rear-Admiral Doorman had signalled Vice-Admiral Helfrich: 'Enemy retreating west. Where is convoy?' It is noteworthy that during the battle, reports of enemy forces *outside the battle area* kept coming in, but not a single report referring to the enemy whom he was actually engaging was received by Rear-Admiral Doorman.

By this time, the enemy was no longer in sight, and the *De Ruyter* led the Allied forces to the north-east and subsequently as requisite (presumably), to try and work round the enemy escort and get at the convoy. Speed 22 knots. The situation was not clear. Cdr. H.E. Eccles, USN, Captain of the *Edwards*, says, 'Darkness set in and we followed the main body endeavouring to regain station and having not the slightest idea as to his [Admiral Doorman's] plans, and still only a vague idea as to what the enemy was doing.'

The *Jupiter* and the *Encounter* were then about 1 mile astern of the *Java*, and in the gathering darkness were endeavouring to get ahead of the Allied cruisers and form a searching force. The cruisers were gradually altering course to the north-west. According to Commander Binford in the *Edwards*, 'There were no more signals and no one could tell what the next move would be. Attempts were made to communicate again with *Houston* and *De Ruyter* with no results.'

At 1850, evidently in response to Rear-Admiral Doorman's 1830, asking the whereabouts of the convoy, a US Catalina flying-boat from Captain Frank D. Wagner's Patrol Wing Ten was sent from Surabaya to find the convoy and signal its position. It was located at 2235, but the information was not passed to the *De Ruyter* until too late to be of any use.[22]

---

21. Admiral Doorman replied that the *Houston* was to use her ammunition sparingly.
22. According to the *Dutch Account*, p. 16. the Catalina located the transports at 2235, as follows: '16 ships at 06° 07′ S., 112° 05′ E., course 300°. One cruiser and one destroyer 4 miles to the east, course 300°. 12 ships 10 miles to the east, course 330°, speed 12 knots.' This information reached Admiral Koenraad at Surabaya at 2352 and was passed to Admiral Doorman; it could have reached him at about 0010 on the 28th. Admiral Helfrich remarks, 'This delay in communications was really intolerable. If C.C.S.F. had received the signal in time, it would have given him a good chance to find the convoy.' At the time that Admiral Helfrich wrote those words, the *De Ruyter* was thought to have been sunk about 2315.

By 1856, the Allied fleet was on course 290°, altering gradually to the north; it was a bright moonlight night.

55. Night action, 1927

After dark, the enemy force was augmented by two 7–8-in, cruisers, the *Mikuma* and the *Mogami*, and a light cruiser, the *Natori*, leading the three destroyers of the 5th Destroyer Flotilla. The *Naka* and the 4th Destroyer Flotilla receive no earlier mention in the Japanese report of the night action and appear to have withdrawn.

At 1927, four ships were sighted on the port beam (i.e., to the westward). at a range of about 9,000 yards; they were the light cruiser *Jintsu* and three destroyers of the 2nd Destroyer Flotilla. About the same time, an enemy aircraft dropped a flare on the disengaged side of the Allied force. At about this time, the *Jupiter* having managed to get into a position 1 mile on the *De Ruyter*'s port bow, course 350, speed 28 knots, sighted 'three ships, bearing 300°, distant about 5 miles'; she made long red flashes to the *Encounter* which was by then 1 mile on the *De Ruyter*'s starboard bow.

56. Fourth Japanese, torpedo attack, 1936

Shortly afterwards, the Japanese launched another torpedo attack. At 1933, the *Perth* opened fire with her main armament; she then fired starshell, but these fell short. The *Houston* also opened fire. 'Two greenish starshells were fired at our cruisers, and simultaneously our own starshells were seen to burst short of the enemy.' Seeing a row of explosions at 1936 in one of the enemy ships, the captain of the *Perth*, suspecting torpedoes, 'turned away', and all ships followed. The *Jupiter* (on the port bow) moved in.[23] The correctness of the *Perth*'s suspicion is confirmed by the Japanese, who state that at about 1936, the *Jintsu*, on approximately a parallel course, fired four torpedoes at 10,500 yards running range, her point of aim being the leading ship of four cruisers. It was probably the opportune 'away' by the *Perth* that rendered the attack abortive.

The Allied cruisers then formed up again in line ahead and were led on various courses by the *De Ruyter* to intercept the enemy. According to Captain Waller, 'we seemed to drop a couple of destroyers in this last move.' Finally, at about 1945, '*De Ruyter* … led the column round on a large circle to a course

---

23. The *Melbourne Report*, p.6, states that the *Perth* turned away onto course 060°, and that: 'for the next 20 minutes course was frequently altered course between north and east in an attempt to close the enemy.'

of 170°. *Jupiter* maintained her position to the northward until it was obvious that course 170° was going to be steered for some time; she then increased to 30 knots to regain her position ahead of the line.' The *Encounter*'s movements at this stage are not known, but she appears temporarily to have lost contact with the Allied force.

The reason for this alteration to the southward has not been stated and remains obscure. 'Why CCSF went south and the motives for this manoeuvre, as stated by Captain of the *Perth*, are not clear,' says Vice-Admiral Helfrich.[24] It seems probable, however, that Rear-Admiral Doorman had decided that it was impracticable to work round the enemy to the northward, and that it was preferable to interpose his force between the enemy and the coast of Java, and to work round to the southward.

This fourth Japanese torpedo attack may well have been one of the occasions when the enemy found difficulty in handling his various formations, for the Commander of the 2nd Destroyer Flotilla remarks, 'During the first stage of the war, in order to capture many strategic points … various forces were organized into a temporary force inconvenient and disadvantageous to unity of command … and to the maintenance of communications.' More specifically, the Commander of the 5th Destroyer Flotilla, in the *Natori*, speaking of the disadvantage of 'excessive concentration of attack' in a night engagement, remarks that: 'In the night engagement off Surabaya … [owing

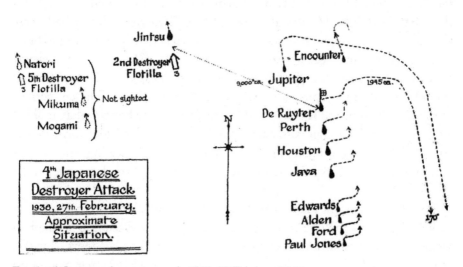

Fig. 5. 4th Japanese destroyer attack, 1936, 27 February 1942.

---

24. The Captain of the *Perth* made no statement on this matter in his report, but *U.S.C.N.*, p. 73, states: 'Why Admiral Doorman so easily abandoned this attempt to reach the convoy is not clear.'

to] the attack carried out under starshell illumination ... [being] excessively concentrated, it was extremely difficult to carry out the night battle.'[25]

57. Reconnaissance reports

It seems clear that the communications system ashore and afloat was functioning badly. At 1930 on 27 February, the Commander of the Naval Base at Surabaya asked the Commander Air Defence Surabaya for information, and was informed that at 1700 that day a US Army bomber had attacked a convoy of 45 transports, 3 cruisers and 12 destroyers, course west, 20 miles west of Bawean. Rear-Admiral Koenraad passed on the information to Rear-Admiral Doorman. 'I am afraid', says Vice-Admiral Helfrich, 'that this signal did not reach Admiral Doorman.'[26]

At 1955, the US Catalina flying boat which had been sent out at 1850 to locate the enemy convoy (see Section 54), saw starshells above three cruisers and eight destroyers, on a northerly course, about 30 miles S.W. of Bawean. Unfortunately, the pilot thought these were our own and made no contact report, while Rear-Admiral Koenraad only received the information later, after the plane had landed at Surabaya.

58. Night action, 2000

The Allied cruisers continued on course 170°, and, at 2000, Rear-Admiral Doorman, evidently unaware that the *Electra* had been sunk, signalled to her, the *Jupiter* and the *Encounter*, 'Report your position, [course] and speed.'

At 2023, what appeared to be four enemy destroyers were observed on the port bow attempting a torpedo attack, and the Allied cruisers altered course to port. At 2043, an enemy destroyer attack was again thought to have been delivered, this time from starboard, and course was altered to 175°. Neither torpedoes nor torpedo tracks were observed, and the Japanese make no mention of any of their destroyers having fired torpedoes during the night action, though the CO of the 2nd Destroyer Flotilla 'felt keenly' that such an attack should have been made. He said: 'A night battle against an enemy cruiser squadron ... [of equal speed] ... and free to practice evading tactics presents difficulties, especially when visibility is [good]. This was the cause of the inconclusive pursuit in the night ... Having made contact near the limit of

---

25. *Japanese Report*, p.5.
26. Offcially, this information was not received by Admiral Koenraad at the Naval Base, Surabaya, till 2125. (*Dutch Account*, p. 13.)

visibility, upon estimating the enemy's course, it is … [felt keenly] that even against a cruiser division it is necessary to carry out 'O' torpedo firing.'[27]

Furthermore, it appears that Section 2 of the Japanese 7th Cruiser Division (the *Mikuma* and the *Mogami*) thought that a destroyer division had fired torpedoes, for the Commander reported that, 'in the night naval action off Surabaya … [his] cruisers carried out firing action after [destroyer division had attacked.[28] At that time the enemy [i.e. the Allies] was already in a damaged and confused condition and the two Japanese cruisers were experiencing difficulty in firing. It is recognized that 'O' fire should have been carried out if possible *before the attack of the destroyer division*.'[29]

At about 2100, the Allied cruisers turned west, leading round to about 280°, and the *Jupiter* decided to take station astern of *Java*, the last cruiser of the line. The four American destroyers, which had been following the cruisers all the time, formed about one mile astern of *Jupiter*.

59. US destroyers withdraw

The US destroyers' fuel supply was running low, and shortly after 2100, Commander Binford decided that as he had no more torpedoes, further contact with the enemy would be useless, since his speed and gunpower were less than anything he would encounter. He therefore retired to Surabaya, which was about 50 miles away. Outside the Surabaya minefield, the US destroyer *Pope*, en route to join the Combined Striking Force after completing repairs, was met and was ordered to return with the other US destroyers to Surabaya;[30] as they entered the channel in the minefield an enemy plane dropped a flare above them. Commander Binford's action anticipated a signal sent at 2133GMT (i.e., 1403Z) by Rear-Admiral Doorman to the US destroyers, 'DD58, C.Z.M, Comsowespac, *Edwards*, *Alden*, *Whipple*,[31] *Ford*: Proceed to Batavia to replenish with fuel and to receive orders as to obtaining new torpedoes'.

Commander Binford received this signal in the Western Channel off Surabaya, and accordingly turned back and proceeded in the direction of

---

27. 'O' firing may refer to the Japanese method of firing a salvo of torpedoes which converged on the enemy ships.
28. It seems probable that it was the torpedo attack by the *Jintsu* (see Section 56), flotilla leader of the 2nd Destroyer Flotilla, at about 1936, which gave rise to this apparent misconception.
29. *Japanese Report*, p.2.
30. Admiral Helfrich remarks: 'It is not certain whether the US destroyers were ordered to return to Surabaya. Though all their torpedoes were fired, they could have been useful as A/S ships. It is possible that shortage of fuel was the main motive'. (*Dutch Account*, p. 27.)
31. This should have been *Paul Jones*.

Batavia. At 2350, unaware that the *De Ruyter* had by that time been sunk, he signalled to Rear-Admiral Doorman: 'With reference to your message 1403[Z]: Followed by aircraft and enemy forces. With the disposition of enemy forces as they are[32] have considered the impossibility of reaching Batavia to-night. Now in channels off Surabaya. Will fuel immediately. Will proceed as directed. Entire communications between E.C. [i.e. Admiral Doorman] and *Houston* were lost after dark. All torpedoes fired.'[33]

After the departure of the American destroyers at 2100, the remaining ships of the Allied striking force turned westward along the north coast of Java. They were in 'single column led by *Encounter*',[34] followed by the *De Ruyter*, the *Perth*, the *Houston*, the *Java* and the *Jupiter*.

60. *Jupiter* sunk, 2125

The *Jupiter* was then in shallow water off the coast, course of about 280°, she followed the *Java*'s gentle zig-zag. Occasional greenish starshell were being sighted well to the northwards. At 2057, Vice-Admiral Helfrich had made a signal: 'Mines will be laid to-night 27th off Rembang [50 miles west of Toeban, on the north coast of Java] in 20 meters.'

At 2125, the *Jupiter* in position lat. 06° 45.2′ S., long. 112° 05.5′ E. (about 8.5 miles north-north-east of Toeban) 'was torpedoed from the starboard side, abreast the forward bulkhead of No. 2 boiler room. The ship stopped almost immediately, and a V/S signal, "*Jupiter* torpedoed", was made to *Java*. The signal was not acknowledged. No W/T signal was made as it was obvious that the fleet was trying to pass unnoticed along the coast.'[35]

No one saw the track of the torpedo which is said to have struck the *Jupiter*, and the enemy does not record having fired torpedoes at her. She sank in 8 fathoms at 0130/28, approximately in the position in which she was hit. The explosion killed 12 ratings, and wounded seven, of whom two subsequently died. Five officers and 78 ratings landed on the Java coast in ship's boats, but before the boats could carry out a second trip the *Jupiter* had sunk. An off-shore current set in, and 6 officers and 161 ratings were unable to reach the shore. Of these, the Captain (Lt.-Cdr. N.V.J.T. Thew, RN), one officer, and

---

32. On this point it has been stated that the *Encounter*, with survivors of the *Kortenaer* on board, was proceeding westward to Batavia, when, at about 2330, she turned back to Surabaya, because the Captain received information that there were very strong enemy forces to the west. It is not known where Captain of *Encounter* got this information from. (Statement by the Captain of the *Kortenaer*, *Dutch Account*, p. 17.)

33. *Dutch Account*, p.15.

34. It seems doubtful, however, that the *Encounter* could have been leading the Allied line at 2100.

35. *Jupiter*'s Report, p.15.

95 ratings (of whom one subsequently died) were captured by the Japanese. Four officers and 66 ratings were missing.

61. Enemy aircraft shadow

The course steered by the Allied fleet after the *Jupiter* was torpedoed is not known; it was probably northward. 'At 21.50', the Captain of the *Perth* states, 'another aircraft flare appeared overhead and shortly afterwards a line of about six brilliant calcium flares in the water straddled our line at right angles. This happened every time we steered a new course, and it was soon obvious that our every move in the moon-light was being reported, not only by W/T, but also by this excellent visual means.'

62. *Kortenaer*'s survivors

At 2217, the fleet passed the spot, approximately 06° 25′ S., 112° 08′ E. where the *Kortenaer* had been sunk, and the survivors, standing on or clinging to their rafts, saw the Allied cruisers steam past at full speed. The *Houston* dropped a raft and a flare, and the *Encounter* was told by the *Perth* to pick up survivors. The *Encounter*, no longer with the cruisers,[36] (see Section 56), at about 2330 picked up 113 of the survivors, including the Captain, Lt.-Cdr. A. Kroese, RNethN, and subsequently proceeded westward toward Batavia.

63. Fifth Japanese torpedo attack, 2245–46

In a position which is not exactly known, but whilst the Combined Striking Force was still apparently on a northerly course, two Japanese cruisers were seen in the moonlight. The Captain of the *Perth* says, 'At 2230, I sighted two cruisers on the port beam. *Houston* reported them at the same moment.' These two cruisers were the *Nachi* and the *Haguro*, and they were on approximately a parallel course. 'They had not been sighted since about 1830.' (see Section 54). Captain Waller continues: 'They were a long way off, but one of them fired a salvo shortly after I sighted. I immediately opened a heavy fire on him and both cruisers opened up on us. This fire was extremely accurate again but very slow. Two of my salvoes at least, and possibly three, struck home (we were spotting by moonlight). The same ship opened up with a stream of starshell and obliterated the target as they fell short. One enemy shell hit the

---

36. At 2222, the *Perth* signalled the *Encounter*, 'Pick up survivors we just passed in a boat.' (*Dutch Account*, p.15).

De Ruyter on the quarter deck. The *De Ruyter* turned 90° away, and I followed as I thought he might have seen torpedoes. Whilst the line was halfway round this turn [i.e. at about 2250], the whole of the *Java*'s after part blew up and she stopped, heavily on fire although she had completed her 90° turn ... almost at the same moment the *De Ruyter* blew up with an appalling explosion and settled aft, heavily on fire.'

The two Dutch cruisers had been torpedoed by the Japanese 5th Cruiser Division, which reports this climax of the battle as follows: '[The 5th Cruiser Division] received enemy starshell fire four minutes after detecting the enemy approximately 15 kms [16,250 yards] away. Confronting action [sic] was conducted with slow, unilluminated fire, and O torpedo firing action was executed when at length the general situation of the action was stabilized. Then (20 minutes after detecting them) two enemy naval vessels were sunk.'[37]

The enemy's point of aim was the *Houston*; two torpedo hits are claimed on the *De Ruyter*, and one on the *Java*. Other details of this torpedo attack, allowing for the discrepancy of about 37 minutes between Japanese and Allied times are as follows:

2245   *Nachi*, torpedoes fired 8, range 5,200 yards
2246   *Haguro*, torpedoes fired 4, range 7,700 yards

64. Sinking of the *De Ruyter*, 2250

The *Perth* just avoided colliding with the *De Ruyter* by the use of full helm and stopping one engine. The *Houston* hauled out to starboard. The *De Ruyter*'s crew assembled forward, as the after part of the ship as far as the catapult was in flames. Almost immediately the 40 mm. ammunition began to explode, causing many casualties, and the ship had to be abandoned; there was no panic or excitement. The *De Ruyter* sank within a few minutes. For some time, her foremast structure remained above the water, until after a heavy explosion she disappeared beneath the waves. The position in which the Dutch cruisers were sunk appears to have been approximately 06° 11′ S., 112° 08′ E. (35 miles south-west of Bawean). No details of any Dutch survivors of either the *De Ruyter* or the *Java* have been received.[38]

37. *Japanese Report*, p.2
38. *U.S.C.N.*, p. 76, states: 'On the afternoon of the 28th, the US s/m *S.37* found a lifeboat crowded with
    60 survivors of the *De Ruyter*. She took on board US Signalman Sholar and another of the American
    liaison group, but could not take more. She left 5 days' rations and water for the others. There is no
    mention of their reaching Java and it seems likely that they were taken by the Japanese.'

65. *Perth* and Houston withdraw

Rear-Admiral Doorman's verbal instructions before the battle had been that any disabled ship must be left 'to the mercy of the enemy'. The *Perth* therefore took the *Houston* under her orders, feinted to the south-east, and turned direct for Batavia, some 300 miles distant, at high speed. Captain Waller's reasons for this are given in his report: 'I had now under my orders one undamaged 6-in. Cruiser, one 8-in. Cruiser with very little ammunition and no guns aft. I had no destroyers. The force was subjected throughout the day and night operations to the most superbly organized air reconnaissance. I was opposed by six cruisers, one of them possibly sunk, and 12 destroyers. By means of their air reconnaissance they had played cat and mouse with the main striking force and I saw no prospect of getting at the enemy (their movements had not reached me since dark, and even then the several reports at the same time all gave different courses). It was fairly certain the enemy had at least one submarine operating directly with him, and he had ample destroyers to interpose between the convoy and my approach – well advertised as I knew it would be. I had therefore no hesitation in withdrawing what remained of the striking force and ordering them to the pre-arranged rendezvous after the night action – Tanjong Priok.'

Captain Waller's decision was communicated by the *Perth* at 0050 on 28 February, in the following signal, 'Striking Force, (R) C.-in-C. E.I., C.C.C.F.: Returning to Batavia. *De Ruyter* and *Java* disabled by heavy explosions, in position 06° 00' S., 112° 00' E.'

After receiving the *Perth*'s signal, Rear-Admiral Koenraad at Surabaya ordered the hospital ship *Op Ten Noort* to proceed to sea; some hours later, however, this ship was sighted under the escort of two enemy destroyers and had presumably been captured.

Chapter IV

Allied Naval Command Leaves Java

66. US Catalina report

Meanwhile, the convoy which Rear-Admiral Doorman had been striving to reach was steering north. Lieut. Campbell, American pilot of a Catalina flying boat sighted it at 0100/28, consisting of 39 transports led by a cruiser. It was flanked on the port side by two destroyers and two cruisers in line ahead, and on the starboard side by one cruiser or destroyer and three destroyers, also in line ahead. Seeing gunfire and flashes bearing 120°, in approximate position 06° 00′ S., 111° 40′ E., the pilot flew in this direction and saw two cruisers and four destroyers steaming north-west. Thinking they were Allied ships, he gave the recognition signal, but received no reply; the ships then closed the convoy and circled south of it.

67. Dutch Catalina report

A Dutch Catalina was also scouting for the convoy. The pilot, at 2300 on 27 February, had been ordered by Rear-Admiral Koenraad to make a reconnaissance flight to locate it. The terms in which the pilot was briefed seem to indicate a good deal of doubt as to the situation. At 0200 on 28 February, the Catalina sighted the enemy convoy in position 05° 50′ S., 111° 40′ E., i.e. about 54 miles west of Bawean, and about 29 miles north-west of the position in which the *De Ruyter* and the *Java* were sunk. The pilot's report generally confirmed that of the American Catalina, though differing as to the strength of the escort.

68. *Perth* and *Houston* reach Batavia

On 28 February, the *Perth* and the *Houston* arrived at Batavia at 1400 to refuel, after a Japanese torpedo aircraft formation possibly intending to attack them had been broken up outside the harbour by Hurricanes. After refuelling, the cruisers proceeded westward at 2121 for Sunda Strait during darkness, en route for Tjilatjap on the southern coast of Java.

69. Destroyer *Evertsen* lost

The Dutch destroyer *Evertsen* had been directed to accompany the *Perth* and the *Houston*, but she did not sail with them, nor until about two hours later. About midnight on 28 February, the *Evertsen* reported a sea battle in progress off St. Nicholas Point, at the northern entrance of Sunda Strait. Sometime later, she reported that she had been intercepted by two cruisers and had beached herself in a sinking condition on Sebuku (Seboekoe) Island, off the south coast of Sumatra.

70. *Perth* and *Houston* sunk

The sea battle reported by the *Evertsen* was evidently the one fought by the *Perth* and the *Houston*. They were sunk at about 0035, 1 March, in a night action lasting about an hour and a half, 'off Batavia'. The enemy force comprised two 7.8-in. cruisers and 10 destroyers.

The only damage sustained by the enemy was to three destroyers, the *Shirayuki*, the *Shikinami* and the *Harukaze*. The *Shirayuki* received 'a shell hit below the control station and [had her] electrical communications … put out of action. Torpedo firing was carried out relying (for control) on an emergency bamboo speaking tube'. The *Shikinami*'s port propeller was damaged by a near miss. The *Harukaze* suffered damage and casualties from shell fire and consequently fired only five torpedoes instead of six.

The odds were overwhelming, and during the action 42 torpedoes were fired at the *Perth* and 43 at the *Houston*. Each of the Allied cruisers seemed to be hit by a total of four torpedoes, says the *Japanese Report*.[1] This *Report* also states that as the naval engagement took place in an area very close to their own convoy anchorage, they were apprehensive of inflicting damage on their convoy and minesweepers, and subsequently several torpedo wakes were in fact seen, believed to have been fired by their own cruisers. The convoy had just been escorted to the anchorage when the Allied ships were sighted, and the flagship ordered, 'The enemy is to the east, attack!' Presumably, because there was no time to form in any organized disposition, the attack was made by small sections or by individual ships.

Nothing further had been heard of Captain Waller, but of the *Perth*'s complement, 22 officers and 285 ratings were picked up by the Japanese. No precise details of survivors of the *Houston* have been received.[2]

---

1. Survivors of the *Perth* state that the ship was abandoned in a sinking condition after the third torpedo hit.
2. Survivors from the *Houston* 'numbered upwards of 300 officers and men'.

71. *Exeter, Encounter, Pope* sunk

On 28 February, the centre of naval activity shifted from Tanjong Priok to Tjilatjap. During the night of 28 February/1 March, Japanese landings took place at Indramayoe (100 miles east of Batavia and Rembang), and at Banten (40 miles west of Batavia). Surabaya was under frequent air bombardment. On the evening of the 28th, the *Exeter*, still able to steam only 16 knots, had sailed from Surabaya accompanied by the *Encounter* and the *Pope*, with orders to proceed to Colombo via Sunda Strait. After clearing harbour, she was to proceed east along Madura coast for about 20 miles, and then steer north, passing east of Bawean Island. She was then to steer north-west before altering course for Sunda Strait.

Soon after leaving Surabaya, the *Exeter* and the two destroyers were discovered by an enemy reconnaissance plane, and at about 1000 on 1 March, the *Exeter* reported that three enemy cruisers were approaching. The *Exeter* was, however, intercepted by four 7–8-in. cruisers and three destroyers. The ensuing action took place 'off Surabaya', and was a gun duel against overwhelming odds.

The Japanese 5th Cruiser Division records that two of the heavy cruisers the *Myōkō* and the *Haguro*, fired 8,000 rounds in an hour and a half.[3] By about 1126, the *Exeter* had almost completely stopped,[4] and the destroyer *Inazuma*, aiming at the *Exeter* amidships, at 3,700 yards range, fired two torpedoes. One of these hit and sank the *Exeter*. This was the only torpedo that scored a hit out of the 19 fired at her.

Captain O. I. Gordon, 44 officers and 607 ratings of the *Exeter*, and Lt.-Cdr. E. V. St. J. Morgan, 6 officers and 143 ratings of the *Encounter* were picked up by the Japanese. Details of survivors of the *Pope* have not yet been received.

72. Japanese torpedo expenditure

During the period 27 February–1 March, the Japanese fired 255 torpedoes, as follows:

---

3. It may be noted that this would mean an establishment or stowage of over 250 rounds per gun, particularly as the *Haguro* had been in action throughout 27 February and would not have had time to 'ammunition'.

4. 'In the second naval engagement off Surabaya, the continued deflection to the right of our shells was due to the enemy's sudden reduction of speed … (this was learned afterwards), and according to observations made by aircraft, it seems that at about 1256 [ie. 1126GH] the enemy had already almost completely stopped.' (*Japanese Report*, p. 16).

27 Feb	Daylight action	135 torpedoes fired	*Kortenaer* sunk
27 Feb	Night action	16 torpedoes fired	*De Ruyter* and *Java* sunk
28 Feb/ 1 March	Off Batavia	85 torpedoes fired	*Perth* and *Houston* sunk
1 March	Off Surabaya	19 torpedoes fired	*Exeter* sunk

Total expenditure: 255 torpedoes

All the enemy cruisers were equipped with torpedo tubes, but among the Allied cruisers, only the *Exeter* and the *Perth* were similarly armed. There is no record of either of these Allied cruisers having fired torpedoes during the battle of the Java Sea, though *U.S.C.N.*, p.79, states that the *Perth*, when she set out for Tjilatjap on what proved to be her last voyage, 'had fired all her torpedoes'. The only Allied destroyers which are known to have fired torpedoes are the *Edwards*, the *Alden*, the *Ford* and the *Paul Jones*, which expended all their torpedoes at about 1814 and 1819/27, in the course of firing port and starboard broadsides of six torpedoes in the American destroyers' counter-attack.

73. American destroyers sail for Australia

The *Edwards*, the *Alden*, the *Ford* and the *Paul Jones* left Surabaya in the late afternoon of 28 February: the *Pope* did not accompany them, having been ordered to report for duty to the *Exeter*. The Dutch destroyer *Witte de With*, having damaged her propellers was also unable to accompany them, and was lost in dock when bombed the next day.[5] Hugging the Java coast, the American destroyers proceeded via Madura and Bali Straits.[6] Off the southern end of the Bali Straits, at about 0210 on 1 March, they sighted an enemy destroyer, and shortly afterwards two others. About 0230, the enemy sighted them and opened fire. A gun duel ensued at about 6,000 yards range, the Americans maintaining a rapid volume of fire with the object of keeping the enemy outside torpedo range. Having no torpedoes, they simulated torpedo fire by means of primers and dummy charges, and after a few minutes the increasing range put an end to the action. At 0321, the enemy, then astern, could be seen still firing.

---

5. The Dutch destroyer *Banckert*, which had been damaged by bombs on 24 February, received further bomb damage at Surabaya on 1 March, and had to be destroyed by her crew.
6. The reason why the *Exeter* was not also routed through Bali Strait, is mentioned by Admiral Helfrich: 'The fact that the small US destroyers made their escape through Bali Strait ... was only possible because they took the route through the Eastern Channel (*Oostervaarwater*), which is too shallow for cruisers; also because of their high speed as compared with the *Exeter*'s 16 knots and because they had luck.' (*Dutch Account*, p. 23.)

The US 58th Destroyer Division arrived at Fremantle at 1645 on 4 March without further incident.

74. British auxiliary craft

Between 19 and 26 February, 36 merchantmen had been cleared from Tanjong Priok. On 26th, the Commander-in-Chief, Eastern Fleet, represented to the Admiralty the danger of losing ships at this port where they were exposed to air attack without shore AA defences or fighters. On 27 February, therefore, all the remaining British auxiliary craft were ordered to clear from Tanjong Priok, and the *Scott-Harley*, the *Wo Kwang* and the *Seram* sailed at 1600 for Tjilatjap.

Shortly after midnight on 27th, the Western Striking Force sailed from Batavia, and after a sweep northwards in a vain search for an enemy convoy from Muntok (Banka Island), proceeded in accordance with orders, via Sunda Strait, to Trincomalee; they arrived at Colombo on 5–6 March. At about the same time, the auxiliary minesweeper *Anking* (with about 70 ratings), the tankers *War Sirdar* and *British Judge*, escorted by the sloops *Jumna*, *Yarra* and *Wollongong* sailed for Tjilatjap. They were not, however, so fortunate; on 28 February, these auxiliaries and their escort were heavily dive-bombed in Sunda Strait. The *War Sirdar* was set on fire, beached on Agenieten Island (one of the Thousand Islands), in 05° 31′ S., 106° 36′ E., and abandoned; the *British Judge* was torpedoed after dark on 28th by a submarine (but subsequently reached Colombo under her own steam).

75. Decision to evacuate

At 0710 on 1 March, Commodore J.A. Collins, RAN received orders from Dutch Naval HQ at Bandoeng to leave Batavia. At 0930, a conference was held at Bandoeng, of Vice-Admiral Helfrich, Rear-Admiral Palliser and Commodore Collins's Chief Staff Officer, to consider a reconnaissance report of Japanese heavy ships and destroyers located 80 miles south of Tjilatjap, steering north at 0800. It was decided that the best chance of saving some of the shipping at Tjilatjap was to sail it all after dark that day; Dutch ships to hug the coast to the westward, and British ships to the eastward of the port, and then to break independently for Colombo or Australian ports. Orders were passed to Tjilatjap to have all ships fuelled and ready to sail by nightfall.

The only secret means of communication at this time with ships at sea was by an American W/T set at Bandoeng, and American cyphers. The fate of the *Perth* and the *Houston* being then unknown, these ships were ordered by signal to avoid Tjilatjap and to proceed to Fremantle.

76. Vice-Admiral Helfrich resigns command

Later in the day, Vice-Admiral Helfrich sent for Rear-Admirals Palliser and Glassford, and formally resigned the command of British and American naval forces in the ABDA area. These forces thereupon reverted to the respective commands of Commodore Collins and Rear-Admiral Glassford. The surviving Dutch vessels were to proceed to Colombo.

77. US warships leave Java

Rear-Admiral Glassford at once ordered all US surface ships of his command, then in Java waters, to proceed to Australia. At Tilatjap were two destroyers, the *Pillsbury* and the *Parrott*; four gunboats, the *Tulsa*, the *Asheville*, the *Lanaka* and the *Isabel*; and two minesweepers, the *Whippoorwill* and the *Lark*. The two destroyers, the *Whipple* and the *Edsall*, were operating south of Java. A cruiser, the *Phoenix*, was en route for Java, as was a submarine tender, the *Otus*. Of these ships, the *Edsall*, the *Pillsbury* and the *Asheville* have not been heard of and are considered lost. Rear-Admiral Glassford, with his staff, left Bandoeng for Tjilatjap by car. Thence 'he proceeded to Australia by plane, while others followed by plane and submarine.'

78. British warships diverted from Tjilatjap

About 1600 on 1 March, two Australian minesweepers, the *Burnie* and the *Bendigo* arrived at Tjilatjap, and refuelled. By 1900, Commodore Collins's staff, accompanied by Rear-Admiral Palliser, also arrived. A signal was immediately made, as from Commodore Collins, on HMAS *Bendigo*'s W/T, ordering all British warships to avoid Tjilatjap, and to make for Fremantle or Colombo.

79. British warships leave Tjilatjap

All British officers and ratings remaining were embarked in SS *Zaandam* and USS *Seabelle* which were already full of evacuees; both these ships sailed before midnight on 1 March, the destroyer HMS *Stronghold* having sailed earlier, with instructions to escort the *Zaandam*. Survivors and details continued to arrive at Tjilatjap.

At 2015 'a party of 75 survivors of the *Jupiter*' arrived at Tjilatjap by train from Surabaya, and at about 2030, Commodore Collins arrived from Batavia. At 2200, HMAS *Bendigo* sailed with the *Jupiter*'s survivors and the majority of the Commodore's staff. At 0130 on 2 March, a car convoy from Batavia arrived at Tjilatjap with 15 officers and 43 ratings. Owing to a collision on the line, the train party from Batavia, due the previous day, did not arrive until 1630. The number of naval ratings at Tjilatjap was further increased by the arrival, by train from Surabaya, of '10 further survivors from the *Jupiter*, and 45 from the *Electra*'. Small numbers of British civilians from Surabaya were also arriving throughout the day.

By arrangement with the Dutch authorities, SS *General Verspyck* was made available, and 41 officers, 108 ratings, HBM Consul-General at Batavia, and 27 other British subjects were embarked in her. The end was then approaching, and the remaining British naval officers and ratings were embarked in HMAS *Burnie*, for passage to Fremantle.

At 1130, four Australian corvettes, the *Goulburn*, the *Toowoomba*, the *Maryborough* and the *Ballarat*, of the 21st MSF, unexpectedly arrived. The *Ballarat* was short of fuel, and she and the *Maryborough* refuelled. HMAS *Goulburn* and *Toowoomba* sailed from Tjilatjap at 1800 with orders to hug the coast to the eastward. The *General Verspyck* escorted by the *Maryborough* sailed at 2230, hugging the coast to the westward. They were immediately followed by HMAS *Ballarat* and *Burnie*, the latter wearing the broad pennant of Commodore Collins. Rear Admiral Palliser proceeded to Australia by plane.

Just as the last group was leaving, the auxiliary minesweeper HMS *Gemas* arrived, with the unwelcome report that she was unseaworthy and her engines and boilers incapable of making the journey to the Australian coast. The *Ballarat* was detached to escort her into deep water outside the harbour, take off her crew, and sink her. This was done, and the *Ballarat* then proceeded independently. By 2300, all British ships and the majority of Dutch ships were clear of Tjilatjap.

80. Vice-Admiral Helfrich leaves Java

During the day of Monday, 2 March, Vice-Admiral Helfrich reported to the Commander-in-Chief, Eastern Fleet, that he was proceeding to Colombo, with his staff, in four Dutch Catalina flying boats.

He reached Colombo on 3 March.

81. *Stronghold, Yarra, Anking* sunk

On 4 March, at 0615, the *Yarra* (Lt.-Cdr. R. W. Rankin, RAN), the *Anking*, the tanker *Francol* and *MMM 51*, having presumably been sighted by enemy aircraft, were intercepted by an enemy force of three cruisers (two of the *Nachi* class), and four destroyers, in 11° 30' S., 109° 03' E., some 250 miles from the south coast of Java, and sunk by gunfire. A few survivors were picked up by the Dutch submarine *K.10*[7]and by Dutch merchant vessels and landed, some in Colombo, some in Western Australia. HMS *Stronghold* (Lt.-Cdr. G. R. Pretor-Pinney) was also sunk on 4 March, but this may well have been the case when this report was written, but in fact Stronghold was attacked by the enemy heavy cruiser Maya which succeeded in sinking her after firing 635 shells from her main guns. You may wish to consider adding a footnote to that effect, rather than leaving Stronghold's fate up n the air.

82. The end

This was the end of the Java Sea campaign, which temporarily sealed the fate of the Netherlands East Indies. The Battle of the Java Sea constitutes a melancholy page in the history of the war, but not an inglorious one. An Allied force deplorably deficient in air power, deprived of a secure base, hastily assembled without any previous combined training proved powerless to stem the enemy's advance. Misfortune attended them, for of the only two 8-in. cruisers, the *Exeter* was knocked out early by an unlucky shot; the *Houston* was short of ammunition and three of her nine guns were out of action from an air attack prior to the battle. The Japanese, after years of careful preparation directed to a single end, swept in an overwhelming flood to the southward, over-running the Philippines, Malaya, Burma and Singapore, the Netherlands East Indies and New Guinea, and standing finally at the gates of India and Australia. The Allies had received a heavy blow and were faced with the colossal task of checking this advance; the situation was desperate, but in the hearts of the Allies there still shone the spirit of Tromp's last words, '*Ik heb gedaan. Houd goeden moed*!'[8] An immense programme of preparation was undertaken, involving the construction of supply bases and airfields in jungles and the transport of great armies and huge quantities of supplies, tanks, guns and planes over 7,000 miles of ocean. The people of the United States girded them together to the task. As early as June 1942, the preparations began to mature. The rush to the south was stemmed and gradually turned back. The Battle of the Java Sea received an answer at Midway.

---

7. At 14.30, 9 March, *K10* picked up 13 survivors from the *Yarra*; 15 others had died from exhaustion. She also picked up 3 ratings from the *Anking*, and one Dutch officer.
8. 'I am finished. Keep up your hearts!' Maerten Tromp was a Dutch Admiral of the 16th and 17th centuries famous for his defeat of the Spanish navy and his battles with the English fleet.

APPENDIX A

Report by survivors of HMAS *Perth*

On 12 September 1944, the Japanese transport *Rakuyo Maru*, carrying prisoners of war from Singapore to Japan, was torpedoed in the China Sea. Among the 151 prisoners of war rescued by 4 US submarines were four survivors of the *Perth*. Their account of the *Perth*'s last fight is as follows:

> At about 2310, on 28 February, in Sunda Strait, the starboard look-out sighted a dark object bearing Green 10, and a few minutes later the *Perth* opened fire with 'A' and 'B' turrets. The ship appeared to have run into a convoy. Destroyers were passing at such close ranges that they were engaged by the .5 machine guns.
>
> The *Perth* was first hit at about 2330, when a shell passed through her foremost funnel and exploded. Thereafter, numerous shell hits were sustained, and then the *Perth* was torpedoed on the starboard side, before 'A' turret. Ten minutes later, a second torpedo hit the starboard side, in the forward engine room, and Captain Waller ordered 'Stand by to abandon ship.'
>
> The *Perth* continued to be hit by gunfire, which came from several bearings, and at about 0025, 1 March, a third torpedo hit aft, on the port side, under 'X' turret. When the ship was sinking Captain Waller ordered 'Abandon ship: every man for himself.' The *Perth* sank at 0035.
>
> During the action, the *Perth* fired 4 torpedoes to port and 4 to starboard with unknown result, but the following morning 3 transports and one converted aircraft carrier were seen down by the stern, practically on the beach in Banten Bay (east of St. Nicholas Point, Java).

APPENDIX B

Vice-Admiral Heltrich's comments on the *Perth*'s withdrawal

Commenting on the withdrawal of the *Perth* and the *Houston*, Vice-Admiral Helfrich says (*Dutch Account*, p. 28): 'Strictly speaking, the return of *Perth* and *Houston* was against my order 2055/26 "You must continue attacks till enemy is destroyed." This signal was intended to make it quite clear that I wanted CSF [Combined Striking Force] to continue action whatever the cost, and till the bitter end. *Perth* did receive this signal. Both cruisers were undamaged, and it was not right to say in anticipation, "It is no use to continue action", considering the damage inflicted upon the enemy cruisers, which in my opinion must have been severe. However, it is possible that other facts had to be considered, such as shortage of fuel or ammunition.

'The decision of Capt. of the *Perth* is even more regrettable as, after all, both cruisers did meet their end. Probably on the night of [27/28 February] they would have sold their lives at greater cost to the enemy.'

APPENDIX C

Comments on the sinking of the Jupiter

The entry in the *Jupiter*'s log to the effect that she was torpedoed, was evidence, in Vice-Admiral Helfrich's opinion, that she was not hit by a Dutch mine. Rear-Admiral Palliser, his Chief of Staff, did not, however, consider this could be accepted as conclusive evidence, unless any of the survivors were certain that they had seen the track of a torpedo. On the contrary, Rear-Admiral Palliser considered that as the *Jupiter*'s position at the time, according to the Dutch track chart, was only 3 miles north of the mines laid by the *Gouden Leeuw* if either the mines or the *Jupiter* were slightly out of position, it might have been a mine. In view of this contention, Vice-Admiral Helfrich agreed that the possibility of mines must not be excluded.

The minefield referred to by Rear-Admiral Palliser was laid on 27 February by the Dutch minelayer *Gouden Leeuw*, off Toeban. The *Dutch Account*, p.6, refers to this minefield as follows: 'At 0047, 27 February, CMR signalled position of minefields to be laid by *Gouden Leeu*, to *O.19* and *K.8* (ships of CSF were not informed of the position of these mines: only CCSF got the information just before sailing). The mines have been laid within the 10-meter line.'

No Japanese destroyers fired torpedoes during the night of 27/28 February. The *Japanese Report* records no firing of torpedoes by Japanese cruisers within from one to two hours of the time that the *Jupiter* was sunk; further, the *Report* makes no mention of Japanese submarines being present during the battle of the Java Sea.

The only Allied submarines operating in the vicinity of the battle area were:

(i)   Dutch s/m *0.19*, off Rembang.
(ii)   U.S. s/m *S.38* off Toeban (long. 112° 04' E.). *Jupiter* was sunk in this area. *S.38* eventually rescued the *Electra*'s survivors.

APPENDIX D

Vice-Admiral Helfrich's comments on the disposition of Allied cruisers

Vice-Admiral Helfrich, after referring to Rear-Admiral Doorman's alteration of course of about 20 to port on engaging the enemy at 1617/27, in order to bring a full broadside to bear, makes the following remarks (*Dutch Account*, pp.31 and 32):

'The distance however, ... [was] very great and a good chance of hitting for the 6-in. guns of the light cruisers [was] out of the question ... he should have shortened the distance rapidly by continuing on the same course for some time. The disadvantage that the (foremost) guns only could be fired and the enemy... [was] crossing the T, had to be accepted. Undoubtedly the Japanese could have prevented a shortening of [the] distance by turning off, but this would have been disadvantageous to their own firing. Furthermore, the battle area would have been moving towards the north, i.e. towards the convoy which would have been favourable to the Allies

'In my opinion, there was still another way, considering the event in the light of what actually happened, i.e., to split the formation into one group of heavy cruisers (*Exeter* and *Houston*) and a second group consisting of the three light cruisers. Whilst turning off to port, the heavy cruisers could have kept the Japanese heavy cruisers engaged on a westerly course. Meanwhile the light cruisers could have tried to reach the convoy by steering northwards, staying out of the gun range of the Japanese heavy cruisers. Then they would have found against them only two light Japanese cruisers, which were considerably inferior (22 6-in [Allied] guns against ten 5-5-in. [Japanese] guns). This splitting would have forced the Japanese Commander-in-Chief to make a difficult choice. If he ... [continued] fighting on a westerly course, the Allied cruisers ...[would] reach their object. If he [returned] to the north to assist his own cruisers, he ... [would have] to let go the Allied heavy cruisers. ... [If] Admiral Doorman did hit upon this idea of splitting, he probably rejected it because of the rather poor means of communication and because his cruiser force was not working together very well.'

APPENDIX E

Vice-Admiral Helfrich's comments on Rear-Admiral Doorman's proposed night formation

Vice-Admiral Helfrich says (*Dutch Account*, p.24): 'The formation for the night as ordered by C.C.S.F. [Admiral Doorman] had some disadvantages.' Vice-Admiral Helfrich's further remarks, however, seem to show that it was not Rear-Admiral Doorman's proposed night formation which was contrary to Vice-Admiral Helfrich's normal practice, but Rear-Admiral Doorman's action on sighting the enemy. Rear-Admiral Doorman's proposed night formation was in effect the same as Vice-Admiral Helfrich's approved day formation, as advocated by Vice-Admiral Helfrich for adoption at night in bright moonlight (which prevailed at the period under review); the only difference was that for a particular reason Rear-Admiral Doorman proposed to place the American destroyers in the rear of the cruiser line.

Vice-Admiral Helfrich further remarks, 'In 1936/37, during the time that I was in command of the Netherlands squadron in the East Indies, I ordered the following formations:

'*Formation for the night* – In front, the cruisers in single line ahead, and astern of them at visibility distance the destroyers in a quarter line formation.

'The advantage of this formation was that the cruisers could open fire immediately, when a sudden contact with the enemy was made without being disturbed by their own destroyers. Whilst the enemy was engaged, the destroyers could launch a torpedo attack from a favourable position.

'*Formation for the day* – Destroyers in a screen ahead of the cruisers' visibility distance ... of the cruisers ... [and] of each other ... As soon as the enemy is sighted ... the destroyers [to] gradually withdraw and close in towards the cruisers.

'*In case of bright moonlight* – Formation for the day ... [is] to be taken up and the destroyers must withdraw to close in towards the cruisers.' (*Dutch Account*, p. 24.)

APPENDIX F

Disposition of Allied submarines

On 27 February, at 0130, the US submarine *S. 37* arrived at Surabaya from Madura with orders to leave immediately and patrol between the western approaches to Surabaya and Bawean Island. On that date, too, the Dutch submarines *O.19* and *K.8* were at sea, in the Java Sea, in the respective positions 08° 13′ S., 112° 00′ E., and 06° 14 'S., 113° 8′ E. The US submarine *S. 38* was at sea in position 06° 20′ S., 112° 41′ E.

HMS *Truant* was routed through the Western Channel (*Westervaarwater*) Surabaya, north-west to 112° E, and then to the north. She had been on patrol in the north entrance to Lombok Strait and was ordered to proceed to Ceylon, under operational command of the Commander-in-Chief, Eastern Fleet. The remaining Dutch submarines were disposed as follows:

On patrol, west Java Sea: *K.14*, *K.15*.
Repairing at Surabaya: *K.11*, *K.12*, *K.13* and *K.18*.
Under operational command of C.M.R. at Surabaya: *K.9*, *K.10*; the latter was sent north of Madura.

Commenting on the disposition of American submarines Vice-Admiral Helfrich says, 'After I assumed command as Abdafloat [14 February), the US submarines were ordered to concentrate in the eastern part of the Java Sea and had to take up position on a line between Makassar and Lombok Strait, and in Lombok Strait except two of the S type which were operating in the South China Sea, north of Karimata Strait. On 25 February it was ordered to move them to the north coast of Java and Madura, to cover the landing places between Rembang and Sapoedi Strait. Except for *S.37* and *S.38* ... I did not know whether the submarines had already reached their new positions. After 27 February ... no reports about these ... submarines reached me.'

Commenting on the disposition of Allied submarines, *U.S.C.N.*, p. 51, says, 'All available submarines were ordered into the Java Sea and were drawn into close-in defensive positions ... [though] American experience since the invasion of the Philippines had indicated the difficulty of attacking the Japanese close-in, and the move further had the effect of depriving us of scouting information from our submarines. It seemed unlikely that our undersea craft could seriously impede the Japanese.'

APPENDIX G

Last sighting of the enemy on 97 February, 942

The last time recorded in the Captain of the *Perth*'s report refers to the sighting of two enemy cruisers on the port beam at 2230/27. The time of sighting is of importance. Captain Waller was quite definite about it and said that the *Houston* reported the two cruisers 'at the same moment'. Captain Waller's report cannot lightly be disregarded, for throughout the whole report the time of almost every important incident in the battle, and particularly the times of sighting the enemy, were carefully noted; yet after 2230, Captain Waller recorded no other time, nor any subsequent sighting of the enemy. It is also evident from Captain Waller's report (which comprised 16 numbered paragraphs), that the two Dutch cruisers were torpedoed shortly after this sighting, as both incidents, i.e. the sighting and the torpedoing, are recorded in his paragraph numbered 14.

No mention, however, is made by the Dutch, American, Melbourne or Commodore Collins's reports of Captain Waller's sighting at 2230. On the other hand, all these four reports mention, or imply that there was, a sighting of the enemy at, or about, 2315 or 2330; thus:

(a) The *Dutch Account*, p.16, states that at 2315, Admiral Doorman signalled 'Target to port 4 points'.

(b) *U.S.C.N.* p.75, states that at 2315, the *De Ruyter* signalled 'Target at port 4 points'.

(c) The *Melbourne Report*, p.7, states that two enemy cruisers were sighted on the port beam at 2315.

(d) Commodore Collins's report, p. 3, says, 'At 2330GH, contact was made with two cruisers on the port beam of the Allied force ...' and quotes this time of sighting, 2330GH, in a message, 0123/10 March, when reporting this phase of the battle.

None of these four reports, however, state on what authority this time of sighting, 2315 or 2330, is based. It seems probable that it was an estimate based on Captain Waller's report of having passed the *Kortenaer*'s survivors (in approximate position 06° 25' S., 112° 08' E at 2217) and on his subsequent report that the *De Ruyter* and the *Java* were 'disabled' in 'lat. 06° S., long. 112° E.,' i.e., 25 miles, or about one hour's steaming, to the northward. If so, the probability that the position 06° S., 112° E. was only an approximation, was overlooked. At the time when these reports were compiled, the *Japanese Report*, with the Japanese statement that they sank the Dutch cruisers 20 minutes after they sighted them, which tends to confirm Captain Waller's report, was not available.

Part Three

The Battle of Midway

Chapter I

Situation After Battle of the Coral Sea

1. US inferiority in carriers

After the Battle of the Coral Sea the Americans found themselves in a serious situation in the Pacific. It is true that a valuable base for the reconquest of New Guinea had been saved for the Allies, and there were indications that the Japanese had, temporarily at least, renounced any designs they might have had on Australia.

This was the interpretation which the Americans put on the absence from southern waters of Japanese warships other than occasional submarines, and a husbanding of Japanese air strength so marked that during the weeks following the battle the shore-based aircraft of the Allies delivered against enemy bases in the Solomons and New Guinea a total weight of attacks two or three times as heavy as those of the Japanese on Port Moresby and other Allied bases. But the victory had been dearly bought with the loss of one carrier and damage to a second so severe as might require a considerable period of repair and possibly even a visit to a West Coast Navy Yard; and in a region where the air was now clearly demonstrated to be of paramount importance the Americans found themselves outnumbered in the Pacific as to fleet aircraft carriers by two to one; with naval aircraft which the Battle of the Coral Sea had shown to be inferior in performance to those of the enemy; and with screening forces insufficient in number to enable their battleships to be operated in support of their carriers.

This was the difficult situation of the Americans in the Pacific during the lull following the repulse of the enemy attempt on Port Moresby. Most of the available carriers were in the South Pacific, as the Americans knew the Japanese were well aware; for although the *Enterprise* and *Hornet* which with their supporting cruisers and destroyers composed Task Force 16, had arrived too late to take part in the battle, they had been sighted by a Japanese reconnaissance aircraft in southern waters about the middle of May, a fact to which the immunity of Nauru and Ocean Islands from occupation by the enemy was ascribed. With regard to the two carriers of Task Force 17, although the Japanese could have no certainty that the *Lexington* had sunk after the battle, they could not fail to be aware that both this carrier and the

Yorktown had been damaged. The remainder of the air groups of these two carriers were on board the *Yorktown* and urgently in need of reorganization and rest. The force had been at sea continuously since 16 February.

The only other important American naval force in the Pacific was Task Force 1 containing battleships and a small destroyer screen, which was on the west coast of the United States. The concentration of United States naval strength in the South Pacific seemed to invite a blow against the US positions in mid-Pacific, and when before long it became evident that Japan was concentrating her fleet for movements of major importance, the Americans correctly appreciated that Midway Island and the Aleutians would be the threatened areas.

2. The objective, Midway

Midway, the westernmost but one of the Hawaiian Islands, acts as a sentry for Hawaii, as Commander-in-Chief of the Japanese First Air Fleet succinctly stated in his appreciation. Its importance as an American outpost was further enhanced after the seizure of Wake Island by the Japanese on Christmas Eve 1941. The Japanese intended to use it after capture as a base for long-range reconnaissance aircraft and submarines.

It consists of an atoll on which are two small islands, Eastern Island and Sand Island. There is an anchorage for deep draught ships, and the islands could support an air force of about the size of a carrier group. They were defended by fixed defences.

About 56 miles westward of Midway Islands is the atoll Curé or Ocean Island, where the Japanese planned to establish a seaplane base.

3. Japanese plans to occupy Midway

The occupation of Midway Islands and establishment of a base in the Aleutians were an integral part of the plan of expansion of the defensive perimeter of which the seizure of Port Moresby was to have been the first installation. Though foiled in the latter object, the Japanese refused, even in their secret reports, to regard the battle of 7–8 May as other than a victory for themselves; and certainly from a material point of view their losses were both lighter than those of the Allies and had proportionately far less effect on their all-important carrier strength.

Japanese intelligence of the disposition of the American carriers was far from complete. They knew of the presence of the *Enterprise* and *Hornet* in the Pacific and placed them in the Hawaiian area. They believed the

Ranger was in the Atlantic but could get no reliable information as to the whereabouts of the *Wasp*. Some of the prisoners taken in the Battle of the Coral Sea stated that the *Lexington* had been sunk, though others claimed that she was under repair on the west coast of the United States. The two or three American auxiliary (escort) carriers which were placed in the Pacific were known to be slow and were not considered by the Japanese to be capable of effective employment in offensive operations. The Japanese did not expect that the Americans had any powerful unit, built round aircraft carriers, in the neighbourhood of Midway.

A sortie by the American naval forces in the Hawaii area, in the event of an attack on Midway, was expected. The strength of these forces was estimated as follows:

Aircraft carriers	2 to 3
Escort carriers	2 to 3
Battleships	2
Cruisers	7 to 9
Light cruisers	4
Destroyers	about 30
Submarines	25

Unburdened by the problem of two-ocean warfare the Japanese felt no doubts as to their ability to defeat this or any other force with which the Allies might be able to counter-attack.

The reinforcement of the air strength of Midway which was undertaken by the Americans after the Battle of the Coral Sea, did not escape the notice of the Japanese, who made a fairly close estimate of the American air forces on the island, as follows:

Reconnaissance flying boats	2 squadrons
Army bombers	1 squadron
Fighters	1 squadron

They believed that strict air patrols were maintained both day and night to a distance of about 500 to 600 miles from Midway and that about three fighters were kept over the islands at all times. Air reconnaissance was believed to be conducted mainly to the west and the south, and to be less strict to the north-west and the north. It was also thought that patrols by surface vessels were maintained, with submarines active to the west.

Air strength in the Hawaii area, which could be used for the speedy reinforcement of Midway, was estimated at the following:

Flying boats	2 squadrons
Bombers	1 squadron
Fighters	1 squadron

It was considered that combat air patrols and ships' AA fire could deal successfully with any attempt to counter-attack by US shore-based aircraft.

Midway was believed to be very strongly defended, with powerful fixed batteries and high angle guns, and a garrison of marines. The Japanese intended to land on Curé, Eastern and Sand Islands.

4. Organization of the Japanese expedition

The Japanese force for the MI (Midway) Operation comprised the main strength of the Japanese Combined Fleet and was organized in groups; the Main Body, Striking Force, and Occupation Force, under the command of Admiral I. Yamamoto.

OCCUPATION FORCE

Midway Island is very small, and no more than six transports were needed to carry the special naval landing force, consisting of some 1,500 marines for Sand Island and 1,000 Army troops for Eastern Island, together with engineers and ancillary units. Two seaplane carriers conveyed the 11th Air Flotilla which was to establish the seaplane base at Curé Island. Close escort of this transport unit was carried out by the 2nd Destroyer Flotilla, consisting of the light cruiser *Jintsu*, flagship of Rear-Admiral R. Tanaka who commanded the unit and its close escort, and 11 destroyers. A tanker was in company.

The assault forces apparently were ill-supplied with landing boats. They carried many different kinds but were not sanguine as to the ability of most of them to cross the reefs, in which case rubber boats were supposed to be used. Distant cover for the force was provided by the 2nd Fleet, formed at this date by part of the 3rd Battle Squadron (*Kongo* – flagship of Vice-Admiral Kondo, Commander-in-Chief of the Occupation Force – and *Hiyei*), the 4th Cruiser Squadron (*Atago* and *Maya*), 5th Cruiser Squadron (*Myoko* and *Haguro*) and the 4th Destroyer Flotilla (light cruiser *Yura* and seven destroyers). A supply group and tankers accompanied the 2nd Fleet. The four cruisers of the 7th Cruiser Squadron (*Kumano*, Flagship of Rear-Admiral T. Kurita, *Suzuya*, *Mikuma* and *Mogami*) constituted a fast support force which took up a position between 75 and 100 miles ahead of the transports during the approach to Midway. It was intended that this force should shell Midway prior to the landing.

STRIKING FORCE

The landing on Midway Island was to be preceded by an air attack carried out from the four carriers *Akagi* (flagship of Admiral C. Nagumo, Commander-in-Chief 1st Air Fleet), *Kaga*, *Hiryu* and *Soryu*, which also had the dual role of attacking the US Fleet, if located, and supporting the invasion force. The carriers were supported by the 2nd Division of the 3rd Battle Squadron (*Haruna* and *Kirishima*), 8th Cruiser Squadron (*Tone* and *Chikuma*), and the 10th Destroyer Flotilla (light cruiser *Nagara* and 16 destroyers). Two supply groups accompanied the force, which was under the command of Admiral Nagumo.

MAIN BODY

A powerful force under Admiral Yamamoto, Commander-in-Chief Combined Fleet, consisting of the 1st and 2nd Battle Squadrons (three and four battleships respectively), the 9th Cruiser Squadron (two cruisers) and the 3rd Destroyer Flotilla (light cruiser *Sendai* and 12 destroyers), together with the light carrier *Zuiho* and two supply groups, was in support.

5. Operations of the Japanese submarines

In connection with the Midway Operation the Japanese intended to carry out a reconnaissance of Pearl Harbor by submarines of the 6th Fleet based on French Frigate Shoal, halfway between Midway and Honolulu, about the end of May. However, when the submarines arrived at French Frigate Shoal they found that the Americans were using it as a seaplane base, and the plan had to be abandoned.

French Frigate Shoal was also to have been a land-based aircraft refuelling station and two submarines of the 13th Submarine Flotilla (*I-121*, *I-123*) carried supplies of aviation spirit to refuel aircraft of the 24th Air Flotilla which had the duty of giving air cover and carrying out reconnaissance from the Marshall Islands during the operation. This plan, too, had to be abandoned.

The submarines reported by radio the changed situation at French Frigate Shoal and proceeded to carry out a patrol between the Shoal and Midway, keeping to the southward of Lisyanski Island.

In the hope of intercepting the US fleet a patrol was established by submarines of the 3rd Flotilla off Hawaii and of the 5th Flotilla between Midway and Hawaii. Only one of these boats encountered any ships. This was *I-168*, which was ordered by wireless to search for a damaged aircraft carrier, and on 7 June discovered and sank the damaged *Yorktown*. This submarine, whose patrol line ran close to Midway, kept the Commander-in-Chief informed as to the air strength and absence of US surface craft at the island, and reconnoitred and reported on Curé Island, and at 0130 on 5th it shelled Midway.

Two submarines of the 3rd Flotilla were stationed in the Hawaii area on life-saving duty. Japanese aircraft were unable to communicate directly with the submarines.

6. The Aleutian diversion

Intimately connected with the Midway operation and acting as a diversion for Operation MI the Japanese planned an attack on the Aleutians, Operation AL. This was carried out by a small but powerful force consisting of two aircraft carriers, two heavy cruisers, and three destroyers, termed the Second Mobile Force or Second Task Force.

On 3 June (West longitude date), the day before the carrier attack on Midway, an air attack was carried out on Dutch Harbor, followed on the 6th 7 June respectively by the occupation of Kiska and Attu.

The Americans appreciated the likelihood of an attack on their Aleutian bases concurrently with an operation against Midway. To meet the threat, a new Task Force 8 was formed out of the five cruisers and four destroyers which were the only spare ships within reach. This was despatched to reinforce the sea frontier forces being assembled in the Alaskan area.

7. Japanese preparations for the operation

The carriers detailed for the Midway operation returned to their home ports from the raid on Ceylon, on 22–23 April, and immediately set about repair and maintenance and urgently needed flight training.

During the operations which had lasted for more than five months there had been a considerable turn-over in flight personnel, and there was time for no more than basic training for most of the airmen. Some experienced flyers had lost much of their skill. Only one carrier was available for take-off and landing drills. The Commander-in-Chief of the Japanese 1st Air Fleet, in his *Battle Report*, paints a picture of rudimentary conditions of training almost incredible in a power which had presumed to challenge the might of the United States. Inexperienced flyers barely reached the point where they could make daytime landings on carriers, and only the more experienced pilots carried out about one dusk landing apiece. No opportunity was available for joint training, thus precluding co-ordinated action between contact units, illumination units, and attack units. Consequently, night attacks were practically ruled out. There was no opportunity for bomber leaders to participate in formation level bombing drills. The only target ship, the old battleship *Settsu*, was limited to waters in the western Inland Sea, causing waste of time by flyers in coming and going, to the prejudice both of their dive bombing and of their basic training. Even this minimum practice could not be conducted satisfactorily since the men were kept busy with maintenance work. In air combat tactics only the more experienced got further than lone air combat training and even they were limited to about a three-plane formation. Only the fundamentals of night flying were learned by the inexperienced.

The need for replacements and transfers of personnel had greatly lowered the fighting efficiency of the ships of the striking force. Maintenance and repair work went on until a few days before departure, which affected the men's efficiency. The ships did not assemble from their home ports until a few days before the scheduled date for sortie, and the squadron as a whole had no opportunity to carry out joint drills. Limitations in time prevented satisfactory training in group formations. This was particularly true of the newly formed 10th Destroyer Flotilla, some of the units of which underwent training as AA screening ships, others as AS screens; but the squadron as a whole had no opportunity to carry out joint drills.

8. Organization of the US forces

The Americans were well aware that if their appreciation of a Japanese intention to attack Midway was correct, the situation was most serious. Midway was unable to defend itself without support; their carriers were far away, and perhaps only two would be fit in time to fight. Task Force 17 had already been recalled to Pearl Harbor for replenishment and for repair of the *Yorktown*. Task Force 16 was now immediately ordered north; it arrived at Pearl Harbor on 26 May and sailed on the 28th under Rear-Admiral R. A. Spruance, for a rendezvous north-east of Midway. Task Force 17 reached the base on 27th and excellent work by the Navy Yard, the Service Force, and supporting services placed the *Yorktown* and her aircraft in reasonable fighting condition in three days; and the force sailed on the 30th for the rendezvous, under Rear-Admiral F. J. Fletcher.

Task Forces 16 and 17 made rendezvous at 1530 on 2nd June as arranged in 32° 04′ N., 172° 45′ E., about 350 miles north-east of Midway, having fuelled at sea en route; and the combined force, under the command of Rear-Admiral Fletcher, moved to an area of operations north of Midway, Task Force 16 operating about 10 miles to the southward of Task Force 17.

Task Force 17 contained now the single carrier *Yorktown*, two heavy cruisers, and five destroyers. The *Yorktown's* aircraft were made up by the addition of squadrons from the *Saratoga* to a total of 36 scout bombers 12 torpedo bombers, and 25 fighters. The *Enterprise* and *Hornet* in Task Force 16 each carried 35 scout bombers, 14 torpedo bombers, and 27 fighters. The lesson of the Battle of the Coral Sea, when the American fighters were outnumbered at every encounter, had resulted in a 50 per cent increase in the number of fighters borne, bringing them to numerical equality with the Japanese, ship for ship.

Consideration was given to the employment of Task Force 1 in the defence of Midway. It was not moved out from US waters, however, because of the undesirability of diverting to its screen any unit which could add to the long-range striking power of Task Forces 16 and 17 against the enemy carriers; and events proved that none of the air units which were employed could have been spared from the purpose for which it was used.

The Commander-in-Chief, United States Fleet, Admiral E. J. King, believed that the Japanese plans were designed to trap a portion of the US fleet. For this reason, he gave orders that only strong attrition tactics were to be employed, and that the US carriers and cruisers were not to be unduly risked. This, and the fact that the Americans were defending a fixed point against a superior enemy force, dictated the American tactics.

A submarine cordon was established to cover the approaches to Midway on an arc from 210 degrees to 000 degrees on 3–4 June. Six submarines patrolled sectors of the 150 miles circle[1] and three were stationed on the 200 miles circle from Midway.[2] The *Flying Fish* and *Cachalot* were on station patrols some 60 miles north-north-west and north-west of Midway respectively, and the *Cuttlefish* 700 miles west of Midway. Three were placed in support on the 800-mile circle north-west of Oahu,[3] and four 300 miles north of that island,[4] and the last ones to become available on the 100 miles circle from Oahu. Nineteen of the 26 submarines in the Central Pacific, all that could reach the Oahu-Midway area by 3 June, were employed, the consequent cessation of their offensive patrols being accepted.

Admiral C. W. Nimitz, Commander-in-Chief, United States Pacific Fleet, retained in his own hands the broad tactical direction of all forces in the Midway area.

---

1. *Gudgeon, Grouper, Nautilus, Grayling, Trout, Tambor*
2. *Grenadier, Gato, Dolphin.*
3. *Plunger, Narwhal, Trigger.*
4. *Growler, Finback, Pike, Tarpon.*

9. Preparations at Midway

Measures were taken to strengthen Midway to the maximum extent possible.

The problem at Midway for the Americans was to hit the enemy before they were hit. The danger against which they had to guard was that their aircraft might be surprised on the ground and destroyed, and their runways put temporarily out of action by bombing before the enemy was damaged. There were two essential requirements to prevent this: effective search and long-range striking power.

For long-range search 30 Navy patrol bombers (Catalinas) were sent to the island and for long range strikes 17 B.17s of the Seventh Air Force and four Army B.26s fitted with torpedoes were sent to Midway from Hawaii, in spite of the difficulty of protecting these aircraft on the ground. Major-General C. L. Tinker, US Army, Commander of the Army Air Force in Hawaii, himself came to the scene of action.[5] To provide close-in air striking power the marine air group was brought up to a strength of 28 fighters and 34 scout bombers, though only 30 pilots were available for the latter type. This group was augmented by six new Navy torpedo bombers. Because of overcrowding of the facilities at Midway there was considerable interchange between that island and Hawaii, so that the number of aircraft available varied from day to day. The figures given above were those for 3 June. The radio and communication personnel at Midway were reinforced for the control of the additional aircraft.

All Navy and Army aircraft sent to Midway and all B.17s of the 7th Bomber Command whose duties involved landing on or basing aircraft at Midway, operated under the control of the Commanding Officer, Naval Air Station, Midway, Captain C. T. Simard; but there was no co-ordinating authority for the operations of the aircraft based at Midway and those of the US carriers respectively; moreover, the carriers normally operated under conditions of radio silence.

In the belief that the Japanese planned a rendezvous about 700 miles west of Midway B.17s flew searches to a distance of 800 miles on 31 May and 1 June, and on the 2nd a B.17 without bombs searched 800 miles to the west without making any contacts. From 30 May to 3 June Catalinas searched 700 miles from bearing 200 degrees through west to 020 degrees.[6] Cover was

---

5. He was lost on 9 June when the long-range bomber in which he was searching for the enemy was forced down at sea.

6. The Commander, Patrol Wing 2 on 23 May recommended that searches by PBY-5 seaplanes (twin-engine patrol bombers, boat (Catalinas)). should be carried out over a 180 degrees sector, radius 700 miles; search to start at dawn daily, proceed out at average speed of 100 knots, returning at 111 knots or better in order to get back by dark. Assuming 25 miles visibility which might reasonably be expected in the Midway area at that time of year for a large force or single ship proceeding at such speed as to leave a conspicuous wake, each PBY could cover an 8 degrees sector, so that about 23 aircraft would be required. Comment by the Head of BAD Washington, that the search, though not watertight, appeared to be the best possible provided it was not judged to be perfect.

good except beyond 300 miles to the north and north-west, where visibility was very poor. It was precisely this area of low visibility and fog that concealed the approaching Japanese carriers from the Americans for some 30 hours, until they came within 650 miles of Midway.

On account of this unsearched area it was thought possible the enemy would escape detection on the day before reaching attacking range if they approached from that direction, though it was appreciated that the same weather would no doubt affect accuracy of navigation and prevent the Japanese from launching a night attack. It was thought that on passing from the bad weather area early in the morning they would fix their position at dawn before sending off an attack. This would occur between 0430 and 0500, and Midway could consequently expect to be attacked about 0600. In the event, the American appreciation was correct: Midway was attacked at 0630.

To counter the threat of dawn attack, search aircraft were sent off as early as possible each day, usually about 0415. To safeguard them from destruction and to ensure that a striking force would be available as early as possible each day, usually about 0415. To safeguard them from destruction and to ensure that a striking force would be available immediately if a target was located, the B.17s took off directly afterwards. They remained in the air for four hours, by which time the progress of the search and the reduction of their fuel load rendered landing possible and desirable. The four B.26s, the six TBFs and the other aircraft remained on the ground but fully alert until the search had reached a distance of 400 miles.

The garrison of Midway was increased to the maximum. The Marine Sixth Defense Battalion was reinforced by part of the Second Raider Battalion, with special equipment for opposing a mechanized landing, and by the AA and Special Weapons Group of the Third Defense Battalion. The troops worked day and night to strengthen the defences of the islands. Underwater obstacles were installed, and anti-tank and anti-personnel mines planted.

For the local defence of Midway Motor Torpedo Boat Squadron One, consisting of 11 MTBs, was sent from Hawaii and placed under the direction of the Commanding Officer, Midway. These boats assisted in meeting the enemy air attack on the islands and carried out rescue work of airmen down at sea. Rescue boats were also stationed at Pearl-Hermes, Lisyanski, Gardner, Laysan, and Necker Islands in the Hawaii Group.

Chapter II

Preliminary Movements, 3–4 June

10. Japanese expedition sails

The striking force sailed from Hashira Jima in Hiroshima Wan (Inland Sea) at 0900 on 26 May (Z + 12). The supply unit was met at 1500 on 27th in about 28° 30′ N., 139° 30′ E., and the force turned north-eastward and headed for the area to the north-west of Midway. The ships fuelled at sea on 31 May and 1 June. Visibility steadily decreased from about 1300 on 1 June, so that fuelling had to be broken off before all ships had completed. By 1400 on the 1st the force was completely closed in by fog. Course was altered to the south-eastward at 1630 on the 2nd in 37° 20′ N., 171° 40′ E., for the run down towards Midway, but visual signalling was impossible and radio silence had to be broken at 1300, the orders for alteration of course being made on long wave. By the morning of the 3rd, however, surface visibility had proved greatly, though there were scattered clouds overhead.

The main body was apparently about 30 hours astern of the carriers and took a shorter route towards the operating area. At 1500 on 3 June in 35° N., 165° E., Admiral Yamamoto detached a considerable portion of his force, termed the Aleutian Screening Force, to screen him to the northward. Simultaneously, the main body altered course to the eastward, to be within supporting distance of the carriers coming down from the north. The Aleutian screening force steered to the north-eastward till 1200 on the 4th, when it altered course to rejoin, though it did not make junction till the operation had been abandoned and all detachments had turned for home.

The reinforced Second Fleet (distant cover and screening force for the Occupation Force) sailed from the Inland Sea with the main body and continued to the south-eastward to close the transport unit at the appointed rendezvous in 26° 15′ N., 175° 40′ E., when the main body turned north-easterly.

The transport unit with its close escort sailed from the Inland Sea and was serviced at Saipan whence it sailed at 2100 on 27 May with the intention of assaulting Midway from the south. Passing west of Tinian, it picked up some of the slowest transports[1] which had sailed from Eniwetok, the westernmost of

---

1. It is thought that the Japanese word which is translated 'transports' includes also supply ships and oilers.

the Marshall Islands, and proceeded towards the rendezvous with the Second Fleet, in 26° 15′ N., 175° 40′ E. Owing to submarine report, however, the unit, which should have altered course to the eastward when in 24° 30′ N., 161° 30′ E., continued on course 058 degrees until reaching the 165 degrees meridian in 26° 30′ N. The naval units zigzagged, but the transports, unless under attack, steered a steady course at their maximum speed of 10 knots. Air cover was given by the 24th Air Flotilla from the Marshall Islands and the 26th from Marcus Island.

11. Occupation force sighted, 0904 3 June

The air searches which had been carried out from Midway for the past few days were rewarded on 3 June. On that day the usual search was made. By 0430 all aircraft fit for service were in the air, in order to clear the runways. As on the previous days, coverage was good except beyond 400 miles to the north-north-west. A few hours later reports began to be received at the island from the Catalinas, indicating that an enemy surface force was approaching from a bearing of 265 degrees. This was the Japanese Occupation Force.

First contact was made with the transport unit at 0904 by an American patrol bomber which reported two cargo ships in 25° 08′ N., 174° 30′ E. At 0924 a large number of ships, later reported as 11, was sighted by a Navy patrol aircraft bearing 261 degrees, distant 700 miles from Midway, steering an easterly course at 10 knots. Several smaller groups of ships were reported about the same time and were correctly interpreted as belonging to the Occupation Force and its escort, converging on a rendezvous for the final advance on Midway.

The reporting Catalina was ordered to return to base on account of shortage of fuel and the probability of its being shot down if it attempted to shadow; and at 1230 a special long-range B.17, which it was thought could look after itself, with no bombs, but with a Naval observer on board, took off to shadow[2] the enemy forces now reported 500–600 miles SW of Midway, and to direct a striking force out.[3] The B.17 sighted only two transports and two destroyers bearing 261 degrees distance 700 miles at 1640.

---

2. The Catalinas, whilst excellent for long range search, did not possess the performance or defensive characteristics required to stand up against strong enemy air opposition; consequently, when the latter was to be expected, they failed in their primary requirement of continuous shadowing.

3. The US *Combat Narrative*, p. 9, says the B.17 was also to search the expected enemy rendezvous at 800 miles, but this is not mentioned as one of its duties in the B.17's report.

12. B.17s attack transport unit, 1623 3 June

None of the sighting reports included the enemy carriers,[4] consequently the Commanding Officer of the Midway defence forces was unwilling to commit his long-range striking force of B.17s pending the receipt of more definite news. About noon the enemy reports crystallized into positive information, and at 1230 the striking force of nine of the 17 B.17s of the Seventh Air Force at Midway was despatched to attack.

Interception was effected at 1623 of a force reported bearing 265 degrees 570 miles from Midway. The actual position was probably about 60 miles further to the south-eastward, viz., approximately 261° N., 17° E. The bombers estimated the force to contain five battleships, cruisers or destroyers with about 40 transports and cargo ships, but in point of fact no battleships or cruisers (other than the light cruiser *Jintsu*) were present, for the enemy that had been sighted was the Occupation Force and its close escort; and the particular formation which the bombers attacked comprised the transport unit, viz., six transports and the tanker *Akebono Maru* escorted by the *Jintsu* and six destroyers. The seaplane carriers had quit the force about 1½ hours earlier and proceeded at 17 knots for Curé Island, and if they were sighted they were apparently not recognized for what they were.

The B.17s were loaded with demolition bombs, seven with 4 × 600 lb. and two with 4 × 500 lb. They carried out a high level horizontal bombing attack in flights of three aircraft at altitudes of 8,000 and 10,000 and 17,000 feet respectively, dropping their bombs with 1/10 seconds delay. Three 500 lb. failed to release.[5] No enemy aircraft opposed them, but at the bomb release line very heavy but inaccurate anti-aircraft fire was encountered throughout the attack. Bursts were from 5,000 to 18,000 feet, but in this as in practically all future attacks in the battle the fire was mainly behind the attacking aircraft, none of which was hit.

The attack came as a surprise to the enemy, who were not fitted with radar, and their first warning was when the first bombs fell. Nevertheless, the AA fire they put up was so heavy that the bombers did not consider it wise to remain in the area for close observation. They estimated the damage caused as: 1 heavy cruiser or battleship hit, burning; 1 transport hit, burning; 1 heavy cruiser believed hit at the stern, no evidence of damage except some smoke from the stern.

---

4. One carrier was reported among the forces sighted on the 3rd, but the sighting was not verified.
5. Some of the equipment of the aircraft was received too late for the crews to become familiar with their material, and it was thought that the cases of malfunctioning of bomb releases could be attributed to this cause.

The attack demonstrated the relative ineffectiveness of high level horizontal bombing against ships which retain speed and manoeuvrability for the Japanese reported that no ship was hit and no bomb fell nearer than 200 yards, despite the fact that the transports steered a steady course, without zigzagging until it was recognized that they were under attack.

The B.17 flights returned individually to Midway, landing at 2040. On that day, as throughout the operation, owing to the lack of space at Midway and the short time available for preparation of the Seventh Air Force crews had had to reservice their own aircraft and carry out essential maintenance, and as a result in some cases they went into the air in an exhausted condition.

13. Night attack transport unit by patrol bombers

At 2115 four Navy patrol bombers (Catalinas), three of which had flown from Pearl Harbor, a ten-hour flight, that afternoon, were despatched to make a night torpedo attack on the Japanese force approaching from the westward. The night was clear, with broken cumulus clouds at 1,000 feet. The third and fourth aircraft were lost from the formation in passing through cloud about 2400 and 0100 hours respectively, though one of them succeeded in finding the target alone and attacking, but the other turned back and eventually landed in the sea near Lisyanski Island, short of fuel, the crew being rescued 53 hours later.

At about 0015 on the 4th radar indicated a group of some ten ships 10 or 12 miles to port of the group, and soon the silhouettes of, apparently, ten or more large ships (actually seven or eight including the *Jintsu*) in two columns, escorted by six destroyers became visible in the moonlight. This was the transport unit which had been attacked by B.17s during the afternoon, and the reported position was about 261 degrees 500 miles from Midway. There were indications of another large group nearby, close to Midway.

The attackers approached down moon with engines throttled back. At 100 feet altitude the leader launched his torpedo at 800 yards range at the largest ship, which was leading the northern column. The second aircraft dropped his torpedo at 200 yards and opened machine-gun fire on his target, causing some casualties. The result was not observed, but it was apparently this torpedo which made the only hit obtained in the attack; it struck the tanker *Akebono Maru* forward, killing 11 men and wounding 13; but the damage merely caused the tanker to slow down, and she was able to keep with the unit, and was capable of 13 knots after the battle. The third aircraft found the target visually; he was attacked by a fighter directly after releasing his torpedo and escaped in the clouds. The Americans estimated that one transport or cargo ship has been sunk and one severely damaged. 'This night attack by Catalinas was a daring and historical feat' wrote the Commander-in-Chief, U.S. Pacific Fleet in his report.

The three patrol bombers returned from the attack individually, and landed at Laysan, being warned by radio that Midway Island was under air attack.

At 0700 the *Cutllefish* reported contact with an enemy tanker bearing 260 degrees 600 miles from Midway. Commander Submarines Pacific Fleet ordered her to shadow, but she was forced down and lost contact. Two hours later all submarines were given the position, course and speed of the Occupation Force, as reported by aircraft, and were ordered to close the enemy. This attack on the Japanese transport force was the prelude to the Battle of Midway itself which may be taken as beginning at dawn on 4 June. The battle fell into three well-defined phases.

(a) Air attack on Midway Island by the Japanese striking force and attempts of the Midway shore-based aircraft to halt the enemy advance (0430–0830, 4 June).

(b) Sinking of the four carriers of the Japanese striking force by US carrier-borne aircraft, and Japanese counter-attacks on the *Yorktown* (0900–1800, 4 June).

(c) Attacks on the defeated Japanese during their withdrawal, by US shore-based and carrier-borne aircraft (5–6 June). These successive phases of the battle will be described in the following chapters.

Chapter III

Air Attack on Midway, 4 June

14. Japanese attack group takes off from carrier, 0430

While the Occupation Force was approaching Midway from the westward the Japanese striking force, 650 miles to the northward, had altered course to the south eastward at 1630 on 2nd in 37° 15′ N., 171° 07′ E. From 1500/2 to 1500/3, however, only some 220 miles were made good, and consequently the force never emerged from the unsearched area of low visibility during the daylight hours of 3 June. Some doubtful sightings of American aircraft were made by the force in the evening and early part of the night of the 3rd–4th, causing fighters to take off from the *Akagi* at 1940 on the 3rd, whilst at 2330 ships went to action stations, in each case for false alarms.

At dawn on 4 June the Japanese forces were converging on Midway Island according to plan, their striking force about to fly off its air groups to attack the island from a position some 230 miles to the north-westward. About 200 miles to the north-east of this force was the American carrier force, steering to the south-west. Neither carrier force had been located by its opponents, and the Japanese were unaware of the strength the Americans had been able to concentrate. The Americans knew the approximate position of the Japanese transport force, and the attacks of the night before had revealed to the Japanese that they could not hope for tactical surprise. On Midway Island, all aircraft were standing by and the dawn reconnaissance was just taking off.

At 0430 on the 4th an attack group of 36 naval fighters, 36 bombers, and 35 torpedo aircraft (armed with bombs), made up as follows: *Hiryu* – 17 torpedo, 9 fighters; *Soryu* – 18 torpedo, 9 fighters; *Akagi* – 9 fighters, 18 bombers; *Kaka* – 9 fighters, 18 bombers, under the command of the flight officer of the *Hiryu*, Lieut. Tomonaga, took off for Midway from the Japanese carriers which were then some 210 miles to the north-westward of Midway, in approximately lat. 30° 45′ N., long. 179° 40′ E.[1]

---

1. The Japanese reported that some of their fighters were sent on ahead to gain control of the air over Midway. The Americans, however, did not encounter these fighters separately.

15. Discovery of the Japanese carriers

Meanwhile the Americans had not succeeded in locating the Japanese carriers, and at about the same time the usual search group of Naval Catalinas took off from Midway, covered by a Marine fighter patrol. Their orders were to search to 425 miles for the four enemy carriers which the Americans evidently appreciated were riding the weather front to the north-west, after which they were to return to Laysan and Lisyanski, to avoid exposing them unnecessarily at Midway where attack was now believed to be imminent.

The Catalinas made contact with the Japanese attack group about an hour after it had taken off from the carriers. One or more of the American flying boats was shot down,[2] but at 0545 they sent a report to Midway of many aircraft heading for the island, bearing 320 degrees distant 150 miles, and five minutes afterwards the Midway radar picked up aircraft at a distance of 93 miles, altitude about 10,000 feet. Only seven minutes later, at 0552, the impatiently awaited news of the enemy carriers arrived, when another flying boat sighted two carriers and a number of supporting ships, including battleships, on the same bearing as the enemy aircraft, distant 180 miles, coming in at 25 knots on course 135 degrees.

16. The air battle

The alarm was sounded at Midway at 0555, and in a few minutes every serviceable aircraft was in the air. Bombers and torpedo bombers made for the enemy carriers while between 0556 and approximately 0620 the 1st, 4th and 5th Division of Marine fighters (eight F2A Brewster and six F4F Grumman) were vectored towards the target, and the 2nd and 3rd Divisions (ten F2A Brewster) were vectored out on 310 degrees for 10 miles and instructed to orbit, being temporarily withheld in case another group of enemy aircraft should appear on another bearing. As none appeared, they were shortly after ordered to join the air interception of those aircraft already reported. The group was also joined by two fighters (F4F) which for some reason had remained in the air from the early morning covering patrol and now landed, refuelled, and took off again. One fighter returned with engine trouble, leaving a total of 25 which proceeded to meet the Japanese attack.

Contact was made at 12,000 to 15,000 feet, at 0616, about 30 miles from Midway. The Japanese bombers were in a tight 'V' formation, with the fighters apparently at a lower altitude, for they were not at first seen by the

---

2. The US Summary of Air Operations shows that one Catalina was shot down and four forced down, whereas the Japanese claimed to have shot down two aircraft.

Americans[3] who consequently attacked the bombers in separate divisions from 17,000 feet. These Marine fighters, although shore squadrons, were of the carrier type, and found themselves not only outnumbered by the Japanese Zero fighters, but markedly outclassed in speed, manoeuvrability and climb, though superior in armour, armament, and in the possession of leak-proof tanks. Each American fighter, after one or two passes at the bombers, found himself attacked by Žero fighters which outmanoeuvred him, and from which there was little possibility of escape other than in cloud cover, though it is reported that in two cases pilots successfully led the enemy into the fire from light AA guns ashore and on board the MTBs It is clear from the reports that the individual American pilots fought gamely, single aircraft going after Zero fighters even though the hunter inevitably became the hunted. To repulse or break up the attack on Midway was not in their power, however.

Their losses were heavy. Of 27 fighters of the Marine air group that intercepted the Japanese, including interceptions over the island during the attack, only 12 returned in answer to the message broadcast at 0715, 'Fighters land, refuel by division, Fifth Division first' and of these seven were severely damaged.[4] They estimated they had destroyed eight fighters and 25 bombers, but the Japanese reported that they lost no more than one fighter, one bomber and three torpedo aircraft.[5] They too, grossly overestimated the number of American fighters destroyed, which they put at 41.

17. Bombing of Midway

Meanwhile, at Midway, despite the efforts of the American fighters, considerable damage had been done. The weather was good, with excellent visibility, though there appears to have been a small amount of cloud above 1,600 feet. The first battery got on to the target at 50,000 yards range, and at 0631 the observation post reported that all AA batteries had opened fire.

The attack was opened about 0630 by the torpedo aircraft from the *Hiryu* and *Soryu* which each dropped one 805 kg. (1,700 lb.) land bomb from 3,400 m. (11,150 feet), followed by the dive bombers from the *Akagi* and *Kaga*, which each dropped one 242 kg. (550 lb.) land bomb. Targets were reported by the Japanese to have been as follows:

---

3. Presumably this is the reason why the Americans did not attempt to hold off the Japanese fighters with a portion of their force while the remainder dealt with the bombers.
4. Two were missing.
5. S.E. Morison, *History of U.S. Naval Operations in World War II*, Vol. IV, says the Japanese were vague about their losses in their official reports (since they lost all by the next day) and that at least a third of the attackers were destroyed by the Marine fighter squadron or by anti-aircraft fire.

Hiryu and *Soryu* ... Neutralization of AA fire, attacks on airfield and installations on Sand Island, though the *Soryu*'s aircraft also attacked the Eastern Island airfields.

Akagi and *Kaga* ... Enemy aircraft both in the air and on the ground.

Most of the structures above ground were considerably damaged, the most serious at the time being the destruction of the power plant on Eastern Island, necessitating fuelling of aircraft by hand from tins and drums. Little damage was caused to the runways, and it was thought the Japanese wished to leave these intact for their own future use, though the available evidence suggests that the opposite was the case. The attack lasted for about 17 minutes, though at 0701 two batteries opened fire again for a few seconds on a single aircraft appearing to the south. Smoke from the burning oil tanks interfered with AA. The Americans reported that ten enemy aircraft were shot down by us, but the Japanese reported only three so lost.

19. Japanese cancel second air attack on Midway

After the take-off of the Midway attack group, the remaining torpedo aircraft of the Japanese striking force were ordered to arm and stand by in readiness to attack any surface vessels located by the searches then being made.

The striking force had launched altogether seven reconnaissance aircraft shortly before dawn, between 0430 and 0500, to search to the east and south as follows:-

Akagi and *Kaga*	One ship-based torpedo aircraft each
Chikuma	One seaplane
	One seaplane
Tone	One seaplane
	One seaplane
Haruna	One seaplane

All aircraft were ordered to go out 300 miles, then turn left-handed for 60 miles except the *Haruna*'s, which went out 150 miles and 40 miles to the left. One of the *Chikuma*'s seaplanes turned back at 0635 on account of bad weather when 350 miles from her launching point.

At 0715 the command aircraft of the attack group (Air Officer, *Hiryu*), reported that a second attack on Midway would be necessary; this was decided upon, and the attack aircraft were ordered to remove torpedoes and replace them by 805 kg. land bombs.

The order had barely been given before a report came in from the pilot of one of the *Tone*'s reconnaissance aircraft that he had sighted what appeared to be a force of ten enemy surface ships, in position bearing 010 degrees distant 240 miles from Midway, steering a course of 150 degrees at a speed over 20 knots. The weather was cloudy, and the *Chikuma*'s first aircraft (No. 5) through whose sector of search the US force was passing, failed to sight the Americans. The aircraft was ordered to report the enemy types, preparations for air attack were made, those attack aircraft which had not yet exchanged their torpedoes for bombs being ordered to retain their torpedoes. Half an hour later, the reply from the *Tone*'s aircraft arrived: 'Enemy is composed of five cruisers and five destroyers', followed, at 0820, by 'The enemy is accompanied by what appears to be a carrier.' This was the *Yorktown*. Two additional cruisers were reported a few minutes later, astern of the larger force, steering a similar course. The shore-based American aircraft had been attacking Admiral Nagumo's force at intervals for over an hour, and an air attack was in progress at the moment (see Chapter IV), but directly a lull occurred the Admiral altered course and headed for the enemy.

The second wave of attack on Midway gave place to the new and more important object of attacking the American carrier. Owing, however, to the necessity for re-equipping the torpedo aircraft it was not immediately possible to send off a strike against the *Yorktown*. The Midway attack group was expected back very shortly, and it was therefore decided to await their return and then to despatch the strongest possible group to attack the reported carrier.

Before this could take place, however, the situation underwent a dramatic and, for the Japanese, a disastrous change. The last aircraft of the Midway attack group was safely on board and it was confirmed that substantial results had been obtained; preparations were hastily going forward for a 'grand attack' by 93 aircraft on the *Yorktown*. Though the striking force had been under attack since 0710, first by American Army, Navy and Marine shore-based torpedo aircraft and bombers, followed at 0920 and again at 20 by carrier-based torpedo aircraft, it had suffered no hits or damage whatever. Then, at 1022, antagonists of a very different calibre appeared – the American carrier-borne dive bombers. Seldom in war can a situation have been more swiftly and suddenly reversed; within a few minutes three out of four of the carriers had been reduced to flaming wrecks and Japanese sea power had suffered a blow from which it never recovered for the remainder of the war.

Before describing these devastating attacks, however, it is necessary to give an account of how the American shore-based air attacks had fared.

Chapter IV

Midway Aircraft Attack Japanese
First Air Fleet 0710–0820, 4 June

19. Army (B.26) and Navy torpedo (TBF) aircraft attack, 0710

To return to Midway Island. When the Japanese carriers were sighted at 0552, the four Army B.26s, under Captain J. F. Collins, Jr., and the six Navy torpedo bombers under Lieut. F. K. Fieberling, were already manned, with engines warmed, and they were at once despatched to attack. History was made by the fact that for the first time the B.26s each carried a torpedo.

The Army aircraft took off at 0625, and at 0705 they sighted the Japanese striking force which they reported as three carriers, one battleship, several cruisers, and about six destroyers. Sighting by the Japanese was simultaneous at about 27,000 yards range and all carriers flew off fighters. Approaching from the south-east, the Americans were met by heavy anti-aircraft fire from the Japanese striking force, which steered directly towards them; and just before reaching the enemy formation six Zero fighters were met head on at 700 feet. As Captain Collins manoeuvred, first to the left and then to the right, to find the best path through the enemy's AA fire, he caught sight of six Navy torpedo aircraft which had left Midway fifteen minutes earlier than his own group; they were just going in for their attack, approaching from his right and across his course. To avoid the Japanese fighters the B.26s dived steeply to 200 feet, and most of the enemy's fire passed overhead. It was probably at this point that two of the Americans were shot down.

Captain Collins chose as his target the carrier *Hiryu*, in the centre of the formation, releasing his 2,000 lb. torpedo, with depth setting 12 feet, at 200 feet and 200 mph from 25 degrees off the bow, range 800 yards, as the carrier turned across his path. His No. 4 slightly below and to his left, released at about 450 yards from 150 feet, and then pulled up over the carrier. One of the two B.26s shot down was reported to have launched its torpedo, and was then thought, though incorrectly, to have struck the *Hiryu*'s flight deck and hurtled into the sea. None of the three torpedoes fired by the B.26s found their mark, and the only damage reported by the Japanese was two men killed by strafing aboard the flagship *Akagi*. The last of the Japanese fighters, 50 of which were reported to have been disposed over the enemy ships,[1] at altitudes from 20,000 feet downwards, was not shaken off until the B.26s entered cloud cover on the way home, 15 to 20 minutes later. In both the surviving American aircraft the machine guns gave trouble, and Captain Collins reported that all his guns were unsatisfactory during the entire fight. One of the two machines crashed on landing, and both were so badly damaged as to be unserviceable. The six Navy torpedo aircraft attacked simultaneously with the Army bombers. Both the *Akagi* and *Hiryu* reported being attacked, the former by four and the latter by 13 aircraft. The Navy aircraft, like the B.26s, encountered heavy AA fire and an overwhelming number of fighters, for which the unescorted TBFs, despite their excellent armament, were no match, particularly since they had to slow down to limiting torpedo releasing speed. Two were shot down before they could release their torpedoes; it was estimated that the remaining four fired torpedoes but none of them hit, their slow speed enabling the Japanese ships to avoid them. Only a single badly damaged aircraft survived to make a landing with one wheel retracted, and the pilot could give no clear account of the attack.

20. Douglas (SBD) Marine scout bombers attack, 0755

Fifty minutes later, the Marine scout bombers of squadron VMSB-No.1 at Midway attacked. Thirty took off on signal, and were already in the air orbiting, 20 miles east of Eastern Island, when the report of the Japanese carriers came in; instructions to attack were sent but no acknowledgment was received, and the orders were repeated periodically for over an hour, though as events proved they had been acted upon at the first transmission. The scout bombers proceeded in two groups, the one commanded by Major L. R. Henderson, with 18 SBD-2[2] aircraft, the second under Major B. W. Norris with 12 SB2U-3s.[3] Two of the SBDs developed engine trouble and one SB2U was forced to return with a loose cowling. Ten of the pilots had joined the squadron only a week before, and there had been very little opportunity for training flights.

As only three of his pilots had experience of the SBDs, the Commander decided to make a glide bombing attack, for although less effective and more hazardous than dive bombing it permitted lower pull outs.

---

1. This was probably an over estimate, for the Japanese report that the total number of fighters which opposed the attacks of the Midway aircraft between 0710 and 0820 was 20 of the Combat Air Patrol assisted by the returning fighters of the Midway Attack Group, though the latter did not, however, arrive back over the carriers until 0810.
2. Douglas Dauntless scout bomber.
3. Vought-Sikorsky Vindicator scout bomber.

The SBDs sighted the enemy striking force at approximately 0755 and began to come down in a wide circle from their height of 9,000 feet to get into position for glide-bombing attack from 4,000 feet. The squadron was attacked once by several enemy fighters, and the enemy ships opened violent anti-aircraft fire. Major Henderson's own aircraft, on which the Japanese fighters apparently concentrated, was quickly set on fire and he himself was put out of action; the fighter attacks were so heavy that Captain E.G. Gliddon, Jr., who then took charge, led the squadron into a heavy layer of cloud from which it emerged at 2,000 feet and dived in close formation on the *Hiryu* under heavy AA fire and renewed attack by fighters. Bombs were released at 500 feet or less, and it was thought three direct hits were made, but the Japanese subsequently stated that there were no hits. The *Hiryu* had a number of casualties from near misses, but no damage was reported. Eight of the American bombers returned to base, but only six remained fit for service. Two were seen to go down in flames, and one went out of control before reaching Midway. The pilot jumped and was picked up by a PT boat. Another was forced down 100 miles west of Midway, but both pilot and gunner were rescued two days later.

21. Army B.17s attack the carriers, 0814

About 20 minutes after Major Henderson's attack, and before Major Norris's group of Marine scout bombers reached the target, Army B.17s of Flight 92 under the Commanding Officer of the 431st Bombardment Squadron, Lieut.-Col. W. C. Sweeney, Jr., attacked the Japanese striking force.

The 16 available Fortresses had taken off directly after the reconnaissance group and cleared Midway about 0415. To occupy them usefully during the four hours before they could safely land, they were ordered to attack the Japanese Occupation Force to the westward, which it was estimated they would find at a distance of about 480 miles. There had been no report of the latter since the night attack by patrol bombers; and it was not until five hours after the Army aircraft took off that the force was again picked up. At 0916 three cruisers in column were sighted in about 28° 00′ N., 176° 35′ E.; and at 0945 a force of four heavy cruisers, two oilers, and two cargo ships with destroyers in about 27° 35′ N., 175° 10′ E.; and at 0952 large vessels, including perhaps a battleship, in 26° 30′ N., 176° 30′ E. All were proceeding on course about 077 degrees towards Midway. The B.17s had the benefit of prolonged experience with naval forces obtained during co-ordinated patrol operations. They had been warned to be prepared for a change of objective if the enemy carriers should be discovered; and orders to this effect were sent to them as soon as the report of the carriers came in. The Fortresses were about 200 miles from Midway when they received the message, in plain language, stating that another enemy task force, including many carriers, was approaching Midway on a bearing 325 degrees, distance 145 miles.

Climbing to 20,000 feet, the Americans altered course for the carriers. The enemy were met at 0732, but it was not until 0810 that two carriers were seen

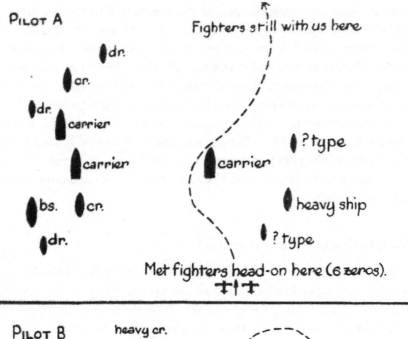

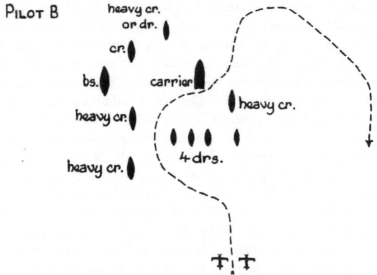

Fig. 6. Attacks on *Hirya* and *Agaki* by Army and Navy torpedo aircraft, 0710, 4 June.

through the broken clouds. The circling of the Fortresses had brought them to the north-westward of the Japanese fleet, and they attacked from astern from 20,000 feet.

The attack was made by flights of three aircraft (only two aircraft in flight 5). The first two flights dropped a total of 40 × 500 lb. demolition bombs and reported one hit on the stern of a carrier. The third and fifth flights attacked a second carrier, the third flight reporting one hit on the port bow, one waterline hit, one possible hit and five near misses; and the fifth flight one hit, one possible hit and two near misses. The fourth flight reported one hit and two near misses on a third carrier. In all, 16 × 600 lb. and 92 × 500 lb. bombs were dropped; the remainder hung up through failures of releasing gear. No Japanese ship appears to have noticed any bombs, except the *Soryu* which reported about 11, the nearest 50 yards away. No ship suffered any damage, and the relative ineffectiveness of high altitude horizontal bombing on ships which retained freedom of manoeuvre was again amply demonstrated.

The enemy AA fire was heavy and at the proper altitude, but generally behind the target. The Japanese fighters displayed no desire to close their formidable antagonists though the Fortresses reported that they were able to shoot down two Zeros.

22. Vought-Sikorsky (SD2U) Marine scout bombers attack, 0820

The second unit of the Marine group, eleven SB2Us under the command of Major Norris, flying at 13,000 feet, sighted the Japanese striking force at 0820, just as the Fortresses were finishing their attack. Japanese fighters were encountered at 13,000 feet, before the unit was in position to attack, and their opposition was so severe that the Americans were unable to search for the main objective, the carrier; and consequently, a secondary target, the battleship, *Haruna*, was chosen. The unit attacked in a long flat glide through the clouds at 2,000 feet and pulled out at a low altitude. One aircraft which was out of position attacked a destroyer and the bomb of one machine hung up. The Americans estimated two bombs hit the *Haruna* but this was not the case, though two fell very close. The *Haruna* reported that only five or six bombs in all fell near her, and it is possible that the three bombs which the carrier *Kaga* reported dropped by carrier-based bombers at 0830, the nearest no more than 20 yards from her stern, were dropped by the SB2Us. However, the carrier was not damaged.

Two of the SB2Us were lost through forced landings in the sea before reaching Midway, the two pilots and a gunner being rescued: the other gunner was apparently killed in the attack.

Chapter V

Destruction of First Air Fleet by Carrier Aircraft and Attacks on *Yorktown*, 4 June

23. Situation after the attack on Midway, 0710

The outlook on this June morning, as the last of the Midway aircraft withdrew from the scene of the attacks on the carriers was most unfavourable to the Americans. Indeed, had they known, it was even more serious than they supposed; for in place of the ten or so ships which they believed their air attacks to have damaged, actually only a single ship, a tanker, had suffered slight damage. On the island, nearly everything above ground had been destroyed or badly damaged by the Japanese air attack. The Midway bombers and torpedo bombers had struck with full strength but had not checked the great force of about 80 ships, including three (actually four) undamaged carriers reported to be converging on the island base. Most of the American fighters as well as the torpedo aircraft and dive bombers which were the only types capable of making a high percentage of hits on ships, were destroyed or out of action.

This was the situation when the United States aircraft carrier force rode into the battle.

24. Task forces 16 and 17 launch attack groups, 0716

The American carrier Task Forces 16 and 17, after making rendezvous on 2 June north-east of Midway in 32° 04' N., 172° 45' W., had moved westward during the night 2nd–3rd, Task Force 16 being about 10 miles south of Task Force 17. On the 3rd they turned north, and received reports, both from Midway and from the Commander-in-Chief, Pacific Fleet, of the enemy force sighted to the westward of Midway. It was clear, however, that this was not the Japanese Striking Force, which was expected to approach from the north-westward, so Rear-Admiral Fletcher turned eastward once more and whilst the *Enterprise* and *Hornet* held their aircraft in readiness as an attack force, the *Yorktown*'s aircraft conducted a search of a sector between 240 degrees and 060 degrees. Rain squalls and low visibility rendered the search difficult, and it was without result.

Throughout 3 June the American task forces remained undiscovered. During the approach, the Japanese striking force had maintained anti-submarine air patrols, but the thick weather which concealed the carriers from the American reconnaissance aircraft also prevented the enemy from sending out air searches, whilst the denial of French Frigate Shoal as a fuelling base limited the aircraft from the Marshall Islands to searching south of Midway. It is an interesting fact that during the whole of 3 June, too, Task Forces 16 and 17 were in the area patrolled by Japanese submarines, without being sighted.

Rear-Admiral Fletcher moved south-southwest during the night 3–4 June, to a position about 200 miles north of Midway, on the flank of the enemy striking force whose attack on the island was expected to take place shortly. At 0420 on the 4th the flagship launched a security search of the sector to the north and put a fighter patrol in the air. The *Enterprise* of Task Force 16 took over the direction of fighters.

The carrier force intercepted the report at 0545 of Japanese aircraft heading for Midway and a few minutes later the report of sighting two enemy carriers. Orders were at once sent to Rear-Admiral Spruance, five or ten miles to the south-west, to move westward and launch attacks when he came within range of the Japanese striking force. Since only two enemy carriers had been reported and the *Yorktown* had aircraft in the air, her attack group was temporarily held in reserve.

Task Force 16 increased to 25 knots and headed for the enemy. By 0700 Rear-Admiral Spruance estimated that the Japanese striking force, bearing 239 degrees, was about 155 miles distant. This was only 20 miles less than the combat radius of his torpedo aircraft. Nevertheless, as the reports of the enemy air attack on Midway came in, he decided to launch at once, in the hope, which in the event was fulfilled, of catching Nagumo's carriers with their aircraft on deck being refuelled for a second strike. He turned into the light south-east wind to launch his strike groups. Every aircraft not needed for combat patrol and A/S patrol was put into the air. Launching commenced at 0706 and required about an hour, deferred departure being used, the order of launching being (1) fighters for patrol, (2) dive bombers, (3) torpedo aircraft, (4) fighters to escort torpedo aircraft. The *Hornet* launched 35 scout bombers armed with 500 lb. bombs, 15 torpedo aircraft with torpedoes, and ten fighters; the *Enterprise* 32 scout bombers (15 with 1 × 1,000 lb. bombs and 17 with1 × 500 and 2 × 100-lb, bombs), 14 torpedo aircraft, and 10 fighters.

By 0840 there had been no report of further enemy carriers other than the two already sighted, and it was decided to launch the *Yorktown*'s attack group, lest she should be caught with her aircraft on deck. The entire torpedo squadron (12 aircraft each carrying one torpedo), half the bomber squadron

(17 scout bombers each with one 1,000-lb, bomb), and six fighters were launched. The 17 scout bombers that remained were held in reserve in case two more enemy carriers were sighted. The slower torpedo aircraft headed for the target at once. The scout bombers were ordered to circle for 12 minutes before proceeding to overtake the torpedo squadron. To economise fuel, the fighters were not launched until 0905. The three squadrons effected rendezvous at 0945 as they proceeded towards the target, which they found at the same time as the *Enterprise* group.

It was intended to co-ordinate the attacks of the torpedo aircraft and the dive bombers but owing to the inherent difficulties exact co-ordination was not achieved.

25. Enemy alters course, 0917

Meanwhile, the Japanese scouts had sighted the American task forces and Admiral Nagumo had altered course towards them at high speed (see Section 18). One of the two seaplanes, either the *Tone*'s or *Hiryu*'s, which made the sighting, was sighted by the Americans, who thus knew they had been reported and must consequently expect attack unless their own attack could be made before the enemy carriers could refuel and despatch once more the aircraft which had returned from the strike on Midway.[1]

The change of course to the north-eastward by Admiral Nagumo had taken place about 0917. It was reported to the American carriers, but the latter did not break wireless silence to inform their attack groups, with the consequence that some of the latter, on arriving at the estimated position of the Japanese carriers found the area void of enemy ships.

The 35 scout bombers from the *Hornet* on finding an empty sea turned southward to search along the enemy's reported course. With them were the ten fighters. No contact was made, and shortage of fuel forced all the fighters down in the sea before reaching Midway on the return journey, though eight of the pilots were rescued. All but two of the dive bombers eventually returned to the *Hornet*, 11 of them via Midway where they refuelled. Two landed in the lagoon.

26. The *Hornet*'s torpedo squadron attacks, 0920

The *Hornet*'s torpedo squadron, led by Lieut.-Commander J. C Waldron, had proceeded at a lower altitude than the remainder of the attack group, from which it became separated although there were only scattered clouds. The

---

1. It was thought probable that the Japanese did not know the position of the US carriers until the *Yorktown* broke R/T silence on power to vector fighters on to aircraft which subsequently proved to be friendly. But it is evident that the *Yorktown* was discovered by air R/C.

squadron turned north to search and found four Japanese carriers dispersed in a wide roughly circular formation accompanied as they estimated by two or three battleships, four cruiser and six destroyers. Warning of their approach was given by the *Tone* reconnaissance aircraft. The *Akagi*, *Kaga* and *Soryu* were close together, with the *Hiryu* standing off some distance to the north. The Japanese carriers had just completed landing-on the Midway attack groups and the Americans believed incorrectly that the *Soryu* and one other ship resembling a battleship were smoking from the attacks of the Midway aircraft an hour earlier.

The group attacked at once (0920) unsupported. Heavy fighter opposition was encountered, the *Chikuma* opening fire with her main armament at the same time. Almost immediately the group ran into heavy AA fire from the supporting ships, which soon ceased as it was seen that the Japanese fighters were shooting them down. Not one of the 15 aircraft survived the attacks, and only one pilot, Ensign G. H. Gay came through. After attacking a carrier believed to be the *Kaga* he crashed in the sea near the *Akagi*, while he watched the subsequent attacks of the *Yorktown*'s and *Enterprise*'s aircraft, hidden under a floating seat cushion and refraining from inflating his life raft until dark. Five of their aircraft were thought by the Americans to have been shot down before releasing their torpedoes, the other ten were believed to have been launched and to have made one hit each on the *Kaga* and another carrier. The Japanese reported that the attacking squadron apparently consisted of 17 aircraft, and that four torpedoes were seen, of which two very nearly hit the *Soryu*, one missed forward and one to starboard. No hits were made either on this carrier or the *Kaga*.

27. The *Enterprise* and *Yorktown* torpedo groups squadron attack, 1020

The torpedo and dive-bombing groups of the *Enterprise* and *Yorktown* attacked almost simultaneously, an hour after the *Hornet*'s. First in point of time to deliver their attack were the torpedo groups of the two carriers.

The *Enterprise*'s torpedo squadron, under Lieut.-Commander E. E. Lindway, escorted by 10 fighters, proceeded to the target independently of the dive bombers. On the way it became separated from its fighter escort, which inadvertently joined the *Hornet*'s torpedo squadron, and launched its attack without support. The altitude of the aircraft was too low to enable them to see more than three of the four Japanese carriers when they sighted the enemy about 1000 and first came under fire. It was not until 1020 that the aircraft were able to gain a position for attack on the beam of the carriers, for the violent manoeuvring of the enemy who altered course to starboard through

24 points of the compass from 270 degrees (the course which the attackers reported they were steering when sighted) to 180 degrees, kept them on the quarter of the carriers and forced them to make a wide circle. During this time, the torpedo group were under both AA gunfire and attack by enemy fighters, and the Americans estimated that six of their number were shot down before launching their torpedoes at the westernmost carrier, apparently the *Hiryu*. Only four aircraft survived the attack.

The *Yorktown's* torpedo squadron under Lieut.-Commander L. E. Massey made its attack simultaneously with that of the *Enterprise*, despite the difference of an hour in launching time. The squadron had been overtaken en route as planned, by the *Yorktown's* dive bombers and had proceeded at about 1,500 feet, with two of the six fighters 1,000 feet above them and four at 5,000–6,000 feet. They too, like the *Enterprise's* torpedo squadron, sighted the enemy ships about 1000. At about 14 miles from the target Zero fighters attacked them and they dropped to 150 feet to avoid anti-aircraft fire. The superior numbers of the Japanese fighters soon resulted in the heavily outnumbered American fighters becoming separated from the torpedo aircraft, which turned in to attack one of the enemy carriers from a point about a mile to the east. Seven of the twelve aircraft were shot down before reaching release point, and three of the remaining five almost immediately after launching.

It was estimated by the Americans that two hits were obtained on one carrier and one or two on a second. The Japanese reported that the attacks of both torpedo squadrons were directed against the *Hiryu*: in the first attack, at 1013 by the Japanese carrier's reckoning, by 16 aircraft, seven torpedo tracks were seen; in the second attack, at 1030, by five aircraft , five torpedoes were reported. None of the torpedoes hit, their slow speed enabling them to be avoided.

In repulsing the attacks of the torpedo aircraft, the escorting cruisers *Tone* and *Chikuma* employed their main armament in addition to their AA guns, opening fire with the former at ranges up to 45 km. (nearly 50,000 yards). Only two of the 12 aircraft in the *Yorktown's* torpedo squadron survived the attack. Two of the fighters were lost, one crash-landed on board the *Hornet*, and the remainder returned to the *Yorktown*.

28. *Enterprise* dive bombers attack, 1022

The torpedo squadrons had been cut to pieces; out of 41 aircraft only six survived the attacks. Nevertheless, although exact co-ordination of the torpedo attacks with those of the dive bombers now coming in had not been achieved and not a single torpedo hit had been made on the enemy, the unsupported attacks of the torpedo aircraft had the effect of attracting the Japanese fighters, so that few were in position to oppose the dive bombers when their attacks commenced, two minutes later.[2]

The *Enterprise* dive-bombers took departure at 0730 and climbed to 20,000 feet. Some of the pilots experienced trouble with their oxygen masks; and observing this, the commander of the group Lieut.Commander C. W. McClusky, Jr. removed his own mask in order to have the same reaction as other pilots.

Like the *Hornet*'s dive bombers an hour earlier, the *Enterprise*'s failed to find the enemy carriers in the estimated position, because of their alteration of course. The commander turned northward, however, and about 1005, after searching for about hour, the Japanese fleet was sighted.[3] All four carriers were in view, disposed in a diamond shape, the *Hiryu* considerably to northward of the remainder. With them were seen four heavy ships, battleships or cruisers, and eight to ten destroyers. The entire fleet was steering a northerly course.

No damage to any of the carriers was visible at the time of sighting or during the dive, thus substantiating the Japanese report that no hits were made by any of the American high level bombing, glide bombing or torpedo attacks by either land-based or carrier-based aircraft.

The weather was clear and visibility excellent. There were scattered cumulus clouds between 1,500 and 2,500 feet, and the ceiling was unlimited. A surface wind of five to eight knots was blowing from the south-east.

Approaching from the south, the attack was made by sections on the two westernmost carriers, targets were ordered by voice radio and there was some confusion. The group commander and Scouting Squadron 6, armed with 500 lb. and 100 lb. bombs, attacked the left-hand (i.e. most westerly) carrier, as did the second division of Bombing Squadron 6 armed with 1,000 lb, bombs, whilst the five aircraft of the first division of Bombing Squadron 6 attacked the right-hand carrier and the third division attacked both carriers. Each squadron leader was convinced that the carriers his men attacked were of the *Kaga* or *Akagi* type, both of which were converted, the *Kaga* from a battleship and the *Akagi* from a battlecruiser.

---

2. The Americans believed the Japanese recognized the torpedo aircraft as the greater menace and concentrated their fighters on them. But the evidence is that at this date the Japanese considered dive bombing to be more dangerous than torpedo attacks. The Americans also thought that the attacks of the *Enterprise* and *Yorktown* torpedo groups, by compelling the Japanese carriers to manoeuvre, prevented them from launching bombers to attack TF16 and TF17, but this was not the case; they were not completely ready to take off, for the Midway attack groups had not yet all been serviced.

3. The reports on this attack were rendered by the commanders of the two squadrons and not by the commander of the group; and reasons which caused Lieut.-Commander McClusky to make the most important decision to turn north ward are not stated.

Anti-aircraft fire was light, and no fighter opposition was experienced until all bombs had been dropped, though the American torpedo aircraft were seen to be under heavy attack as they came in. As the dive bombers pulled out, however, many of them were attacked by Zero and Messerschmidt type fighters and came under the AA fire of the screening vessels which up to now had largely been concentrated on the torpedo aircraft. Eighteen of the Enterprise dive bombers failed to return to the carrier; it is thought that most of these were not shot down but were forced to come down in the sea when they ran out of fuel.

29. *Yorktown* dive bombers attack, 1025

The *Yorktown*'s 17 scout bombers, each carrying one 1,000 lb. bomb, sighted the enemy about 1000. The bombers were still in touch with the torpedo squadron, with which it had proceeded to the scene; but they lost contact when the latter attacked.

The bombers opened their dive at 1025 from about 14,500 feet, on a carrier estimated by the pilots to be of the *Akagi* class which was turning to the southward into the wind to launch her aircraft. This was probably, however, the *Soryu*. This ship, though officially displacing only 10,050 tons, little more than a third of the tonnage of the *Akagi* and *Kaga*, was actually a 17,500 ton ship and not noticeably smaller than the *Akagi* and *Kaga*, having been designed as a carrier from the first, and not as an armoured ship. The first bomb exploded amongst the aircraft assembled on the flight deck, turning the after part of the deck into a mass of flames. Four aircraft of the squadron, seeing the carrier so badly damaged, transferred their attack to a nearby cruiser and a battleship, neither of which was, however, reported hit by the Japanese.

No fighter opposition was experienced until after the dive, and the aircraft withdrew at high speed low over the water, avoiding heavy AA fire. The entire squadron returned safely to the *Yorktown*.

30. Sinking of the *Soryu*, 1913

In the attacks just described, the *Soryu* reported the number of dive bombers that attacked her as 13. Three hits were made, and fires spread with great rapidity and caused induced explosions in the bomb storage magazine, AA and MG ammunition magazines, and gasoline tanks. Both engines stopped and the ship was abandoned at 1045. The captain, Ryusaku Yanagimoto, remained at his post and lost his life. About 1600, when the fires had died down somewhat, the air officer, who was acting commander, organized fire fighters with the intention of re-boarding the ship. Before this could be done, however, at 1913 the *Soryu* sank in 30° 42 5′ N., 178° 37.5′ W., torpedoed by the US submarine *Nautilus*.[4]

The US submarines had been notified that morning of the Japanese striking force north-west of Midway, and nine of them were ordered to close the enemy. The *Grouper* sighted the Japanese force but was prevented by air attacks from attacking. The *Nautilus*, Lieut.-Comdr. W. H. Brockman, Jr., after shadowing a force of enemy battleships and cruisers, made an unsuccessful attack and was heavily depth charged. At 1029 she sighted on the horizon columns of smoke from the Japanese carriers under attack. On closing, the *Nautilus* encountered the *Soryu*, on an even keel, with hull apparently undamaged, smoking but with flames apparently under control, and accompanied by two ships believed to be cruisers, but actually no doubt the destroyers *Hamakaze* and *Isonami*, to which the crew had been transferred. At 1359 the *Nautilus* fired three torpedoes at the *Soryu* and the destroyers at once retaliated with a depth charge attack. When this was over, at 1610, the *Nautilus* rose to periscope depth and found the carrier completely aflame and abandoned. At 1840 heavy underwater explosions occurred accompanied by a cloud of black smoke. At 1941 the *Nautilus* surfaced. No ship, smoke, or flame was in sight.[5]

31. *Kaga* sinks 1925 4th June, *Akagi* scuttled 0500 5 June

The *Kaga* was still engaged in evasive action against the attacking American torpedo squadrons when nine dive bombers were suddenly sighted amongst the clouds at 1022. Her manoeuvres enabled her to avoid the first three bombs, but four of the next six hit her. The third hit (bomb No. 8) almost completely destroyed the bridge and killed everyone thereon, including the captain. Although it was recognized that there was little hope of getting the fires under control, the crew continued their efforts until 1640, when the situation was recognized as hopeless and orders were given to abandon ship, and the destroyers *Hagikaze* and *Maikaze* took off the crew. By 1925 the fires had spread to both forward and after fuel tanks, causing two great explosions which sank the ship in 30° 20.3′ N., 179° 17.2′ W.

Only three bombs hit the *Akagi*, none of which would under ordinary circumstances have been fatal; but caught as she was with her aircraft on deck,

---

4. The Americans gave the time of sinking as 1840.

5. It later transpired that it was not *Nautilus* which had sunk *Soryu* nor as the C-in-C US Fleet claimed in his *Official Report* that it was carried-based aircraft which finished her off. It was actually the Japanese destroyer *Isokaze* which sank *Soryu* with torpedoes. See Parshall, Jonathan & Tully, Anthony, *Shattered Sword: The Untold Story of the Battle of Midway* (Potomac Books, Dulles, 2005), pp. 334–36.

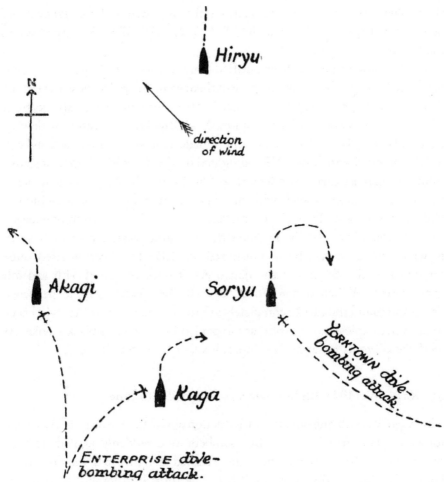

Fig. 7. Dive bombing attacks on *Soryu Akagi* and *Kaga*, 1020, 4 June.

they sufficed to destroy her. The fire quickly engulfed the entire hangar area and aided by induced explosions spread with great intensity to the immediate vicinity of the bridge; and at 1046 the flag was shifted to the light cruiser *Nagara*. Orders were given to flood the magazines, but the pump system failed, and although every effort was made to get the fires under control it became increasingly evident that there was little hope of success. At 1925 orders were given to abandon ship, and the crew began to transfer to the destroyers *Arashio* and *Nowake*. At 0500 on 5 June, by order of the C-in-C Combined Fleet the ship was sunk by torpedo in 30° 30′ N., 178° 10′ W.

There can be little doubt that the destruction, by no more than four and three bombs respectively, of two ships as strong as *Kaga* and *Akagi*, was due to their being caught before they could fly off their aircraft which were on deck fuelled and armed for attack on the US force.[6]

32. Bombing attack on *Yorktown*, 1208

The fourth Japanese carrier, the *Hiryu*, had not been troubled by the attacks of the *Yorktown* and *Enterprise* dive bombers; as soon as the torpedo attack was over, about 1058, she was therefore free to despatch her aircraft to attack the carrier *Yorktown* which one of the reconnaissance aircraft from the cruiser *Tone* had discovered two hours earlier. At 1058 the ship flew off 18 bombers armed with 500-lb. bombs, escorted by five or six fighters, and despatched them to attack the *Yorktown*.

About an hour later, at 1150, the *Yorktown* launched 12 fighters to relieve the combat air patrol which was up at the time, together with 10 scout bombers, each armed with one 1,000-lb. bomb, to search a sector between 280 degrees and 030 degrees to 200 miles, for the reports which Rear-Admiral Fletcher had of the number and positions of the enemy carriers were incomplete. Almost simultaneously, at 1152, the ship's radar picked up a large number of aircraft approaching from the westward, 32 miles distant, which were later calculated to number 18 dive bombers and 18 fighters.[7]

At that moment, the six aircraft of the combat air patrol that had just been relieved and the surviving fighters of the group returned from attack on the Japanese carriers were on deck being refuelled and the scout bombers were still in the landing circle. The latter were ordered to fly clear, fuelling of the fighters was suspended, and the fuel system was drained and CO_2 introduced.

The 12 fighters were ordered out in two waves to intercept the Japanese attack group, which they met at about 9,000 feet, 15 or 20 miles out. Only seven or eight of the enemy bombers succeeded in breaking out of the mêlée and diving on the *Yorktown*, but three of their bombs made hits; one bomb from an aircraft which had been cut to fragments by automatic gunfire fell and exploded on the flight deck abaft the island; one made a hit in an uptake and forced the *Yorktown* to stop, largely because boiler gases were drawn into the stokeholds rendering them uninhabitable; and a third landed in the forward lift well starting fires adjacent to the forward aviation fuel tanks without igniting them. The screening vessels circled the *Yorktown* at 2,000 yards,

---

6. The carriers apparently had the following numbers of aircraft on deck being refuelled and rearmed at the time of the dive-bombing attack: *Akagi* 3 fighters, 18 torpedo aircraft; *Kaga* 3 fighters, 27 torpedo aircraft; *Soryu* 3 fighters, 18 bombers.
7. The Report of C-in-C 1st Air Fleet states, however, that only six fighters were launched, and the *Hiryu*'s signal gives the number as five.

zigzagging at high speed and putting up heavy AA fire. Of the 18 enemy bombers 13 were destroyed, at least 11 of them by the fighters. Three of the Japanese fighters were shot down. By 1215 the attack was over

The *Hiryu*'s attack group considered they had made six hits, three on the starboard side abreast the island, one on the starboard side a little further aft, and two aft, all being made with general purpose bombs, except one hit aft by a land bomb. Damage to the *Yorktown* was not serious. The hole, 10 feet in diameter, in the flight deck caused by the first bomb, was covered in less than half an hour. By 1412 repairs to the uptakes were completed, and the ship with two boilers disabled was able to steam at 19 knots, all fires had been extinguished and refuelling of fighters on deck was again possible. At 1320 the cruisers *Vincennes* and *Pensacola* and destroyers *Benham* and *Balch*, from Task Force 16, joined to reinforce her escort. The position of the ship at 1402 was 33° 51' N., 176° 00' W., course 090 degrees.

33. Torpedo attack on *Yorktown*, 1441

When the report of sighting an enemy carrier came in to the *Hiryu* from the *Tone*'s seaplane, a type 13 experimental ship-based bomber was despatched from the *Soryu* (0830), to maintain contact with the carrier; owing, however, to a wireless breakdown the Japanese did not learn until the return of this aircraft that in addition to the *Yorktown*, there was a task force (TF 16) that included a carrier of the *Enterprise* class and another of the *Hornet* class. Task Force 16 had also been sighted by the *Hiryu*'s bombers, but the signal reporting the force, though timed 1140, which was not received by the *Hiryu* until nearly an hour later.

At 1331 the *Hiryu* flew off against the *Yorktown* a second attack group, composed of four fighters and nine torpedo air force, supplemented by two fighters from the *Kaga* and one torpedo aircraft from the *Akagi*. They were picked up by the radar guardship *Pensacola* at 1427 at 33 miles distance, on bearing 340 degrees, and the combat air patrol which was overhead at the time, six *Yorktown* fighters which had been rearmed and refuelled on board the *Enterprise*, was vectored out to intercept. The first four aircraft, flying at 10,000 to 12,000 feet, overran the Japanese who were coming in at 5,000 feet, and had to turn back to find them. The other two which took off a few seconds later, met the enemy 10 to 14 miles out.

Once again, the *Yorktown* suspended fuelling her aircraft and introduced CO_2 into her fuel lines. Eight of the 10 fighters on deck had sufficient fuel in their tanks to fight, but there was only time to launch four of them before the guns opened up. The American force was in circular formation, with the carrier in the centre of the reinforced screen of four cruisers and seven destroyers, steering a course of 90 degrees, at 20 knots, the enemy approach being from the port quarter. The Americans apparently again over-estimated the size of the attack group, which they considered to number 12 to 16 torpedo bombers and about the same number of fighters, though the Japanese reported the actual figures to be 10 and six respectively.

Fire was opened at 1441 at a range of 12,000 yards by the cruisers *Pensacola* and *Portland* on the side of the screen towards the enemy aircraft, nine of which got through the fighter opposition and had already begun their glide to torpedo release point. They were in two groups; five aircraft headed to pass astern of the *Pensacola* towards the *Yorktown*, and two or three to pass ahead of her through the heavy curtain of fire thrown up by the screening ships. Although the Japanese reported that all nine fired their torpedoes only four torpedoes were seen and only five aircraft survived the attack. The *Yorktown* avoided two torpedoes which crossed her bow, but the last two, released at about 800 yards, struck her on the port side amidships at about 30 seconds' interval at 1445:

> 'By 1447 firing ceased. The *Yorktown*, listing heavily to port, was losing speed and turning in a small circle to port. She stopped and white smoke poured from her funnels. The screening vessels began to circle.
>
> 'The diesel generators were cut in, but the circuit breakers would not hold, and the ship remained in darkness. The list gradually increased to 26 degrees. Without power nothing could be done to correct it. The Commanding Officer and the Damage Control Officer thought it probable that the ship would capsize in a few minutes, and at 1455 orders were given to abandon ship. Inside, men clambered over steeply sloping decks in total darkness to remove the wounded. After an inspection in which no living personnel were found, the Commanding Officer left the ship.
>
> 'Destroyers closed in to pick up survivors.'[8]

Only half the Japanese attack group, viz., five torpedo bombers and three fighters (two of the *Hiryu*'s and one of the *Kaga*'s) survived to return to the *Hiryu*, where preparations were at once made for a third attack on the U.S. carriers at dusk by the six fighters, five bombers and four torpedo aircraft which were all that remained. It was now known that the American force included three carriers, but it was thought that the bombing and torpedo attacks respectively had been made on two different carriers both of which had been damaged, the first by five or six bomb hits, the second by two torpedoes,

8. *U.S. Combat Narrative*, p.31.

for when the Japanese torpedo bombers attacked at 1441 the *Yorktown* showed no sign whatever of the damage she had sustained in the recent bombing.

Before the third attack group could fly off, however, the *Hiryu* herself came under the attack which destroyed her.

34. Attack on *Hiryu*, 1705

The *Hiryu* had been sighted about 1430, a few minutes before the torpedo attack on the *Yorktown*, by one of the ten scout bombers sent out on reconnaissance by the flagship at 1150. Her position was given as 31° 15′ N., 179° 05′ W., and she was stated to be accompanied by two battleships, three heavy cruisers (actually two and one light cruiser) and four destroyers, steering a northerly course at 20 knots.[9]

At 1530 the *Enterprise* began launching an attack group of 10 of her own scout bombers and 14 from the *Yorktown*, 11 of them armed with one × 1,000 lb. and 13 with one × 500 lb. bombs. The *Hornet* at 1603 began launching a squadron of 16 scout bombers. Both groups appear to have proceeded independently to the attack.

The *Enterprise* bombers sighted the enemy at 1650, steering a course 280 degrees and well spread out. Three columns of smoke to the southward marked the three Japanese carriers attacked earlier in the day. The *Hiryu* had fighters overhead, and they shot down one of the American bombers before it began its dive and two as they were pulling out. The Americans dived in from the sun from 19,000 feet, and four direct hits soon rendered the *Hiryu* a mass of flames. One bomber attacked a battleship, apparently the *Haruna*, without success.

35. Attack by *Hornet*'s bombers on *Tone* and *Chikuma*, 1730

By the time the *Hornet*'s squadron arrived 25 minutes later, the *Hiryu* was burning so fiercely that it was obviously unnecessary to damage her further, and the attack was diverted to a battleship and a cruiser as the American airmen believed, though actually it would appear to have been directed at two cruisers, the *Tone* which reported ten and the *Chikuma* five bombs, all within 50 to 100 yards of the ships, neither of which suffered any damage.

36. B.17s attack Japanese striking force, 1810–1830

Elimination through serious damage of four Japanese carriers had given the Americans command of the air, though they were by no means certain

---

9. According to the Japanese plan the position of the *Hiryu* at the time of sighting was some 30 miles further east.

whether there were any further enemy carriers in the area. Meanwhile, it had been an anxious day at Midway. Owing to the great distances over water between landing grounds it was impossible to get fighter reinforcements to the island, after practically all the fighters there had been put out of action in the course of the single Japanese raid. At 1115 there was a false air raid alarm caused by the return of 12 of the *Hornet*'s dive bombers that had failed to find the target, coming in to Midway short of fuel; they dropped their bombs on the edge of the airfield causing considerable confusion, then landed, with the exception of one which fell in the lagoon. The seven B.17s with defects that were fuelled and ready for flight took off for Hawaii, leaving only eight on the island, of which half were ready for service though later two more were repaired. In the early afternoon, before the news of the naval air attacks on the Japanese carriers arrived, the estimate at Midway was that Army aircraft had damaged one enemy carrier; the losses of the Marine air group were so heavy that it appeared their attack had been broken up before reaching the enemy; the *Yorktown* had been hit; the enemy with three undamaged carriers was still coming on and it seemed possible that before sunset Midway would be under bombardment by surface vessels. At the airfield, all confidential papers were ordered to be burned at noon.

Damage to the fuelling system and other equipment at Midway rendered refuelling and servicing of aircraft so slow that the aircraft still remaining were unable to make repeated attacks on the enemy during the afternoon as would have been so desirable. At 1500, however, four serviceable B.17s which were ready were sent out under Lieut.-Colonel W. C. Sweeney Jr., US Army Air Corps, to attack the Occupation Force approaching on bearing 265 degrees and thought to be then about 265 miles distant. Whilst on the way to the target, orders were received to attack a carrier on bearing 334 degrees, 185 miles distant from Midway, and the Fortresses accordingly turned to the northward.

Contact was made about 1810, but the carrier found in the area was burning and apparently abandoned, and another ship believed to be a battleship was also thought to be on fire. Attack was consequently made on a heavy cruiser, on which 28 × 500 lb. demolition bombs were dropped from 20,000 to 25,000 feet altitude, one hit being (incorrectly) reported.

Two more B.17s were made ready and took off about an hour later under Captain C. E. Wurtele, US Army Air Corps. They found the same force, estimated as two damaged carriers, two battleships or heavy cruisers, and six or eight light cruisers or destroyers. Bombs were dropped from 9,600 to 12,000 feet on various ships of the force and two hits on a battleship and two on a damaged carrier were (incorrectly) reported.

Meanwhile, during this latter attack six more Fortresses were seen to be engaged in bombing the enemy force from a lower altitude. These six aircraft, under Major G.A. Blakey, US Army Air Corps, had been sent from Barking Sands Airfield, Molokai (Hawaiian Islands), each with half a bomb load and one bomb bay tank, to reinforce Midway and were ordered at 1610 to attack the Japanese striking force before landing. To save fuel, the squadron attacked from its cruising altitude of 3,600 feet. A large burning carrier was seen surrounded by a screen of a battleship, two heavy cruisers and destroyers; and pilots also reported (incorrectly) a second, or even two more, smaller carriers. The aircraft attacked out of the sun, on course about 60 degrees. Heavy AA fire was encountered, and several enemy fighters were met, four of which were reported shot down. Eight bombs were dropped on a carrier which was already aflame, and one destroyer; the latter was (incorrectly) believed hit and sunk. All six aircraft came safely to Midway after sunset.

In all, these 12 Fortresses dropped 52 × 500 lb. bombs; 18 further bombs failed to release. No hits were made and no damage was caused to any of the Japanese ships.

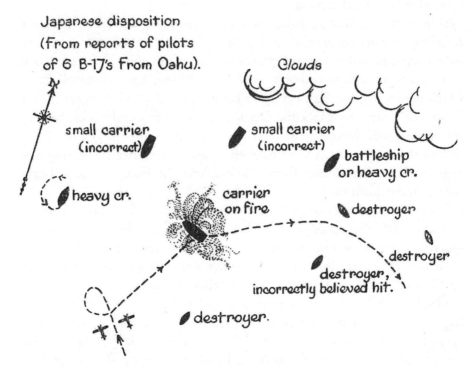

Fig. 8. Attack on striking force by Army B.17s, 1810-1830, 4 June.

37. Midway aircraft attempt night attack, 1900

After the Fortresses at Midway had been refuelled and serviced, the eleven Marine dive bombers remaining fit to fight were got ready. About 1700, when the report of the successful dive bombing attack on the *Hiryu* came in, Major B. W. Norris, commanding Squadron 241, was ordered to attack the enemy carrier, reported burning bearing 338 degrees distance 200 miles from Midway. In order to avoid enemy fighters, it was decided to make a night attack, and about 1830 to 1900 six SBDs under Captain M. A. Tyler and five SBD3s under Major Norris took off.

Rain squalls were encountered, and at sunset cloud increased; and although the position of the Japanese had been reported with considerable accuracy and the striking force was still in the same general area where it had been engaged for some time in rescuing tighter aircraft crews, the bombers searched without success. All aircraft returned safely except that of Major Norris, which plunged into the sea on the return.

38. MTBs attempt to attack, 1930

A final endeavour to attack the damaged carriers and other Japanese ships in the area was made by the 11 MTBs which left Midway about 1930 for their 200-mile trip. However, the squally weather and low visibility which provided excellent conditions for attack also operated adversely on the chances of finding the target. The MTBs searched until dawn and then returned to Midway. A Japanese reconnaissance aircraft bombed and machine gunned one of the boats in the morning without causing serious damage.

39. The *Hiryu* sinks, 0510 5 June

Though the American attempts to attack during the night of 4/5 June had not produced any results, the enemy was destined to suffer yet another serious blow before daybreak. The *Hiryu*, though heavily on fire, had remained capable of steaming for some four hours after the dive bombing attack at 1705 on the 4th; during this time she made every effort to escape from the area and fight the fires. These could not be got under control, however; one after another the men in the engine rooms were killed at their posts: the list gradually increased to 15 degrees; further operation of the ship became impossible.

About midnight, there were hopes that the fires might yet be got under control, but another explosion re-kindled them; by 0315 on the 5th it was evident that further fire-fighting was useless, and all hands were ordered to abandon ship. The crew were taken off by the destroyers *Kazegumo* and *Makigumo*. Rear-Admiral Yamaguchi and Commanding Officer, Captain T. Kaki, shared the fate of the ship when she was sent to the bottom at 0510 by a single torpedo from the *Makigumo* in 31° 27.5′ N., 17° 23.5′ W.

With her went the last of the 253 aircraft lost by the striking force on this disastrous day.

Chapter VI

Pursuit of the Enemy, 5 June

40. Movements of the U.S. force, night 4–5 June

When the six B.17s under Major Blakey landed at Midway after sunset on 4 June the situation was by no means clear. Information as to the strength and position of the Japanese forces in the bad weather area to the northward was incomplete. The Fortresses had encountered several Japanese fighters, and although these might have been, and actually were, the protective cover left in the air from the *Hiryu* when she was attacked, the possibility of a fifth Japanese carrier in the area could not be disregarded. A fifth carrier, the light carrier *Zuiho*, did in fact take part in the Midway operation, but was never sighted; she was detached with the Aleutian screening force which had not yet rejoined the main body. There was every indication that the enemy was continuing to close and no certainty that the loss of air support would deter him from the landing on Midway which it was the concern of Task Forces 17 and 16 to prevent. Battleships had been reported with the enemy force, and the latter might be superior to Task Force 16 which was now operating independently of Task Force 17 and was the only American force remaining in the area.

Rear-Admiral Fletcher with Task Force 17, after leaving the destroyer *Hughes* to stand by the abandoned *Yorktown*, moved off to the eastward, despatching the *Pensacola* and *Vincennes* to re-join Rear-Admiral Spruance. His intention was to transfer the survivors from the destroyers to the cruiser *Portland*, which would then proceed to Pearl Harbor, whilst the *Astoria* and destroyers would return next morning to salvage the *Yorktown*. These plans were modified by a message from Admiral Nimitz that the submarine tender *Fulton* had been despatched to take over the survivors. Captain Buckmaster (*Yorktown*) with 180 key officers and men therefore returned with the destroyers *Hammann*, *Balch* and *Benham* to the *Yorktown* whilst the remainder of Task Force 17 moved on to refuel and subsequently to join the carrier *Saratoga* for operations in the Solomon Islands. In order to avoid a night action with possibly superior forces and yet to be in a position next morning either to pursue the enemy if retreating or to break up an attempted landing on Midway, Rear-Admiral Spruance decided to move east for a time during the night 4–5 June.

At 2115 on the 4th orders had been sent to the US submarines to form on a circle radius 100 miles from Midway; they were to arrive on station and dive before dawn. The wisdom of the move was soon apparent, for it was from one of these submarines that the next intelligence of the enemy was received, when at 0205 on the 5th the *Tambor* reported many unidentified ships about 90 miles west of Midway. The *Tambor* failed to report the course and speed of the enemy, nor did she shadow or attack. The contact indicated to the Americans that the enemy was persisting in his plans for a landing on Midway. All submarines were directed to close the island in order to be in position to attack the enemy transports and supporting ships at a time when they would be most vulnerable.

But the expected assault never materialized. The enemy was the Japanese fast support consisting of the 7th Cruiser Squadron and two destroyers, steering for Midway, to bombard the island; and the appearance of the *Tambor* was destined to have a decisive effect on the operation.

41. Japanese movements, night 4-5 June

The Japanese, who were planning a night attack with all their surface forces on the American ships, at 1728 noticed the general easterly course which Task Force 16 had steered during the afternoon of the 4th. A few minutes earlier, one of the *Chikuma* reconnaissance aircraft had sighted what was estimated to be four enemy carriers, six cruisers, and 15 destroyers, in addition to the burning and listing *Yorktown*, though fighters prevented the aircraft from shadowing. What had happened was that, unknowingly, the aircraft had sighted Task Force 16 twice, with an interval of six minutes, and failed to recognise the two forces as identical. The report was not received until 1830, and it was the first inkling Admiral Nagumo, Commander of the striking force, had of the overwhelming American carrier strength.

To an Admiral who had just lost the whole of his carrier force, the blow must have been severe, and at 1915, to his further dismay, he received from the Commander-in-Chief, Admiral Yamamoto, a signal beginning: 'The enemy fleet has practically been destroyed and is retiring eastward,' and concluding: 'The Striking Force, Occupation Force (less 7th CS) and Advance Force[1] will immediately make contact with and destroy the enemy'. Such a mistaken appreciation of the situation clearly called for correction, and Admiral Nagumo pointed out unequivocally, in two separate signals, that the American force contained five carriers, four of which were still undamaged, and that all four

---

1. Presumably the Submarine Force.

Scene on the main deck of a *Cimarron*-class fleet oiler USS *Neosho* in early May 1942, as she refuelled USS *Yorktown* (CV 5) in heavy seas shortly before the Battle of Coral Sea. (*NHHC 80-G-16444*)

View on the flight deck of USS *Lexington*, at about 1500 hours on 8 May 1942, during the Battle of the Coral Sea, with Grumman F4F-3 fighters nearest the camera. SBD scout bombers and TBD-1 torpedo planes are parked further aft. (*NHHC 80-G-16802*)

The cruiser USS *Minneapolis* shown here on 9 November 1943. During the Battle of the Coral Sea, *Minneapolis* had the task of screening *Lexington*. (*NHHC 80-G-276720*)

Damage in the port forward 5-inch gun gallery of USS *Lexington* (CV-2), from a Japanese bomb that hit near the gallery's after end during the Battle of the Coral Sea, 8 May 1942. (*NHHC 80-G-16803*)

A heavy explosion on board USS *Lexington* blows an aircraft over her side, 8 May 1942, during the Battle of the Coral Sea. This is probably the great explosion from the detonation of torpedo warheads stowed in the starboard side of the hangar, aft. At the left is the bow of USS *Hammann*, which was backing away with a load of the carrier's survivors on board. (*NHHC 80-G-11916*)

View on the flight deck of USS *Lexington* at about 1700 hours on 8 May 1942, as the crew prepares to abandon ship. (*NHHC 80-G-16811*)

Survivors of USS *Lexington* are pulled aboard a cruiser (probably USS *Minneapolis*) after the carrier was abandoned during the afternoon of 8 May 1942. (*NHHC 80-G-7392*)

USS *Yorktown* arrives at Pearl Harbor after the Battle of Coral Sea, 27 May 1942, with her crew paraded in whites on the flight deck. After repairs, she departed on 30 May to take part in the Battle of Midway. (*NHHC 80-G-21931*)

HMS *Exeter* sinking after engaging Japanese heavy cruisers in the Java Sea, 1 March 1942. (*NHHC 80-G-179020*)

USS *Marblehead* under repair at the New York Navy Yard, circa June 1942, after she had been damaged by Japanese high-level bombing attack in the Java sea on 4 February 1942. This view shows new deck plating on the cruiser's stern. Her after 6/53 gun turret is in the centre. (*NHHC 80-G-254938*)

USS *Marblehead* in the Netherlands East Indies, Tjilatjap, Java, after being damaged by Japanese air attack during the Battle of Java Sea, on 4 February 1942. Chinese cooks at work in the cruiser's bomb-wrecked wardroom pantry. (*NHHC 80-G-237444*)

The Dutch destroyer *Witte de With* photographed at Den Helder, Netherlands, circa 1935. *Witte de With* was attacked and damaged by Japanese planes on 1 March 1942. The next day she was scuttled. (*NH 87863*)

The Dutch Light Cruiser, *De Ruyter* photographed in Netherland East Indies waters circa 1939. She was hit by a single torpedo fired by *Haguro* in the Java Sea at about 2340 hours on 27 February 1942 and sank at about 02.30 the next morning with the loss of 367 men, including Admiral Doorman. (*NH 80900*)

Japanese heavy cruiser *Nachi* experienced considerable success at the Battle of the Java Sea, being responsible for the sinking of the Dutch ships *Kortenaer* and *Java* and participated in the sinking of the British ships *Exeter* and *Encounter*. (*NH 111605*)

An SBD-3 scout bomber, probably flown by the Bombing Squadron Three (VB-3), ditches alongside USS *Astoria* at about 1348 hours on 4 June 1942. This was one of two VB-3 planes that ditched near *Astoria* after they were unable to land on the damaged USS *Yorktown* during the Battle of Midway. (*NHHC 80-G-32307*)

USS *Yorktown* lists heavily after she was abandoned during the afternoon of 4 June 1942 during the Battle of Midway. (*NHHC 80-G-21666*)

The Japanese heavy cruiser *Mikuma*, photographed from a USS *Enterprise* SBD aircraft during the afternoon of 6 June 1942, after she had been bombed by planes from *Enterprise* and USS *Hornet* during the Battle of Midway. (*NHHC 80-G-414422*)

SBD Dauntless dive bombers from USS *Hornet* approaching the burning Japanese heavy cruiser *Mikuma* to make the third set of attacks on her, during the early afternoon of 6 June 1942. (*NHHC 80-G-17054*)

USS *Portland*, at the right, transfers USS *Yorktown* survivors to USS *Fulton* on 7 June 1942, following the battle of Midway. *Fulton* transported the men to Pearl Harbor. (*NHHC 80-G-312028*)

The Japanese Aircraft Carrier *Akagi* shown here in 1941 with three Mitsubishi A6M Zero fighters parked forward. *Akagi* was scuttled on 5 June 1942 after being fatally damaged by US aircraft during the Battle of Midway. (*NH 73059*)

US Marine Corps LVT(1) amphibian tractors move toward the beach on Guadalcanal Island, during the 7-9 August 1942 initial landings. (*NH 97749*)

The USS *George F. Elliott* burning between Guadalcanal and Tulagi, after she was hit by a crashing Japanese aircraft during an air attack on 8 August 1942. (*NH 69118*)

The Australian heavy cruiser *Australia* underway off the north shore of Guadalcanal as the invasion task force leaves the area on 9 August 1942, following the Battle of Savo Island. (*NHHC 80-G-13492*)

A view of USS *Portland*'s two forward 8/55 gun turrets. *Portland* was damaged by a torpedo off Guadalcanal on 13 November 1942. (*NH 82031*)

Beached Japanese transports burn at Guadalcanal, as an SBD bomber flies by in the foreground on 16 November 1942. (*NHHC 80-G-30517*)

USS *South Dakota* and two destroyers alongside USS *Prometheus* for repairs. *South Dakota* was damaged in a gun battle in the night action off Guadalcanal on 14/15 November. (*NHHC 80-G-36088*)

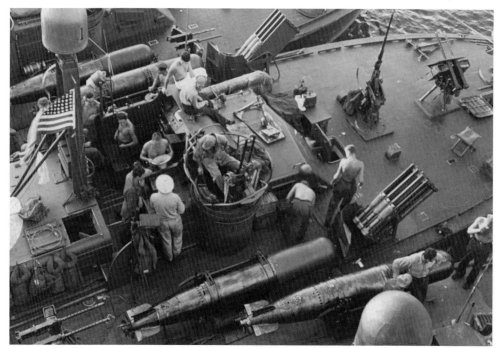

USS *PT-131* (foreground) and other ELCO type motor torpedo boats preparing for the Battle of Surigao Strait, about 24 October 1944. (*NHHC 80-G-345819*)

USS *Intrepid* photographed from the rear seat of an SB2C, after taking off to attack the Japanese Fleet in the Battle of Sibuyan Sea, 24 October 1944. (*NHHC 80-G-K-2198*)

The bow area of *Musashi*, photographed from the forward superstructure during sea trials in June 1942. The uncluttered deck would be changed during the war following the addition of large numbers of 25mm anti-aircraft guns. (*NHHC L42-08*)

Yamato manoeuvres frantically under attack as a bomb explodes off its port side. The fire in the area of the 6.1-inch turret can be clearly seen. (*NHHC L42-09*)

The Japanese aircraft carrier *Zuiho* under attack by planes from USS *Enterprise* during the Battle of Cape Engano, 25 October 1944. (*NHHC 80-G-281768*)

USS *Tennessee* in all her glory in May 1943. At the Battle of Surigao Strait, *Tennessee* fired 69 armour-piercing shell in the course of twelve minutes of shooting. (*NHHC 19-N-45071*)

of his own carriers were out of action. Although the Admiral commanding his own 8th Cruiser Squadron, whose seaplanes had been doing all the useful reconnaissance, signalled that the enemy consisted of two carriers, and there was the suspicious circumstance that the aircraft which made the original report of four undamaged carriers was unable on demand, to supply the class and speed of more than two of them, Admiral Nagumo apparently paid no attention. At least half his destroyers were away assisting his crippled carriers and he was in no condition to undertake a night action against an enemy with which moreover, he was not in touch. He therefore abandoned the idea of a night attack, continued his north-westerly course, and bent his energies to attempting to save his last remaining carrier, the *Hiryu*, and getting her out of the danger area.

Meanwhile, Vice-Admiral Kondo, having sent back the transport unit and air group at 1300, to be out of harm's way, was bringing the fighting units of the Occupation Force northward to co-operate with the striking force in attacking the US ships, and he so informed Admiral Yamamoto. It seems probable that the Commander-in-Chief was uncertain whether Admiral Nagumo was still in company with his battleships and cruisers; he was aware that the C-in-C 1st Air Fleet (Commander Striking Force) had transferred to the *Nagara* and he had just learned that he was retiring to the north-west with the *Hiryu* whose damage apparently was not very severe since she was able to steam at 28 knots. Perhaps, therefore, it was as a precautionary measure, so that he should not lose the services of these heavy ships in the prospective night engagement, that he placed the striking force, less the *Hiryu*, *Akagi* and ships escorting them, under the command of the Commander-in-Chief Second Fleet, and called for clarification of the present whereabouts and movements of Admiral Nagumo's heavy ships, the 8th Cruiser Squadron and the 2nd Division of the 3rd Battle Squadron.[2]

The immediate result of this was an order from Vice-Admiral Kondo, for the striking force, less the *Hiryu*, *Akagi* and their escorts, to reverse course immediately and co-operate with him in attacking the American task force that night; the Vice-Admiral, who was coming up at 24 knots on course 065 degrees, with cruisers and destroyers spread in search disposition, had already some hours previously explained to all concerned his tactical intentions in the anticipated night engagement. This peremptory order was addressed,

2. The correctness of this reading of the signals depends on the interpretation of the Japanese word translated 'Escorting' in signal 176. HS/TSD works perforce on translations of the original Japanese signals, and consequently it is uncertain whether the C-in-C referred to the destroyers supporting the *Hiryu* and *Akagi* or their supporting ships, the 3rd BS and 8th CS It is presumed that Admiral Yamamoto would not have placed Admiral Nagumo's force under the command of an officer junior to him, if he thought the Admiral was still in company with his ships.

not to the C-in-C 1st Air Fleet, but to the Commander Striking Force, for Vice-Admiral Kondo was obviously unaware that Admiral Nagumo (C-in-C.1st Air Fleet) was still with the striking force.[3] In any event, it elicited no response from Admiral Nagumo, who continued to assist the *Hiryu*; a few minutes later, however, there came an order from the Commander-in-Chief of the Combined Fleet, that the forces with Admiral Nagumo and Vice-Admiral Kondo were both to rendezvous with the main body, and after some delay Admiral Nagumo reversed course and informed the Commander-in-Chief that he was preparing to carry out his instructions.

42. *Mogami* damaged; Japanese abandon the operation, 0255, 5 June

It had been arranged that the 7th Cruiser Squadron, the fast support group of the Occupation Force, should bombard Midway at 0200 on the 5th, and the four cruisers, under Rear-Admiral Kurita in the *Kumano*, had continued to steer towards the island when the second Fleet turned to a north-easterly course at 1200 on the 4th. This bombardment was now cancelled and the 7th CS was ordered to join the main body.

At 0200 on the 5th, prior to receipt of the order cancelling the bombardment of Midway, the four cruisers with two destroyers were proceeding in line ahead in the order *Kumano* (flagship), *Suzuya*, *Mikuma*, *Mogami* in approximately 281° N., 179° W., when a submarine was sighted on the starboard bow of the flagship. All ships turned to port together, but the *Mogami* was late in receiving the order. The *Mikuma* had turned 60 degrees to port, but the *Mogami* had only turned four points when she collided with the port quarter of the *Mikuma*. The force of the collision damaged the *Mogami*'s bow, so that some of the plates below water were bent to port, reducing the ship's speed by a third or more. The *Mikuma* was also damaged. In consequence of this, the squadron abandoned the intended bombardment and retired.

The news of this mishap, coming on top of the loss of his entire air power, decided the Commander-in-Chief that the operation must be abandoned and at 0255 a signal to that effect went out. All forces were to rendezvous and refuel during the morning of 6th June in position 33° N., 170° E., with the exception of the *Hiryu* and ships escorting her, and the landing force which was to move westward, out of air range of Midway. The three destroyers of the 15th Group accompanied the transports, whilst the *Jintsu* and the eight destroyers of the 16th and 18th Divisions had already approached the battle

---

3. 'Obviously', because his next signal 20 minutes later, *re* the prospective night engagement and participation of the striking force, which was not only likewise addressed to the Comdr. Striking Force but was *repeated* to the C.-in-C. 1st [Air] Fleet for information.

area in readiness to co-operate in the night engagement so closely that they saw one carrier burning.

43. *I-168* bombards Midway, 0130 5 June

At 2030 on the 4th orders had been sent to the Japanese submarine *1-168*, whose patrol line passed close to Midway, to shell and destroy the air base on Eastern Island. *I-168* fired a few rounds at 0130 on the 5th, which caused no damage, and were answered by the batteries, which (erroneously) claimed a hit. To the defenders of Midway it seemed probable that this bombardment constituted a diversion to cover the attack of a landing party. However, when no further developments followed, it was thought, in view of the Japanese losses, that the bombardment had been carried out by a submarine which had failed to receive the order to abandon the operation and retire.

44. Contact with the enemy, 0545 5 June

It was not long before American aircraft from Midway discovered the retirement of the Japanese forces. All night long men had worked hard on the island servicing the remaining aircraft. The fuelling system had not yet been repaired, and 45,000 gallons of aviation spirit in 55-gallon drums were supplied by hand to the hand pumps from which the aircraft tanks were filled. Eighty-five 500-lb. bombs were loaded.

The morning of 5 June was overcast and visibility poor. The first reconnaissance aircraft took off before dawn, search being concentrated in the sector 250 degrees to 20 degrees, to a distance of 250 miles. Within two hours enemy sighting reports began to come in, the most important of which were as follows:

(*Mikuma* and *Mogami*)
0630   2 battleships bearing 264 degrees, distance 125 miles, course 268 degrees, speed 15 knots, ships damaged, streaming oil.

(*Kumano* and *Suzuya*)
0700   2 enemy cruisers, bearing 283 degrees, distance 174 miles, course 130 degrees, speed 20 knots.

(Striking Force)
0719   5 ships, bearing 325 degrees, distance 200 miles.
0735   5 ships, course 38 degrees, speed 25 knots, 31° 15′ N., 179° 55′ W.
0800   2 battleships and 1 carrier on fire, 3 heavy cruises, bearing 324 degrees, distance 240 miles, course 310 degrees, speed 12 knots.

0815   Cruiser and destroyer screening burning carrier, battleship well ahead.

08.20   1 carrier, bearing 335 degrees, distance 250 miles, course 245 degrees.

The two damaged heavy cruisers were of course the *Mikuma* and *Mogami* and in company with them were the destroyers *Arashio* and *Asashio*. The other two ships of the 7th Cruiser Squadron, the *Kumano* and *Suzuya*, had drawn ahead of the damaged vessels during the early morning hours, and altered course to the north-westward to rendezvous with the main body after the abandonment of the operation.

The main body of the enemy escaped detection since it never approached nearer to midway than 350 miles. The Second Fleet, also, only came within the extreme range of search for a short period, before altering course at 0330 on the 5th for the rendezvous with the main body after the cancellation of the operation.

45. Marine aircraft group attacks *Mikuma* and *Mogami*, 0805

The Commanding Officer of the Midway Naval Air Station gave orders for attack on the two 'battleships' of the 0630 report, bearing about 270 degrees, distance 150 miles.[4] Only 12 aircraft of the Marine group remained fit for action; these took off about 0700–0730 in two groups of six, armed with 500-lb. bombs. One group of six SBD2s under Captain M. A. Tyler was to make a dive-bombing attack from 10,000 feet, followed by a glide bombing attack by six SB2Us, under Captain R. E. Fleming from 4,000 feet.

The weather was clear with scattered clouds at 8,000 feet. After flying about 100 miles the wide oil streak left by one of the damaged ships was picked up and the attackers were able to follow it for 40 miles to the target, which Captain Tyler's group reached soon after 0800.

The SBDs. dived out of the sun on the *Mogami* from about 10,000 feet. Heavy AA fire was encountered, but no aircraft was hit. In the glide bombing attack by SB2Us. that followed, however, Captain Fleming's aircraft was hit, but he held to his glide and released his bomb before bursting into flames and being destroyed. It was perhaps this aircraft which, as the Japanese reported, dived into the *Mikuma*'s after turret and started fires and caused damage which reduced the ship's speed somewhat, The second section of SB2Us. made

---

4. The various reports give the bearing of the enemy as 241–278 degrees, distance 130–180 miles, composition one or two 'battleships' but it is clear that the *Mikuma* and *Mogami* were indicated. Capt. Tyler's report is not available, and Capt. Fleming was killed in the attack.

their glide from out of the sun, broadside to the target. The glide bombers believed they had made some direct hits, but the Japanese reported this was not so, though some near misses were made, causing slight damage. Captain Fleming's was the only aircraft to be lost.

46. Attack on *Mikuma* and *Mogami* by B.17s, 0830

Captain Fleming's group had barely drawn clear when the *Mikuma* and *Mogami* once more came under attack. Twelve B.17s that remained at Midway had taken off[5] armed with 500-lb. bombs and pursued a westerly course. At a distance of about 100 miles, when they had climbed to 10,000 feet, they received orders to attack two enemy battleships bearing 270 degrees, distance 130 miles from Midway.

Only eight of the Fortresses found the target, about 0830, after a period of considerable difficulty during which at one time they had turned back towards Midway. They attacked in two groups of four, one group the *Mikuma* and the other the *Mogami*, the two cruisers now being four or five miles apart. The attacks were made from 20,000 feet, the groups dropping 19 and 20 bombs respectively, whilst a further 13 hung up. The first group did not observe the results of their attack; the second group reported one hit and one near miss. The Japanese, however, reported that no hits were made. Heavy AA fire was experienced, but no damage was caused to any aircraft.

47. B. 17s attack *Tanikaze*, 1635 and 1840

After servicing at Midway on return from the attacks just described the Fortresses were again sent out. At 1320 seven, of Flight 92, each armed with eight 500-lb. demolition bombs, set out to the north-west under Lieut.-Colonel B. E. Allen, US Air Corps, to continue the attacks on the remnant of the retreating Japanese striking force. One ship, estimated to be a heavy cruiser, was sighted on the outward journey, but no other enemy were seen. On the return, at 1636, the Fortresses attacked what they took to be the same heavy cruiser, in position reported to be 32° 20′ N., 178°. Actually, the ship was the *Tanikaze*, one of the destroyers of the striking force, but it is not known why she was alone.

Four of the Fortresses attacked from 16,000 feet and dropped 32 bombs, making as they estimated, two hits and three near misses; the other three

---

5. It is not known at what time they took off. The only available report that mentions the time gives 0430 (Midway time), which seems reasonable, since much time was spent in trying to find the target.

Fortresses dropped 24 bombs from 14,500 feet, reporting one hit and one near miss. The *Tanikaze* was not hit, however; and only five bombs were seen. Her anti-aircraft fire caused no damage to any of the bombers.

Five further B.17s (Flight 93) under Captain D.E. Ridings left Midway at 1545 for the last attack of the day on the carriers by Midway aircraft, taking a more northerly course than Flight 92. By this time, clouds had gathered in the north to a heavy overcast at 12,000 feet and the group failed to find the target, but on the return journey they attacked a supposed carrier in position about 310 degrees, 420 miles from Midway, at 1840.[6] This may have been the *Tanikaze*, which reported being bombed at 1845, though all bombs fell wide. The squadron dropped 15 × 600-lb, and 8 × 300-lb, bombs from altitudes ranging from 9,000 to 12,500 feet. The results were not seen. Very heavy AA fire was encountered, and it was probably this which caused one of the Fortresses to drop its bomb bay tank; this aircraft about 2330 reported 'out of gas and landing' and was not seen afterwards. One other aircraft was also lost through shortage of fuel though all but one of the crew were picked up. The remainder became separated in the clouds on the return and were guided into Midway by radar.

The failure of the air searches from Midway on the morning of the 5th, to sight the Japanese striking force, was due largely to the weather, though there was an additional reason, namely the change of course of the remnant of the striking force, viz. the 8th CS and Section 2 of the 3rd BS, to the westward during the small hours of the 5th, after the cancellation of the Midway operation, in order to make rendezvous with the main body in about 31° N., 179° 45′ E., at 1155 that morning. Consequently, the Fortresses were searching across the enemy's course, rather than along it. The *Akagi* was scuttled at 0500 and the *Hirya* sank at 0510, so that by the time the air searches reached the area where yesterday four damaged carriers had been seen, the sea was empty of ships.

48. Carrier aircraft search for Japanese striking force, 5 June

Meanwhile, successes of the US carriers, but the retirement of the enemy during the night, had put the opposing forces too far apart for attack to be possible until the later afternoon.

---

6. The report of the Air Force Commander, Hikam Field gives the position as 320 degrees, 425 miles from Midway, and the time as 1825, but the only two available pilots' reports, viz, those of Capt. Ridings and Lt. Bird give the position 310 degrees, 420 miles from Midway, and Capt. Ridings gives the time as 1840. Lt. Bird gives no time.

When the *Tambor*'s enemy sighting report came in at 0217 Task Force 16 had just altered course (0200) to 270 degrees, after a short detour to the northward during which there was radar contact with an unknown craft about 60 miles off to the north-west, and in the belief that it betokened a landing Rear-Admiral Spruance increased speed to 25 knots and set a course to close Midway to attack the enemy. At 0600 he was on a south-westerly course about 130 miles north-east of Midway, position 29° 50′ N., 175° 44′ E.,

The enemy reports sent in by the Midway aircraft between 0630 and 0820, indicating that an enemy retirement was in progress, were presumably intercepted by Task Force 16 who estimated that there were two principle enemy groups as follows:

(a) a transport group west of Midway followed by two damaged heavy cruisers [*Mikuma* and *Mogami*] (reported as battleships).
(b) the striking force attacked on the 4th, of two battleships (one reported damaged), three heavy cruisers, and four destroyers, followed by a burning carrier [*Hiryu*], to the north-west.

Rear-Admiral Spruance was faced with a choice of two objectives, both of which contained good targets, and he chose the one to the north-west; for although it was further away, it contained the crippled carrier and two battleships, one of which was reported already damaged. The existence of a belt of bad weather about 500 miles to the north-west of Midway was known, and the possibility that the remnants of the retreating Japanese force might find concealment therein, was accepted. At 1100 course was altered to 300 degrees to close the enemy; and except for turning into the wind when the *Enterprise* and *Hornet* launched attack groups between 1500 and 1530, this course was maintained until sunset at 1900, when course was altered to the westward, shortly after crossing the 180th meridian.

'The chase continued at 25 knots throughout the afternoon,' says the *U.S. Combat Narrative*, elaborating the few words of Task Force 16 in attempting to retrieve the situation caused by the retirement eastward during the first half of the previous night. During the forenoon of the 5th the only incident was the rescue of the crew of a patrol aircraft found on the water about 0900 by the destroyer *Monaghan*, which was then detached to join the *Yorktown*'s screen. Four MTBs were sighted at 1232, returning from their unsuccessful night's search for the enemy. At 1420 Rear-Admiral Spruance received from Admiral Nimitz a sighting report of two battleships, three cruisers, five to ten destroyers, one burning carrier and one carrier smoking badly in latitude 32° N., longitude 179° 32′ E., at 0800, course 310 degrees, speed 12 knots. At about 1400 a flight of B.17s passed over. Rear-Admiral Spruance signalled his intention of launching an attack about 1500. The planes did not reply, but were heard reporting the position of the task force to Midway Later Rear-Admiral Spruance received the disputing information that the B.17s had failed to find the enemy force. His last report of the enemy's position was based on a morning contact, and as the afternoon wore on prospects became less and less promising.

49. Attacks on Japanese destroyers, 1804 and 1830, 5 June

At 1500, when the enemy force was estimated to be about 230 miles away, launching of two strike groups began. The *Enterprise* launched 32 scout bombers, armed with 1 × 500-lb. bombs, the *Hornet*, at 1512, 26 scout bombers. The sky was heavily overcast and visibility poor.

Rear-Admiral Spruance's retirement eastward during the night of 4th–5th had lost too much time. The hour was too late and the range too long, and the Japanese had escaped out of reach of the American carrier aircraft.

The *Hornet*'s group searched to 315 miles without finding the enemy. At 1804 they attacked what was believed to be a light cruiser or destroyer in approximately 33 N., 177 E. The enemy ship was apparently the destroyer *Tanikaze*, which reported being attacked at 1807 and very near missed by 11 bombs from 26 bombers. The attackers saw no hits.

The *Enterprise* group searched to 265 miles, then turned to port for a leg. They too, encountered what was believed to be a light cruiser or destroyer in 33° 00′ N., 177° 00′ E., and between 1830 and 1900, at dusk, they attacked her with 32 bombs, none of which hit. The enemy destroyer manoeuvred at full speed and her AA fire was stated to be unusually heavy, and one scout bomber was shot down.[7]

The US aircraft had little fuel left when they returned to their ships and landed after dark. One of the *Hornet*'s attack group had to make a water landing near the *Enterprise*, but the *Alywin* rescued the crew.

---

7. The ship attacked cannot be identified. No attacks other than those already described were reported by any of the ships of the Japanese Striking Force, and the attack was presumably therefore made on one of the ships of the Occupation Force, for instance, the *Jinstu* and Destroyer Divisions 16 and 18 may well have been in this area at the time.

Chapter VII

Last Contacts, 6 June,
Sinking of the *Yorktown*, 7 June

50. *Mikuma* and *Mogami* sighted, 0640 6 June

Nightfall on 5 June found Task Force 16 approaching the bad weather area into which it was useless to follow the enemy. No Japanese forces had been found for 250 miles to the north-westward. There remained the possibility that the striking force might either turn westward towards Japan, or south-west to join their transports. Rear-Admiral Spruance consequently set a course 280 degrees for the night and reduced speed to 15 knots, both to economize his destroyers' fuel and to avoid overtaking any enemy battleships in the dark.

After the retirement of the enemy became apparent, the fastest US submarines were sent in chase and others retuning from western patrols were directed to the expected lines of retirement of the enemy. About 0510 on 6th the *Enterprise* launched a search group of 18 scout bombers, each armed with one 500-lb. bomb, to search to a distance of 200 miles in the entire western semi-circle, between 180 and 360 degrees. A light wind from the south-west facilitated launching and recovery of aircraft throughout the day with minimum deviation from the south-westerly course (230 degrees) to which Task Force 16 altered at 0800.

It was not long before the first enemy sighting reports came in. Two contacts were made almost simultaneously. The first at 0640 was of two heavy cruisers and two destroyers on course south-west, speed 15, bearing about 275 degrees, distance 400 miles from Midway. The second at 0645, bearing about 280 degrees, distance 435 miles from Midway, though variously identified appears to have been the *Mikuma* and *Mogami*, with three or four destroyers, on course west, speed 10 knots. Rear-Admiral Spruance estimated that there were two enemy groups, the second about 50 miles south-east of the first, though as the hours passed and further reports came in, both from the *Enterprise* search groups, from the two scout observation aircraft which the *Minneapolis* and *New Orleans* each launched at 0720, and from the crews of returning attack groups, the positions and composition of the enemy forces became more and more confused. Actually, the whole of the reports referred to the same enemy group, namely the *Mikuma* and *Mogami*, which with the destroyers *Asashio* and *Arashio* were making what speed westward the damaged condition of the two cruisers permitted.

Rear-Admiral Spruance took as his target what was believed to be the more northerly of the two enemy groups, which was, by report, the closer, and by some reports contained a battleship. It was believed to be a remnant of the striking force. The southern group was left for attack by long-range aircraft from Midway.

51. First attack on *Mikuma* and *Mogami* by *Hornet* group, 0930–1000

At 0800 Task Force 16 altered course to south-west and the *Hornet* began launching an attack group of 26 scout bombers, 18 armed with 1,000-lb. bombs and eight with 500-lb, bombs. Eight fighters escorted the group, in case of air opposition.

The attackers found the enemy force without difficulty. To the pilots, the group of two heavy cruisers and two destroyers appeared to consist of a battleship, a heavy cruiser, and three destroyers.[1] The aircraft attacked about 0930, taking as the principal target the supposed battleship, the *Mikuma*, on which they believed they obtained three hits and two near misses, an estimate which accords with the Japanese report. Her navigation was affected, and she was left turning to starboard in uncontrolled circles. The *Mogami* was also correctly estimated to have been hit twice: the first 1,000-lb. bomb landed on to top of No.5 turret, penetrated the armour, and killed the entire turret's crew; the second hit the ship amidships, damaged torpedo tubes, and started fires below decks, which were, however, extinguished. One of the destroyers was also hit in this attack, but the ship remained navigable, though the attackers believed they sank her.

There was no air opposition, so the fighters occupied themselves by machine-gunning the enemy destroyers. Anti-aircraft fire, however, shot down one of the American dive-bombers.

52. *Enterprise* group attacks *Mikuma* and *Mogami*, 1200–1300

The *Enterprise* about 1115 sent off a group of 31 scout bombers armed with 1,000-lb. bombs, escorted by 12 fighters. The target was given as two

---

1. There were certain points of just possible resemblance between the two heavy cruisers and some of the older Japanese battleships: for the *Mogami* class had a 'pagoda' bridge structure (though not very high) and a tripod mast and the ships appeared to the US aircraft crews to be far larger than their listed tonnage of 8,500, as indeed they were, being 13,000-ton ships.

battleships, two heavy cruisers, and several destroyers in 29° 33′ N., 175° 35′ E., course 270 degrees, speed 15 knots. The scout bombers proceeded independently and climbed to about 19,000 feet. At 1200 they sighted a force estimated to consist of one heavy cruiser, one light cruiser, and two destroyers. Part of the group searched ahead for the reported battleships. One dive-bombing squadron, however, began about 1200 an attack on the *Mikuma*, the more easterly of the two cruisers. The other squadrons came in later, and the attack on both heavy cruisers continued in this manner until after 1300, the aircraft diving out of the sun from 21,000 feet.

The *Mogami* was again hit twice, once amidships and once forward of the bridge, which started fires and slowed her down. The *Mikuma* was hit several times and was set on fire. The *Arashio* tried to go alongside to rescue the crew, but the fires were too fierce, so she lowered her boats and picked up the men from the water.

Three torpedo aircraft were sent from the *Enterprise* to take part in the attack, but they failed to make contact with the scout bombers and made no attack.[2] All the *Enterprise*'s aircraft returned safely.

53. Second attack by *Hornet*'s group, 1500; sinking of *Mikuma*

The *Hornet*'s attack group had returned to their ship at 1045 and refuelling and re-arming for a second attack began at once. At 1330 this group of 24 scout bombers armed with 1,000-lb. bombs took off to attack the enemy now reported bearing 264 degrees distance 110 miles from the *Hornet*. All four of the Japanese ships were still afloat when they were sighted at 1500 and the attack by 23 aircraft commenced.

The *Mogami* received another hit amidships. The bomb penetrated the deck and killed men fighting the earlier fire and also damaged the doors leading to the engine room so that a number of men were trapped in the fire. About 93 men were reported killed in this attack, but the *Mogami* was still able to steam.

The *Mikuma* was hit several more times and was left a shambles. One bomb hit the *Arashio* in the stern, killing almost all the survivors of the *Mikuma* who were on deck; but the *Arashio*, like the *Mogami*, remained navigable, and both ships, as well as the *Asashio*, which apparently suffered no damage, escaped. The *Mikuma* was still afloat at 1730 when one of two photographic aircraft

---

2. The *U.S. Combat Narrative*, p. 46 footnote 43, says: 'These torpedo planes were ordered to attack only after the bombing attack. After failing to make contact with our bombing planes they found an enemy ship independently and circled an hour awaiting our bombers which did not appear. Finally lack of fuel forced them to return to the *Enterprise*. This clearly indicates the presence of two enemy groups'

sent out from the *Enterprise* returned with a photograph showing her gutted and abandoned. She sank that night at some time unknown, the position of sinking being estimated by the Joint Army-Navy Assessment Committee as approximately 30° N., 173° E.

54. B.17s bomb *Grayling* in error, 1640

One other air attack took place on 6 June, by part of a flight of B.17s despatched at 1145 to attack the southern group of the Japanese transport force. The enemy were not found, but on the return by separate routes one section of six of the Fortresses, at 1640, in a position bearing about 262 degrees, 400 miles from Midway (approximately 27° 20′ N., 175° 05′ E.) sighted a vessel. The Fortresses were at 10,000 feet altitude, and in spite of the unlimited visibility identification of type was difficult.

The first section of three aircraft dropped four bombs each and thought they had hit the target, which disappeared in 15 seconds. No bombing run was made by the second section, since no attack signal was given. The wing aircraft, believing that a bombing run was in progress, released her bombs, which were considerably off the target; the leading aircraft returned with his bombs.

The vessel attacked was the US submarine *Grayling* which crash dived when the first bombs fell near her bow and was not damaged. This was the only attack made by Midway aircraft on 6 June.

55. Escape of the Japanese

The main body, the striking force (less the four sunken carriers), and the Second Fleet (less the *Mikuma* and *Mogami* and accompanying destroyers) met at 1155 on the 5th in approximately 31° 30′ N. 176° 50′ E. The exact route by which the main body reached this position is not known. The combined force made good its escape by a considerable detour to the westward. A rendezvous for refuelling during the forenoon of 6 June was ordered in position 33° N., 170° E. By 0900 on the 6th, however, the various forces had already made rendezvous and were in position 33° 30′ N., 172° 50′ E. The Aleutian screening force had joined up shortly before, and the 3rd Battle Squadron and 4th Cruiser Squadron of the 2nd Fleet here met the *Kumano* and *Suzuya*.

The combined force steered a course 270 degrees whilst fuelling, during which it fully expected to be attacked from the air. Nothing happened, however, and the main body with the remnant of the striking force turned south at 1500 on the 6th in 33° 30′ N., 169° 10′ E., to a position in 25° 0′ N.,

169° 10′ E., where it turned westerly and returned to the Inland Sea with the transports of the Occupation Force. The Second Fleet turned south some hours earlier and met the damaged *Mogami* with the two destroyers at 0900 on the 7th in 28° N., 171° E., when the *Kumano* and *Suzuya* escorted the *Mogami* to Truk and the 4th Cruiser Squadron on went to Saipan, whilst the battleships went on to Japan.

Rear-Admiral Spruance did not pursue the enemy further. The long period of high speed steaming had reduced his destroyers' fuel, and the *Maury* and *Worden* had to be detached to refuel from the *Cimarron*. With the *Benham*, *Balch* and *Monaghan* also away screening the *Yorktown*, Task Force 16 was left with only four destroyers. Enemy submarines were reported in the area, and moreover it would have been dangerous to come within range of Wake, where the Japanese were known to have concentrated an air force in readiness for transfer to Midway, consequently. after the *Hornet* landed on her attack group at 1720, Rear-Admiral Spruance turned north-east and began to retire.

56. Sinking of the *Yorktown* and *Hammann*, 6–7 June

Whilst Task Force 16 was endeavouring to follow up the successes of 4 June, some 400 miles to the eastward the stricken *Yorktown* was making but little progress. Prematurely abandoned[3] on the afternoon of 4 June, she continued to float during the night of 4th–5th whilst the *Hughes* stood by her. Her list remained about constant. On the morning of the 5th the destroyer rescued two wounded men who had been overlooked when the ship was abandoned, and also picked up a fighter pilot, shot down in action, who rowed up in his rubber boat.

The minesweeper *Vireo* and fleet tugs *Seminole* and *Navajo* had been despatched to assist.[4] The *Vireo* from Pearl Harbor and Hermes Reef arrived about noon on the 5th and at 1436 began towing at about two knots on course 090 degrees, for Pearl Harbor. The flooded carrier, with rudder jammed, proved too heavy for the *Vireo*, which by next day was barely able to keep the *Yorktown* on her course. During the afternoon of the 5th the destroyers *Monaghan* and *Gwin* arrived, the latter having been diverted whilst on passage to join Task Force 16. The *Gwin* put a salvage party aboard, but it was removed at dusk, before being able to accomplish much. The *Hammann*, *Balch* and *Benham* returned to the carrier about 0200 on the 6th.

---

3. *Yorktown* might have been saved if she had not been completely abandoned during the night but salvage work carried on. *Secret Information Bulletin No.1*, comment by HQ of C-in-C US Fleet, p.12.
4. The latter did not arrive before the *Yorktown* sank.

About 0415 on the 6th, as soon as there was sufficient light, the *Hammann* went alongside and transferred to the *Yorktown* a salvage party of 29 officers and 130 men under Captain Buckmaster. In order to supply power for operating submersible pumps, and foamite and water for firefighting, it was found necessary to secure the *Hammann* alongside, as she could not lie clear and keep position accurately, and she was secured on the starboard side forward. The remaining four destroyers circled the two ships at 12 to 14 knots as an A/S screen.

By the afternoon the salvage party had made considerable progress, and the *Yorktown*'s list had been reduced some 2 degrees. But that morning (6 June) the *Yorktown* had been sighted listing and drifting by a reconnaissance aircraft from the *Chikuma*, and submarine *I-168*, whose patrol line was near Midway, was ordered to attack her. This she lost no time in doing.

At 1335 the wakes of four torpedoes were sighted to starboard of the *Yorktown*. The *Hammann* went full speed astern on her starboard engine, but in the minute that elapsed before the torpedoes struck there was insufficient time to pull the ships clear. Apparently two torpedoes hit the *Hammann*, one of which broke her back, and two struck the *Yorktown* below the island. The hole tom in the carrier's side by the resulting explosion apparently flooded the starboard fire rooms, for the list was reduced to 17 degrees and the ship settled a little.

The *Hammann* sank within three or four minutes, most of the crew managed to get clear, but about a minute after she disappeared a heavy underwater explosion occurred, which killed and injured a great many men. As the depth charges were known to be set to safe it was surmised that the explosion may have been caused by the *Hammann*'s torpedoes, one of which was said to have been seen running hot in its tube as the ship sank.

Destroyers hunted the submarine all the afternoon. At about 1845 a submarine surfaced on the horizon and was attacked. But *I-168* escaped undamaged. The destroyers being thus preoccupied, it was decided to defer further salvage attempts on the *Yorktown* until next day. The *Vireo* took off the salvage party and all water-tight doors remaining undamaged were closed. At 0501 on the 7th, however, before the salvage party boarded her again, the *Yorktown* capsized to port and sank in 3,000 fathoms in about 30° 36′ N., 176° 34′ W.

Chapter VIII

Lessons and Effects of the Battle

57. Experienced gained

The Americans were not slow to recognize the lessons of the battle. Some of these concerned material, such as the inferiority of the Navy fighter aircraft to the Japanese in speed, manoeuvrability and rate of climb; the fatal inadequacy of the Douglas torpedo bomber and the necessity for developing long range fighters to support the Grumman torpedo bomber which was unable to attack ships defended by fighters, whilst the aerial torpedo itself needed a larger warhead and to be designed for much higher release speed.

US carrier task forces were re-organized to provide stronger close screen of cruisers and destroyers in consequence of the demonstrated value of such a screen in the torpedo attacks on the *Yorktown*; Admiral Nimitz considered that had the *Yorktown* not been slowed down by previous bombing damage she might have avoided all the torpedoes fired by the only four Japanese aircraft that succeeded in penetrating the screen.

On the operational side, both Admiral Fletcher and Admiral Spruance stressed the vital importance of timing the first attack on enemy carriers whilst the latter had their aircraft on board. In so far as the Americans were able to do this, Midway was a victory of pre-battle intelligence resulting in a tactical situation in their favour. Once battle was joined, however, there was a failure to maintain continuous contact with the enemy, one cause of which was the unsuitability of the Navy patrol bombers for carrying out their important function of shadowing due to their inability to face fighter opposition. 'The lack of information on the enemy's surface forces between 0623 and 1000 [on 4th June] was serious and jeopardized the tactical advantage we enjoyed over the enemy', wrote Admiral Nimitz.[1] The delay of the *Enterprise*'s air group attack against the enemy carriers and the failure of the *Hornet*'s scout bombers to make contact with the enemy can be attributed to this lack of information. Further, the loss of aircraft from the *Hornet* and *Enterprise* by water landings from lack of fuel can be partly attributed to the same cause.

---

1. Lessons and conclusions from the action by C-in-C Pacific Fleet, *Secret Information Bulletin* No.1, p. 31.

The Japanese were guilty of the fatal omission to scout to the eastward of their striking force prior to launching their air attack on Midway, their planning having been based on the assumption that they need not fear the very thing that destroyed them, namely carrier air attack. There were two marked failures of co-ordination in the US air attacks on 4 June. The first was apparently due to lack of time not permitting adequate study and thought. On the morning of the 4th all the four groups of Midway aircraft, the Army B.26s, the Navy torpedo aircraft (TBF) and the Marine dive bombers, though flown off at about the same time, attacked separately between 0710 and 0720. Experience indicated that had they attacked together there would have been greater likelihood of damaging the enemy.

The second instance, the failure to co-ordinate the carrier dive bombing and torpedo attacks between 0920 and 1025, as had been so successfully done at the Battle of the Coral Sea a month earlier, probably had little effect on the damage caused to the Japanese, though it resulted in the loss of 35 out of 41 torpedo aircraft.

The escape of the Japanese main body and survivors of the striking force, without being brought under air attack by Task Force 16 dive bombers on 5 June, consequent on Rear-Admiral Spruance standing to the eastward during the first part of the previous night, can certainly be attributed to the orders of the Commander-in-Chief, US Fleet, not to risk ships unduly, and to the fact that the Americans were defending a fixed point, and had been warned against a probable enemy trap.

Midway was the only defensive battle of the war in the Pacific in which American submarines were extensively employed. Lack of search radar for night shadowing was held to be a primary reason for failure; directional (SJ) radar was installed in most of the submarines within a few months.

Effects of the battle

The Americans repulsed the attempted invasion of Midway at a cost of the *Yorktown* and *Hammann* sunk and 307 men and 150 aircraft lost. The Japanese lost the carriers *Akagi, Kaga, Hiryu* and *Soryu* and the heavy cruiser *Mikuma*; whilst the heavy cruiser *Mogami,* the destroyer *Arashio,* and tanker *Akebono Maru* suffered major, and the destroyer *Tanikaze,* minor damage. Losses of Japanese officers and men were about 3,500 and aircraft 253.

The loss of four carriers, 250 naval aircraft and 100 pilots was crippling to the Japanese. The striking force with which they had achieved their conquests, and on which they relied to repulse American attempts to counter-attack, was destroyed. Their shipbuilding capacity and air training organization were too limited to enable them to make good their losses, with consequential effect on their future operations throughout the war.

This great American victory completely reversed the strategic situation in the Pacific. It put an end to the long period of Japanese offensive action, removed any threat to India, stopped Japanese expansion to the east, and saved Midway Island as an important US outpost. It was perhaps the decisive battle of the war in the Pacific.

Part Four

Naval Operations of the Campaign for Guadalcanal Aug. 1942–Feb. 1943

Chapter I

First Japanese Offensive

1. Introduction

The campaign for the capture of Guadalcanal and the adjacent area, which opened with assault landings by US Marines on 7 August, 1942, and closed with the final withdrawal of the Japanese in the first week of February, 1943, was of great importance in the whole war in the Far East. Apart from the intrinsic value of the area to both sides, owing to its strategic importance, this was the first offensive operation undertaken by the Allies after the impetus of the initial Japanese rush to the south had been checked. Hitherto, the effects of the surprise attack on Pearl Harbor and the years of pre-war preparation had given the initiative to the Japanese: the role of the Allies had been restricted to attempts to delay the enemy operations, usually with totally inadequate forces hastily assembled to counter particular dangers as they occurred. The Guadalcanal campaign represented the first fair trial of strength, and as such a foretaste of things to come. Would the Americans working from distant bases be able to consolidate their position obtained by the surprise of 7 August? Or would the hitherto invincible Japanese army with its high standard of efficiency and ripe experience of combined operations be able to recover what it had lost? It took six months to obtain the answer to these questions. During that period, four major attempts were made by the enemy to re-capture Guadalcanal, while minor operations to reinforce and supply the troops on shore were carried out continuously by both sides. Desperate fighting at sea, in the air and on land took place, in which very heavy losses were suffered by both sides. At one time the enemy came within an ace of success.

This battle summary gives some account of the salient features of the naval operations of the campaign. No detailed tactical analysis of the actions has been attempted, partly because sufficient information is not yet available and partly because such detail is outside the scope of a general survey of the campaign as a whole.

The original American landings at Tulagi and Guadalcanal took place on 7 August, 1942. The enemy were taken completely by surprise, and by 10 August, Tulagi was firmly in American hands and all the Japanese accounted for in that area. In Guadalcanal, some 10,500 American troops held the area around Lunga Point on the North Coast, including the fine airfield at Kukum recently completed by the enemy. Lack of fighter cover had however, compelled the withdrawal of the American store ships before unloading had been completed, and the consequent shortage of heavy equipment prevented the American troops from dealing with the considerable Japanese forces still at large in the island. Heavy losses had been sustained by the Allied surface forces in a night action off Savo Island on 9 August, and as a result the enemy had obtained local command of the sea, and the American Forces on shore in Guadalcanal, though in superior strength, were virtually cut off. Japanese surface forces bombarded with impunity day and night, but apparently no land reinforcements were immediately available. Within a fortnight, however, the Americans were operating dive bombers from the airfield – known as Henderson's Field – and the Japanese, who had no airfields within immediate supporting range of Guadalcanal, suffered sufficient casualties to surface ships by day to restrict them to night operations.

2. Allied Naval Forces, South Pacific

Vice-Admiral Ghormley, USN, the Commander of the South Pacific was in general charge of the Allied operations, with his headquarters at Noumea. The effective naval forces at his disposal consisted of three carriers (*Saratoga*, *Enterprise* and *Wasp*), the battleship *North Carolina*, six heavy cruisers (*Minneapolis, New Orleans, Portland, San Francisco, Salt Lake City, Australia*), four light cruisers (*San Juan, Atlanta, Phoenix, Hobart*) and 20 destroyers. During the period following the occupation of Tulagi the *Australia* (Flag Rear-Admiral Crutchley, VC), *Hobart* and six destroyers, which had been present at the landing operations, were at Noumea; the remainder known as Task Force 61 under the command of Vice-Admiral Fletcher, USN, were cruising in the area to the west of the New Hebrides.

Allied aircraft based on Espiritu Santo, Efate, and New Caledonia, as well as those of the south-west Pacific area based in Australia and New Guinea were keeping up a constant reconnaissance of the Bismarck-Solomons area.

3. Japanese preparations

By 20 August 1942 – just a fortnight after the American landing – the Japanese were ready for their first large-scale counter-attack. A strong striking force of carrier borne aircraft was to neutralize Henderson's Field, after which strong reinforcements were to be landed from a convoy escorted by powerful surface forces. In the event, the presence of American aircraft carriers forced them to divide their air effort between the carriers and the airfield with disastrous results.

It had not been possible to conceal from the Allies the concentration of the necessary forces at Rabaul, and by 17 August it was clear to them that the greater part of the enemy naval forces was committed to the South Pacific. This was estimated as two battleships (*Kongo* class) seven heavy cruisers, four light cruisers and between 20 and 30 destroyers. No intelligence had been received as to aircraft carriers, but it was suspected that two or even three might be used in support; in addition, it was necessary to reckon on about 160 shore-based aircraft.

When the scale of the threatening attack was appreciated by the Americans, the carrier *Hornet* was ordered from Pearl Harbor to join Vice-Admiral Ghormley's forces, and she sailed on 17 August. On the same day, a diversionary operation was carried out, designed to draw part of the enemy forces away from the Solomons area and induced the Japanese to detach a relief force. This consisted of a raid on Makin (Gilbert Islands[1]).

4. Movements of Task Force 61

As the reports received began to indicate that the Japanese preparations were nearing completion, Vice-Admiral Fletcher's carrier forces moved to the northward. On 21 August they were joined by Rear-Adm. Crutchley, V.C., with the *Australia*, *Hobart* and three US destroyers. During the next two days, Task Force 61 operated to the south and east of Guadalcanal within 100 miles of the island.

On 23 August a reconnaissance aircraft reported an enemy force of two cruisers, three destroyers and four transports at 1030 near Ontong Java (Lat. 5° S., Long. 160° E.), steering a southerly course at 17 knots. That afternoon the *Saratoga* launched a striking force of 37 torpedo and dive bombers to attack this force then estimated 320° 260 miles from Task Force 61; nine dive-bombers, escorted by fighters, were also sent from Guadalcanal. But the enemy, on being sighted, had made a drastic alteration of course to the north-westward which the reconnaissance aircraft omitted to report and neither of these striking forces made contact. Both landed on Henderson's Field, the *Saratoga*'s aircraft rejoining her next forenoon.

---

1. Two submarines – *Narwhal* and *Argonaut* – landed 215 Marines who killed a number of Japanese and destroyed the radio station, a petrol dump and stores, and two seaplanes, while the submarines sank a gunboat and a transport.

In the course of the day (23 August) a signal was received from the Commander-in-Chief, Pacific pointing out that the spearhead of Japan's naval attack had been aviation and designating 'carriers and all other ships' as prime objectives for destructive attack. As it could not be foreseen exactly when the enemy would make their attempt, a fuelling program had been worked out for Task Force 61, and in pursuance of this the *Wasp* (Flag, Rear-Admiral Noyes), *San Juan* (Flag. Rear-Admiral Scott), *Salt Lake City* and *San Francisco* were detached in the evening of 23 August to re-fuel at sea from tankers in Lat. 13° S., Long. 164° E.

5. Battle of the Eastern Solomons, 25 August, 1942

At daybreak, 24 August, Vice-Admiral Fletcher was about 50 miles to the eastward of Maramasike (Malaita Island); the *Wasp*, some 250 miles to the southward had just commenced fuelling. When the reports from the dawn air reconnaissance began to come in, they showed that a wide-spread enemy movement was under way. Five ships in convoy, escorted by a cruiser, to the south of Bougainville; two cruisers and destroyers were reported in the New Georgia-Ysabel area, and later strong naval forces including at least one aircraft carrier were sighted steering to the southward near Ontong, Java, some 300 miles north of the American carrier groups. Vice-Admiral Fletcher ordered steam for full speed, preparing air striking forces to send against the enemy.[2] The aircraft enemy reports were confusing, and they were not amplified or kept up to date. It was clear, however, that there was a considerable naval force, including at least one carrier to the northward, and that it was apparently organized in groups, spread roughly east and west.

Meanwhile the American Force had been under observation by Japanese aircraft since 1100,[3] or earlier, and there could be no doubt that the Japanese Commander was receiving full and frequent reports of its movements. The information received by Vice-Admiral Fletcher, on the other hand, was so vague that at 1300, 24 August, he ordered the *Enterprise* to send out a search group, and a force of 29 bombers and torpedo-bombers was flown off to the northward. Half an hour later a similar force was launched from the *Saratoga*, with orders to attack the carrier reported during the forenoon. At the same time (1330), the *Saratoga*'s radar detected a large group of unidentified aircraft bearing 350°, distant 112 miles, flying in the direction of Guadalcanal. An

---

2. Frequent flying on and of operations, necessitating turns into the south-easterly wind, made it difficult to close the enemy to the northward. At noon, 24 August, Vice-Admiral Fletcher's Force was in latitude 9° S. longitude 163° E. still 250 miles from the enemy.

3. Four of these were shot down by the American Combat Patrol.

attack on Henderson's Field by twin and single-engine bombers, protected by Zero fighters, developed at 1440. Ten bombers and 11 fighters were shot down for a loss of three fighters.

Meanwhile the *Enterprise* search group had sighted the carrier *Ryujo*, a heavy cruiser and three destroyers bearing 317° 198 miles from Task Force 61 at 1410, and 20 minutes later two carriers, four heavy cruisers, six light cruisers, eight destroyers bearing 340° 198 miles. Owing to faulty communications the first of these reports only reached Vice-Admiral Fletcher at 1518; the second not at all, but a subsequent report of an unsuccessful attack on a carrier possibly the *Zuikaku*, made known to him the presence of this force at 1525. At 1440, a third group of four heavy cruisers, with destroyers, bearing 347° 225 miles from Task Force 61 was sighted; this report got through without delay.

The *Saratoga*'s striking force brought off a successful co-ordinated attack on the *Ryujo* at 1530. Four of the dive bombers made hits, and the torpedo bombers, attacking as the last dive bombers were coming down, obtained one certain and one probable hit. In addition, a destroyer was sunk and a heavy cruiser damaged by torpedoes. On its way back to the *Saratoga*, the striking force fell in with seven Japanese dive bombers (probably returning after an attack on the *Enterprise* which had taken place during its absence) and shot down four, or possibly five, of them.

About an hour later (1640) the Japanese counter-attack, which cost them so dearly in aircraft as to defeat the whole attempt on Guadalcanal, struck at Task Force 61. The first warning came at 1602 when the *Enterprise* picked up a large flight bearing 302°, 83 miles distant; the contact was then lost for 17 minutes, but reappeared on the screen at 1619 on the same bearing 44 miles distant, and preparations were made to meet the impending attack. Both carriers flew off their remaining striking forces, the *Saratoga*'s (three dive bombers, five torpedo bombers) to attack the enemy's battleship group and the *Enterprise*'s (11 dive bombers, seven torpedo bombers, seven fighters) to finish off the *Ryujo*; the fighter patrol over the Task Force was strengthened, and the *Enterprise*'s returning search group was ordered to keep clear.[4]

At this time, Task Force 61 was in two groups, steaming at 27 knots, with frequent alterations of course. The *Entrerprise* with the *North Carolina* 2,500 yards from her, was some 10 miles to the north-west of the *Saratoga*. Each group had its screen in close support, the cruisers 2,000 yards distant, and the destroyers inside 1,800 yards. Fifty-three fighters were in the air over the force. The weather was fine with excellent visibility; a moderate south-easterly wind was blowing and there was a slight swell. The sun was bearing about 325°. The first visual contact occurred at 1625, when one section of

---

4. Some of these aircraft did not receive this order and it is possible that the enemy followed them in.

the fighter patrol sighted 36 bombers and many Zero fighters, bearing 300°
33 miles from the *Enterprise*. When they had closed to about 25 miles, the
enemy split into numerous sections, veering to the northward, and from
then on became lost to the ships' radar screens, owing to confusion resulting
from the great number of aircraft – friendly and hostile – operating in the
neighbourhood.

Previous estimates had placed the enemy at 12,000 ft. altitude, but when
they were within 14 miles of their objective, one of the fighter patrols
amended this to 18,000 ft. The fighter patrol, therefore, had to climb, and
this combined with faulty communications with the Fighter Director Officer
in the *Enterprise* resulted in the majority of the enemy being unmolested till
they were in their dives.[5]

The initial attack was concentrated on the *Enterprise*. This was first
observed in the *North Carolina* when the aircraft were beginning to dive at
15,000 ft. A few seconds later a 20 mm. Battery Officer in the *Enterprise*
sighted them at 12,000 ft. And 'very properly opened fire without delay, thus
giving immediate warning and point of aim to the other batteries.' At the
same time the *North Carolina* and screening ships opened fire with 5-in guns.
This first dive resulted in a near miss at 1641; for the next four minutes,
except for two short breathing spaces, there was a continuous roar of aircraft
diving on to the carrier.

The AA fire of the Americans was excellent. Three dive bombers
disintegrated in mid-air; others pulled out of their dives at 6,000 to 4,000 ft.
or were so jolted by the bursting shells that they were thrown off their point of
aim; a few jettisoned their bombs. Out of the 25 to 30 aircraft which attacked,
15 came down in determined dives, which were pushed home to 1,500 ft. or
lower before release.[6] For nearly three minutes the *Enterprise* was unscathed;
then a near miss damaged her port quarter. A few seconds later she received
three direct hits in quick succession, one on the corner of No. 3 elevator which
penetrated to the third deck before it burst, and caused considerable damage,
besides starting fires and killing 35 men; one which struck about 20 ft. from
the first, putting two 5-in. guns out of action and killing their entire crews,
and one – a lighter bomb – which exploded just abaft the island superstructure,

5. A lack of radio discipline on the part of the fighter pilots was noted, many talking simultaneously,
   or making non-essential remarks. Few of the orders of the Fighter Director Officer reached them
   and but little of their information reached him. Only five to seven fighters engaged the enemy dive-
   bombers on the approach and about ten during their dives. The remainder were either engaged by
   Zeros, or first attacked the dive-bombers during their retirement.
6. The dives were carried out in sections of as many as five aircraft with very short intervals between
   them – in many cases below seven seconds. Thus the AA gunners had only the minimum time in
   which to clear jams, replenish ammunition and recover from shock or near misses.

and narrowly missing the after two 1.1 mounts, put No. 2 elevator out of action. Two blazing enemy aircraft just missed landing on the flight deck; at least ten crashed into the sea nearby, and others flew away smoking heavily.

Two minutes after the initial attack on the *Enterprise* (at 1643) the *North Carolina* was attacked by about 10 dive bombers from the starboard bow. So heavy was the fire with which she greeted them – while still engaging a group attacking the *Enterprise* – that only three succeeded in getting through to drop their bombs, two of which landed within about 20 yards of the battleship. During this attack about eight low-flying aircraft either attacked with torpedoes, or simulated torpedo attacks from various directions, in order to draw the *North Carolina*'s fire from the dive bombers. Their movements were well co-ordinated, but achieved no success, and some of them venturing too near were shot down. At this time practically all the *North Carolina*'s AA armament was firing and, to eye-witnesses in other ships, she appeared 'to be ablaze throughout.' At 1645 in the midst of this widespread firing a second dive bombing attack was made on her by six aircraft from the port quarter. Two of these were shot down by the after 20 mm; the remaining four placed their bombs within 150 yards of the ship one close enough to knock down the gun's four crew and flood the deck. Simultaneously eight to 12 heavy bombers carried out an unseen high-level attack from 15,000 ft.;[7] their bombs fell harmlessly between her and the *Enterprise*, which by this time had opened to about 4,000 yards. This ended the attacks on Task Force 61, though firing at detached low-flying aircraft continued for some minutes longer. Out of 80 Japanese aircraft which had attacked not less than 70 had been shot down, about 23 by ships' gunfire and 47 by the carrier air groups.[8]

By 1649, 24 August, the firing was over, and the interest of Task Force 61 centred on the damaged *Enterprise*. So efficient was her damage control and fire-fighting that within an hour she was steaming at 24 knots and landing on aircraft. Just after sunset (at 1821) her steering gear broke down, but after 38 minutes she was once more under control. Reports were coming in of another

---

7. This attack was unobserved partly because the high-level bombers were able to make use of cloud cover, and partly because attention on board the *North Carolina* was distracted by the low altitude and dive-bombing attacks in progress. The incident emphasizes the necessity for maintaining an overhead lookout at all times. The *Enterprise* had increased speed to 30 knots when the attack commenced. This, taken together with the avoiding action, had caused the *North Carolina* to fall astern. It was subsequently remarked that when a fast battleship is present with a carrier task force, speed should not be increased above 27 knots, because by so doing battleship support will be lost. The difference between 27 and 30 knots makes no appreciable difference in the manoeuvrability of ships in avoiding bombs.

8. These figures were Vice-Admiral Fletcher's final estimate. Claims for aircraft shot down amounted to about 50 by aircraft and 30 to 40 by ships fire. Some of these were clearly duplications, but it is equally clear that the enemy suffered very heavy losses.

strong Japanese air striking force,[9] apparently seeking for the Task Force; this, however, failed to make contact, and at 1940, 24 August, the whole Force withdrew to the southward.

While all this was happening, the *Saratoga*'s small striking force flown off at 1625 had brought off a successful attack on the enemy's surface force, hitting a battleship[10] with a 1,000-lb. bomb, and torpedoing a cruiser, despite heavy AA fire from the 16 to 18 ships forming the squadron. All the American aircraft returned to the *Saratoga*, except two torpedo bombers, which subsequently landed in Cristobal Island. The force sent off at the same time from the *Enterprise* failed to find the *Ryujo*; the dive bombers proceeded to Guadalcanal for the night, and the torpedo bombers returned to the carriers landing on after dark.

Summing up the day's operations, the enemy had lost a carrier (*Ryujo*), a destroyer and probably a cruiser; in addition, a battleship and a cruiser had been damaged. On the debit side, the *Enterprise* had been damaged. But the real importance of the victory lay in the virtual destruction of the Japanese air striking power. In the air, including the results achieved by shore-based aircraft, the enemy had lost 101 aircraft against the American loss of 11 pilots. Not only was the enemy landing expedition robbed of all hope of success, but the Americans had definitely won control of the air. Though one of their carriers was damaged, they still had intact two practically full carrier air groups; the *Wasp* Task Force was re-fuelled and proceeding north to re-join Task Force 61, and the *Hornet* was approaching from the eastward.

The Battle of the Eastern Solomons ended the first attempt of the enemy to recapture Guadalcanal. Henderson's Field was ineffectively bombarded for about an hour that night by four ships believed to have been destroyers, one of which was damaged – perhaps sunk – by a moonlight air attack; and during the forenoon of 25 August, many groups of enemy ships continued to close Guadalcanal.[11] But the staggering air losses inflicted on them the previous day had weighted the scales too heavily against them, and by that afternoon

---

9. At 1700 the *Saratoga* aircraft returning from attacking the *Ryujo* sighted at least 18 enemy dive bombers, nine torpedo bombers and three fighters in latitude 7° 45′ S, longitude 162° 10′ E., on course 140°. This course would have led them to Task Force 61 within an hour, but they altered to the south, and at 1721 were picked up to the westward by radar. They passed about 50 miles to the westward, then turned due east, till about south of the Task Force, when they altered to the north-west. Had they steered north, they would have made contact just when the *Enterprise*'s steering gear broke down. Later on in the evening they were heard trying to find their carrier; it is possible that some or all of them were lost.
10. Probably the *Mutsu*.
11. Some of these were attacked by shore-based aircraft from Guadalcanal, which sank a light cruiser or destroyer and damaged a heavy cruiser and 14,000-ton transport.

all surface craft had turned round and were retiring to the northward at high speed.

How serious was the predicament of the enemy does not seem to have been fully appreciated at the time. It now seems clear that if the Americans had followed up their victory, the Japanese reverse might have been turned into a defeat which might have finally ended the struggle for Guadalcanal. No serious counter-offensive, however, was undertaken.

During the night, 24–25 August, Task Force 61 continued to the southward, passing Task Force 18, returning after fuelling, at 0300, 25 August.

During 25 August, Task Force 18 cruised in the area to the southeast of Guadalcanal, ready to repel further Japanese attacks, while the remainder of Task Force 61 was fuelling well to the southward. Two enemy submarines were sighted and probably sunk while this was in progress, one by the destroyer *Grayson* and one by a dive bomber from the *Enterprise*, which secured a direct hit with a 1,000-lb. bomb. On completion of fuelling the injured *Enterprise*, escorted by the *Portland* and destroyers, was detached for repairs, the remainder of her Task Force (the *North Carolina*, *Atlanta* and two destroyers) joining the *Saratoga*'s group, which then returned to the northward and reinforced Task Force 18.

Chapter II

Second Japanese Offensive

6. Vice-Admiral Ghormley's policy 27 August, 1942

The Battle of the Eastern Solomons was followed by a period of small-scale reinforcements to Guadalcanal by both sides, the enemy being restricted by the American command of the air to running in troops and supplies in destroyers by night, while the Japanese superiority in surface ships seriously reduced the flow of American supplies. It seemed clear that despite the failure of his first attempt the enemy would make another powerful effort before long, and on 27 August Vice-Admiral Ghormley informed his Task Force Commanders of his policy: 'Until hostile strength and intentions are determined we must employ to the utmost of our limits land based aircraft, while improving the Tulagi-Guadalcanal position. What we would wish to achieve is the combination (no matter where the enemy may strike) of our shore-based planes and carrier aircraft against the following targets in order of priority, carriers, transports, battleships, cruisers, destroyers. Therefore the Carrier Task Forces should operate generally south of latitude 10° S. unless a promising target is located within striking distance, meanwhile covering the movement of supplies and reinforcements into the Guadalcanal area. Shore- and tender-based planes should continue as extended and intensive a search as operating conditions permit ...'

Vice-Admiral Fletcher's Carrier Forces accordingly cruised in the area between latitudes 10° 30 'S., and 13° S. and longitudes 163° 30′ E, and 164° 30′ E., in order to cover the line of communications between Espiritu Santo, where an advanced supply base had been established, and Guadalcanal. The importance of this line of communication was appreciated by the enemy, who by means of a well-planned submarine offensive inflicted serious damage on the carrier forces in the course of the next few weeks.

7. U.S.S. *Saratoga* torpedoed, 31 August, 1942

On 29 August, Vice-Admiral Fletcher was joined by Task Force 17, consisting of the carrier *Hornet*, the cruisers *Northampton*, *Pensacola* and *San Diego* and screening destroyers, and the three carrier forces cruised in company during 30 August.[1]

Shortly after midnight, 30–31 August, the *Wasp*'s group was detached to Noumea to take in fuel, provisions and stores. The other two groups remained in company, steering to the northward at 13 knots. There had been several reports of enemy submarines in this general area recently, and at 0330, 31 August, several ships obtained radar contacts of an unidentified object, which faded from the screens at 0345. A destroyer ordered to investigate failed to search the correct area owing to a communication error, and rejoined the formation an hour later. At 0639, 31 August, the *Saratoga* altered course to the south-eastward, to conform with the *Hornet* which was then launching the dawn search into the wind. At 0655 the Fleet shaped course 140°, 13 knots, and half an hour later commenced zigzagging. At 0746, while steering 180° on the starboard leg of the zigzag, the *Macdonough*, 3,500 yards on the starboard bow of the *Saratoga*, sighted a periscope about 10 yards off, abreast of No.1 gun. She dropped two depth charges and broadcast a warning that a torpedo was approaching the *Saratoga* on course 050°. Full speed was at once ordered in the carrier, the rudder being put hard to starboard, but she swung sluggishly at the slow speed at which she was moving and at 0748 a torpedo struck her on the starboard side just abaft the island superstructure. By the end of two minutes she had swung to 290° and built up speed to 16 knots; but three minutes later (0753) power failed and she came to a standstill. During this time another torpedo was seen passing astern from starboard to port, and three torpedoes broached approximately 4,000 yards off (indicating a run of about 7,000 yards at 30 knots). The *Saratoga* had suffered serious structural damage and was listing about 4°; but she was able to proceed at 6 knots at 0836. Power again failed, however, shortly before 1100, and she was then towed by the *Minneapolis* for four hours while she reduced the list and effected temporary repairs. It is noteworthy that while in tow she was able to launch aircraft.

Immediately after the attack, the destroyers were ordered to circle around the wounded *Saratoga*. Later a depth charge attack on the submarine was

---

1. 'Our intelligence has advised that the Japanese now have in this southern area many of their naval commanders-in-chief. The Commander-in-Chief, Combined Fleets, is thought to have reached the Rabaul area recently; the Commander-in-Chief, First Air Fleet, is reported to be commanding the aircraft carrier striking force now in the Bismarck-Solomons area: the Commander-in-Chief, Second Fleet, is reported to be in command of a strong task force based on Truk; the Commander-in-Chief, Sixth Fleet, is reported en route to Jaluit; and the Commander-in-Chief, Eighth Fleet, is reported in the heavy cruiser *Chokai*, which has now been in the Bismarck-Solomons area for some weeks. The presence of all this talent must be an indication of the magnitude of the effort the Japanese are preparing to make ...' (Rear-Admiral Crutchley).

organized, which is believed to have been sunk by the *Monssen* about 1000 that forenoon, though there was no evidence of success apart from air bubbles.[2]

8. Operations of Carrier Forces, 31 August–15 September 1942

After this mishap, the *Saratoga* proceeded to Pearl Harbor for repairs, while Rear-Admiral Murray with Task Force 17 (*Hornet*), to which the *North Carolina* was now attached, withdrew to a position about 150 miles to the eastward of Espiritu Santo where fleet oilers were awaiting him. When complete with fuel, Task Force 17 returned to a covering position just south of the cruising area of the previous week.

At 1251, 6 September, when in Lat. 13° 20' S., Long. 162° 40' E. one of the patrolling aircraft sighted a torpedo approaching the *Hornet* and dropped a depth bomb near it. This caused the torpedo to broach and explode, and a few seconds later another torpedo exploded about 100 yards from the first. A third missed the carrier and passed to port of the *North Carolina* as she was swinging to starboard. Later that afternoon two aircraft returning from an extended search sighted a submarine on the surface in Lat. 13° 29'., Long. 163° 25' E. Each dropped a depth bomb, which fell within 25–30 ft. of the submarine and may have inflicted damage. Task Force 17 then cleared the suspected submarine area to the south-westward and, returning to the eastward during the night, spent 7 September cruising in an area 120–180 miles south-east of the scene of the attack the previous day. While in this area the force manoeuvred to avoid four different contacts, which may or may not have been submarines. At 0800, 8 September course was shaped to the northward till 2000 that evening and then for the fuelling position to the east of Espiritu Santo, where Rear-Admiral Noyes' Task Force 18 (*Wasp*) from Noumea was met on 11 September. Having completed with fuel, both Forces – now known as Task Force 61 – proceeded to the westward, embarking about 20 fighters from Espiritu Santo for Guadalcanal *en passant*. These were flown off at 0700, 13 September, from a position about 250 miles east-south-east of Guadalcanal (about 50 miles from where the *Saratoga* had been torpedoed), and the Force then withdrew to the eastward down the channel between Santa Cruz and Banks Islands, altering to the westward again early on 14 September in order to cover an important convoy under Rear Admiral Turner which was leaving Espiritu Santo with reinforcements for Guadalcanal that morning.

---

2. The fact that the Japanese never claimed the torpedoing of the *Saratoga* is an indication that the submarine did not survive.

About noon, 14 September, a report was received of an enemy battleship and cruiser group to the north-westward on a southerly course; Task Force 61 altered course to 330° to get within range and at 1430 the *Wasp* launched a tactical scout group and the *Hornet* an attack group. Soon afterwards, however, the enemy reversed their course, and neither group made contact. Flying Fortresses from Espiritu Santo found the enemy, however, and reported making two or three possible hits on one of the battleships. After recovering aircraft Task Force 61 retired to the east till about midnight 14–15 September, when course was altered to the west in order to keep in supporting distance of the transports.

9. Loss of USS *Wasp*, 15 September 1942

During the forenoon of 15 September, Task Force 61 continued to the westward on a mean course 280°, 16 knots. Soon after noon the fighter patrol shot down a shadowing aircraft, which was passed in the water at about 1300 in Lat. 12° 30' S., Long. 164° 30' E.; it is probable that this aircraft got off a report before being destroyed.

At 1420 the *Wasp*, which was duty carrier, turned into the wind (about 120°) for flying operations reducing speed to 13 knots during recovery of aircraft. The *Hornet*'s Force, 5 to 6 miles to the north-eastward, conformed to the *Wasp*'s movements. By 1442 flying operations were completed, and the *Wasp* began turning back to the westward, increasing to 16 knots. Two minutes later, while she was swinging to starboard, three torpedoes were sighted close aboard, 3 points before the starboard beam. The rudder was put hard to starboard, but almost immediately the torpedoes hit in the magazine and petrol storage areas forward, while a fourth torpedo passed ahead on a course 060°. The shock of the first torpedo ruptured petrol lines and started fires, and immediately afterwards a petrol explosion sent flames 150 ft. Into the air. Planes on the flight and hangar decks were lifted and dropped with such force that their landing gear was broken. 'Planes triced[3] to the hangar overhead broke loose and crashed on those below. Fires started on the hangar deck and in many places forward. Ready ammunition began to explode. Water mains forward broke under the shock. The ship listed to starboard 11° but was soon brought back to 4°. Fires spread in oil and gasoline on the water alongside. In a few minutes a heavy internal explosion shattered the ship forward.[4] The

---

3. Lashed or secured.
4. It is believed that this explosion was the foremost magazine as it was accompanied by a column of dense white smoke similar to one seen when the *Arizona*'s magazines blew up at Pearl Harbor on 7 December, 1941.

ship was stopped, and then went astern, so as to get the wind on the starboard quarter; but violent internal explosions were taking place, and within half an hour the flames had spread to such an extent that she had to be abandoned, the Commanding Officer leaving at 1600.[5]

10. USS *North Carolina* and *O'Brien* torpedoed

Meanwhile the *Hornet*'s force also had been attacked. At the moment the *Wasp* was hit (1444) Task Force 17 was just beginning to alter course from 120° to 280°. While the ships were turning the *Wasp* was seen to burst into smoke and flames. The *North Carolina* had just steadied on 280° at 1450 when she intercepted a broadcast warning from one of the *Wasp*'s screening destroyers that a torpedo was heading directly for the force, course 080°. She started turning to starboard under 10° of helm, and half a minute later the *Mustin*, then about 500 yards 60° on her port bow reported: 'Torpedo passed astern headed for you.' Full speed was ordered and the rudder was put hard to starboard, but she had only swung 15° when at 1452 a torpedo struck her port side. A heavy column of oil and water rose nearly as high as the tops and immediately a 51° list developed. The list was removed in six minutes, but extensive flooding took place, and flash from the explosion penetrated to No. 1 turret handing room and spaces in the vicinity. As a precaution the magazines were flooded. The hole in the hull was 32 ft. long by 8 ft. high, extending from just below the armour belt, and severe structural damage was suffered. Five men were lost. Despite the damage to the *North Carolina* built up speed to 25 knots, and retained her position in the formation, manoeuvring radically to conform with the *Hornet*.

At the time the *North Carolina* was hit, the destroyer *O'Brien* was a few hundred yards on her port quarter, steaming at 19 knots to regain her station after the alteration of course to the westward. Two minutes later she sighted a torpedo two points before the port beam, distant about 1,000 yards, running at 27 knots, course 350°. This torpedo just missed her stern by 4 or 5 ft., but simultaneously another was sighted close aboard, which struck the stem blowing away the forefoot from about frame 10 up to the main deck. There was shock damage throughout the ship and flooding forward, but the *O'Brien* was able to proceed under her own power for Noumea; she broke in two, however, and sank while on passage.

---

5. There were about 26 officers and 167 men killed or missing out of 201 officers and 2,046 men on board.

11. US Reinforcement of Guadalcanal, 14–18 September

Meanwhile, the second Japanese attempt on Guadalcanal had been launched and repulsed. On this occasion the plan was to capture Henderson's Field by land forces, which had been built up by infiltration, after which large reinforcements were to be landed to drive the Americans into the sea. A heavily escorted convoy of transports put to sea and lay off to the northward outside bombing range, ready to land after the capture of the airfield. The land assault on Henderson's Field commenced on the night of 13/14 September, and after heavy fighting was defeated by the US Marines. The convoy thereupon withdrew to the northward.

The losses suffered by the American carrier forces on the 15th September, left Rear-Admiral Turner's convoy in an awkward position. The general situation on leaving Espiritu Santo on the 14th had been far from reassuring. There was a considerable enemy concentration at Faisi; almost nightly raids by surface forces were taking place on Guadalcanal, and the strength of enemy air attacks had increased; clearly, another strong effort to recapture the island was about to take place.

It was particularly important that the convoy should not be detected, since, in addition to the air menace, strong enemy surface forces were known to be to the north-west, north and north-east of Guadalcanal, all within less than one day's steaming. The route chosen was south of San Cristobal and thence through Indispensable Strait and Lengo Channel. In approaching San Cristobal, the force kept well to the eastward in spite of the submarines as giving the best chance of evading enemy air reconnaissance.

The reports which came in on the 14th and 15th were not encouraging, and at 1100, 15th, the convoy was located and shadowed for an hour by a 4-engined bomber. Since the troops embarked were the only reinforcements in the South Pacific which could be available for some weeks, Rear-Admiral Turner considered that he was not justified in risking an attack by strong surface force during disembarkation and decided to withdraw temporarily to await a more favourable opportunity. In the hope of drawing the Japanese surface forces within reach of the US shore-based aircraft, he held his course till after dark, and then sending one transport (the *Zane*) on with orders to signal by wireless during the night a report of his change of plan, altered course to the south-eastward.

That night (15/16) enemy cruisers and destroyers landed troops in Guadalcanal. On the 16th the picture was not clear to Rear-Admiral Turner, but the failure of the enemy to make his expected large-scale landing or other attacks on the island induced him to turn to the northward towards the eastern end of San Cristobal at 1500, 16th, in order to be in a position to arrive at Guadalcanal on the morning of the 18th if conditions then warranted the attempt. Hazy weather and high winds from the south-east prevailed and the force was not sighted either by submarines or aircraft.

Early on the morning of the 17th the decision was taken to proceed with the plan. Conditions appeared to be shaping fair. It seemed probable that the enemy surface craft which had raided Guadalcanal on the night of 15th/16th would not be able to return in time to interfere with the landing on the 18th; news arrived of the destruction of a number of aircraft by Australian bombers on the airfield at Rabaul; and a message from Vice-Admiral Ghormley expressed the opinion that the enemy had temporarily withdrawn from the area.

During the afternoon a report was received that scouting aircraft had sighted at Gizo (200 miles from Guadalcanal) at 0900 that morning 10 four-engine flying boats, several fighters on floats, four cruisers, destroyers and transports – a total of about 20 vessels. Rear-Admiral Turner considered that 'there was no great danger of attack from this enemy, since his surface escort would probably be employed in large part to protect his own transports.'

Once the decision to carry out the reinforcements had been taken, all went well. The night was very dark, with frequent rain squalls, but the approach through the narrow and inadequately charted waters was skilfully accomplished and the transports arrived off Kukum Beach at 0550, 18th September and immediately commenced disembarkation. This was reported by enemy radio within three quarters of an hour.

A very careful organization for unloading had been worked out, one-third of the embarked troops being detailed for handling cargo, and assistance in trucks and boats being rendered by the troops already ashore. While this was going on two of the destroyers – the *Monssen* and *MacDonough* – at the request of the General, bombarded various enemy positions to the westward of Kukum. Fires were started, but otherwise the results could not be estimated. By the close of the day the disembarkation of the 7th Marines, with all its weapons, essential equipment, most of its motor vehicles, three units of fire and 40 days' rations had been completed. In addition, about 150,000 gallons of much needed petrol, oil and stores had been landed at the same beaches from three auxiliaries which arrived during the day. At 2030 all ships got under way, and withdrew through Lengo Channel, arriving at their bases without incident between 20 and 22 September.

At 0015, 19th, as expected, an enemy force of cruisers and destroyers arrived off Kukum, but it was far too late and beyond bombarding the shore positions there was nothing for it to do.

Chapter III

Third Japanese Offensive

12. US Carrier-borne raid on Shortlands Islands, 5 October 1942

Between the second and third major Japanese efforts to recapture Guadalcanal there was an interval of about three weeks. The enemy continued to land small reinforcements and bombard the American positions in the island by night, while 300 miles to the north-westward his expeditionary force was getting ready at his advanced base in the Buin-Faisi (Shortlands Islands) area. On 1 October 1942, Task Force 17,[1] under the command of Rear-Admiral Murray, consisting of the *Hornet*, four cruisers and six destroyers was ordered to leave Noumea the next day to launch an air attack on the concentration of shipping there. The raid was planned to take place on 5 October, and arrangements were made for attacks by shore-based aircraft of both the South-west and South Pacific areas to be carried out on Rabaul and the Buka-Kieta area, in order to contain the enemy air force and to prevent a counter-attack on Task Force 17 during its retirement. Rear Adm. Murray left Noumea on 2 October and arrived in a position about 120 miles to the southward of Buin at 0430, 5 October.[2] There was a 16-knot wind from the south-east, with light cumulus cloud at 2,000 to 3,000 ft. A careful study of weather maps had led to the expectation of unsettled weather in the launching area, but improved conditions in the target area. The attacking aircraft were divided into two waves, the first consisting of 18, and the second of 15 bombers. Each group was escorted by eight fighters. About halfway to the target the weather got steadily worse; heavy rains were encountered, and the ceiling at the target 'became a solid overcast, with some clouds as low as 2,000 to 3,000 ft., prohibiting dive bombing against any objective'. The bombers became separated and the escort also lost touch, but all proceeded independently. Three overran the target area, and finding themselves over Kieta, bombed

---

1. Task Force 17, carrier *Hornet* (Flag Rear-Admiral Murray), 8-in. cruisers *Northampton*, *Pensacola*, AA cruisers *San Diego* and *Juneau*, plus six destroyers.
2. The endurance of the destroyers was insufficient for them to carry out the whole operation at the high speed necessary to reach the launching position in time. The heavy ships therefore increased to 28 knots at 1000, 4th, and went on alone, leaving the destroyers to follow at 19 knots, which would enable them to rejoin after the raid in time to increase the AA fire against a possible enemy counter-attack.

the airfield there; 9 others flying through rain and murk found neither land nor enemy ships and returned to the carrier with their bombs. Those which did reach their objective seem to have taken the enemy completely by surprise and claimed to have scored 1,000-lb. bomb hits on an 8-in. cruiser (*Nachi* class) and a transport, and 500 lb. bomb hits on a large seaplane tender and two transports. In addition the 8-in. cruiser may have been damaged by near misses. All the American aircraft returned safely to the *Hornet*, and Task Force 17 withdrew without incident.

Commenting on the operation, Rear-Admiral Murray remarked that 'in the employment of a carrier task force in raids on enemy objectives, the state of the weather is one of the most important, if not the most important, consideration.' On this occasion the forecast for the 24 hours preceding the raid indicated unsettled weather conditions in the launching area, with promise of improvement and possibly clear weather at sunrise in the target area. This led to the decision to equip the torpedo bombers with bombs instead of torpedoes. Actually, the weather was the reverse of what was predicted. The damage which might have been inflicted on the enemy had torpedoes been carried instead of bombs, is, of course, a matter of conjecture: but 'had the assumption been that the ceiling at the target would be so low as to prohibit dive bombing, at least six and possibly all the torpedo bombers would have carried torpedoes.'

13. Battle of Cape Esperance, 11/12 October, 1942

Early in October, 1942, the American strength in surface ships in the South Pacific had increased sufficiently to allow a striking force of cruisers and destroyers to be formed for the purpose of countering the enemy's night activities off Guadalcanal. This force, known as Task Force 64.2, was placed under the command of Rear-Admiral N. Scott, USN.

On 7 October Task Force 64.2 sailed from Espiritu Santo for the Guadalcanal area. The intention was to remain well to the southward of the island by day beyond the range of enemy bombers, and to close the Western Approaches by night, in order to intercept enemy reinforcements.

These dispositions coincided with the opening moves of the third great Japanese effort. The recapture of Henderson's Field was still considered by the enemy an essential preliminary to landing the main occupation force, but to build up his forces ashore sufficiently by his methods of infiltration was a slow business, so he decided to bring in transports at night, run them aground on the unloading beaches, and trust to getting the personnel and as much material as possible ashore before the ships were destroyed by air attack in daylight. The first operation of this nature which was planned for the night of 11/12 October was defeated by Rear-Admiral Scott in the night action known as the Battle of Cape Esperance.

Task Force 64.2 had arrived in its cruising area on 9th October. For two days there was no special news of the enemy, but at 1347, 11 October, a reconnaissance aircraft reported an enemy force of two cruisers and six destroyers 210 miles to the north-westward of Guadalcanal, approaching the island at high speed. A further report at 1810 placed it 100 miles nearer.

Rear-Admiral Scott calculated that the enemy would reach the landing area about 2300, 11 October, and accordingly at 1600 steered to the northward at 29 knots from position lat. 11° 30' S., long. 161° 45' E., to establish a patrol to the westward of Guadalcanal and Savo Island.

At 2333 the squadron had reached a position about four miles due west of the northern point of Savo Island, and course was altered to port from 050° to 230°. Ships were in column in the order *San Francisco, Boise, Salt Lake City, Helena*, with three destroyers (*Farenholt, Duncan, Laffey*) ahead and two (*Buchanan, McCalla*) astern of the cruisers. It was a dark night, with no moon and a clear atmosphere; there was a 7-knot wind from the south-east, and a calm sea, with an easterly swell.

There had been several vague radar contacts from 2100 onwards but at 2325 – just before the alteration to the south-westward – the *Helena* obtained a definite contact on SG radar of ships bearing 315°, 27,700 yards off, and tracking commenced. The *San Francisco* was unfortunately not fitted with SG radar, and Rear-Admiral Scott therefore had to wait for other ships' reports. This caused him considerable inconvenience and uncertainty during the action which followed.

At 2342 the enemy was estimated to be bearing 285°, 12,000 yards, steering 140° at 26 knots; three minutes later ships were sighted to starboard and at 2346 the Americans opened fire at a range of 4,000–5,000 yards. The Japanese were caught unawares and the *San Francisco* and *Boise* sank the leading ship, tentatively identified as a *Nachi* class cruiser in six minutes; two destroyers were sunk, one by the *Boise* with her secondary armament and one by the *Helena*, which then shifted her fire to a burning heavy cruiser which was sunk at the same time. The *Salt Lake City* first engaged a light cruiser *(Natori* class) and then a heavy cruiser; the *San Francisco* and *Boise* each sank another destroyer, and the latter then opened fire on a heavy cruiser. As she did so she received a hit. This occurred at 2354 and was the first damage suffered by the Americans. After engaging a burning destroyer for some minutes, the *Boise* came under a heavy fire from an 8-in. cruiser and another destroyer at 0009, 12 October; she received seven hits in three minutes, and was forced to discontinue the action. Meanwhile the *San Francisco* had sunk another destroyer, and then engaged in turn a *Nachi* class cruiser at 7,000 yards range, which she left burning fiercely, and another cruiser 1,000 yards beyond; the *Salt Lake City* sank an auxiliary and a destroyer, the *Helena* sank a cruiser to the northward and the *Duncan* and *Buchanan* each hit a cruiser with two torpedoes. The *Duncan* was herself set on fire and subsequently sunk, most of her crew being saved. At 0025 all firing ceased. 'By this time the enemy had been crushed. Except for several ships burning (two of these were an 8-in. cruiser and a destroyer, that ultimately blew up) …. Our force had received indeterminate damage, the formation was disorganized after a half-hour of heavy action, and the destroyers were still out of position, so that there was danger of our ships engaging each other.' Under these circumstances Rear-Admiral Scott decided to withdraw, and at 0027, 12 October, set course to the south-westward. By 0305 all the American ships had rejoined the flag. The *Boise*, *Salt Lake City* and *Farenholt* had suffered damage and *Duncan* had been lost. Against this, two enemy 8-in cruisers, one light cruiser, one auxiliary and five destroyers had been sunk, and an 8-in cruiser and other destroyers had been damaged. Aircraft from Guadalcanal followed up the victory after daylight and damaged – probably sank – an 8-in cruiser and a destroyer.

The exact number of enemy ships engaged is not known. It seems probable that there were two groups: the first consisting of three 8-in. cruisers and three destroyers, and the second of the two cruisers and six destroyers tracked during the previous afternoon. There may have been some auxiliaries and destroyers between these groups. After this most successful action, Rear-Admiral Scott returned to Espiritu Santo, covered by shore-based aircraft of the South Pacific Air Force.

The next day (13 October) the American Marines in Guadalcanal were reinforced by the 164th Infantry Regiment, US Army, which was landed without interference by the enemy.

14. Preparations and Assault, 13–24 October, 1942

Undeterred by their defeat at the Battle of Cape Esperance, the Japanese continued to press on their preparations for their third great assault on Guadalcanal. They still enjoyed local command of the sea by night, and two nights after the engagement (13/14 October), a force of two battleships, a light cruiser and eight destroyers bombarded Henderson's Field for an hour and twenty minutes, destroying a large number of aircraft. The bombardment was repeated with less effect by cruisers and destroyers on the two succeeding nights. Numerous air attacks increased the damage, but cost the enemy heavily in aircraft.[3]

On 15 October, before dawn, the enemy succeeded in landing about 10,000 troops and much equipment from six transports to the west of Kokumbona; aircraft from Henderson's Field sank three or four of these transports and damaged an escorting 8-in. cruiser after daylight.

To the south-east submarines and carrier-borne aircraft operated as far as lat. 13° S. against the American lines of communication: the auxiliary *Meredith* was sunk on 15 October, and the cruiser *Chester* was torpedoed and seriously damaged on 20 October. Far to the north-west, Japanese troops and aircraft were being steadily moved from the Philippines, the Netherlands East Indies and other places towards the Solomons, and the concentrations in the Rabaul and Shortlands Islands areas were increasing daily.

To meet this threatening situation the Americans concentrated submarines in the Bismarck area, and increased the number of heavy land-based bombers and patrol aircraft in the South Pacific. Aircraft of the South West Pacific area collaborated and intensified their attacks on Rabaul and the airfields in the Bismarcks, doing considerable damage. The main naval forces were held in readiness to intercept the enemy expeditionary force as it approached Guadalcanal.

On the evening of 23 October, after a heavy artillery bombardment of the American lines, the Japanese land forces attacked with tanks and massed infantry along the Matanikau River, with Henderson's Field as their objective. Hard fighting took place throughout the 24th and 25th. For the opening stages the airfield was out of action, owing to damage and heavy rains, and on the 25th the enemy troops were supported by cruiser and destroyer gunfire, as well as by bombers. By noon (25th) the weather had improved, and American aircraft could be operated again; they broke up many bomber attacks and damaged two cruisers, in the course of the afternoon. That night (25th) came the crisis of the battle; the enemy actually broke through the American lines, but after desperate fighting were driven back with heavy losses. The great attack had failed; the all-important airfield remained in American hands, and the main Japanese occupation forces, which had left Buin during the night of 24–25 October once again turned back. The attempt, however, had very nearly succeeded, and if the Japanese had moved in their main occupation forces while Henderson's Field was unserviceable, without waiting for its capture, it would have been difficult for the Americans to have held out.

---

3. Between 1 and 27 October, approximately 200 (out of 600) aircraft were shot down by aircraft and AA fire from Guadalcanal.

On the following day (26 October), the enemy's discomfort was completed at the Battle of Santa Cruz. This, like the Battle of the Eastern Solomons, was fought out by carrier-borne aircraft, and again the Japanese air forces were practically annihilated, though on this occasion the Americans suffered heavier losses in both air and surface craft, than on 24 August.

15. Battle of Santa Cruz, 26 October 1942

Meanwhile, as the Japanese preparations advanced, the following naval dispositions had been taken up by the Americans. The fast battleship *Washington*, with three cruisers and ten destroyers (Task Force 64), under Rear-Admiral W. A. Lee, Jr., cruised to the westward of Guadalcanal, ready to attack enemy forces supporting landings. Beyond the New Hebrides, some 800 miles to the eastward, Task Force 61 consisting of the carrier *Hornet* with the remaining cruisers and destroyers, under Rear-Admiral Murray, awaited news of the departure of the enemy main occupation forces from the Shortlands area. The *Enterprise* (Flag Rear-Admiral Kincaid) was at Pearl Harbor, repairing the damage suffered at the Battle of the Eastern Solomons; by great exertions, she was able to join the *Hornet* in lat. 13° 45' S., long. 171° 30'E., on 24th October – the day after the Japanese launched their land assault on Henderson's Field. With her came the battleship *South Dakota*, and Rear-Admiral Kincaid, who was the senior officer present, assumed command of the whole force.

On receipt of the news that the Japanese offensive had begun, Task Force 61 shaped course to the north-westward to close the Guadalcanal area, passing north of the Santa Cruz Islands. During 25 October, air reports were received of strong enemy forces, including battleships and carriers some 360 miles to the north-westward; Rear-Admiral Kincaid steered for the contact at 27 knots, and flew off an attack group of 18 bombers and 11 fighters, which, however failed to reach the enemy, who had altered course to the northward.

During the night (25–28 October), Task Force 61 continued to steer towards the enemy at 20 knots. At 0410, 26 October, a shore-based aircraft reported a large carrier and six other vessels about 200 miles from Task Force 61's position. This report did not reach Rear-Admiral Kincaid till 0612, when the *Enterprise* was flying off fighter patrols and a search group of 16 aircraft. At 0730 the first report of the search group was received – two battleships, one heavy cruiser and six destroyers, steering north, had been sighted at 0717 at a distance of 170 miles 275° from the *Enterprise*. Half an hour later, at 0750, a second report placed two carriers and escort steering 330°, 75 miles north of the squadron first sighted. At the same moment a Japanese aircraft was reporting Task Force 61. Two of the American search planes attacked one of the carriers (*Shokaku*) and obtained 2 hits; two others probably hit the stern of a cruiser.

At 0800, 26 October, Task Force 61 was in position Lat. 8° 45' S., Long. 166° 38' E. (about 100 miles north of the Santa Cruz Islands), steering 270° at 23 knots. Between 0830 and 0910 both carriers flew off striking forces, totalling 51 bombers and torpedo bombers, and 23 fighters.

At 0930 the *Enterprise* group, when some 60 miles out, was surprised by fighters of an enemy striking force on its way to attack Task Force 61, which shot down three torpedo-bombers and two fighters, and damaged one torpedo bomber and two fighters so seriously that they returned to the *Enterprise* and landed in the water. The remainder went on, and failing to find the enemy carriers, dive bombed a *Kongo* class battleship at 1040, obtaining two 1,000-lb. bomb hits. The torpedo planes attacked an *Atago* class cruiser but claimed no hits. About 16 enemy aircraft were shot down.

The *Hornet* group found the carrier group and attacked at 1050. dive-bombers secured four 1,000-lb. bomb hits on a large carrier (*Shokaku*) and two hits on the 8-in. cruiser *Chikum* leaving both heavily on fire, while the torpedo planes hit an 8-in. cruiser (*Nachi* class) with two or three torpedoes and made four or five 500-lb. bomb hits on a light cruiser (*Tone* class).

Meanwhile the enemy striking force had attacked the *Hornet*. Soon after 0920 two large groups were picked up by radar, bearing 280° 60 miles distant. The *Hornet* was then in position Lat. 8° 38' S., Long. 166° 43' E., closely screened by her cruisers and destroyers, the *Enterprise* group being 8 or 10 miles to the north-east. There were 15 American fighters overhead. These encountered the enemy shortly before 1000 and shot down a number of them. About 15 dive-bombers got past, however, and at 1012 concentrated their attack on the *Hornet*. At the same time 12 or more aircraft carried out a well co-ordinated torpedo attack from various directions. Flying low over the water, they got in unopposed by American fighters, but suffered heavily from AA fire.[4] Within three minutes the *Hornet* was hit by a bomber, which dived into her and exploded, by three 500-lb. bombs, and by two torpedoes.[5] The latter especially caused very serious damage. Two boiler rooms and the forward engine room were flooded; all propulsion, power and communications failed; large fires broke out, and the ship listed 7° or 8° to starboard. Two minutes later an unarmed torpedo plane crashed into the ship and blew up, starting

---

4. The *Pensacola* estimated that 20 aircraft took part in this torpedo attack, and that over half were shot down before releasing torpedoes.
5. This bomber was armed with two 100 lb. and one 500 lb. bombs. Both the 100 lb. bombs burst, but the 500 lb. one failed to detonate.

another large fire. By 1017 – five minutes after the first bombs had fallen – the attack was over. AA fire had accounted for eight or more torpedo planes and about 12 out of the 15 dive bombers which got through the fighter umbrella.

The *Hornet* was dead in the water by this time. A circular screen was formed round her by the cruisers and some of the destroyers, while others went alongside and despite a heavy roll, did excellent work in assisting to fight the fires. By 1100 these were all under control, and the *Northampton* commenced to take her in tow.

Just at this time, another enemy striking force was opening an attack on the *Enterprise*. When the attack on the *Hornet* started, Rear-Admiral Kincaid had turned to the northward to take advantage of a rain squall. Between 1031 and 1048, the *Enterprise* recovered her search group, which reported having shot down seven enemy fighters and one torpedo bomber. At 1107, the destroyer *Porter*, while rescuing survivors of a friendly aircraft which had crashed, was torpedoed by a submarine, and about five minutes later, the force was heavily attacked from the air.

It appears that the enemy had been unaware of the presence of the second carrier until 1027, when it was revealed by radio voice transmission. He lost no time in taking action, and during the next two hours launched three heavy attacks on her.

The first attack was carried out by about 24 dive bombers between 1115 and 1119. Owing to broken clouds, and confusion on the radar screen due to the large number of aircraft friendly and hostile, the enemy were not seen till well in their dives. About 10 of them were shot down, but the *Enterprise* suffered damage from a near miss and two direct hits, which put the forward lift out of action, and caused heavy damage.

Half an hour later, at 1145, 15 torpedo planes accompanied by fighters, commenced a drawn out attack. This was immediately followed by 12 dive bombers, most of which attacked the screening ships. There were no torpedo hits or bomb hits during the main attack, but some minutes later a solitary bomber slipped through the clouds, and obtained a direct hit on the *South Dakota*, which put two guns of number 2 turret out of action. The destroyer *Smith* was also damaged by a torpedo plane which crashed on her.[6] *Enterprise* was saved from torpedo hits by clever ship handling and well directed AA fire; about 12 torpedo planes and five or more dive-bombers were shot down.

Just after this attack (at 1155), a submarine fired four torpedoes at the *Portland*; one passed ahead, the others probably hit, but failed to explode. Ten

---

6. Although ablaze, the *Smith* maintained her position on the screen. By steering his ship under the stern of the *South Dakota* her captain made use of the spray from the high speed wake to help bring the fire under control.

minutes later the *San Juan* sighted a periscope; torpedoes were fired at her, but she succeeded in combing their tracks.

From 1221 to 1233, 20 dive-bombers attacked the *Enterprise* in shallow dives. They got no hits, though a near miss caused damage, and about nine of them were shot down. They were followed by 15 dive-bombers and nine fighters, which inflicted considerable damage on the *San Juan* with five near misses and a direct hit; 10 of them were shot down. This was the last attack on Task Force 16; over 80 aircraft had taken part in the three attacks; at least 60 had been destroyed,[7] and the damage sustained by the American ships had been remarkably light. As soon as the last attack was over, the *Enterprise* was able to resume landing on aircraft, which by this time were running very short of fuel. Many ran out and had to land in the water.

While these attacks on Task Force 16 were taking place, Task Force 17 – except for a harmless attack by a lone aircraft at 1109 – had not been molested. Soon after noon the *Northampton* had the *Hornet* in tow; later there was a delay owing to the tow parting, but by 1420 they were moving at about three knots, and there were good hopes of saving the ship.[8] But it was not to be.

At 1620 Task Force 17 was attacked by nine torpedo planes and six dive-bombers.[9] The *Northampton* cast off the tow as the torpedo planes came in, and just avoided all torpedoes. Three or four of the aircraft were shot down but one torpedo hit the *Hornet*, flooding the remaining engine room. The list to star board gradually increased to about 20°, and the order was then given to abandon ship, but before this could be done, nine twin engine bombers – unseen in the broken clouds – carried out a high level attack from 8,000 ft.; one bomb struck the *Hornet*, the remainder falling close astern of her and the *San Juan* at 1655. An hour later (1805) just as the last survivors were being picked up, four dive bombers, two of which were shot down, attacked the stricken carrier; one bomb exploded in the hangar just before the island.

Meanwhile Japanese air reconnaissance had sighted Rear-Adm. Lee's Task Force 64 (*Washington*) to the southward of Guadalcanal. Estimating that this force would move east to cover the damaged carrier, the Japanese Commander ordered a night attack by cruisers and destroyers, supported by

---

7. The American fighters shot down about 18 of the enemy, of which 10 were torpedo bombers. On only one occasion did they get into position to attack dive-bombers before they were in their dives. AA fire was effective against the dive bombers, many of them being set on fire in their dives, while others turned away at high altitudes.

8. The engine room department was making progress in regaining power at this time. As a precaution, however, all hands not required for handling and fighting the ship were removed by destroyers.

9. An appeal to the *Enterprise* for fighter protection could not be complied with owing to congestion, caused by the large number of aircraft from both carriers on board, and aggravated by one elevator being out of action.

a strong force of battleships, on the American forces in the Santa Cruz area. Rear-Admiral Murray realized that attack was imminent, and at 1905 ordered the destroyers *Mustin* and *Anderson* to destroy the *Hornet*, withdrawing with the remainder of Task Force 17 to the south-eastward. Badly damaged though she was the *Hornet* resisted the efforts of the destroyers to sink her for two and a half hours. During this time they hit her with nine torpedoes and 369 rounds of 5-in. She was still afloat, burning fiercely and sinking, when at 2140 they ceased fire and followed after Task Force 17 at high speed. The two destroyers were shadowed by flare dropping enemy aircraft until 0100, 27 October; unknown to them they were being pursued by a force of cruisers and destroyers, probably less than 40 miles off, which, however, gave up the chase about midnight, 26–27 October.

To sum up the day's operations, two enemy carriers (*Shokaku* and *Zuikaku*), one battleship (*Kongo* class), two heavy cruisers (*Tone*, *Chikuma*), and a light cruiser had been damaged by bombs, and one heavy cruiser (*Nachi* class) had been hit by two or three torpedoes.[10]

Against this, the Americans had suffered more serious losses: the *Hornet* and one destroyer (*Porter*) being sunk, and the *Enterprise*, South Dakota, *San Juan* and *Smith* damaged. The loss of personnel amounted to 29 officers and 254 ratings. In the air, as at the Battle of the Eastern Solomons, the enemy had suffered shattering losses, at least 123 carrier-borne aircraft having been shot down by fighters and AA fire; the Americans lost 74. Of these only about 20 were shot down, with a loss of 23 officers and 10 ratings, the remainder being lost in the carriers, or owing to the inability of the *Enterprise*, itself damaged, to cope with the large number of her own and the *Hornet*'s aircraft wishing to land on, after the latter had been put out of action.

That night (26/27 October) Task Forces 16 and 17 retired independently to a position about 185 miles south-east of Espiritu Santo, where they re-joined each other and fuelled the next day. Japanese aircraft searched for them in the Santa Cruz area during the 27th, while their surface forces withdrew to their usual position north-east of Guadalcanal. But the fate of the island had already been decided by the failure of their land forces to capture Henderson's Field, and late that day with battered ships and denuded of carrier aircraft they set course for their northern bases.

---

10. In addition, between 24 and 27 October, two heavy cruisers and two light cruisers had been damaged by aircraft from Espiritu Santo and Guadalcanal; and about 10 ships, including a light cruiser and a destroyer had been damaged at Rabaul by bombers of the South West Pacific Command.

Chapter IV

Fourth Japanese Offensive

16. Events Following the Battle of Santa Cruz

After their repulse at the Battle of Santa Cruz, the Japanese began assembling ships and troops for yet another attempt on Guadalcanal. On shore in the island, unsuccessful assaults on the American lines had cost the enemy dear during the last days of October and, before they had time to make good these losses by reinforcements, the Americans launched a counter-attack. Beginning at 0030, 30 October, the *Atlanta* and four destroyers bombarded the Japanese positions behind Point Cruz for eight hours. At dawn the marines, heavily supported from the air, struck across the Matanikau River, and by 3 November had advanced beyond Point Cruz, killing many of the enemy and capturing much equipment. During the night of 2–3 November, however, Japanese cruisers and destroyers managed to land about 1,500 troops with artillery east of Koli Point and the American offensive to the westward was checked to meet this new threat. The force east of Koli was effectively bombed by the *San Francisco*, *Helena* and *Sterett* on 4 November, and after several days fighting, most of it was surrounded at Tetere, and had been annihilated by 11 November.

Meanwhile the Americans had not been slow to take advantage of the retirement forced on the Japanese surface forces by the Battle of Santa Cruz. Appreciating that the retention of Guadalcanal depended on getting enough troops on shore to sustain an offensive, they landed additional troops at Lunga early in November. A force was also landed to the east at Aola Bay to begin a supporting airfield; and arrangements were made for a further 6,000 men with ammunition and supplies to arrive about the middle of the month in two convoys under Rear-Admiral Turner. The airfields in the Lunga area were being developed rapidly; and aircraft operating from them attacked an enemy force of one light cruiser and 10 destroyers on 7 November. One bomb and two torpedo hits were claimed on the cruiser, besides damage to two destroyers: in addition 16 enemy aircraft were shot down.

During the first fortnight of November, too, a decision which had been taken just before the Battle of Santa Cruz to operate 24 submarines – known as Task Force 42 – in the South Pacific Command, bore good fruit. Attacking the enemy's supply line to the Solomons they inflicted the following damage: one destroyer sunk, one probably sunk, one damaged; one torpedo hit on an armoured cruiser and two on a *Natori* class light cruiser; one minesweeper and four transports or oilers had been sunk, and at least three others damaged, and a *Chiyoda* class seaplane tender, had received two torpedo hits.

But almost nightly Japanese troops and supplies were reaching Guadalcanal in destroyers or small boats and though the motor torpedo boat squadron based at Tulagi, aircraft and ships' gunfire took their toll, considerable reinforcement was effected. And the enemy concentration in the Rabaul-Buin area was increasing daily.

17. Naval Situation, 10 November 1942

On 10 November, a coast watcher reported at least 60 ships, including four battleships, six cruisers and 33 destroyers in this area, and the enemy was estimated to have available besides two carriers and six light cruisers. A grand scale attack on Guadalcanal was evidently imminent, and, despite their previous successes, the situation appeared critical to the Americans. Their land forces may have been superior to the Japanese, but the enemy had been constantly bringing in small reinforcements and a large assault force was known to be ready in the north. The Japanese naval and air forces, however, were numerically far stronger.

Their carrier situation was uncertain but it seemed probable that three – the *Hayataka*, *Hitaka*, and *Zuiho* – were present, and possible that the *Zuikaku* would be sufficiently repaired to take part. The only available US carrier was partly repaired *Enterprise*[1] which would not be fully ready for action till 21 November. She was at Noumea, and with the battleships *Washington* and *South Dakota*, cruisers *Northampton* and *San Diego* and eight destroyers formed Task Force 16 under Rear-Admiral Kincaid. The remainder of the American surface forces were operating under the command of Rear-Admiral R.K. Turner, who with his flag in the transport *McCawley* was on passage from Noumea to Guadalcanal, where he was due on 12 November with the reinforcements for the garrison embarked in four transports escorted by the cruisers *Portland* and *Juneau* and four destroyers (Task Force 67). A smaller convoy (Task Group 62.4) consisting of three transports escorted by the

---

1. The *Saratoga* was just leaving Pearl Harbor on completion of repairs after being torpedoed 31 August, and extensive improvements to her AA armament. Immediately after the Battle of Santa Cruz the Americans had requested that a British carrier should be sent to the South Pacific, but this could not be done so long as the result of the Allied landings in North Africa (8 November 1942) was in doubt. The *Victorious* left European waters 16 December, and arrived at Pearl Harbor early in March 1943.

cruisers *Atlanta* (Flag, Rear-Admiral Scott) and four destroyers was due at Guadalcanal next day, 11 November, from Espiritu Santo. Covering these movements was Task Group 67.4 under Rear-Admiral Callaghan consisting of the cruisers *San Francisco, Pensacola* and *Helena* and six destroyers.

18. Japanese Attack on Guadalcanal, 11 November 1942

The Japanese plan on this occasion was to immobilize Henderson's airfield by air attack and bombardment by battleships and then to run in a large troop convoy under powerful escort. On 11 November enemy land-based aircraft began a heavy attack on the airfield. That same day Rear-Admiral Scott's transports commenced landing 6,000 men with much equipment, ammunition and supplies. These were attacked by enemy bombers but only one (the *Zeilin*) was hit. About 13 aircraft were shot down by fighters, and several more by AA fire.

It was clear that the Japanese had started another large scale attack on Guadalcanal, and Rear-Admiral Turner determined not only to land the remainder of the reinforcements due the next day, but also to protect Henderson's Field – the key to the whole position – by engaging the bombarding forces with his escort forces. This bold decision to accept heavy risks for an adequate object was amply justified in the event.

At sunset, 11 November the transports withdrew from the unloading area to Indispensable Strait and joined the second convoy which was approaching. The surface units under Rear-Admiral Callaghan swept east and west of Savo Island during the evening but nothing was seen of the enemy and the convoys then proceeded to the anchorage. At dawn, 12 November unloading was recommenced. This was interrupted by a heavy air ride by 21 torpedo bombers escorted by 12 fighters at 1405: able manoeuvring, good gunfire and fighter protection from Guadalcanal enabled all the ships to escape unscathed.[2] It is believed that all but one of the torpedo bombers and several of the fighters were destroyed.

Numerous enemy reports during the day led to the belief that the enemy intended to attack the transports or bombard Henderson's Field during the night, with a force likely to consist of two battleships, four to six cruisers and ten or more destroyers. At 1815, 12 November, Rear-Admiral Turner left Lunga Roads, and proceeded to Espiritu Santo with the transports and three escorting destroyers, leaving Rear-Admirals Callaghan and Scott with five

---

2. The *San Francisco* was damaged by a torpedo plane which crashed into her fire, and the *Buchanan* was hit by a 5-in. projectile fried by one of the American ships.

cruisers and eight destroyers[3] (Task Group 67.4) to deal with the approaching enemy force.

At this time Task Force 16 under the command of Rear-Admiral Kincaid, the *Enterprise*, two battleships, two cruisers and eight destroyers,[4] was steaming north from Noumea with orders to be in a flying off position south of Guadalcanal on the morning of 13 November. From this setting developed the decisive actions known as the Battle of Guadalcanal, which settled the issue of the whole campaign. This battle consisted of two entirely separate night actions – on the nights of 12/13 and 14/15 November – between strong surface forces on each side, with a series of air operations over the whole period. The net result was so severe a defeat of the Japanese that they gave up hope of recapturing the island and from then on confined their efforts merely to delaying the final expulsion of their forces.

19. Battle of Guadalcanal, 12–15 November, 1942

(i) Night Action, 12–13 November.

After escorting Rear-Admiral Turner's transports to the south-eastward, Rear-Admiral Callaghan's Force re-entered Lengo Channel at midnight, 12–13 November. Ships were in line ahead in the order *Cushing* (Commander, 10th Destroyer Division), *Laffey*, *Sterrett*, *O'Bannon*, the light cruiser *Atlanta* (Flag Rear-Admiral Scott), heavy cruisers *San Francisco* (Flag Rear-Admiral Callaghan), *Portland*, light cruisers *Helena*, *Juneau*, destroyers *Aaron Ward* (Commander, 12th Destroyer Squadron), *Barton*, *Monssen* and *Fletcher*. The night was dark and overcast.

First contact with the enemy was obtained at 0124, 13 November when the *Helena*'s SG radar picked up three groups of ships bearing 310°-312°, range 27,000–32,000 yards. There were indications that the enemy consisted of heavy ships, screened ahead on either flank by light forces. The American column was at the time near Lunga Point, steering 280°; Rear-Admiral Callaghan altered course to 310° and shortly afterwards to 000°. The enemy was closing rapidly on a south-easterly course. Besides these three groups, there seems to have been a further formation of three or more ships to the north-east, range 10,000 to 15,000 yards when the action started. Unfortunately, Rear-Admiral Callaghan's flagship was not equipped with SG radar, and

---

3. Task Group 67.4, *San Francisco* (Flag Rear-Admiral Callaghan), *Portland*, *Atlanta* (Flag Rear-Admiral Scott), *Helena*, *Juneau*, eight destroyers.

4. Task Force 16, *Enterprise* (Flag Rear Admiral Kincaid), *Washington* (Rear-Admiral W.A. Lee), *South Dakota*, *Northampton*, *San Diego*, eight destroyers, had left Noumea at noon, 11 November, when it became clear that the enemy was committed to a full scale attack, but this was too late for it to arrive in time to interfere with the threatened bombardment, 12–13 November.

much of the advantage to be expected from the superiority of the American radar equipment was therefore wasted. Before Rear-Admiral Callaghan could get a clear picture of the situation the head of his column became mixed with the enemy and confusion arose before the firing began. At 0148 he ordered odd numbered ships to open fire to starboard, even numbered to port; simultaneously enemy ships close aboard on both hands switched on searchlights, and one of the fiercest actions of the war commenced.

The three approaching enemy columns were 2,000 to 3,000 yards apart, with the two flank columns advanced. The screen of the northern column had just passed ahead of the American van destroyers; Rear-Admiral Callaghan therefore found himself about midway between the flank columns, and directly in the path of the main body which contained battleships.

The American fire was very effective. Within five minutes one ship in the northern column, believed to be a light cruiser, blew up, and others were damaged before they could retire on the main body. In the southern column, which also retired, the *Portland* and *Atlanta* each sank a destroyer, the *Helena* heavily hit a target believed to be an armoured cruiser and saw ships in the column were damaged.

Most of the American ships received hits during this brief engagement; the *Atlanta*, however, which was hit by one or two torpedoes, was the only one seriously damaged, possibly because the enemy were firing bombarding ammunition from their main armament. But the formation was no longer an organized force. Considerable confusion existed, and it was difficult to distinguish friend from foe. At 0155, Rear-Admiral Callaghan, in the belief that some of his ships were firing on the *Atlanta*,[5] ordered 'cease fire'.

Within a minute or so the second phase of the action began with the arrival of the enemy main body. A *Kongo* class battleship passed close to port of the *Cushing* and through the van destroyer column astern of the *Laffey* (the original second ship in the line). She was being hit repeatedly by gunfire, probably from the *San Francisco* and *Portland*. The *Laffey* increased speed to avoid being rammed by the battleship and then fired torpedoes, but the range was too short: just afterwards she was herself hit by a torpedo and within a few minutes blew up with heavy loss of life. The battleship reversed her course; she was then struck by three torpedoes from the *Cushing* and disappeared slowly to the westward. At about the same time the *O'Bannon*

---

5. There is reason to believe that the *Atlanta* was in fact engaged by the *San Francisco*. She reports being hit by three or four salvoes and received 19 8-in. hits at a range of about 3,500 yards. The *San Francisco* fired two salvoes at 'an enemy small cruiser or large destroyer', 3300 yards, just forward of the starboard beam at the time. Reported movements and relative positions are so incomplete that no conclusions can be reached from them.

also scored three torpedo hits on a battleship, already badly damaged by gunfire; there was a tremendous explosion 'and the battleship was enveloped from bow to stern in a great sheet of flame'. During this second phase of the action (from 0155 to 0200), a large enemy ship rolled over and sank 1,500 yards to starboard of the *Aaron Ward* (leading the rear destroyers): the *Helena* nearly rammed a large capsized vessel with a beam greater than her own and observed an enemy ship larger than the *San Francisco* burning from bow to stern and apparently sinking: and the *Monssen* (two ships astern of the *Aaron Ward*) made two torpedo hits on a *Kongo* battleship about 4,000 yards to the starboard.[6] The *Barton* was sunk by two torpedoes, the *Cushing* was heavily hit by gunfire and brought to a standstill, and the *Portland* was hit by a torpedo aft, which damaged her steering gear, so that she could only steam in circles. While doing so she continued to fire with good effect on a battleship. The *Juneau* had by this time been put out of action by a torpedo hit in her forward engine room.

In the third phase of the action, which lasted from 0200 to 0230, the *San Francisco* engaged a battleship, whose upper works she seriously damaged; most of her own secondary battery was knocked out by 14-in. shell, but one gun in local control detonated the depth charges of a destroyer, which probably sank as a result.

The *San Francisco* herself came under a crossfire, and was severely damaged, sustaining 15 hits of major calibre and many of smaller calibre. She lost about 85 killed, including Rear-Admiral Callaghan and most of his staff, and her Commanding Officer, Captain Young, during this engagement. Her situation was somewhat relieved by the *Helena*, which heavily hit one of the larger ships engaging her, and also set two destroyers on fire. By this time the enemy ships were probably firing at each other. Between 0205 and 0220 the *Sterrett* got two torpedo hits on the stern of a damaged *Kongo* battleship, part of whose crew were seen abandoning ship, and at about 0230 she torpedoed a *Fubuki* class destroyer, which blew up. The explosion illuminated the *Sterrett*, which at once came under a heavy fire and was damaged. The *Monssen*, meanwhile, had been abandoned at about 0220, after being wrecked by about 40 hits;[7] and the *Cushing*, already dead in the water, having fired her torpedoes, came under a heavy fire, and was abandoned. The *Aaron Ward* had passed through the entire enemy formation at some time after 0205, receiving three 14-in. hits, two 8-in. hits and five smaller. She sank or helped to sink a cruiser

---

6. The enemy losses appear higher than they actually were owing to the duplication of the reports of various observers, and the confusion inseparable from night action. It is also possible that some ships engaged 'phantoms', i.e. their own shadows thrown by gun flashes, etc., on low lying cloud banks.
7. She continued to burn throughout the night and blew up about noon 13 November.

and damaged two destroyers, then lost power and remained stopped until after daylight, when she was towed to Tulagi. The *Fletcher* torpedoed a heavy cruiser during this period.

When firing finally ceased the enemy retired to the north west. Nine ships were left burning on the scene of the action. Three of these were the *Atlanta*, *Cushing* and *Monssen*.

The remnant of the American Force capable of steaming withdrew towards Espiritu Santo at 18 knots. This consisted of the *Helena*, *O'Bannon* and *Fletcher*, which were not seriously damaged, and the badly damaged *San Francisco*, *Juneau* and *Sterett*. The *Portland* and *Aaron Ward* remained immobilized in the battle area; the *Laffey* and *Barton* had been sunk.

(ii) Operations, 13–14 November.

Dawn broke on the scene of the battle at about 0530, 13 November. The *Portland*, still not under control, found herself within range of a damaged *Shigure* class destroyer, which she promptly sank at 12,500 yards range. She could also see a cruiser on the northern horizon and a *Kongo* battleship steaming slowly in circles north-cast of Savo Island. The latter fired four 2-gun salvos at the *Aaron Ward* at 25,000 yards range; then she was attacked by American aircraft and ceased fire on the destroyer. The *Portland* eventually succeeded in reaching Tulagi with the help of a tug, but the *Atlanta*, which had lost 40 per cent. of her personnel, including Rear-Admiral Scott, after being towed to the vicinity of Lunga Point, sank at 2015 that evening.

During the forenoon of 13 November an enemy carrier[8] with a battleship and other warships, was sighted about 250 miles to the northward of Guadalcanal apparently as cover for their damaged ships, or possibly to attack those of the Americans. Anxiety on this account was felt for the ships on passage to Espiritu Santo, but no interference was encountered from these forces. The *Juneau*, however, fell a victim to submarine attack. She was struck by a torpedo at 1101, 13 November, when in Lat. 10° 32' S., Long. 161° 02' E. and the whole ship disintegrated, nearly all her crew being lost.[9]

Air attacks on the damaged Japanese battleship off Savo Islana, which proved to be the *Hiyei*, were carried out intermittently throughout the day. Seven torpedoes[10] and two 1000 lb. bomb hits were claimed, but when

---

8. No Japanese carriers were in fact present at these operations, though frequently reported from the air. It is possible that some of the troop transports were camouflaged with the deliberate intention of simulating the appearance of carriers from the air.
9. The Senior Officer present altered course away from the area, reporting the position by signal through an escorting aircraft for which he had asked. This signal did not get through and in consequence many of the 60-odd who survived the explosion perished on rafts.
10. The torpedoes were all set for 10 ft. depth.

last seen she was still afloat, with a cruiser and five destroyers standing by. She sank during the night. Air reconnaissance sighted another damaged battleship (*Fuso* class), between Florida and Santa Isabel Island, which was hit and further damaged by B.17s from Espiritu Santo; a destroyer beached on Olevuga Island (north of Florida Island) was also sighted. An unidentified ship blew up and sank south-west of Florida Island, in the course of the day.

Large enemy troop convoys which had closed Guadalcanal on 12 November ready for a landing next day returned to Buin after the defeat inflicted on their surface forces by Rear-Admiral Callaghan. They put to sea again during the night of the 13–14 November for another attempt.

Meanwhile, Task Force 16 from Noumea had reached the position to which it had been ordered, some 300 miles south of Guadalcanal in the morning of 13 November. As one of the *Enterprise*'s lifts, damaged at the Battle of Santa Cruz, had not yet been repaired, it was decided to reduce the number of aircraft on board and nine torpedo bombers, with six fighters, were flown off to Guadalcanal. These fell in with the damaged *Hiyei* en route, which they attacked and hit; they proved of great value in subsequent operations, working from Henderson's Field.

Early that forenoon the *Pensacola* (Flag/Rear-Admiral M.S. Tisdale) joined Task Force 16, and at 1110 orders were received from Vice-Admiral Halsey, who had relieved Vice-Admiral Ghormley as Commander, South Pacific, to proceed to the support of the ships damaged in the action of the previous night, but to remain south of Lat. 11° 40′ S., unless conditions required otherwise. Rear-Admiral Kincaid increased speed to 23 knots and steered to the northward. Further orders from the Commander, South Pacific, received at 1653, 13 November, directed him to organize a battleship striking force to intercept enemy bombarding forces, expected off Lunga Point during the night; this force, however, was not to proceed on this duty without express orders from the Commander, South Pacific. The battleships *Washington* (Flag) *South Dakota* and four destroyers were at once detailed under Rear-Admiral Lee, and at 1929 orders were received for them to attack that night, but it was then too late for them to reach the Lunga area in time, and an enemy force of unknown strength bombarded Henderson's Field from 0120 to 0240, 14 November, unopposed, except by six MTBs from Tulagi. These scored at least one torpedo hit and caused the enemy to withdraw. The bombardment destroyed three aircraft and damaged 17 fighters – most of them slightly – on the airfield.

The enemy was apparently determined to push reinforcements through to Guadalcanal on 14 November regardless of loss. Early in the day American air reconnaissance reported a convoy of 12 ships escorted by three light cruisers and eight destroyers steaming down New Georgia Sound direct for Guadalcanal.

An enemy cruiser force had also been sighted to the westward. This force was attacked by aircraft from Henderson's Field, which made three torpedo hits on a light cruiser and two 1,000 lb. bomb hits on an *Atago* class cruiser; search planes from the *Enterprise* subsequently reported that both these ships sank. The *Enterprise* had closed Guadalcanal during the night and at dawn, 14 November, was in a position about 200 miles to the southward. On receipt of the report of the cruiser group, she ordered 17 bombers and 10 fighters – already launched – to attack it, and then go on to Guadalcanal. Later, she sent another striking force of eight bombers and 12 fighters to attack the large convoy, and then with only 18 fighters for her own protection on board withdrew to the southward, taking no further part in the operations. Both striking forces reached their objectives, and after inflicting damage, landed at Henderson's Field and with the shore-based aircraft, participated in repeated attacks on the convoy during the day. Details of these attacks are not available, but many transports and warships suffered damage. By 1900 14 November, of 12 ships reported in the convoy 'one or more were sunk, six were seriously damaged, and with others were milling around about 60 miles north-west of Savo Island.' These were attacked again before dark, when several were sunk and three were left heavily on fire.[11]

(iii) Night action, 14–15 November.
Meanwhile Rear-Admiral Lee's battleship force had arrived some 50 miles to the S. by W. of Guadalcanal towards the close of the forenoon of 14th November. From the reports received throughout the day it seemed almost certain that the enemy would renew their bombarding operations that night, probably using capital ships, and in the hope of surprising them Rear-Admiral Lee remained in this vicinity till late in the afternoon, when he shaped course to the northward, passing between Russell Island and Savo Island in the early evening. Nothing was seen of the enemy north of Savo Island, and a south-easterly course was then steered till 2253, 14 November when course was altered to 270° the Force then being due north of Lunga Point. The Force was in column formation, the four destroyers led by the *Walke* 2 miles ahead of the *Washington*. The distance between the battleships was 1,700 yards; the speed 17 knots. The moon was in the first quarter and visibility was good.

---

11. The total damage claimed by aircraft operating from Guadalcanal (including the *Enterprise* group) on 14 and 15 November was: one heavy cruiser (*Nachi* class), two light cruisers, twelve transports sunk, one heavy cruiser and one destroyer damaged.

At 2307 the *South Dakota* sighted three ships bearing 330°, dimly illuminated by the setting moon. The leading ship was a battleship or heavy cruiser, the other two light cruisers. They were to the eastward of Savo in almost the same water as the American ships had traversed on their run to the south-east. At 2317 the *Washington* opened fire on the leading ship, at radar range 18,000 yards, and immediately afterwards the *South Dakota* engaged the next astern. Both targets were hit and set afire by the first or second salvos; after seven or eight salvos, within seven minutes of opening fire, both targets sank. The rear ship of the enemy column may have retired, or may have been a ship which appeared some five minutes later on the *South Dakota*'s starboard quarter, and was engaged by her at a range of 10,000–11,000 yards. After a few salvos, the enemy was seen to break in two and sink at 2333.

Soon after first contact, Rear-Admiral Lee had ordered an alteration of course to 300°, and the column was at this time heading midway between Cape Esperance and Savo Island. At 2326 the leading American destroyers opened fire on a group of enemy destroyers, possibly accompanied by a cruiser, which had stood south close to the coast of Savo Island.[12] The battleships joined in and at least two of the enemy were damaged, but not before firing torpedoes which at 2334 sank the *Preston* and *Walke* with heavy loss of life. The *Benham* was also torpedoed but was able to retire. At this time the *Washington* and *South Dakota* came under fire from an unidentified enemy force to starboard; neither ship was hit, most of the enemy's shot going over. The *South Dakota*, however, was having electrical trouble which deprived her of all power for three minutes and put her SG radar out of action from 2333 to 2346. At 2340 speed was increased to 26 knots. During the next five minutes the *South Dakota* engaged targets close to Savo Island. By that time, the formation was drawing to the westward of the island and targets were fine on the starboard quarters.[13]

The Washington, meanwhile, had been following on her radar screen a group of eight enemy ships closing on her starboard bow. Rear-Admiral Lee did not know the exact position of the *South Dakota* because of a blind arc astern in the *Washington*'s SG radar, nor was he aware of the breakdown of the *South Dakota*'s radar and her consequent ignorance of the enemy approaching from the north-west. At 0000, 15 November, the *South Dakota* was illuminated by searchlight from just before the starboard beam and came under a heavy fire from three or four ships at about 6,000 yards range. The *Washington*

---

12. 'The gunfire of our destroyers forced the enemy to fire his torpedoes prematurely and at our destroyer formation instead of our battleships.' – Rear-Admiral Lee's report.
13. One salvo from No. 3 turret set fire to the *South Dakota*'s aircraft on her stern; the next salvo fortunately blew two out of the three aircraft over the side and extinguished most of the fires.

immediately opened fire on the leading enemy ship, a battleship, subsequently identified as the *Kirishima*, and the *South Dakota* shortly afterwards engaged the second ship – the illuminating ship – which broke in two and sank. The first and third ships were hit and heavily smoking, and the fourth ship was believed to be damaged when the action came to an end at about 0010, 15 November.[14]

During this short engagement, the *South Dakota* received many hits, including 14-in., 8-in., 6-in. and smaller. About 30 men were killed and 60 wounded; five oil fuel compartments were holed, and much damage done to radars, guns and equipment. For the time being, she had become more of a liability than an asset, and her Commanding Officer 'wisely decided to retire – to the great relief of the Task Force Commander', and set course to the south-westward at 0010, 15 November.

The *Washington* continued to the north-westward and northward, seeking enemy transports or other suitable targets, until at 0033 she altered course sharply to starboard to avoid a smoke screen laid by some Japanese destroyers. Appreciating that by this time the transports had been sufficiently delayed to prevent their reaching Guadalcanal before daylight, Rear-Admiral Lee decided the time had come to withdraw, and shaped course to the south-westward. Several torpedo attacks – mostly from the port quarter – were made on her during retirement, and 'four or five torpedoes came uncomfortably close and were avoided only by bold and skilful ship handling'. After clearing Russell Island, radar contact was established with the damaged *Benham*[15] and *Gwin*, who were directed to proceed independently to Espiritu Santo while the *Washington* herself re-joined the *South Dakota*.

The enemy, completely foiled in their attempt, were retiring to the northward. All they had managed to do during the night was to beach three transports and a store ship on the Japanese-held coast off Cape Esperance. These were attacked and damaged by aircraft early next morning, and finally destroyed by the destroyer *Meade*, which had arrived at Tulagi the day before escorting a fleet auxiliary, and now found herself the only warship in the area. She also rescued 266 survivors from the *Walke* and *Preston* and one man who had been blown overboard from the *Benham*.

Thus ended the Battle of Guadalcanal, and with it the Japanese hopes of recapturing the island. They had made their great effort, with the strongest

14. The *South Dakota* states this took place at 2348, 14 November, the *Washington* at 0000 15 November. The discrepancy cannot be reconciled, but the plot of the action on the chart tends to confirm the *Washington*'s estimate.
15. The *Benham* began to break up while en route for Espiritu Santo that afternoon. After taking its crew on board, the *Gwin* sank her by gunfire.

force available;[16] beyond landing negligible reinforcements, with no supplies, they had achieved nothing, and had suffered such losses in surface ships that for the first time since 9th August the Americans achieved superiority in this respect.

In the words of the Commander-in-Chief, Pacific Fleet, 'In four days the fate of Guadalcanal and the fate of our campaign in the South Pacific for months to come were decided. There were many courageous decisions, from lowest to highest commands, and heroic actions without number. First place among them however, belongs to the decision of the Commander, Task Force 67, well knowing the odds and possible destruction of his forces, to send his cruisers and destroyers against the Japanese battleship bombarding force, and the resolute manner in which our ships were led into the resulting battle.'

---

16. In a captured Japanese combat report, covering the widespread sea and air operations of the last three weeks of October, there appears this statement: 'Consequently, it must be said that the success or failure in recapturing Guadalcanal Island, and the results of the vital naval battle related to it, is the fork in the road which leads to Victory for them or for us. The Imperial army and navy must forget the countless hardships they bear together, for this is the time when we must dash forward to attain our goal.'

Chapter V

Japanese on the Defensive

20. Events following Battle of Guadalcanal.

After the Battle of Guadalcanal there was a lull of about a fortnight. Thoroughly defeated, the Japanese naval forces temporarily abandoned their advanced base in the Shortlands Islands, and fell back to the Rabaul area, while the American Naval Forces withdrew to Espiritu Santo and Noumea to reorganize and make good damage, a striking force of cruisers and destroyers (Task Force 67) under Rear Adm. Kincaid being held in readiness at Espiritu Santo.

During this period the enemy pressed on with their efforts to strengthen their position in the mid-Solomons, and commenced a new airfield at Munda, New Georgia (about 200 miles from Guadalcanal[1]); two escorted cargo ships were damaged in this area by American aircraft on 28 November. On shore at Guadalcanal, the American Marines had taken the offensive and by the end of November had driven the main Japanese forces well to the westward of Point Cruz. At the same time they had dispersed the enemy detachments to the east of the Tenaru River. For these operations they had been supported by naval bombardment. At this stage, American Army Units arrived to take over from the Marines, and during the change-over, active shore operations were suspended. To the enemy however, the situation must have appeared very serious, and on 24 November a marked increase in shipping[2] in the Buin-Faisi area indicated to the Americans that an attempt at reinforcement was in preparation.

The attempt took place on the night of 30 November-1 December and was frustrated in the night action known as the Battle of Lunga Point, at a heavy cost in American cruiser strength as the result of torpedo attack.

21st Battle of Lunga Point, 30 November–1 December 1942
On the evening of 29 November Rear-Admiral Wright who had succeeded Rear-Admiral Kincaid in Command of Task Force 67[3] only the day before,

---

1. The construction of the airfield was so cleverly concealed by the use of natural camouflage of coconut trees that its existence, though suspected, was not definitely verified until early December, when it was nearly complete.
2. By 27 November about 25–30 ships were reported in this area, as compared with about a dozen a week earlier.
3. Task Force 67: cruisers *Minneapolis* (Flag Rear-Admiral Wright), *New Orleans, Pensacola, Honolulu* (Flag Rear-Admiral Tisdale), *Northampton*; destroyers *Perkins, Drayton, Fletcher, Maury*. The destroyers *Lamson* and *Lardner* joined the Force while on passage.

received orders to proceed to sea as soon as possible, in order to intercept an enemy force of eight destroyers and six transports expected to be off Tassafaronga (Guadalcanal) at 2300, 30th November. Task Force 67 sailed that night at high speed and reached Lengo Channel by 2145, 30 November.

Rear-Admiral Wright's intention was to engage by radar at a range of about 12,000 yards, after his destroyers had delivered an unseen torpedo attack, also by radar. For this purpose the destroyers were stationed two miles on the 'engaged' bow; after launching their torpedoes they were to clear the range quickly, and engage with gunfire when the cruisers opened fire.[4]

Task Force 67 cleared Lengo Channel at 2245, 30 November, and shaped course 320°, 20 knots in the order *Minneapolis* (Flag), *New Orleans, Pensacola, Honolulu* (Flag, Rear-Admiral Tisdale) *Northampton*, the destroyers *Fletcher, Perkins, Maury* and *Drayton* being stationed 300° 2 miles from the flagship, and the *Lamson* and *Lardner*, which had joined too late to receive the plan of attack, astern of the *Northampton*. It was a dark night, with overcast sky and surface visibility of about 2 miles. At 2238 the cruisers formed line of bearing 140° on course 280°. At 2306 the *Minneapolis* obtained an SG radar contact of ships off Cape Esperance bearing 284°, 23,000 yards, and three minutes later the Squadron turned together to 320°, bringing the cruisers into line ahead. There seemed to be seven or eight ships in the enemy group, steering a south easterly course at 15 knots. At the same time, another group of six vessels, about 4 miles to the south eastward of those picked up by radar, was reported by aircraft to be approaching Tassafaronga close inshore but this report did not reach Rear-Admiral Wright.[5]

At 2314 course was altered to port to 300°; at the same time, the commander of the destroyers in the van asked permission to fire torpedoes but was ordered to wait till the range had closed.[6] Five minutes later (2319) the torpedo attack began; the *Fletcher* fired 10, and the *Perkins* (her next astern), eight torpedoes

---

4 Arrangements had been made for aircraft from Guadalcanal to illuminate the enemy with flares after action was joined. The aircraft, however, did not arrive in time, and the fares dropped by them actually illuminated damaged American ships rather than the enemy. Both sides made use of the star shell.

5. Rear-Admiral Wright had received no definite intelligence of the enemy since the original signal ordering the operation, except a coast watcher's report of the departure of 12 destroyers from Buin on the night of 29 November, and a signal from the Commander, South Pacific, that the enemy force might consist of destroyers only. Aircraft searches on 30 November, including special ones from Guadalcanal, had failed to locate any approaching enemy ships, despite good weather and 100 per cent coverage of search sectors. It is still (March,1944) unknown exactly what enemy forces were present in the battle.

6. By radio-telephony. It was subsequently thought that this may have been intercepted by the enemy, and thus have given away the presence of Task Force 67.

at ranges of 7,300[7] and 5,000 yards respectively. The *Drayton*, the third in the line, owing to an erratic radar plot, fired two torpedoes only, and the *Maury*, which was not fitted with SG radar and could not identify targets, fired none. Almost simultaneously the *Minneapolis* opened fire (2320) and the action became general. The results of the destroyer attack are unknown; some minutes afterwards a target 4,000 yards on the port beam disappeared in a violent explosion and a number of 'terrific explosions occurred along the beach', towards which the American ships were firing by that time, the destroyers retired at high speed to the westward of Savo Island, exchanging gunfire with the enemy until out of range, and took no further part in the action.[8]

The cruisers, meanwhile, were engaging the enemy to the southward. For seven minutes all went well. The *Minneapolis* opened fire at 2320[9] on the right-hand (rear) enemy ship, bearing 260° at a range of 9,200 yards; she saw her 'disintegrate', and then sank a destroyer coming in to attack from the westward; the *New Orleans* and the *Northampton* engaged the leading ship of the formation – a destroyer bearing 220°, range 8,700 yards, which blew up – while the *Pensacola* hit a three-funnelled cruiser, which capsized. Then things began to go awry. The *Minneapolis* had just fired a salvo at a large cruiser or destroyer being engaged by the *New Orleans*, when at 2327 she was hit on the port side by two torpedoes; one exploded in No. 2 boiler room, causing extensive damage and flooding, and the other blew off the bow and started large petrol fires forward. One minute later, a torpedo struck the *New Orleans*, port side forward, detonating her fore magazines, and causing very serious damage. The entire bow, including No.1 turret disappeared, and the whole crew of No. 2 turret was killed. The *Minneapolis*, though apparently sinking, continued firing for five minutes after being hit; then, at 2333, all power failed, and she came to a standstill. With his flagship immobilized and communications failing Rear-Admiral Wright directed Rear-Admiral Tisdale in the *Honolulu* to take over the conduct of the battle.

Deprived at a stroke of its two leading ships, the American formation was thrown into some confusion, the third in the line, the *Pensacola*, hauled out to port to clear the *New Orleans*, while the *Honolulu* and *Northampton* altered sharply to starboard, steadying independently on northerly courses. *Pensacola* continued to the westward roughly parallel to the coast, engaging two enemy

---

7. Commander-in-Chief Pacific Fleet, (Admiral Nimitz) subsequently considered these ranges at night excessive and remarked that ranges at night of more than 4,000 to 5,000 yards were not acceptable.
8. While on a north-westerly course rounding Savo Island, the *Drayton* detected the vessels to the westward, and fired four torpedoes at them, with unknown results.
9. 'At 2320, after receipt of report that our destroyers in the van had fired torpedoes, and when range from *Minneapolis* to right-hand target was 10,000 yards, I ordered commence firing with guns.' Rear-Admiral Wright's Report.

targets – both retiring at high speed – with unknown results. At 2339 her last target had just disappeared when a torpedo struck her port side abreast the main mast. Many compartments, including the after engine room, were flooded; a 13° list developed, and fires were started which were not fully under control 12 hours later.

Meanwhile the *Honolulu* followed by the *Northampton* had gradually hauled round to the westward. The *Honolulu*[10] had already sunk one destroyer, possibly two, but after her alteration to clear the damaged cruisers, was unable to pick up fresh targets. The *Northampton* sank another destroyer during this phase of the action (2337); then, at 2348, she was herself struck by two torpedoes[11] port side amidships, which wrecked many compartments, started fires, and brought the ship to a standstill with a 10° list. This brought the action to a close. Five fires were burning in the enemy target area; the remainder of their ships had disappeared. They were probably withdrawing to the south-westward, keeping close inshore to Cape Esperance. Rear-Admiral Tisdale in the *Honolulu* searched the area to the west and north of Savo Island, but nothing more was seen of them. He then returned to the scene of action and directed salvage and rescue operations. The *Northampton* was listing 35° by 0245, 1 December, and the order was given to abandon ship; 20 minutes later (0304), just after her Captain had left, she turned over on her beam ends and sank. The other damaged cruisers 'by able seamanship and damage controls'[12] managed to reach Tulagi, where temporary repairs were effected.

Once again the Japanese torpedo efficiency – both tactical and technical – had been demonstrated. Though apparently taken by surprise in the first instance, in under half an hour by their mastery of this weapon they put four 8-in. cruisers completely out of action (one of which subsequently sank). On the other hand, the superiority of the American radar equipment and gunnery received fresh confirmation. Though the actual damage inflicted is still uncertain,[13] there is no doubt that the Americans hit such targets as offered early and hard, while the Japanese gunfire made little or no impression.

Summing up, the Commander-in-Chief, Pacific Fleet, remarked that 'the operation for this engagement was simple and well-conceived. Except for the failure of the illumination planes to arrive on schedule, the TBS

---

10. The *Honolulu*, 3,000 yards astern of the *Minneapolis*, was late picking up a target with her SG radar and did not open fire till about the time the two leading cruisers were torpedoed (2327). In the ensuing six minutes she engaged the two destroyers.
11. Fired, it is thought, either by submarines, or by retiring enemy ships which could not be picked up by radar against the land.
12. Report of Admiral C. W. Nimitz, USN Commander-in-Chief, Pacific Fleet.
13. Result of the Battle of Lunga Point: 4 Japanese destroyers sunk and 2 damaged; 1 US heavy cruiser sunk and 3 damaged.

communications before the torpedo attack, and the long range at which the torpedo attack was delivered, the conduct of the battle was correct. Rear-Admiral Wright led his force into action resolutely and intelligently, and opened fire at a range that should have permitted avoiding surprise torpedo attack. When his flagship was immobilized, he transferred direction of the force to Rear-Admiral Tisdale, who continued the battle and sought the enemy with determination. The fortunes of war and the restricted waters in which we were forced to bring the enemy into action caused our ships to suffer greater loss than their leadership and action merited and prevented them from inflicting heavier damage on the enemy.'

22. Operations in Guadalcanal Area; December, 1942–January, 1943

The Battle of Lunga was the last occasion on which considerable American Naval Forces were engaged with enemy ships in the fight for Guadalcanal. On shore, the relief of the US Marines by the Army proceeded smoothly during December, and by the end of the month preparations for a major offensive were well advanced. This was launched early in the New Year (1943), and continued vigorously throughout January, constantly confining the Japanese to a smaller portion of the island. Four destroyers based on Guadalcanal from 16 January onwards assisted the army by bombarding enemy positions as required, and on 1 February covered a landing at Nugu Point, on the west coast of the island. The landing was unopposed, but one of the destroyers – the *De Haven* – was sunk by air attack to the southward of Savo Island that evening. Two enemy submarines were destroyed during this period, one off Coughlan Harbor by the *Nicholas* and *Radford* on 28 January and another by the New Zealand trawlers *Kiwi* and *Moa* a mile to the westward of Cape Esperance on 30 January.

During all this time the enemy continued to run in small reinforcements and supplies in high speed craft at night. This traffic was known as the 'Tokyo Express', and was constantly attacked by aircraft and the motor torpedo boats based on Tulagi, casualties being suffered by both sides. But the ultimate outcome of the campaign was no longer in doubt, and in January the American Naval Forces were able to carry the offensive into enemy waters and attack their positions in the central Solomons.

23. Bombardments of Munda and Kolombangara Island.

The first such operation was directed against the recently completed airfield at Munda, New Georgia. This was bombarded on the night of the

4/5 January by part of Task Force 67, which was covering the landing of reinforcements in Guadalcanal at the time. The bombardment was carried out by three 6-in. cruisers, the *Nashville* (Flag, Rear-Admiral Ainsworth), *St. Louis* and *Helena*, and the destroyers *Fletcher* and *O'Bannon*. A submarine – the *Grayback* – was stationed off Rendova Island to assist navigation; this, in conjunction with the use of radar, enabled the operation to be carried out exactly as planned. A total of 2,773 rounds of 6-in. and 1,376 rounds of 5-in, was fired, approximately 80 per cent. of which fell in the target area, according to reports from the spotting Catalina; several fires were started, and there were numerous explosions.[14] The bombarding ships rejoined Task Force 67 to the westward of Guadalcanal next morning (5 January). Shortly afterwards the force was surprised by Japanese dive bombers[15] but escaped unhurt, except the *Achilles*, which received a direct hit on No. 3 turret.

Three weeks later, on 24 January, a similar operation was carried out against enemy troops and installations at the Vila and Stanmore Plantations, in the South Kolombangara Island (north of New Georgia). The restricted waters of Kula Gulf would not afford much manoeuvring room, and the plan was therefore to get in unobserved and to withhold fire until headed out but on this occasion the difficulties of an unseen approach were enhanced by the fact that there was a full moon; it was also anticipated – wrongly as it turned out – that so soon after Munda the enemy would be on the *qui vive*.

The bombardment was carried out by the cruisers *Nashville* and *Helena*, and destroyers *Nicholas*, *De Haven*, *Radford*, *O'Bannon*, the cruisers *Honolulu* and *St. Louis*, with three destroyers operating to seaward in support. The Force was picked up south of Guadalcanal by enemy reconnaissance planes at 1030, 23 January, and shadowed all day while making to the westwards,[16] but, just after sunset, the whole sky became overcast, and at 2000, when course was altered to the northward, it was too dark for the turn to be detected. At 0014, 24 January, however, two large Japanese aircraft – tentatively identified as Mitsubishi twin-engine bombers – sighted the force to the northward of New Georgia and remained over it, frequently challenging, for about half an hour; eventually, receiving no reply, they apparently decided it was friendly,

14. The damage was, however, so quickly remedied that enemy aircraft were operating from the field in less than 18 hours. Commenting on the operation, the Commander-in-Chief, Pacific Fleet, remarked: 'As a diversion, as training, and as a deterrent against air attack on Guadalcanal during troop replacement, the operation was of value. Damage to airfields, or other land positions is so transient that ships should not ordinarily be risked to bombard airfields or other positions, except in close support of ground operations.'
15. The Force was exercising guns' crews against friendly fighters at the time. Radar failed to distinguish the approaching enemy from these, and when the attack developed some of the guns' crews mistook it for part of the practice.
16. It is thought probable that the Japanese staff appreciated Munda as the destination of the Force.

and flew off. The last stages of the approach were accomplished without incident, and though no particularly good navigational landmarks existed, radar enabled the cruisers to open fire at 0200, 24 January, exactly as planned. About 95 per cent of the rounds fired fell in the target area. Very large fires and explosions resulted, and there is no doubt that great damage was inflicted. As soon as the bombardment was over, the two spotting aircraft each dropped two 500-lb. bombs, which considerably added to the flames.

During the withdrawal the Force was shadowed by an enemy aircraft, which illuminated its route with flares and float lights for some time and was eventually shot down or disabled by the *Helena*. Later, several groups of enemy aircraft which made half-hearted attempts to close, were detected on radar screens; twice they came within range, and were driven off by gunfire, one at least being shot down. Skilful use of heavy black squalls which blew up at about 0330 enabled the force to avoid a serious attack, and at about dawn the enemy withdrew.

Some six hours after the bombardment, at 0800, 24 January, the same area at Kolombangara was heavily attacked by aircraft from the *Saratoga*.[17] Twenty-five bombers and 17 torpedo bombers, escorted by 24 fighters, dropped 85 500-lb. bombs and 47 100-lb. bombs in the target area, while the fighters 'strafed' housing areas and AA positions. There was no enemy fighter opposition, and all the aircraft returned to Guadalcanal safely, 'there being no personnel or materiel casualties resulting from the sporadic and inaccurate AA gunfire'.

24. Japanese evacuate Guadalcanal

The last week of January,1943, saw an intensification of the enemy air activity in the Solomons area. There were also indications of a movement of strong Japanese naval forces towards the Southern Solomons, and Vice-Admiral Halsey ordered his main forces, including battleships and the carriers *Saratoga* and *Enterprise* to take up dispositions suitable for interception. At the same time, a strong force of cruisers and destroyers, with two auxiliary carriers – Task Force 18 – was to cover an American troop convoy bound for Guadalcanal. Task Force 18 left Efate on 27 January, and had reached a position to the south of Guadalcanal on the evening of 29 January, when it was attacked by Japanese torpedo planes. Two attacks were carried out, about

---

17. Task Force 11, (*Saratoga, San Juan*, six destroyers) had left Noumea on 21 January, and proceeded to the south-west ward of Guadalcanal, where the *Saratoga*'s striking force was flown off to Henderson's Field on 23 January. After the attack on Kolombangara on 24 January it returned to Guadalcanal for servicing, and rejoined the *Saratoga* off Rennel Island that afternoon.

12 aircraft being employed in each. The first took place in late twilight,[18] and was preceded by an aircraft dropping dim white marker floats, and red and green parachute lights; no hits were scored, but shortly afterwards another attack developed, and at 1945 the *Chicago*, which was illuminated by an aircraft which she had just shot down in flames, was hit by two torpedoes. She was subsequently taken in tow by the Fleet tug *Navajo*, but was again attacked next day, 30 January, by about 13 torpedo planes. Ten of these were shot down by fighters from the *Enterprise*, which had made contact from the south; but three of their torpedoes hit the *Chicago*, and she sank 10 minutes later.

The American Forces remained at sea during the first few days of February, but no contact occurred with enemy surface craft. The Japanese heavy forces, which included battleships and carriers, kept well to the northward, apparently as distant cover, while a strong force of destroyers evacuated the remnant of the Japanese troops from Guadalcanal under cover of darkness.

25. Conclusion

To sum up the campaign, the key to the whole position – as was recognized by both sides – was the possession of Henderson's Airfield. By their original occupation of Tulagi, in April, 1942, the Japanese had allowed their sea and land forces to outstrip their air support, their nearest air base being at Rabaul – some 675 miles away. Their carrier losses at the Battle of the Coral Sea, May, 1942, and Midway Island, June, 1942, accentuated this weakness, and the construction of an airfield on Guadalcanal was put in hand in July, 1942. The Americans, however, struck too quickly, and captured the well-nigh completed airfield at the outset of their operations in August. After the cruiser losses suffered by the Allies at the Battle of Savo (8/9 August) the enemy had enjoyed complete local command of the sea; but before he could gather his forces for a large-scale effort at re-capture, the establishment of American aircraft at Henderson's Field wrested from him command of the sea by day. The enemy was thus faced with the alternative of operating by day within range of American shore-based aircraft, or of confining his operations to the hours of darkness. The great superiority in radar equipment enjoyed by the American surface forces rendered his operations by night almost as hazardous as by day; and the net result was a steady drain on his naval and air strength, with no corresponding drain on that of the Americans. This eventually compelled him to acknowledge defeat.

---

18. Sunset, 1849.

The importance of the victory can hardly be over-estimated. Both strategically and tactically the enemy had been out-manoeuvred and out-fought with the Southern Solomons firmly in American hands, the vital line of communications between America and Australia was safeguarded, and the first stepping stone secured on the 3,000 mile route leading through the Bismarck Archipelago and Mandated Islands to China and Japan.

APPENDIX

'Phantom' Contacts

As experience in night fighting increased, it was found that ships were liable to open 'phantoms' i.e, their own shadows, thrown by gun flashes from other ships or illuminants, on to low cloud banks. Rear-Admiral Ainsworth, USN, remarked as follows on this phenomenon in his report on the bombardment of Munda: 'This matter of firing at one's own shadow is much more real than can at first seem possible. With everyone on their toes and all look-outs alerted, we are all prone to see things which do not exist, and these black shadows reflected on cloud masses near the horizon certainly appear to be enemy ships. The *St. Louis*, going across the range, was a ball of fire on the *Nashville*'s port quarter, and the *Nashville* opened fire on a phantom torpedo boat on her starboard bow. The *Fletcher* likewise almost fired a half salvo of torpedoes at her own silhouette. It may well be probable that several of our reports of enemy ships sunk in night engagements may be in error from this cause. Here, again, it behoves us to put our faith in SG and, if time permits, check the phantom before opening fire.' Captured documents show that the Japanese have experienced similar troubles. For example, one of their destroyer squadrons reported chasing American destroyers and torpedo boats out of the area during the battleship bombardment of Guadalcanal on the night of 13–14 October, in point of fact no US surface forces were present on this occasion.

Part Five

The Battle for Leyte Gulf

Introduction

The great triple battle of 23–26 October, 1944, known by the Americans as the Battle for Leyte Gulf, and by the British sometimes as the Second Battle of the Philippines, involved many different forces, both surface and air, and ranged over a wide area. The following summary is given as a guide.

The battle was the outcome of a Japanese attempt to throw the Americans out of the Philippines which they had invaded three days previously at Leyte, in a landing from the Gulf, between the islands of Leyte and Samar. The Japanese fleet sallied out in three detachments, and a series of major surface and air actions developed in and around the Philippine Islands, culminating on 25 October in three almost simultaneous naval battles: the Battle of Surigao Strait, the Battle off Samar, and the Battle off Cape Engano (Luzon Island). The three detachments or groups of the enemy fleet involved in these three engagements are for convenience termed the Southern, Centre and Northern Force respectively.

The Southern Force,[1] mustering two slow old battleships, four cruisers, and destroyers was located in the Sulu Sea on 24 October. It approached Leyte in two groups, to attack the American unloading area, through the Mindanao Sea and its northern exit, the Surigao Strait, and was practically destroyed there by the US Seventh Fleet (Vice-Admiral Kinkaid), early next day.

The Centre Force comprised the main body of the enemy fleet – five modern battleships, 10 cruisers, and destroyers.[2] It sailed from Brunei Bay, passed up the west coast of Palawan, where US submarines attacked it on 23 October, sinking two heavy cruisers and so damaging a third that it turned back to Singapore; it passed through the Mindoro Strait and Sibuyan Sea, where aircraft of Admiral Halsey's Third Fleet carrier groups lined up east

---

1. *Secret Information Bulletin No. 22*, General Recapitulation pp. 78-44 states that the Southern Force carried troops, but there is no confirmation of this and no details are forthcoming.
2. The Centre Force is described in this account of the battle as the main body since it comprised the greater part of the surface fighting strength of the Japanese Fleet. The Japanese termed the Northern (Carrier) Force the main body, as the principal tactical force remaining in the striking force after most of the heavy units had been detached to form the Diversion Attack Forces.

of the Philippines sank a battleship and damaged and caused a heavy cruiser to turn back during day-long attacks on 24th; the still powerful remainder of the force, delayed through damage caused by these attacks, passed through the San Bernardino Strait during the night of 24th–25th and turned south, intending to engage the American Covering Force (Seventh Fleet), whilst the Southern Force emerged from Surigao Strait to clear out Leyte Gulf. The delay on 24th, however, had been sufficient to prevent the two attacks from synchronizing, though between the Japanese Centre Force and Leyte there stood only the American Seventh Fleet Escort Carrier Group, operating off the east coast of Samar Island. The escort carriers, at the cost of heavy losses, held up the enemy for 24 hours, when the Japanese Fleet retired, pursued by aircraft of the Seventh and Third Fleets, who severely handled it until the scattered survivors reached safety on 27 October.

The Japanese Northern Force comprised their carrier force-four carriers and two converted battleship carriers – with cruiser and destroyer screen. It left Japan about 20 October with only a small proportion of its aircraft, the remainder having been transferred to Formosa and the Philippines. The force was first located on the afternoon of 24th approaching the Philippines from the north-eastward; it was attacked by aircraft from the fast carriers of Admiral Halsey's Third Fleet during the whole of 25th off Cape Engano, the north-east point of Luzon, and the four carriers were sunk. In conjunction with the sortie of the Japanese Fleet to relieve Leyte, their land-based aircraft from some of the numerous enemy airfields within range of Leyte made constant attacks on the northernmost of the three fast carrier groups of the Third Fleet east of the Philippines, causing the loss of the light carrier *Princeton*; and they also attacked the escort carriers of the Seventh Fleet operating farther south, and sank the *St. Lo*.

In all, 23 Japanese ships were sunk, including three battleships, four carriers, six heavy and three light cruisers, and seven destroyers. One further destroyer was sunk on 27 October, after the battle was considered to have terminated; and a light cruiser and a destroyer were sunk on 26 October whilst escorting reinforcements to Leyte.

The Americans lost one carrier, two escort carriers, two destroyers, one destroyer escort and one MTB, seven ships in all. The two British ships which were engaged suffered no damage.

Note on Sources

1. This account of the Battle for Leyte Gulf is based mainly on American Action Reports supplemented by the interrogation of certain Japanese officers. Only two British ships, HMAS *Shropshire* and HMAS *Arunta*, were engaged; both rendered reports. The list of American reports which can be traced as having been furnished to the Admiralty, is far from complete. In particular, the despatch of Admiral Halsey, Commander Third Fleet, has not been seen.

2. An account of the Battle for Leyte Gulf is contained in Annex A of *Operations in the Pacific Ocean Areas during the Month of October, 1944* (Commander-in-Chief US Pacific Fleet and Pacific Ocean Areas, 31 May, 1945). This is referred to in this Battle Summary as 'C.-in-C. Pac., Report'. It contains some information which is not available elsewhere to the compilers of this battle summary, but, where discrepancies occur, the date of issue, 31 May, 1945, i.e., before the defeat of Japan rendered enemy sources available, should be borne in mind.

3. Extracts from some of the Action Reports which have not been received by the Admiralty are printed in *Secret Information Bulletin no. 22 – Battle Experience – Battle for Leyte Gulf, 23rd/27th October, 1944* (US Fleet, Headquarters of the Commander-in-Chief, 1st March, 1945); and ... under the heading 'Commander Third Fleet (Supporting Force) reports in part' there are included what are presumed to be extracts from Admiral Halsey's despatch and are quoted as such in this narrative. The extracts stop short at 0730 on 25 October. *Secret Information Bulletin No. 2* contains also plans, photographs and explanatory matter and comments by the compilers.

4. In many of the original action reports the pages have been renumbered consecutively throughout by hand on the photostat film. When referring to action reports in this Battle Summary the continuous pagination is used.

5. The Japanese official account of the battle is contained in 'The Campaigns of the Pacific War' (United States Strategic Bombing Survey (Pacific)), Naval Analysis Division (Government Press). Interrogations of officers concerned in the battle have been printed by the (US) Naval Analysis Division under the title *United States Strategy Bombing Survey [Pacific] Interrogations of Japanese Officials*.

Chapter I

Organization of the Allied and Enemy Forces

1. Situation in the Autumn, 1944

In the autumn of 1944, the advance of the Allies in the Pacific had brought them to a line on which they stood over against the Philippine Islands, the pivot on which they planned to wheel northward and attack the Japanese mainland. In the south-west, General MacArthur's Allied troops and ships, fighting their way northward from Australian and New Caledonian bases to Morotai in the Moluccas gained possession of points from which amphibious forces could assault the Philippines. Further north, in the wide spaces of the Pacific, Admiral Nimitz's great striding drive westward, storming or by-passing one after another the enemy strongholds in the Gilberts, Marshalls, Marianas and Guam, reached, in September, 1944, the airfields of the West Carolines, and anchorages where his supporting ships could find replenishment and shelter.

No breathing space was given to the enemy. From the support of the landings in the West Carolines, the fast carriers of the Third Fleet returned to the Philippines. Consequent upon the revelation of the enemy's comparative weakness in the air during strikes early in September, an immediate decision had been made to advance by some weeks the date of the assault on the Philippines, and a landing on Leyte Island was planned for 20th October.

On 21–22 September, under cover of bad weather the carriers entered the waters to the eastward of Luzon and attacked Manila and other targets. Two days later their aircraft were in the Central Philippines, completing photographic coverage and reaching out as far as the Japanese anchorage at Koron [or Coron] Bay, in the Kalamian group. After a short period spent in replenishing at forward bases, the fast-carrier task force recommenced on 9 October the task of neutralizing as far as possible the hundred or more enemy airfields within striking distance of Leyte. These airfields were too numerous to be effectively neutralized, and too close to Formosa and Japan to be cut off. Nevertheless, the preliminary operations apparently had the effect of enabling the landings on Leyte to be made without difficulty by the American troops. On 20 October the operation for the recapture of the Philippines began.

2. The Allied Forces

This great amphibious operation was under the supreme direction of General of the Army, Douglas MacArthur, Commander Southwest Pacific Area. His naval forces were under the command of Vice-Admiral Thomas C. Kinkaid, Commander Seventh Fleet and Commander Allied Naval Forces, who formed his Central Philippine Attack Force from units of the Seventh Fleet, greatly augmented by ships of the Pacific Fleet. The basic directive was embodied in Commander Seventh Fleet's Operational Order No, 13–44: "This force will, by a ships-to-shore amphibious operation, transport, protect, land and support elements of the 6th Army in order to assist in the seizure, occupation and development of the Leyte area.' This considerable force numbered more than 650 ships, including battleships, cruisers, destroyers, destroyer escorts, escort carriers, transports, cargo ships, landing craft, mine craft and supply vessels. It was divided into the Northern Attack Force (Seventh Amphibious Force, Rear-Admiral Barbey in command) and the Southern Attack Force (Third Amphibious Force, Vice-Admiral Wilkinson commanding) with the addition of surface and air cover groups, fire support, bombardment, minesweeping and supply groups. The tactical units of the Central Philippine Attack Force constituted the covering force, known as Task Force 77. Vice-Admiral Kinkaid, Commander Seventh Fleet, also commanded this task force, for which the principal role envisaged was bombardment, the Fire Support and Bombardment Group being comprised in Task Group 77-2 under Rear-Admiral J. B. Oldendorf with his flag in the cruiser *Louisville*. Together with the Close Covering Group, which during the Battle for Leyte Gulf, operated as an integral part of Rear-Admiral Oldendorf's force, comprised six old battleships, four heavy cruisers, four light cruisers and 21 destroyers. Close air support and air cover was provided by Task Group 77.4, consisting of 18 escort carriers with screen of nine destroyers and 14 destroyer escorts under Rear-Admiral T. L. Sprague, organized as three units. The total aircraft complement on these 18 carriers was 448 machines.[3]

The operation was covered and supported by the Third Fleet and Western Pacific Task Forces, operating under Admiral W. F. Halsey, Jr. The latter operated under Admiral C. W. Nimitz, Commander-in-Chief, US Pacific Fleet and Pacific Ocean Areas.

General MacArthur and Admiral Nimitz were each separately responsible for their particular tasks to the Joint Chiefs of Staff in Washington.

---

3. *Leyte Operation, British Combined Observers' Report*, p. 9.

The Commander-in-Chief US Pacific Fleet's directives to the Commander Third Fleet are shown in the former's Operation Plan No. S-44, briefed as follows:

'The Joint Chiefs of Staff have directed that C. in C. Pacific provides necessary Fleet support to operations (including Leyte and Western Samar) by forces of the Southwest Pacific.

'Forces of Pacific Ocean Areas will cover and support forces of Southwest Pacific. Western Pacific Task Forces (Third Fleet) will destroy enemy naval and air forces in or threatening the Philippines Area, and protect the air and sea communications along the Central Pacific Axis. In case opportunity for destruction of major portions of the enemy fleet offers or can be created, such destruction becomes the primary task (of all POA forces). Necessary measures for detailed co-ordination of operations between the Western Pacific Task Forces and forces of the Southwest Pacific will be arranged by their respective Commanders.'[4]

Admiral Halsey's command was a formidable one of six modern battleships, eight large and seven light aircraft carriers with a total complement of 987 aircraft,[5] six heavy and nine light cruisers, and 59 destroyers. Its internal organization varied from time to time, according to its duties.

In order to ensure early detection of any approach of enemy naval forces, submarines were stationed to guard Brunei Bay, Balabak Strait (the southwest entrance to the Sulu Sea) and Mindoro Strait and Verde Island Passage (the north-western entrances), and to the westward of Luzon, from Manila northwards. Their duties also included lifeguard services and the passing of weather reports.

Air searches from the recently captured airfield on Morotai Island (Moluccas), reaching from Balabak Strait to Verde Island Passage, were extended to a radius of 1,000 miles for the operation. Air searches by Central Pacific forces from Palau in the West Carolines and Saipan in the Marianas were depended upon to supplement Third Fleet aircraft in giving early warning of any approach of enemy forces east of the Philippines.[6]

3. The Enemy Naval Forces

The tactical forces of the Japanese Combined Fleet were re-organized shortly before the Allied landing on Leyte. The Third Fleet comprised the

4. Cincpac, *Report*, pp. 56–7.
5. *Leyte Operation, British Combined Observers' Report*, p. 9.
6. Report of CTF 77 (*Secret Information Bulletin No. 22.* p. 78-10).

four carriers and two converted battleship carriers, *Ise* and *Hyuga*, with their screen, termed the main body of the mobile force or Attack Group. This fleet was based on Japan, and it was this fleet which in the battle for Leyte Gulf constituted the Northern Force. The majority of the remaining ships of the combined fleet were included in the Second Fleet (termed the First Diversion Attack Force), which was organized for the defence of the Philippines in two forces: the Southern Force of two old battleships and one heavy cruiser, with destroyer screen; and the Centre Force comprising the main surface fighting strength of the fleet. On account of shortage of oil in Japan, the home islands could not support the whole of their tactical forces, and the Second Fleet was consequently based on Singapore.

The Fifth Fleet (Second Diversion Attack Force), consisting of two cruiser squadrons (two heavy and two light cruisers) and a destroyer flotilla (one light cruiser and four destroyers), had been brought south from its station at Ominato in Northern Honshu, at the time of the air strikes on Formosa and the Pescadores by the American fast carriers on 12-13 October, in which the cruisers *Canberra* and *Houston* were torpedoed. It appears that the Japanese, believing exaggerated early reports from their airmen, hoped to be able to sink some American cripples, and to rescue some of their own downed aircrews; but they found the Third Fleet too strong and consequently retired to Amami O Shima without becoming involved in an engagement.

4. The Japanese Plan

The defence of the Philippines was part of the plan known as Sho-Go (Sho Operations).[7] It was recognized that the defence of the archipelago could not succeed without the participation of the Combined Fleet. If the Philippines were lost, the southern shipping route, through which a trickle still ran, would be cut and the fleet would consequently be immobilized in Japan for lack of oil, or if it remained in the south, cut off from its ammunition supply. It was therefore decided to risk the entire fleet in one operation.

The plan was designed to make the best use of the Japanese strength in heavy surface ships which at this date preponderated over their light forces and naval air forces, both of which had been diminished through attrition. In the event of threat to the Philippines it was intended that the Southern and Centre Forces should advance from Lingga Anchorage (about 100 miles south of Singapore) to Brunei Bay (Borneo) or the northern Philippines, and time their sortie from here so as to reach the threatened landing beach at the same time as the Allied invasion force. Whilst endeavouring to avoid attack

---

7. Defence plan for the area extending from the Philippines to Japan, inclusive.

by the US fast carriers, they were to fight through any surface opposition and destroy the assault convoys.

The Battle of the Marianas[8] in June, 1944, had broken Japan's carrier-borne air power. Three carriers had been sunk there and one seriously damaged, and the air groups of three carrier divisions were virtually annihilated. With the loss of over 300 carrier-borne aircraft, the Japanese lost the bulk of their trained carrier pilots, and the training of new pilots, increasingly hampered by lack of fuel, was still incomplete; they were insufficiently trained to operate from carriers though trained well enough for operations from land bases. This dictated the future employment of naval air service. In planning, the Japanese High Command intended to use naval air units, flying carrier-borne types but operating mainly from land bases; and in conformity with this, when the American pre-invasion air attacks began on the Philippines on 10 October a high proportion, said to be as much as half the carrier aircraft in training, were sent to reinforce Formosa and the Philippines.

The plan of operations consisted of an attack from two directions on the invasion ships and supporting warships in Leyte Gulf, with a diversion which it was hoped would draw off the powerful American covering force (Admiral Halsey's Third Fleet) and facilitate the penetration of the Japanese attack to Leyte Gulf. The Japanese appear to have received fairly accurate intelligence, from air search on the 23rd, that there were in the Gulf some seven or eight American battleships with cruisers and destroyers appropriate to a balanced fleet, and torpedo boats at the entrance.

The attack on the invasion forces was to be carried out by the Second and Fifth Fleets, the former being divided into two detachments, Centre and Southern, for this operation. The Southern portion of the Force, termed by the Japanese, C Force or Third Group, under the command of Vice-Admiral Shoji Nishimura, consisted of the Second Battle Squadron (two battleships the *Yamashiro* and *Fuso*), the heavy cruiser *Mogami*, and the Fourth Destroyer Division reinforced (four destroyers). The force was to attack Leyte from the south, via the Surigao Strait. The Fifth Fleet (Second Diversion Attack Force) under Vice-Admiral Kiyohide Shima had also the mission of attacking from the south, though its commander was entirely independent both of Vice-Admiral Nishimura and of Vice-Admiral Kurita, Commander-in-Chief, Second Fleet, to whom Nishimura was subordinate.[9] At the time of this operation the Fifth Fleet comprised the 21st Cruiser Squadron (the heavy

8. Also known as the Battle of the Philippine Sea.
9. It seems it had originally been intended that the Fifth Fleet should accompany the Northern (Carrier) Force, but an alteration was made when Admiral Shima moved south at the time of the American Third Fleet air attacks on Formosa. The alteration is said to have disorganized the communications of the Northern Force.

cruisers *Nachi* and *Ashigara*) and the First Destroyer Flotilla (the light cruiser *Abukuma* and four destroyers).[10] It seems that the decision to employ the Fifth Fleet was only taken at the last moment, and Shima at Amami O Shima and Nishimura at Lingga held no communication with one another previous to the operation, and consequently there was no consultation whatever between them on the subject.

The Centre Force was to attack the invasion ships from the east, passing through San Bernardino Strait, down the east coast of Samar Island, and entering Leyte Gulf by the Suluan Island passage. The force was under Vice-Admiral Kurita's own command and comprised the bulk (first and second groups) of the Second Fleet, including the two modern battleships *Yamato* (flagship) and *Musashi*, and three older battleships, three cruiser squadrons (in all, ten heavy cruisers), and two destroyer flotillas each led by a light cruiser.

Combined Fleet Headquarters had at first appointed 22 October as X-day, the date on which the Southern and Centre Forces should make their attacks on the US forces in Leyte Gulf. However, Vice-Admiral Kurita reported that owing to the necessity of fuelling en route he could not attack before the 25th, and this date was accordingly adopted as X-day.

It was intended that the Southern and Centre Forces should attack Leyte Gulf about dawn on 25 October,[11] the Southern Force attacking first, about two hours before the Centre Force, since the waters of the Gulf were too confined for both forces to attack simultaneously.[12] The Fifth Fleet was to co-operate with or support Vice-Admiral Nishimura and was apparently to deliver its attack after those of Nishimura and Kurita. There does not appear to have been a clear-cut plan of attack. After the attack,[13] both the Centre and Southern Forces were to retire via Surigao Strait. The transfer of carrier aircraft of Air Groups 653 and 634 to Formosa and the Philippines on 10 October had left the carriers with so few aircraft, and those with their

---

10. The 16th (Cruiser) Squadron (*Tama* and *Kiso*) also belonged to the Fifth Fleet but were not with it in the present operation.

11. Sunrise was at 0627.

12. The evidence as to the exact timing of the attack is conflicting. SMS 212053 from C-in-C., Second Fleet orders the Southern Force to arrive at the East (sic) entrance to Surigao Strait at sundown on X-1 Day and 'Break through' to the anchorage at dawn on X-Day, and the Centre Force to arrive in vicinity of Suluan Island at 0400 X-Day, 'from whence break through to anchorage.' The distance from Suluan Island. to the landing beaches was about 60 miles.

13. Vice-Admiral Kurita, in reply to questions whether his purpose was to attack the landing ships and the transports and cargo ships rather than the fighting ships, replied that he intended to attack both, giving preference to battleships. His Chief of Staff, Rear-Admiral Koyanagi, stated that stress would have been laid on the transports. His Staff Officer (Operations), Commander Otano, stated that the targets for the operation, in order of importance, were carriers, transports, surface warships. C-in-C Combined Fleet ordered the US surface forces to be destroyed first, and then the landing forces.

training still incomplete, that no more than 116 machines were available for the Third Fleet, Vice-Admiral Ozawa's carrier (northern) force, from the Groups 653 and 634 and such of those of Air Group 601 as were capable of operating from carriers. These were loaded on board the four carriers of the 3rd Squadron during the morning of 20 October at Oita air base, and apart from the meagre attack thus rendered possible, the Japanese Third Fleet was relegated to the role of decoy to draw off the American fast carriers and enable Vice-Admiral Kurita's detachments to get through to the invasion beaches.[14] Ozawa was not optimistic of success, for the only previous precedent was the Battle of the Marianas, where the American task force refused to be drawn from the proximity of the invasion forces until the Japanese carriers had been rendered impotent. The force was to leave the Inland Sea and arrive north-east of the Philippines on X-2 to X-1 day and commence its attack with the few aircraft remaining to it.

Vice-Admirals Kurita and Ozawa were both directly responsible to Admiral Toyoda, Commander of the Combined Fleet. Vice-Admiral Shima's immediate superior was the Commander-in-Chief South-west Area Fleet, Vice Admiral Mikawa at Manila, who was responsible to Admiral Toyoda. The latter had his headquarters in Japan, and consequently exercised little control once the operation had begun, although the co-ordinating command rested with him.[15] In practice, the only co-ordination of this complicated operation which actually took place, was concerned by communication between the units; and this channel failed to fulfil its function.

In view of the importance of maintaining accurate co-ordination, the communications plan had been very carefully made and special radio channels provided; but, in the event, restrictions on communication and the need for radio silence rendered co-ordination between the Second Fleet and the carriers in the north almost impossible.

The employment of submarines in the defence of the Philippines was envisaged in the Sho Plan, and some seven were disposed in the sector between north-east and south-east of Leyte, and three off Lamon Bay on the east side of Mindanao. However, it seems that only three reached the Leyte area by the 25 October, though all 10 of the submarines had arrived by next day.

The employment of shore-based aircraft to attack the American fleet was an important part of the Japanese plan. At the time of the American landing on

---

14. Vice-Admiral Ozawa stated in interrogation that he wished his fleet and Kurita's to be combined for the operation, but the Allied attack came before the training of the carriers was completed.
15. In the interrogation of Vice-Admiral Kurita, it is stated that Admiral Toyoda, not being informed as to the situation did not attempt to direct the operation whilst in progress but merely gave the general orders 'to attack and return.'

Leyte, the land-based naval aircraft in the Philippines, consisting of the First (Navy) Air Fleet, commanded by Vice-Admiral Onishi, had been reduced much below establishment as the result of American attacks; for in October, 1944, alone, the Japanese lost from carrier air strikes approximately as many aircraft as broke the German Air Force during the two months of the Battle of Britain in the late summer of 1940. Most of the Second (Navy) Air Fleet at Formosa, under Vice-Admiral Shigeru Fukudome, was in consequence moved to the Philippines on 22 October and the two air fleets were united to form the Combined Base Air Force. All naval air forces in the Philippines were placed under the command of the Commander-in-Chief South-west Area Fleet, Vice-Admiral Mikawa.

During the summer, 1944, army air units had been subordinated to naval command in Hokkaido and in the Hainan-Formosa area, but no unified air command was established in the Philippines. The majority of the 450 aircraft of the Second Air Fleet flew from Formosa to Clark Field, near Manila, on 23 October. They apparently had orders to attack the American fast carriers on the way, but failed to find them on account of bad weather. In all, about 600 shore-based Japanese aircraft were available in the Philippines.

The operation had a limited object, namely, to delay the American landing for two or three days. There appears to have been no plan to exploit this delay, and indeed no great expectation of success; but to the Japanese with their inferiority in ships and aircraft it seemed to offer the best hope. In particular, it was understood from the beginning, before the plan was put into operation, that they had insufficient aircraft; and this was perhaps one of the basic causes of failure.

The Japanese apparently received warning from their shore observers on the same day, 17 October, that the Americans landed on Dinagat Island, at the entrance to Leyte Gulf, in preparation for the main landing on Leyte Island.[16] The Japanese fleet was then set in motion as planned. Vice-Admiral Kurita moved with the Second Fleet to Brunei Bay where he arrived on 21 October and issued his orders. After fuelling, the fleet sailed on 22nd in two detachments, making a wide swing to the north-westward from Brunei, to avoid suspected submarine areas. The Centre Force, under Kurita, left first, about 0800, and proceeded up the Palawan Passage, whilst Nishimura sailed in the afternoon and steamed through the Balabak Strait into the Sulu Sea, where he made a considerable diversion to the northward, in order to avoid air search from Morotai, before making for the Mindanao Sea and Surigao Strait.

---

16. It is stated that the Japanese on the 18th intercepted an American telephone message from which they learnt that landing was to be made south of Tacloban on Leyte Island.

The Fifth Fleet was brought from Amami O Shima to Bako, and from thence to Koron Bay in the Kalamian group of islands on the south side of Mindoro Strait, for fuelling, and it sailed from here very early on the morning of the 24th by the route west of Negros, to carry out its mission at Leyte. One tanker was sent to Koron Bay, and two tankers from Singapore were brought into the Sulu Sea. Apparently, the tanker was not at Koron Bay when the Fifth Fleet arrived; consequently the cruisers had to supply fuel for the destroyers and the resulting shortage had an effect on the subsequent operation.

5. Appreciation of the Enemy's Reaction to the Leyte Landing

The American estimate of the enemy's strength and dispositions at the end of September differed somewhat from actuality and was as follows: -

	Formosa-Japan	Singapore Area
Battleships	3	4
Battleship carriers	2	–
Carriers	6	–
Light carriers	5	–
Escort carriers	3	1
Armoured cruisers	4	11
Light cruisers	7	several
Destroyers	about 20	about 20

It was recognized by the US Commander South-west Pacific, that the strategic result of capturing the Philippines would be decisive. Nevertheless, the intelligence appreciation upon which his forces were working, anticipated but slight possibility of strong Japanese naval reaction to the landings at Leyte,[17] a view which was not, however, entirely shared by the Third Fleet, by whom some reaction was expected.

---

17. The British Combined Operations Observers S.W. Pacific Area state: 'It was not believed that major elements of the Japanese Fleet would be involved in the present operations, but that fast Task Forces might strike at our supply lines taking full advantage of darkness, surprise and land-based air.'

Chapter II

The Enemy Approach

6. Fragmentary Sighting Reports of 21–22 October

The only considerable information of the enemy available prior to 21 October was of small craft movements, from which it was inferred that reinforcement of the west coast of Leyte by small craft was occurring or about to occur.

On 21 October large enemy warships were sighted to the north, west and south of Leyte, but all sightings were indefinite. There was no evidence of a movement towards the Philippines: but rather the reverse, in fact.

Sightings on 22nd provided no more satisfactory basis for an appreciation of the enemy's intentions. In the Luzon Strait, south of Formosa, a southbound force of some half a dozen ships was sighted at midnight 21st/22nd and was attacked, two hits being reported. During the day, various other sightings occurred in the area north-west of Luzon which seemed to suggest that forces, including heavy cruisers, were moving towards Manila. But these contact reports were deprived of much of their significance because it was thought they were connected with the abortive sortie of the Japanese Fifth Fleet a few days earlier. It was difficult now to determine whether the ships were retiring, re-forming, or standing by.

In the south sightings on 21st and 22nd were equally fragmentary and uncertain.[1]

7. Seventh Fleet Blocks the Approaches to Leyte Gulf, 22 October

Indeterminate though the sightings were, Rear-Admiral Oldendorf, commanding Task Group 77.2, decided already on 22nd to form a battle disposition to defend Leyte Gulf. Under his orders was the force which had been supplying covering fire for the landings in the gulf, namely, six old battleships, three heavy and two light cruisers and destroyers. On Vice-Admiral Kinkaid's instructions, his ships were remaining in the area south of

---

1. The plan of sighting reports 22/24 October includes a single sighting at 2115 of one battleship, three light cruisers, three destroyers and six unidentified ships east of Tarakan, course 170°, speed 15 knots. Three large unidentified warships were shown at 2200 in about 7° 15′ N., 115° 30′ E, course 020° speed 21 knots, but this is the only known sighting of units of the Singapore force.

a line drawn through the centre of Leyte Gulf in lat. 10° 46′ N. Rear- Admiral Oldendorf now stationed his light forces on an east-west line, four miles east of Taytay Point (10° 42′ N., 125° 07′ E.), speed 5 knots, with his heavy forces and destroyer screen to the North-westward, south of lat. 10° 46′ N. He expected the attack, if it came, to be via the southern entrance to the Surigao Strait and it was to this area that he was paying the most attention.

8. First Contact with the Japanese Main Battle Fleet, 0200 23 October

However, in effect it was not Rear-Admiral Oldendorf but Admiral Halsey who first became involved, nor was there long to wait for definite news of the enemy. Early on the morning of 23 October a report came in from a submarine of radar contact on three possible battleships at 0200 steering 040° at 15 knots in 08° 20′ N. 116° 20′ E., at the southern entrance to the Palawan Passage, the narrow channel between Palawan Island and the un-surveyed Dangerous Ground to the westward. An hour later a submarine reported a force of 11 fighting ships in the lower part of the Passage in 08° 47′ N. 116° 37′ E, at 0300, course 039°, speed 15 knots.

These reports came from the American submarines *Darter* and *Dace*, and they appear to have been the first definite indication that the Japanese forces had left Singapore.

9. Sinking of the *Atago* and *Maya*, 0630–0700 23 October

The submarines *Darter* and *Dace* shadowed and attacked the enemy ships as they proceeded up the Palawan Passage, nor were they long in coming into action. At 0630 the *Darter*, in 09° 24′ N., 117° 11′ E. reported three battleships, four heavy cruisers, and three other vessels, and that she had obtained four torpedo hits on one *Atago* class cruiser and damaged a second. Half an hour later, the *Dace*, in 09° 29′ N. 117° 20′ E, reported 11 ships, including three battleships, two heavy cruisers, and a carrier, and that she had obtained four torpedo hits on a *Kongo* class battleship.

The enemy force encountered by the submarines belonged to Vice-Admiral Kurita's Centre Force, comprising the five most modern battleships, 10 heavy cruisers, with light cruiser and destroyer screen. The ships hit were three of the four heavy cruisers of the Fourth Cruiser Squadron, two of which, the *Atago* and the *Maya*, were sunk and the third, the *Takao*, was badly damaged and had to be sent back to Singapore via Brunei, escorted by two destroyers.[2]

---

2. Apparently, the *Takao* was hit in the stern and was unable to navigate. *Takao* was almost certainly the cruiser sighted with two destroyers heading south-west at four knots approaching the southern exit of the Palawan Passage in the early hours of 24 October.

At the time of the attack, the enemy force was cruising in line ahead in two columns, disposed abeam to starboard. Evidence as to the disposition of the ships within the columns and of the screening ships is contradictory, but it is clear that the Fourth Cruiser Squadron in the order *Atago* (fleet flagship), *Takao*, *Chokai*, led the port column, whilst the Fifth Cruiser Squadron (*Myoko* and *Haguro*) with the *Maya* from the Fourth Cruiser Squadron, in that order, composed the van of the starboard column.

The Japanese fleet was zigzagging at 18 knots and had just completed a turn to port when the first attack occurred. This was made, apparently, by the *Darter*, from a position fine on the starboard bow of the leading ship of the port column, the fleet flagship *Atago*, four torpedoes hit the *Atago* and two the *Takao*, second ship in the column.

On the alarm being given, the starboard column turned to starboard, but resumed the course within ten minutes. Almost immediately the second attack occurred, delivered by the *Dace*, from a position broad on the port bow of the Fifth Cruiser Squadron. The change of course of the enemy apparently saved the leading ships, but the *Maya*, which was last ship in the column, was hit by four torpedoes and sank almost immediately.

The Japanese were aware of the presence of American submarine patrols on this route. In planning the operation they had considered three possible routes. First, the most southerly, which would bring their forces under the attack of land-based air from Morotai in the Halmaheras; second, the most northerly route, which was too long; and third, the route adopted. Considering the time and other factors, it was decided to proceed by the middle route.

Before the *Atago* sank half an hour after being hit, the Vice-Admiral and his staff transferred first to the destroyer *Kishinami* and subsequently (at 1623) to the battleship *Yamato*, flagship of the Commander of the First (Battle) Squadron and Second-in-Command of the Second Fleet.[3] The position of sinking of the *Atago* is given as 9° 28′ N., 117° 17′ E.

At 2310 a signal was sent to the Commander-in-Chief Combined Fleet, Mobile Fleet, South-west Area Fleet and Chief of the Naval General Staff, informing them of the situation.

---

3. Interrogation No. (*U.S.S. B.S. No. 47*), *Nav, No. 9*, pp. 47–7, states that the control was improved by the change, although on pp. 47–23 it is stated that when the flag was shifted the communications personnel were divided between two destroyers, one of which was sent back to Brunei with the *Takao*. Vice-Admiral Kurita's operations officer stated that the shift of flag did not interfere much with the operation. Rear-Admiral Koyanagi, Chief of Staff to Vice-Admiral Kurita, states that half the communications personnel was killed in the torpedoing of the *Atago*.

10. Loss of USS *Darter*, 24 October

Unfortunately, the *Darter*, whilst manoeuvring into position for a further attack on the Centre Force, grounded on Bombay Shoal in 09° 26′ N., 116° 56′ E., in the middle of the Palawan Passage, and had to be abandoned next day. The Japanese subsequently boarded the vessel but found that all useful gear had been destroyed by the crew. This was the only US submarine to fall into Japanese hands during the war.

11. Centre Force enters Mindoro Strait, night of 23–24 October

Vice-Admiral Kurita's force was sighted once more on 23rd. At 2130 the American submarine *Angler* in the approaches to Mindoro Strait in 13° 00′ N. 119° 30′ E., reported 15 to 20 ships, including three probable battleships, on an Easterly course at 18 knots. They were tracked into the Mindoro Strait, and at 2400 and again at 2403 two possible carriers were (incorrectly) reported with the three battleships.

12. Cruiser Force reported coming from the North, 0340, 23 October

Simultaneously with these reports of enemy ships proceeding up the Palawan Passage there came reports of contact with a Japanese cruiser force coming down from the northward. At 0340 on 23rd, the submarine *Bream* reported a force of at least two heavy cruisers and several destroyers to the westward of Luzon, in 14° 05′ N., 119° 43′ E. steering at a speed of 10 knots a course for the Verde Island Passage, the northern entrance to the Sibuyan Sea. This was, no doubt, the Japanese Fifth Fleet. The *Bream* reported (apparently incorrectly) one hit on an *Aoba* class cruiser. Two *Aoba* class heavy cruisers (one of them with two hits) and a destroyer were reported 50 minutes later, at 0430 on 23rd, in the same position, steering a course for Manila Bay.[4]

13. Contacts in the South, 23 October

Still further to confirm the violence of the enemy's reaction to the invasion of the Philippines there came contact reports from the southward also. A light cruiser and a destroyer were sighted at 0915 approaching the northern exit of

---

4. This is from the Sighting Reports Plan, where they are incorrectly called two light cruisers (*Aoba*). The Admiralty class these 7-87-in. gun vessels as cruisers. The Americans term them heavy cruisers (CAs). The Sighting Reports Plan shows also 'one *Nachi* (heavy cruiser) damaged 240800' at the entrance to Manila Bay and a *Natori* (light cruiser) damaged 240725 in Manila.

the Macassar Strait from the south-east; two destroyers were seen at 1030 on a south-westerly course off the southern tip of Cebu Island; and in the central part of the Sulu Sea a group composed of one armoured and two light cruisers and four destroyers was reported at 1155 on 23rd in 09° 30′ N., 120° 30′ E. steering an E. by S. course at slow speed. This latter force, though it was not known at the time, was probably the Japanese Fifth Fleet, consisting of the heavy cruisers *Nachi* and *Ashigara*, light cruiser *Abukuma*, and four destroyers, which left Koron Bay on the morning of the 24th, to support or co-operate with the, as yet, undiscovered Japanese Southern Force, south of Negros, late on the 24th.

14. The Fast Carriers move into Position for Search, night of 23–24 October

From the multiplicity of sighting reports on 23 October Vice-Admiral Kinkaid was fairly certain that the Japanese intended an attack on the ships off Leyte, probably through the Surigao Strait. He estimated that the large force moving up the Palawan Passage and the cruiser force reported by the *Bream* to be making for the Verde Island Passage might refuel in the neighbourhood of Koron Bay; the cruiser force could arrive there about 2080/23rd and the other, larger enemy force about 0100/24th.

Chapter III

Air Attack on the Third Fleet Carriers, 24 October

15. Dawn Search and Attack Units Launched, 24 October

Vice-Admiral Mitscher, Commander, Task Force 38, had ordered 'reinforced search teams', consisting of four bombers and four fighter aircraft to be launched at dawn on 24th to cover the Sibuyan Sea and the area from Mindoro Strait in the south to Lingayen Gulf on the west side of Luzon, in the north.[1] Their objective was major units of the Japanese fleet and they were intended as both search and attack units. Both the fighters and bombers carried bombs. and they were launched soon after 0600. In addition, the *Essex* sent off a 20-aircraft fighter sweep to attack enemy aircraft in the neighbourhood of the Manila airfields. A deck load strike was ordered ready on deck of each carrier to strike any enemy units reported by the search. These activities occupied a considerable proportion of the fighter aircraft of the carriers. There remained a barely adequate number to escort the ready strike, and a modest number for combat air patrol over the group.

No search to the north or north-east of Luzon was ordered, consequently the Japanese carrier force coming down from the north remained undetected though within aircraft range. The omission had a definite effect on the rest of the day's action.

16. Air Raid on Task Group 38.3, 0800, 24 October

The first enemy sightings were made by aircraft of Task Group 38.2 who reported, just before 0800, four battleships, eight armoured cruisers and escorts heading into the Sibuyan Sea from south of Mindoro Island. The report was intercepted by the *Essex*, flagship of Rear-Admiral Sherman, commanding Task Group 38.3, consisting of the carriers *Essex* and *Lexington*, light carriers

---

1. The *Essex* launched two teams to search 225° to 245° true, *Lexington* states that she launched five teams to search 10° sectors from 245° to 285° true (? four teams or 245° to 295°) for a distance of 300 miles. In addition, each of these two ships launched one team of four fighter aircraft to act as relay aircraft for contact reports. (*U.S.S. "Lexington" Action Report*, p.5).

Princeton and *Langley*, and screen, who made immediate preparations to launch a strike against the enemy. However, at 0800, just before it could be launched, a group of about 40 Japanese aircraft was reported to be closing on a bearing 250°; and a second large group was reported shortly afterwards closing behind the first. These first attacks came from Luzon, for although shore-based aircraft had reported the enemy to the Japanese Northern Force at 0820, the distance was too great for attacks by the Japanese carriers until it had narrowed. preponderance of carrier types amongst the aircraft was due to the transfer of aircraft in training from the carrier force to the Philippines.

At the time, Task Group 38.3 had combat air patrol of 12 fighter aircraft overhead and an anti-submarine patrol of four fighters and four bombers. This number was considered insufficient to deal with the major air attack which was thought to be pending. Accordingly, at 0805, 12 additional fighters each were scrambled from the *Langley* and the *Princeton*, and seven from the *Essex*. Within a few minutes a third large enemy raid appeared on the screen bearing 240° at a distance of 60 miles. This turned out to be the largest of the three raids, a group of 50 to 80 enemy aircraft divided about evenly between dive bombers, torpedo aircraft and fighters. To meet it, at 0831 the *Lexington* was ordered to launch her remaining 12 fighters.[2] The *Essex*'s Manila fighter sweep was also recalled just as it was arriving over Manila, where it attacked and damaged one of three ships near Bataan. These aircraft returned too late to take part in the battle. Meanwhile, Rear-Admiral Sherman was left with insufficient fighters to escort the strike which it had been his intention to send off against the Japanese fleet in the Sibuyan Sea before the increasing enemy attacks got in too close.

To avoid the oncoming air attack Rear-Admiral Sherman manoeuvred his Task Group to keep within shelter of the rain squalls in the area, emerging into the clear only to launch additional aircraft or land machines requiring fuel and ammunition. 'We were kept pretty busy with the attack for the next several hours,' he writes.

A mêlée soon developed. No directions could be given to the aircraft once they reported 'tally-ho.' Every available fighter was sent up. Commander David McCampbell, the *Essex* Air Group Commander led seven fighters into the large third raid; he shot down nine of the enemy, his wing-man got six, and the remaining pilots got nine between them – a total of 24. The *Lexington*'s fighters shot down 13 for the loss of a single fighter.

---

2. *Lexington*'s fighter Director Narrative does not say how many fighters were launched, merely that '*Lexington*'s planes were vectored out against this raid'. Her track chart shows scramble No.1 launched at 0801 and scramble No. 2 at 1301, with the delayed strike on the enemy in the Sibuyan Sea at 1050. Her Air Operations Narrative states that 11 fighters were launched when the 0800 raid was detected but mentions no further scramble nor any other raid.

17. The "Princeton" hit, 0939/4th

After an hour and a half there was a lull in the fighting. By this time many of the fighters were short of ammunition and fuel and had to be landed. Thanks to their efficient performance and Rear-Admiral Sherman's handling of the Task Group no organized group of enemy aircraft had reached the ships. About 0938 Task Group 383 emerged to the edge of a rain squall in 15° 22' N., 123° 47' E. to land the fighters which needed reservicing – enemy were showing on the flagship's screen within 50 miles. The *Princeton*, to land her fighters, had put her torpedo aircraft which were ready for deck load strike and armed with torpedoes on the hangar deck.   Suddenly, a single enemy aircraft, a Judy, apparently unnoticed by most of the ships amongst the returning friendly fighters, dived out of the low clouds over the *Princeton* and put a small bomb through her flight deck amidships. The AA cruiser *Reno*, on the *Princeton*'s port quarter fired at the Judy and possibly damaged it, and it is believed to have been the Judy which was later shot down by one of the *Lexington*'s fighters.

The bomb started a small fire on the hangar deck. Heavy black smoke came from amidships of the *Princeton* and she commenced to slow, and lost position in the formation which was proceeding at 24 knots at the time.   At 0947 she turned out of formation, and CTG 38.3, drawing clear with the rest of his ships, ordered the *Reno* and destroyers *Cassin Young*, *Gatling* and *Irwin* to stand by her. It seemed to Rear-Admiral Sherman, however, that there was little to fear from one small bomb hitting a ship the ability and strength of the *Princeton*, and that having warded off a major air attack with only one of the enemy getting into the disposition and only one small bomb hit, the Task Group had come off exceedingly well.

About 1001 the *Princeton*, with her flight deck burning furiously, asked the destroyers circling her to pour water into her fire. Almost simultaneously, an explosion occurred on board and about four minutes later a second took place in the after part of the carrier. Further explosions soon occurred. A large fire was raging through the hangar deck and around the island. Smoke was so dense, black and heavy that at times the ship was completely obscured. She lost all way, took a position across the wind, drifting to leeward. Men could be seen abandoning ship,[3] but the work of rescue and assistance was hampered by enemy aircraft who now returned to the attack. The *Reno* quitted the scene for some minutes, to fight off the threat with the *Gatling* and the Combat

---

3. About 1010 the order 'Salvage Control, Phase 1,' which called for all but 490 men to abandon ship, was given, and about 10 minutes later gun crews were also ordered to leave when ammunition in ready service rooms and lockers began to explode.

Air Patrol. Two of the enemy were shot down; one of them, near-missing the *Langley* with a bomb, crashed astern.

About 1030 the light cruiser *Birmingham*, despatched by Rear-Admiral Sherman, joined the group round the *Princeton*, and her Captain, T. B. Inglis, took charge of the operations. The destroyer *Morrison* was also sent. Enemy aircraft were still attacking, but the CAP held them at a distance.

By noon the fire fighting had effected an improvement on board the *Princeton*. It was only temporary, however, for at 1411 the carrier was again smoking heavily. It was raining now, visibility was very poor, as low as 100 yards at times, the wind was about 20 knots, the sea moderate to rough. Once again, enemy aircraft were reported. The Task Group, though in communication, were some miles away, engaged on their own business. Owing to her build, the carrier made more leeway than the lighter craft, consequently it was difficult to keep a ship alongside on the windward (port) side without a line to keep the ships together and causing damage through the crashing of the carrier's projecting sponsons in the seaway. At the *Princeton*'s request, each of the ships in turn had gone alongside to leeward[4] in the dense smoke and heat, but their fire hoses were ineffective up-wind and both the *Morrison* and *Irwin* had been badly, and the *Reno* slightly, damaged in the attempt.

It was clear to Captain Inglis that the only thing to be done was to use his ship as the fire fighter and the others as screen and AA support. Ordering the *Reno* to prepare to tow (1445), he put his ship alongside the *Princeton*'s port side. There were not enough men on board the *Princeton* to handle the hoses, so volunteers from the *Birmingham* clambered aboard with hoses which they led down into the hangar. The *Birmingham* had to cast off once, in order to deal with Japanese aircraft reported to have broken through the screen and with a submarine contact reported 2000 yards away but at 1512 Captain Inglis returned and again put his ship alongside.

18. Sinking of the "Princeton" 1750 24 October

About 12 minutes later the *Princeton*'s after magazines exploded, blowing off her stern and the after part of her flight deck, and hurling fragments and debris over a wide area. Not a single officer or man still on board is known to have escaped injury of some sort in the tremendous blast. Aboard the *Birmingham* the carnage was even more terrible. Her upper deck, crowded

---

4. The CO USS *Birmingham* states (*Secret Information Bulletin, No. 22*, p. 78-93), that he left it to the discretion of the Commanding Officers to comply with *Princeton*'s request if they considered it feasible, but through some misunderstanding the qualification was not transmitted and the directive to these ships was received by them as an unqualified order.

with men fighting the fire and manning the AA guns was raked from stem to stern. Over half of her officers and men were killed or injured in a moment.[5] 'It is impossible, even remotely, adequately to describe the grisly scene of human fragmentation,' wrote her Executive Officer, who took over the Command from the badly-wounded Captain. Nevertheless, within the hour, when the *Princeton* asked the *Birmingham* for a tow the survivors prepared without hesitation to rig their ship for towing. At 1604, however, threatened with another explosion, the *Princeton* had to be abandoned, work which occupied half an hour.

Meanwhile, events elsewhere had been moving rapidly. It was discovered that a concentration of the entire Japanese Fleet for attack on the Leyte beaches was in progress, and Task Group 38.3 was required in the north to deal with the threat coming from that direction.

Fires were raging in the *Princeton*, the weather was getting worse, the ships present were in bad shape, and the carrier after dark would have been a flaring beacon for enemy aircraft. At 1650 Rear-Admiral Sherman, acting on instructions from Commander Task Force 38 ordered the ship to be sunk; but it was not until an hour later, at 1750, after six torpedoes had been fired at her singly, and some shelling, that the *Princeton* blew up and sank in 15° 12′ N., 135° 47′ E. The rescue ships, *Birmingham*, *Morrison*, *Irwin* and *Gatling*, all of them, except the last, damaged to a greater or less degree and crowded with dead and injured, were formed into Task Group 38.3.6, and set course for Ulithi.

The sinking of the *Princeton*[6] cost the enemy about 110 aircraft which were shot down around Task Group 38.3, and in addition 40 Japanese aircraft were shot down by the Americans before the enemy attack.

---

5. Killed 229, missing four, wounded 416, half of them seriously.
6. Casualties of the *Princeton*'s crew were: known killed, one officer and six men missing, nine officers and 92 men; wounded, about 190 officers and men.

Chapter IV

Air Attacks on the Enemy Centre Force, 24 October

19. Contact with the Japanese Centre Force, 0810 24 October

Almost simultaneously with the enemy air attack which resulted in the loss of the *Princeton*, search aircraft from Task Group 38.2 at 0810 on 24th sighted the enemy main body (Centre Force) which had traversed Mindoro Strait in the dark and was now in the Tablas Strait east of Mindoro Island, in position 12° 14′ N., 121° 32′ E., proceeding at 18 knots on a course 015° which would eventually take them to San Bernardino Strait. The force was in two groups of almost similar composition. The first was reported as two battleships. three or four heavy or light cruisers and six destroyers; the second as two battleships, three or four heavy or light cruisers and seven destroyers.

Admiral Halsey intercepted the enemy report and after repeating it to Vice-Admiral Mitscher (Commander Task Force 38) and the commanders of Task Groups 38.3 (Rear-Admiral Sherman) and 38.4 (Rear-Admiral Davison), ordered them at 0827, to concentrate off San Bernardino Strait on Task Group 38.2 (Rear-Admiral Bogan), in which his own flagship, the *New Jersey* was operating and to send off strikes. However, by the time the order was received the *Princeton* had been damaged and, by Vice-Admiral Mitscher's orders, Task Group 38.3 remained with her until the evening when orders came to sink the ship. The remaining Task Group, 38.1, Vice-Admiral McCain's group, had been en route to Ulithi since 22nd and was in approximately 11° 45′ N., 135° 40′ E. A strike at Yap was planned for the morning of 24th, but was cancelled when at 0846 Admiral Halsey ordered the group to reverse course[1] and proceed at best speed towards position in 15° N. 130′ E. and launch a search to the north and north-west at dawn on 25th. A further message instructed the Task Group to fuel at daylight and report completion by urgent despatch.

---

1. McCain's despatch (p. 21). But his flag captain (Capt. O.A. Webber, USS *Wasp*) in his Report (p. 31) says the order to reverse course was received about 1045, though his track chart (which is on a very small scale) shows him reversing course after steaming about 125 miles at 16 knots from 0000/23rd (i.e., at about 0800).

20. The Japanese Southern Force Discovered, 0905 24 October

Shortly before the first air strikes reached the enemy main body, other smaller detachments of the Japanese Fleet were discovered to the southward, in the Sulu Sea. At 0805 on 24th search-strike aircraft from the *Franklin*, one of the fast carriers of Rear-Admiral Davison's Task Group 38.4 reported sighting and attacking three destroyers west of Panay Island, and at 0940 the *Franklin* launched a special strike of 11 fighters and 11 bombers to continue the attack and search for other targets. Only two of the enemy destroyers were found, one of which was strafed, reported hit by rockets and left burning aft, the other slightly damaged. At 0905 aircraft from the *Enterprise*, another of Rear-Admiral Davison's fast carrier group intercepted and attacked a force of two battleships, one heavy cruiser, and four destroyers in the Sulu Sea in 08° 55′ N., 121° 50′ E., south-west of Negros Island. This was Vice-Admiral Nishimura's command ('C' Force), consisting of the old battleships *Fuso* and *Yamashiro*, the heavy cruiser *Mogami*, and the 4th Destroyer Division (four destroyers). The search team reported, apparently somewhat over-optimistically, two bomb hits on each battleship, rocket hits on the cruiser and two of the destroyers, and heavy strafing of the other two destroyers.[2] Admiral Halsey assumed that the Seventh Fleet could take care of this small southern force and adhered to his decision that Task Group 38.4 should concentrate as previously ordered and transfer its attack from this newly-discovered force to the Japanese main body.

21. Air Attacks on the Centre Force, 24 October Sinking of the *Musashi*

Meanwhile Admiral Halsey's carrier aircraft had found and struck the Japanese Centre Force in the Sibuyan Sea, east of Mindoro, and continued throughout the day to batter it as it steered towards the San Bernardino Strait, making a total of 350 sorties in six waves between 0830 and 1730. Cloud cover at 5,000 to 6,000 feet hampered the aircraft somewhat, but there was no air opposition, though AA fire was intense. Task Group 38.2 made a total of 146 sorties, dropped 23 tons of bombs and 23 torpedoes, reporting the battleship *Yamato* damaged by three torpedo hits; another battleship of

---

2. Admiral Halsey's Despatch (*Secret Intelligence Bulletin, No. 22*, p.78-12). But this does not agree with the report received by Vice-Admiral Kinkaid, for which see Section 27. *Cincpac Report*, p. 62, gives 'at least three 500-pound bomb hits, plus several rocket hits on each of the two battleships, *Mogami* class heavy cruiser and the four destroyers were strafed and hit by rockets.' The only surviving Japanese commanding officer (Cdr. Nishino, of the destroyer *Shigure*) states that the *Fuso* received one bomb hit which destroyed her aircraft, and the *Shigure* had one gun damaged by a bomb hit, though her speed and navigability were not affected.

that class (possibly the same one) damaged by a torpedo and two bombs; a *Nagato* battleship hit by torpedo and one bomb; a *Kongo* battleship hit by two torpedoes and six bombs: a *Mogami* class heavy cruiser possibly sunk by a torpedo hit, and a *Nachi* and a *Tone* class heavy cruiser each hit by one torpedo. Task Group 38.4 reported a battleship, believed to be the *Musashi*, hit by torpedo, on fire, down by the bow, and probably sunk; the battleship *Yamato* hit by one to three torpedoes and four bombs; a *Kongo* battleship hit by a bomb; one cruiser damaged; one light cruiser sunk; one destroyer sunk, one probably sunk, and four damaged.

The claims of the aircraft crews of Rear-Admiral Sherman's Task Group 38.3, namely one battleship badly hit and two others damaged, and four heavy and two light cruisers damaged, were comparatively modest. The early morning air attack which necessitated his sending up every fighter he had, delayed his first strike until about 1100, by which time sufficient fighters had been landed and re-serviced to send off a properly escorted attack. Pilots of the reinforced search aircraft landing after the strike was launched reported considerable targets in the Manila area, including two light cruisers, one damaged heavy cruiser,[3] several destroyers and many merchant ships. Apart, however, from the fact that the continued presence of enemy aircraft and insufficiency of fighters precluded sending strikes to Manila he considered the Japanese force in the Sibuyan Sea was the main objective and left the ships at Manila unmolested.

The losses of American aircraft during their attacks on the Japanese Second Fleet were very light. Rear-Admiral Sherman's Task Group, 38.3, lost during the day's operations, including the heavy air attacks made on it, only ten aircraft, five pilots and four aircrewmen. On the other hand, 120 Japanese aircraft were shot down whilst attacking the formation[4] and a further 47 were brought down near Luzon.

22. Lack of Air Support for the Japanese Second Fleet

But in spite of the enthusiastic reports of the American airmen, Vice-Admiral Kurita's force had suffered no crippling loss or damage. Since it was important in the existing situation to slow down the enemy battleships and damage their fire control gear, the American aircraft directed their attacks against

---

3. Some of these were no doubt ships which had been damaged previous to the Third Fleet carrier strikes of 24 October.
4. No reports are forthcoming from TGs 38.2. and 38.4. *Lexington*, however, gives the following figures: Some 100–125 aircraft shot down by CAP and 30–40 by US. search aircraft, sum total 150–160. Admiral King's Second Report says 110 were shot down.

the two battle squadrons which were in the centre of a circular formation. The performance of the American bombs and torpedoes against the Japanese battleships was disappointing. Mixed depth settings of 10ft. and 20ft. were used, though the *Enterprise* reports eight torpedoes dropped against a *Yamato* class battleship, set for 12ft. The great new battleship *Musashi* was hit by torpedoes and bombs[5] and sank later in the day, south of Mindoro Island whilst trying to reach Koron Bay; and the heavy cruiser *Myoko* received damage to two shafts from a torpedo hit at 1135 and returned to Singapore unescorted. With the possible exception of the *Yahagi* no other cruisers were damaged, and although all the other battleships received one or two hits all of them were able to continue to fight.[6] The only destroyer reported damaged was the *Kiyoshimo*.

The Executive Officer of the *Musashi* gave the following account of the sinking of the ship:

> In the first attack, about 1030, the *Musashi* was hit on the star board side by three torpedoes. The second attack about 15–20 minutes later. We received five torpedo hits on the port side from this attack. From about 1300 we gradually fell astern of the main disposition and by 1430 were well separated from the other ships. We were accompanied only by the *Tone*. About 1530 the heaviest attack of the day was made against this ship. The total number of hits received was about 30 bombs and 26 torpedoes. We attempted to beach the *Musashi* on the north coast of Sibuyan Island, but about 1930 it capsized to port and sank. It sank because two torpedo attacks hit in the same place on the port side abreast of No. 4 engine room. Pumping was hindered due to the cumulative bomb damage above, so it was impossible to check the flooding. About 50 per cent of the 2,200 men on board were lost.

Vice-Admiral Kurita received intelligence that American carrier aircraft had been over Manila early that morning, and his own radar gave him warning of attack at about 50 to 60 miles distance. He also learned through a short message from Vice-Admiral Nishimura that his part of the operation was not going well,

---

5. Interrogation No. (*U.S.S. 149) Nav. No. 35, pp. 149–3*) states that she was hit by 18 torpedoes and 40 bombs. Interrogation No. (*U.S.S. B.S. Nar. No. 41. pp. 170–2*, states that she was hit by four torpedoes, only one of which exploded, and by 40 bombs. Capt. Kato, her Executive Officer stated in interrogation that she was hit by about 30 bombs and 26 torpedoes before capsizing. About 1,100 men were lost. The action reports mention five torpedo hits in the first four attacks, and further damage in the fifth attack.

6. Vice-Admiral Kurita's Staff Officer (Operations) (Comdr. Otano) gave the following damage to the remaining battleships *Yamato* – two large bomb hits and two near misses, the latter making a large hole in the bow. *Nagato, Kongo, Haruna* – one bomb hit each, but with the exception of the *Nagato* he was uncertain of the date when these battleships were hit.

and he assumed that the air attack (by the *Enterprise*) at 0905 had caused serious damage. However, he made no alteration in the plan of operations.

The Centre Force sustained the great day-long attacks of Admiral Halsey's fast carrier aircraft without air cover, nor had Vice-Admiral Nishimura's detachment any air protection when attacked from the *Enterprise* that morning. The original plan had made provision for the Second Fleet to be accompanied by Carrier Division 3, consisting of the light cariers *Zuiho*, *Chitose* and *Chiyoda*, with the addition of the carrier *Zuikaku*. These ships were to join Vice-Admiral Kurita at Lingga, but the rapidity with which the Allies struck at the Philippines defeated this intention, for the training of fresh carrier aircraft after the losses in the June engagement off the Marianas was still incomplete.

Admiral Toyoda had given orders for the navy land-based fleets to give cover to Vice-Admiral Kurita, and the latter was empowered to apply direct to the navy air chiefs. On account, however, of shortage of aircraft there were few to spare from the attacks on the American fast carriers; and this factor, together with bad weather and the poor state of training of the Japanese, which was apparently the reason why Vice-Admiral Kurita's repeated requests for air cover were ignored.[7] Army air cover had been arranged for him, and he could apply direct to Field Marshal Terauchi, Commander-in-Chief, Southern Army, who disposed of the Fourth Air Army, but he apparently knew nothing about this.[8]

---

7. *Interrogation of Vice Admiral Fukudone, Nav. No. 11511s, U.S.S. B.S. No. 503*. Captain Inoguchi, Chief of Staff of First Air Fleet, also stated that bad weather prevented air cover being given to the Second Fleet (*Interrogation Nav. No. 12, U.S.S. B.S. No. 62*). Commander Yamaguchi, Operations Officer on the State of the Combined Base Air Force (Philippines) stated that the standard protection for a fleet, viz. 10 aircraft, was ordered for the Second Fleet from a point 200 miles from Luzon until it arrived off Leyte, but this CAP was ineffective against the US aircraft, and the time occupied in returning to Luzon to fuel left the Second Fleet without protection for long periods (*Interrogation Nav. No. 44. U.S.S. B.S., No. 193*). Vice-Admiral Kurita would seem to have been unaware that the C-in-C. Southwest Area Fleet, Vice-Admiral Matsuda, had been placed in command of the Navy Air Fleets in the Philippines, for he states that he addressed his requests for air cover to Vice-Admiral Onishi

8. Vice-Admiral Kurita in his interrogation said: 'No request was made of the Army; I do not know whether there were any army planes there or not. When called upon for planes, the Navy would send planes if they had them; if not, the Navy would request them locally from the Army. That was my opinion.' Captain Ohmae, Chief of Staff to Vice-Admiral Ozawa, stated in his interrogation that the Navy had no satisfactory liaison with Army aircraft in the Philippines and could not call on them for assistance. The reasons he gave for poor co-operation were that on the technical side, Army pilots could not navigate; the Army insisted upon being a defensive machine and would not fight offensively; there was a clash of personalities below the higher levels; and Army maintenance was very poor. Vice-Admiral Kurita's Chief of Staff, Rear-Admiral Koyanagi, stated that it was very difficult to obtain co-operation between the fleet and land-based aircraft. On the other hand, Vice-Admiral Fukudome, who commanded the shore-based Navy Air Fleets in the Philippines, did not think there was any particular friction between the Army and Navy Air Forces. (*Interrogation Navy No. 115, U.S.S. B.S, No. 101*)

23. The Fast Carriers Concentrate, pm, 24 October

In face of the continued strikes the Japanese Centre Force held on its course 'with a determination which commanded respect', although at one time in the afternoon reported to be 'milling around.' At 1749 the *Enterprise* reported that the force consisted of about 25 ships in two groups, position 12° 50′ N., 122° 35′ E. (in the middle of the Sibuyan Sea), heading westward when last seen at 1600.

Vice-Admiral Kurita did, in fact, retire temporarily to the westward about 1600, to avoid air attack. He informed Admiral Toyoda and received in reply an order to continue the advance, though apparently he had already resumed his course for San Bernardino Strait before the order reached him, the air attacks having ceased.[9]

Sunset was at 1805. Between 1715 and 2400 on 24th the night carrier *Independence*, in Admiral Halsey's own Task Group 38.2, spent 30 hours flying time in following the Japanese main body eastward. During these hours Vice-Admiral Kurita passed through the San Bernardino Strait, but the information apparently failed to get through. Communication troubles were experienced by the tracking aircraft, for although there was no indication of deliberate interference these aircraft and the Japanese powerful nearby land stations appear to have shared the same frequency. Sufficient enemy reports were received, however, to show that the main body of the Japanese fleet was continuing to steer for San Bernardino Strait. At 2030 and 2145 on 24th it was sighted by an *Independence* aircraft north of Masbate Island on various courses and trailing much oil.[10] Task Group 38.4 had joined Task Group 38.2 at 1630 in 13° 36′ N., 126° 01′ E., and Admiral Halsey directed Rear-Admiral Davison, who flew his flag in USS *Franklin*, to assume tactical command of the two task groups. Vice-Admiral Sherman, with Task Group 38.3, who had been standing by the *Princeton* all day, did not join until about 2330 24th. It was Admiral Halsey's intention, in the event of the enemy breaking out of the San Bernardino Strait, to form a Task Force (T.F. 34) to engage him.

---

9. His Staff Officer, Operations (Commander Otano) stated that it was hoped the message might bring out land-based aircraft to protect him, and that the same message as was sent to Admiral Toyoda was also sent to Admiral Fukudome and Onishi at Manila.

10. Admiral Halsey's Despatch (*Secret Information Bulletin*, p.78-14.)

Chapter V

The Third Fleet Goes North, 24 October

24. Discovery of the Japanese Northern Force, 1540, 24 October

Meanwhile, the discovery of the Japanese Carrier Force in the north had created a new situation. The air attacks on Task Group 38.3, in which the *Princeton* was sunk, continued during the forenoon of the 24th. Enemy aircraft came from two directions, from Luzon and from a sector roughly between north and north-east. A preponderance of carrier-based types indicated that a Japanese carrier force might be at hand in that direction.

The surmise was, in fact, correct. Vice-Admiral Ozawa had sailed from the Inland Sea with the carrier force on 20 October, leaving Okishima in the Bungo Suido at 1700. American submarines were detected shortly afterwards, both visually by aircraft and by radar, and the force proceeded eastward until 2100 on 20th when it turned south to meet its supply ships from Amami O Shima. Refuelling was carried out during the afternoon of 22nd in about 24° N., 135° E. and at 2000 that day the Vice-Admiral put a fairly long message on the air and subsequently made several contacts with US submarines. Search aircraft were sent out from 0700 on 21st onwards. At daybreak on 24th the force was in position 19° N., 126° 40′ E.; and at 0820 Japanese shore-based aircraft reported the enemy (Rear-Admiral Sherman's Task Group 38.3) bearing 60° distance 90 miles from Manila. It was not until 1115, however, that Vice-Admiral Ozawa's aircraft sighted Rear-Admiral Sherman's group, bearing 120 distance 180 miles; the observer was unable to state whether it included any carriers.

Vice-Admiral Ozawa decided to attack, and at 1145 he sent off 40 fighters, 28 bombers, two reconnaissance and six torpedo aircraft, total 76; Rear-Admiral Sherman's task group was then bearing 210°, distance 150 to 160 miles. Visibility at the target was 20 miles, with fierce squalls to the east and south. The Japanese aircraft were instructed to land at Nichols Field, Luzon or other shore bases if the weather should render return to the carriers too hazardous. Apparently about 40 aircraft reached the target, and 30 to 40 reached Luzon. Only three returned to their ships, and none of them were able to state what results had been obtained. Poor communications prevented any report of the result of the strikes from reaching the Northern Force from the aircraft which landed on Luzon.

'At this time', writes Admiral Halsey, 'it was evident that the Japanese navy was making a major effort, whether for direct attacks or transporting troops, or both, was not apparent. If this was to be an all-out attack by the Japanese fleet, there was one piece missing in the puzzle – the carriers. They were believed to have been in Japan; and there had been sightings which indicated that replenishment measures might have been taken for some important move from Japanese waters. Although our submarines stationed in Japanese waters had not reported a carrier force, it was felt that they were sure to be employed in some manner in any operation as great as that revealed on the morning of the 24th.'[1]

At 1015 on 24th Admiral Halsey had ordered Rear-Admiral Sherman to keep the area to the north under observation.[2] At 1155 Rear-Admiral Sherman, who had been ordered not to leave the neighbourhood of the stricken *Princeton* by Vice-Admiral Marc A. Mitscher (CTF 38) was instructed by the latter to launch a search consisting of two fighters and one bomber aircraft in each sector between the bearings 350° and 040°.[3] However, more than two hours were to elapse before the search got off. Twice the fighters made ready by the *Essex* had to be scrambled to beat off fresh enemy air attacks, and 14 fighter aircraft assembled by the *Lexington* for the search had to be similarly employed. At length, as he had no fighters left, Rear-Admiral Sherman, who strongly suspected the presence of enemy carriers to the north-east, obtained permission from Vice-Admiral Mitscher to send bomber search aircraft on 'single plane search' without accompanying fighters. At 1405, a few minutes after what was to prove the final enemy air attack of the day on the group, these aircraft were launched from the *Lexington*, and at 1640 they reported the missing Japanese carriers (the Northern Force) 190 miles to the north-north eastward.

Vice-Admiral Ozawa had been vainly awaiting information from his aircraft of the result of their strikes; but all contact with his reconnaissance aircraft was lost. Meanwhile, the American air attacks on Vice-Admiral Kurita continued without cessation, and it was apparent that the Northern Force was not succeeding in its task of drawing the enemy northward. It seems that up till now Vice-Admiral Ozawa had received reports of no more

---

1. Despatch, para. 9 (*Secret Information Bulletin, No. 22*, p.78-12).
2. USS *Santa Fe, Action Report*.
3. Report of CTG 38.3. It is not clear whether the directive for the search came from CTF. 38 or from Admiral Halsey. The latter, in his Despatch, in para. 9 commencing 'At this time' (a.m./24th) merely says: 'a search to the north by our carrier planes was ordered.' Admiral King *Second Report*, p. 22 says that Admiral Halsey ordered the search to be made.

than the northernmost (Rear-Admiral Sherman's) Task Group, 38.3, in which his information was that two carriers had been damaged, despite the fact that in the course of this day, 24 October each of the three task groups, 38.2, 38.3 and 38.4 of Admiral Halsey's Third Fleet was reconnoitred by Japanese aircraft.[4] Ozawa determined to send south Rear-Admiral Matsuda, commander of his advance guard, consisting of the 4th Carrier Squadron (*Hyuga, Ise*), the 61st Destroyer Division (less the *Suzutsuki*) and 41st Destroyer Division (*Shimotsuki*), to make contact with Rear-Admiral Sherman and try to draw him northward, and, if opportunity offered, to attack. He himself with the remainder of his force would proceed westward until about 1600, in the hope of taking on his aircraft, after which he would resume his south-easterly course.

Rear-Admiral Matsuda's force made no attack and was eventually recalled, re-joining about sunrise on 25th. To his chagrin, Vice-Admiral Ozawa then learned that about 1900–2100 on 24th the detached force sighted in the distance what it is now thought may have been an electrical storm, though Matsuda at the time considered it to be the American task force, under attack with torpedoes by land-based Japanese aircraft, for his force had radar contact at the time with aircraft though the distance, 50 kilometres (27 nautical miles), was too great for radar contact to be made with ships.[5] On account of the danger of causing confusion if he approached, Rear-Admiral Matsuda sheered off; and when the attack was over the American task force could not again be found. Due to the need for maintaining radio silence the sighting of the supposed fast carriers was not reported back to Vice-Admiral Ozawa at the time.

At 2010 on 24th the latter received Vice-Admiral Kurita's report that the Centre Force had retired to the westward [at 1600], and unwilling to stand alone, Ozawa turned 10 points and retired in his turn until ordered to advance again by the Commander-in-Chief Combined Fleet at 242110. Accordingly, Ozawa turned once more to a south-easterly course. It seemed to him that the Americans would continue their attacks on the Japanese Second Fleet next day, and it was his duty to offer his fleet as a sacrifice to draw Admiral Halsey north.

Amplifying reports to Admiral Halsey of this Northern Force varied. CTF 38 listed the force as three carriers, three to four heavy cruisers, and six destroyers at latitude 18° 10' N., 125° 30' E. coarse 210°, speed 15, and

4. Vice-Admiral Fakudome, Commander Combined Air Fleet at Manila, stated that Vice-Admiral Ozawa's force was outside the area of his command and he was consequently unable to give him any information. (*Interrogation Navy No. 503, U.S.S. B.S, No. 115*).

5. *Interrogation Navy No. 69, U.S.S. B.S, No. 345.*

stated that one of the enemy carriers was of the converted battleship *Ise* class. Later he reported that pilots who had had a good look gave the composition of the force as three carriers, three to four heavy cruisers, and six destroyers at latitude 18° 10' N., 125° 30' E. course 210°, speed 15 speed 15 knots at 1540. One of the battleships was reported to have a flight deck aft. At 1600 two *Terutsuki* class destroyers were reported in 19° 40' N., 123° 00' E., course 240°, speed 12 knots. After studying the reports, Admiral Halsey concluded that the Northern Force was disposed is two groups, estimated to contain a total of at least 17 ships and possibly as many as 24.[6] The former figure was correct for its actual strength was four carriers and two battleship carriers, all now practically devoid of aircraft,[7] with screen of three light cruisers and eight destroyers.

25. Admiral Halsey's Appreciation of the Situation

On one point the contact reports of all the three Japanese forces were agreed: the detachment in the Sulu Sea (Southern Force) approaching Surigao Strait, the main body (Centre Force) in the Sibuyan Sea steering for San Bernardino Strait, and the northern carrier force were all proceeding at moderate speed. The inference was that there was a predetermined rendezvous of geographical location and tim; a co-ordinated plan was being followed, with 25 October as the earliest date of concerted action.

To what extent Admiral Halsey credited the wildly exaggerated aircraft reports of damage to the Japanese Centre Force in the day-long attacks of the 24th is not known, but it is clear from his own words that, as events proved, he did not discount them sufficiently. He concluded that they 'indicated, beyond a doubt, that the Center Force had been badly mauled with all of its battleships and most of its heavy cruisers tremendously reduced in fighting power and life'.[8] He considered that the force was adhering blindly to a plan, and though he recognized that it might 'plod' through San Bernardino Strait and attack the shipping off the Leyte beaches he was convinced that it was so heavily damaged that it could not win a decision. It was from the newly discovered Northern Force that the greater threat came, for the Commander Third Fleet had, of course, no inkling that its teeth had been drawn and that it was both powerless for attack and almost defenceless in face of his overwhelming air

---

6. Admiral Halsey's Despatch, para. 10. None of these reports agrees with those given by Rear-Admiral Sherman which he says he passed on to CTF 38 and Com. Third Fleet. Only one of them agrees with *Lexington*'s report.
7. There were on board 19 fighters, of which 14 could be used only for 'covering operations'.
8. *Despatch*, para. 13.

and gun power. By comparing the number and type of battleships and heavy cruisers reported in the Southern and Centre Forces with the total of the Japanese Navy believed operational, and checking them against the reports of the Northern Force, it would have appeared probable that the latter had few, if any, heavy cruisers, and no battleship strength other than the *Ise* and *Hyuga*, both of which, however, mounted eight 14-in. guns and would have been tough opponents for anything except battleships if brought to gun range.

It was clear to Admiral Halsey that attack was essential if the enemy's plan was to be disrupted and the initiative maintained. Moreover, the attack must come swiftly, before the Japanese carriers could once more fly on their aircraft, which after their strikes on the Third Fleet, were no doubt being re-armed and re-fuelled on the airfields of the Philippines, tactics which the enemy had employed four months earlier, at the Battle of the Marianas. In arriving at this decision the Commander of the Third Fleet considered three alternatives:

(a) To divide his forces, leaving Task Force 34 to block San Bernardino Strait, whilst the carriers, with light screens, attacked the Northern Force.

(b) To keep his fleet concentrated off San Bernardino Strait.

(c) To strike the Northern Force with his entire concentrated striking strength.

Any division of his fleet he rejected as unsound and likely to result in damage to no purpose.

The second alternative was also rejected since it would permit the Northern Force to function unmolested and because the destruction of Japanese carriers would facilitate subsequent operations.

Admiral Halsey, therefore, chose the third alternative. It was strategically sound in that it maintained the integrity of the Third Fleet and afforded the best possibility of surprise and destruction of the enemy carrier force, potentially the most dangerous of the three. Even though the rump of the Japanese Centre Force might emerge from the San Bernardino Strait and inflict some damage, the Commander of the Third Fleet calculated that he could return in time to reverse any advantage gained by the enemy. Taking a long view, swift attack on the enemy carriers would contribute most to the Philippines campaign, even if a temporarily hazardous situation existed at Leyte.

That Admiral Halsey was not altogether easy in his mind is clear. Between the Japanese Centre Force and the mass of defenceless shipping off the Leyte landings there stood two forces. The first consisted of 18 escort carriers, mounting one 5-in. gun apiece, which had been allocated for the operation to Vice-Admiral Kinkaid's Seventh Fleet. The second, Rear-Admiral Oldendorf's Task Group 77.2, comprising the battleship and cruiser strength of the Seventh Fleet was, on paper, a respectable force, and Admiral Halsey had already cast them for the role of 'taking care' of the Japanese Southern Force. There remained only the escort carriers. The success of the Philippines campaign required that these little ships should hold the pass until the Third Fleet, having dealt with the Japanese carrier force, could return to rescue them. 'It was a hard decision to make', writes Admiral Halsey.

26. Task Force 38 Concentrates and goes North, 2330 24 October

After the discovery of the Japanese Northern Force Vice-Admiral Mitscher decided quickly to attack with his fast carriers. Within the hour, at 1723, he informed his Task Force Commanders that he intended to proceed north-eastward during the night, for it was too late to send off a strike that afternoon against Vice-Admiral Ozawa's force, since the aircraft were just returning from the strikes in the Sibuyan Sea. However, if the north-easterly course was maintained during the night the Japanese carriers could not get away. But orders now came through from Admiral Halsey for Task Groups 38.3 and 38.4 to concentrate towards Task Group 38.2. The latter had been operating off San Bernardino Strait all day and was now coming north with Task Group 38.4 which had joined it at 1630. In conformity with these orders, Rear-Admiral Sherman, in Task Group 38.3, who was in the northernmost position, reluctantly turned south-eastward about 1900 to rendezvous with the other two groups.

At 2022 on 24th the Commander Third Fleet sent out further orders for Task Groups 38.2, 38.3 and 38.4 to assemble at a point about 150 miles north-east of San Bernardino Strait, for the run north during the night and to be prepared to attack at dawn. Task Force 38.3 joined up about 2330 and Vice-Admiral Mitscher, Commander First Carrier Task Force, assumed tactical command of the disposition, Task Force 38. This was a formidable fleet, organized in three groups, each containing a carrier unit supported by two battleships and a complement of cruisers and destroyers. Course 000° was set until midnight, when the force was to proceed to latitude 16° N. In order to avoid over-running the daylight circle of the Japanese carriers, which would place them between Task Force 38 and Leyte, a speed of 16 knots was ordered. At 0000/25 the force was in 14° 31′ N., 125° 34′ E., course was altered to 045°, and speed maintained at 16 knots to close the enemy last reported at 1755/24 in 18° 10′ N., 125° 30′ E. Enemy aircraft were about during the night, for search aircraft were regularly launched by the Japanese carriers from the 22nd onwards, but none appear to have closed the fleet nearer than 35 miles.

The hours were pregnant with history, for the coming day was to seal the fate of an empire. Slowly, Admiral Halsey steamed into the night, preceded by planes probing relentlessly for the new antagonist hidden in the northern darkness. Behind him the jaws of the Japanese pincers strained to close on the defenceless shipping off the Leyte landings; for in that midnight hour when the American Third Fleet completed its concentration and set course for the north Kurita, braving the hidden dangers of reef and mine and driving at 20 knots through San Bernardino Strait was making towards Leyte; whilst to the south of him Nishimura, his eyes on the same objective, was approaching the Surigao Straits whose waters were to be his winding sheet.

Chapter VI

The Battle of Surigao Strait, Night, 24–25 October

27. Approach of the Japanese Southern Force, 24 October

Meanwhile the reinforced search group of aircraft of the *Enterprise* (Task Group 38.4) which at 0905 on 24th had attacked Vice-Admiral Nishimura's C Force (two battleships, one heavy cruiser and four destroyers) in the Sulu Sea south-west of Negros Island, in 08° 55' N., 121° 50' E. had reported to Vice-Admiral Kinkaid that four bomb hits had been made on each of the battleships, and rocket hits on the destroyers, actually, only minor damage was caused, however.[1] The force was variously reported as two battleships, two cruisers and four destroyers, and as two battleships, four light cruisers, two heavy cruisers and six destroyers, close to the position of the 0905 report, but Vice-Admiral Kinkaid rightly assumed that all three reports referred to a single force. Vice-Admiral Nishimura's force was again reported by aircraft and attacked about an hour later at 1000, in approximately the same position and on the same course, namely, north-east towards the Surigao Strait.[2] Shortly afterwards, however, Rear-Admiral R.E. Davison informed the Commander, Seventh Fleet, that he was taking his Task Group 38.4, north to effect concentration with the remainder of Task Force 38 north-east of San Bernardino Strait, and would henceforth be out of range of the newly located Japanese Southern Force.

C Force was reported once more, at 1240, close south-west of Negros Island on a south-easterly course, after which it remained unlocated for more than 12 hours.

Meanwhile, a number of sighting reports of other enemy detachments had come in, for from all parts of the archipelago reinforcements were hurrying to Leyte. At 0102 on 24th a force consisting of two heavy cruisers, one light cruiser and four destroyers was reported south of Negros, heading towards the

---

1. Report of CTF 77, *Secret Information Bulletin, No. 22*, p. 78-11. Cm. Third Fleet in his report (p. 78-12), says the search team reported two bomb hits on each battleship, rocket hits on a heavy cruiser and two destroyers, and heavy strafing of two other destroyers. Photographs taken show the *Fuso* apparently on fire from bomb hit aft.
2. The only available Japanese source states that only one air attack was received, namely at 0900.

Mindanao Sea, and at 0931 a light cruiser and a destroyer were reported south-east of Negros Island, entering the Mindanao Sea from the Sulu Sea. Search aircraft from the recently captured airfield on Morotai in the Halmaheras.

The position of the Battle Line was chosen in the northern part of Surigao Strait, in order to avoid the restricted waters further south. To meet the contingency of the enemy attempting to pass east of Hibuson Island or sending a detachment in that direction, the two most heavily armed battleships, the *West Virginia* and the *Maryland*, which each mounted eight 16-in. guns against 12 14-in. of the other four battleships, were placed at the eastern end of the Battle Line, which from east to west was as follows: -

Battleships: *West Virginia*	Destroyers: Aulick
Maryland	*Cony*
Mississippi (Flag)	*Sigourney*
Tennessee	*Claxton*
California	*Welles*
Pennsylvania	*Thorn*

The initial position of the battleships was in latitude 10° 35′ N., steaming east and west at five knots between longitudes 125° 16′ E. and 125° 27′ E., at which points they reversed course. The destroyers were to be used for screening as desired.

The position was chosen so as to allow some freedom of movement to the battle line and yet enable it to train its guns on the enemy whilst the latter was still in the narrower waters of the Strait. Even so, the east to west space was limited, and at a greater speed than five knots the frequent turns necessary would entail a great risk of being on the turn when fire was opened. Rear-Admiral Berkey's force, Task Group 77.3, was assigned duty as Right Flank Force and took station 240° 8,000 yards from the Battle Line at 2000 in approximate position 10° 30′ N., 125° 20′ E., north-east of Kabugan Line at 2000 in approximate position 10° 30′ N., 125° 20′ E., north-east of Kabugan, Grande Island, and patrolled at slow speed on an east-west line on the western side of Surigao Strait. Owing to the crowded conditions on the right flank when the Battle Line was in its extreme westerly (right) position, the Commander Right Flank was authorized to station his destroyers about 8,000 yards to the south and down channel from his westernmost position, on a north-south line between Kabugan Grande Island and Bugho Point.

The cruisers and the remainder of the destroyers of Task Group 77.2, namely the heavy cruisers in the following order, *Louisville*, *Portland* and *Minneapolis*, the light cruisers *Denver* and *Columbia*, and nine destroyers of Destroyer Squadron 56 took station in column on the Battle Line as Left

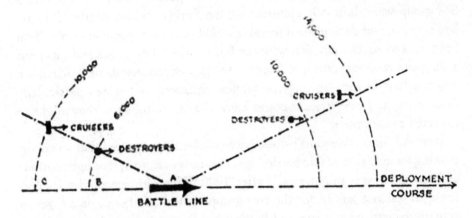

U.S. Type 'A' Battle Disposition for Small Task Forces
A-2
Light Forces Equally Divided

Diagram I. U.S. Type 'A' Battle Disposition for Small Task Forces.

Flank Force, north-west of Hibuson Island. The left flank was made stronger than the right, on account of the possible danger from the eastern end of Surigao Strait as well as from the southern end.

The strong current, the slow speed occasioned by the confined area, and other factors rendered it difficult for all the ships to maintain these dispositions.

The Commander Task Group 77.2 (Rear-Admiral Oldendorf) was in the cruiser *Louisville*, in the Left Flank Force.

The 18 escort carriers of Task Group 77.4 with their escorts, under Rear-Admiral T. L. Sprague, were disposed about 50 miles to the eastward of Homonhon Island (east of Samar Island) in three Task Units within mutually supporting distance and from north to south as follows: 77.4.3, 77.4.1, 77.4.2

Apart from the difficulties inherent in a night action – the difficulty of keeping track of one's own destroyers after releasing them to fulfil their proper function of attacking the enemy with torpedoes, and the danger, in narrow waters, of possible minefields and lurking enemy destroyers – Rear-Admiral Oldendorf's tactics were handicapped by lack of intelligence of the enemy and shortage of ammunition and to some extent, his freedom of action was hampered by the possibility that he might have to defend Leyte Gulf against an attack from seaward as well as holding Surigao Strait.

It was not possible to determine in advance whether the enemy would include his heavy cruisers in his battle line. Between the last sighting report of the Southern Force at 1240 and the next report at 2310, when the Sulu Sea group were definitely approaching the Surigao Strait, nearly 12 hours had elapsed, and during the interval it would have been possible for the Sulu Sea forces to effect a junction with the force in the Sibuyan Sea and carry out a complete re-organization of forces. This lack of continuous reconnaissance was the first factor affecting the tactical situation, and it was particularly disquieting to the Americans not to know the size of the force they might be expected to encounter.

Rear-Admiral Oldendorf's directive to the battle line stated that an enemy striking force of at least two battleships, four heavy cruisers, four light cruisers and ten destroyers might attack after 1900. This estimate of the enemy's strength was not far out for the two groups of the Southern Force together actually comprised the two old battleships *Fuso* and *Yamashiro*, the heavy cruisers *Nachi*, *Mogami* and *Ashigara*, the light cruiser *Abukuma*, and eight destroyers. The leading group ('C' Force) entered the Strait some 20 to miles away from the group in rear (Fifth Fleet).

The second factor influencing the tactics of the battle line was the battleships' ammunition outfits; the outfit required for the dual roles of bombarding and battle called for compromise. The equipment of Rear-Admiral Oldendorf's ships was on the scale usual for bombardment and fire support groups. The employment of the older battleships on bombardment duties had gradually led to their outfits of armour-piercing projectiles and service charges being reduced to a point which proved extremely embarrassing in the present situation. For their main armaments the battleships were carrying no more than 20 to 30 rounds per gun of AP of which a percentage, varying for the different ships, had already been expended in bombardments; whilst of their 5-in. outfits about 40 per cent remained. The destroyers had expended all but about one-fifth of their 5-in. outfits. No replenishment had been effected since the landing on 20 October. Two ammunition ships had been sent into Leyte Gulf, the US Navy ship *Mazama* and the merchant ship *Durham Victory*, but the former was not loaded with any 16-in. ammunition at all and the latter carried only 48 16-in. AP with appropriate service charges, in addition to 1,000 rounds of HC with reduced charges. The situation with regard to 6-in. AP was little better; there were only 1,100 projectiles in Leyte Gulf – less than 15 minutes firing by one light cruiser.

In view of the limited armour-piercing ammunition available – the *Mississippi* had less than 17 rounds per gun – it was necessary to reserve it for use only against battleships, and in order to render it as effective as possible to use it only at the selected moderate ranges of 17,000 to 20,000 yards; it was, therefore, intended to close fast to the latter and fight the action at moderate ranges. Destroyer attacks were to be launched if conditions were suitable prior to the engaging of the battle line.

The weather during the early part of the night was very fine. The wind was easterly, average seven knots, temperature 84°, the sky partly cloudy, sea smooth. In the bright moonlight visibility was at least 8,000 yards, but the moon set at 0007, before the enemy reached the Strait, local squalls then visited the area bringing low overcast clouds and a dark, black night with zero visibility interrupted only by intermittent vivid lightning flashes.

29. Contact with the Enemy, 2310 24 October. The PT Boat Attacks

Vice-Admiral Nishimura was ahead of schedule. In the original plan, he was to enter the Surigao Strait about an hour before daylight on the 25th, but he decided to advance the time by some four hours and make his approach at about 0200, though this gain was subsequently lost through delay caused by the *Enterprise*'s air attack at 0905 on the 24th.[3] He duly informed Vice-Admiral Kurita of his change of plan, but too late on the 24th for the latter to order him to conform to the original plan.

During the approach Vice-Admiral Nishimura at 2100 on 24th, when south of Bohol Island, detached the *Mogami* with the destroyers *Michisio*, *Yamaguma* and *Asagumo*, to reconnoitre ahead of the battleships; they apparently proceeded as far as Panaon Island, then returned and rejoined the flagship about 2330 on the 24th when the approach disposition was assumed, with two destroyers ahead and one on each bow of the heavy ships, the latter being line ahead in the order *Yamashiro*, *Fuso*, *Mogami*.

The first local contact with Vice-Admiral Nishimura's force was made by *PT 131*, who reported at 2215 two radar targets in 9° 33′ N., 124° 26′ E. (22 miles NW of Kamigin Island) steering 80°, speed 25 knots. These were perhaps the *Mogami* and destroyers scouting ahead. At about 2310 *PT 127* sighted three destroyers and two larger ships, 10 miles south-east of Bohol Island, heading north. This message was received by Rear-Admiral Oldendorf's force about an hour later. From now on the MTBs sent regular reports, though these were not received by all ships.[4] Darkness, rain squalls, the short range of the

---

3. The reason for Nishimura's change of plan is not known. The only surviving commanding officer in his fleet, Commander Nishino of the destroyer *Shigure*, hazarded the suggestion that Nishimura was an old style Admiral and preferred a night engagement to a daylight action. The Japanese were certainly aware that darkness reduced the odds against the weaker of two forces, and they had scored some successes in night engagements during the early part of the war, i.e. Battle of the Java Sea.

4 CTG 77.3 considered that much more information could have been obtained from the PT boats had they been used only for reconnaissance purposes, with orders not to attack except in self-defence. (*Special Information Bulletin, No. 2.* pp. 78-107.)

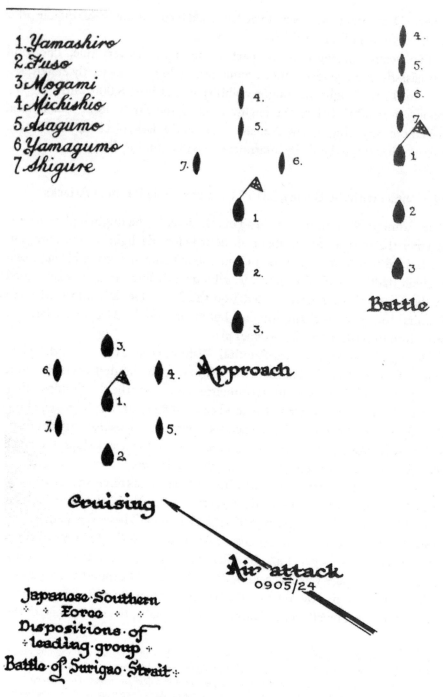

1. Yamashiro
2. Fuso
3. Mogami
4. Michishio
5. Asagumo
6. Yamagumo
7. Shigure

Battle

Approach

Cruising

Air attack
0905/24

Japanese Southern
Force
Dispositions of
leading group
Battle of Surigao Strait

Diagram II. Japanese Southern Force, Disposition of leading group.

torpedo boats, low height of eye, and the interference caused by the enemy's gunfire, all militated against accuracy of reporting. Reports came in of star shells or flares south of Panaon Island about 0110 and then at 0123 of an enemy force in 09° 40′ N., 125° 16′ E., nine miles south of that island. *PT 134* shortly after 0200 reported and attacked a very large unidentified ship off the southern tip of Panaon Island. Other MTBs joined in, but the attacks were not co-ordinated, and the results could not be determined. The enemy opened fire with all guns from 8 in. to 20 mm., illuminating the MTBs with searchlights and star shell and pursuing them with his destroyers. One boat was sunk. Fifteen, however, succeeded in attacking, firing a total of 34 torpedoes, of which 32 ran normally. Seven hits were claimed as possible, and the action of these small craft very probably threw the Japanese command off its balance and contributed to the completeness of their subsequent defeat.[5] It was soon seen that two large ships had successfully passed the line of MTBs These were, no doubt, the Japanese battleships *Yamashiro* and *Fuso*.

30. Special Attack Group 79.11 (Destroyer Squadron 54) attacks, 0230 25 October

By 0230 five destroyers of US Special Attack Group 79.11 (Destroyer Squadron 54, S.O. Captain J. G. Coward, *Remey*) were proceeding down the Strait at 25 knots to attack. These destroyers had been stationed about five miles south of the Battle Line in line across Surigao Strait in approximate latitude 10° 30′ N., where it opens into Leyte Gulf.[6] They were primarily an anti-submarine screen, but with the approval of CTG 77.2, Captain Coward proposed to attack if contact was made with enemy surface vessels. Division 107 (the *Remey*, *McGowan* and *Melvin*) steamed down the eastern and Division 108 (the *Monssen* and *McDermut*) down the western shore. Contact was made about 10 minutes later at 39,700 yards, and at 0242 the *McGowan* reported unidentified ships, subsequently described as three or more, in column heading north, bearing 184°, distant 18 miles. Actually, the Japanese report that they assumed battle disposition, in line ahead with the destroyers leading, about 10 minutes earlier. At 0250 Division 107 began gradually to bear round to a course 120° to gain the firing point. Both groups of destroyers were soon discovered by the enemy and were shortly afterwards straddled by

---

5. Cincpac, *Report*, p. 75. On the other hand, the only available Japanese evidence is that no hits were made and the only effect of the attacks was to cause the Japanese ships to alter course towards the MTBs in order to present smaller targets.

6. *Mertz* and *McNair* of this squadron were guarding the eastern entrance to Leyte Gulf.

his fire. At 0300 the eastern group worked up to 30 knots and then to full speed and commenced to zigzag and to lay a smoke screen.

The eastern group attacked first, firing 27 torpedoes about 0300, followed by the western group, which fired 20 torpedoes a few minutes later, and both groups commenced their retirement to the north at high speed under fire of the enemy, covered by smoke. Salvoes landed near the *Remey* and the *Melvin*, which were not completely screened, but no ship was hit. The enemy also fired torpedoes at the group, without success.

As he retired, ComDesRon 54, Commander of the Special Attack Group, reported that the general consensus of opinion estimated the enemy force at two battleships, one or two cruisers, and one destroyer, though a later estimate put the force correctly at three heavy ships and four destroyers, namely, the leading detachment (Vice-Admiral Nishimura's) of the Southern Force – the *Fuso*, *Yamashiro*, heavy cruiser *Mogami*, and four destroyers. The Fifth Fleet, some miles astern, had not yet come in contact.

It was thought that Division 108 might have made one torpedo hit on a battleship, for several ships of Rear-Admiral Oldendorf's force saw the explosion.[7] Following the torpedo attacks the enemy appeared to separate into two groups of four ships each through the rear ships dropping astern, and to be carried in this disposition when the destroyers of the Right Flank Force on the west side of the Strait, a few minutes later carried out an attack in their turn.

31. Attack by Destroyers of Right Flank Force, 0304 25 October

The destroyers of the Right Flank Force (Destroyer Division 47) had been lying inshore near Pandan Point, but now had come south and reached a position three miles due east of Hinundayan. This Division was organized in two attack groups as follows:

Attack Group 1.2: USS *Hutchins* (ComDes Ron 24) (K. M. McManes), USS *Daly*, USS *Bache*

Attack Group 2.2: HMAS *Arunta* (SO) (Commander A. E. Buchanan, RAN), USS *Killen*, USS *Beale*

---

7. Report of Commander Battle Line, CTG 79.11 in his comments (*Secret Information Bulletin, Ne. 22.* pp. 78-106) states that a number of hits were made and the two heaviest ships were hit and forced to drop astern. Another ship suffered a large explosion. The enemy lost all initiative and his formation was completely disrupted. The only available Japanese source states that no torpedo hits were made in this attack (*Interrogation Nav. No. 79, U.S.S. B.S. No. 90*).

At 0304 Rear Admiral Berkey ordered it to attack. The individual ships had already made radar contact and were plotting the enemy, whose Squadron 24 now led round to the southward in column at 15 knots. After an initial misunderstanding regarding speed, caused by a signal which apparently was received incorrectly by the *Arunta* the two groups separated at 0310 by order of the Destroyer Squadron Commander, Attack Group 1.2 to follow down the Strait the destroyers of the Western Special Attack Group, and *Arunta* to lead Attack Group 2.2 in the wake of the Eastern Special Attack Group. However, the *Arunta*'s group never reached the eastern shore, but proceeded on a general course 150° to the firing.

(a) Attack on the *Yamashiro* by Attack Group 2.2

The *Arunta*'s group received the order from ComDes Ron 24 to attack with torpedoes at 0311. After the torpedo attack by Destroyer Squadron 54 the enemy appeared on the *Killen*'s screen as one large ship and three smaller leading a second, somewhat similar group of about four ships. Unfortunately, the three destroyers *Arunta*, *Killen* and *Beale*, of Attack Group 2.2, had never worked together as a unit. Communications were indifferent. Rapid changes of course and speed were made without notice, and funnel smoke lying in the area added to the difficulties of the two rear ships, *Killen* and *Beale*. The manoeuvring of the group resolved itself into 'a simple follow the leader and reliance on the initiative and skill of destroyers astern', in which, however, a high degree of co-operation was attained.

Since the torpedo attacks were not being supported by gunfire Commander Buchanan intended to reach a firing position between 6,000 and 7,000 yards on the port bow of the enemy. The approach course was such that little adjustment was necessary to fire torpedoes and, communication being difficult, no line of bearing was ordered. The speed of the destroyers was 25 knots, mean course 145°. About two minutes before firing torpedoes the destroyers commenced making smoke.

At 0319 the enemy fired starshell which burst, some to the right and others short. The *Killen*'s radar screen, 15,000 yards (short) scale showed a group of four ships in column, estimated as a battleship leading two cruisers or large destroyers, followed by a destroyer. The second group was not visible on the short scale. In the expectation that, as the enemy was not being engaged a heavy column of fire would follow the starshell, Commander Buchanan gave the order to fire torpedoes to port at 0320, the range being 7,200 yards, and one minute later the *Arunta* fired four torpedoes – all she carried – with spread of 14°, at the large ship, apparently the *Yamashiro*, leading the enemy formation, bearing 120°, depth settings 6 ft. and 8 ft., estimated range 6,900 yards.

No heavy volume of fire followed. The only fire seen was a single salvo, apparently about 4-in, calibre, which fell 300 yards short.

The *Killen* and *Beale* fired their torpedoes shortly after the *Arunta*. The *Killen*, convinced that the target was a battleship and that there were more to come, fired a half salvo of five torpedoes to port, 1° spread, depth setting 22 ft., range 8,700 yards. The track angle was about 90°, giving the maximum chance of hitting. The target was apparently the same as that fired at by the *Arunta*, namely the *Yamashiro*, and the *Killen*'s position at the moment of firing was 10° 19' 30" N., 125° 19' 30" E. The two destroyers then followed the *Arunta* round and made for the western shore. Four and a half minutes later the *Killen* fired two torpedoes at the same enemy ship, then bearing 111°, range 8,100 yards, depth setting 6 ft. As the second torpedo was fired, the target appeared to be altering course, and fire was checked.

Speed was reduced to 20 knots at 0330 and the three destroyers stopped making smoke. A minute later, the enemy fired a salvo or two in their direction. One fell between the *Killen* and the *Beale* immediately following illumination by starshell.

At 0345 ComDes Ron 24's group, which were to the southward and had fired their torpedoes, were heard to engage the enemy with gunfire. Commander Buchanan thereupon turned his group to the south in support. Three minutes later the *Killen* fired her last three torpedoes repetitious at the enemy battleship – evidently the *Yamashiro* again – on her port beam, range 11,300 yards. These torpedoes missed owing to the target altering course before they crossed her path.

The group opened fire with their 5-in. guns at 0352, the *Arunta* at enemy destroyers, the *Killen* at the battleship now bearing 092°, range 12,500 yards. Firing ceased at 0356 and the group continued south at 15 knots until, intercepting erroneously describing them as enemy, Commander Buchanan hastily retired at 25 knots to the north. However, Rear-Admiral Oldendorf was alive to the situation and prevented any untoward happening.

It was considered that in these attacks the *Killen* made torpedo hits on the battleship *Yamashiro* and thus probably contributed to the sinking of the vessel which apparently occurred at 0349.[8]

---

8. Prisoners of war stated that the *Yamashiro* was hit on the port side by four torpedoes before 0400. (Cincpac, *Report*, p.76.

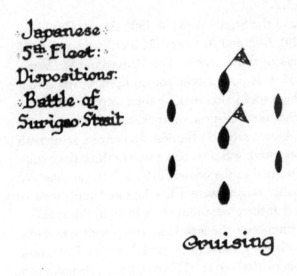

Japanese
5th Fleet:
Dispositions:
Battle of
Surigao Strait

Cruising

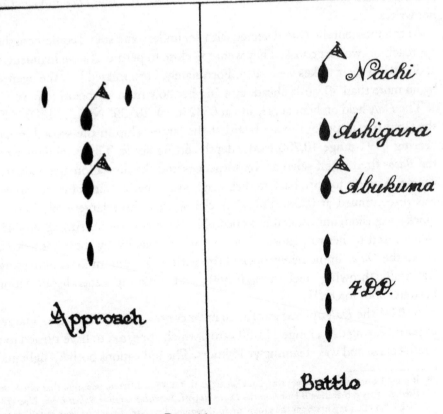

Approach

Nachi

Ashigara

Abukuma

4DD.

Battle

Diagram III. Japanese Fifth Fleet, Dispositions.

(b) Attack by Attack Group 1.2.

Running down the west side of the Strait on course 180°, Attack Group 1.2 the *Hutchins* (ComDesRon 24), *Daly* and *Bache* at 0321 increased speed to 25 knots and steered to attack, making funnel smoke. The *Monssen* and *McDermut* of Special Attack Group 79.11 were passed close aboard to starboard as they retired to the north-west at high speed after making their torpedo attacks.

As seen on the SG radar the enemy disposition consisted of two groups of ships. Ahead were four ships abreast, probably the destroyer screen, at intervals of about 500 yards. Ten cables astern was a second group of three large ships formed on a line of bearing normal to the course, 010°, at intervals of about 500 yards. One or more smaller targets were a few hundred yards west of these ships. It was estimated that there were nine ships in all in this group.

The enemy attempted to illuminate the attacking group with star shells, but all burst short until 0326 when one burst 1,000 yards broad on *Daly*'s bow. The *Hutchins* led round to port to 050° and at 0329 completed a 16-point turn and on course 000° fired five torpedoes to starboard.[9] The *Daly* followed in her wake.

At this moment the *Daly* detected with her underwater sound equipment the approach of two torpedoes. They were too close to permit evasive manoeuvre and at 0330 their wakes were seen. Fortunately, both missed her, the nearest by no more than 50 yards ahead, crossing her bow from starboard to port.

The *Daly* held on her course, and at 0332 in 10° 18′ 30″ N., 125° 18′ 00″ E. she fired five torpedoes to starboard at the largest ship in the second group bearing 099°, range 10,700 yards, depth setting six ft. Three minutes later the *Bache* fired a half salvo of five torpedoes and the formation again altered course 16 points to port, back to their original southerly course. Funnel smoke was discontinued at 0338. The *Daly* claims that three large explosions in quick succession, unmistakably torpedo hits, seen at 0344 bearing about 045° were caused by her torpedoes. 'The ship which was hit by these torpedoes,' stated the *Daly*, 'immediately opened fire with major and minor calibre guns, frantically throwing steel through 360°, and initiating general gun action between both forces.'[10]

At 0341 the *Daly* opened gunfire in radar control at a relatively small target to port, bearing 025°, range 11,000 yards, which appeared to have turned to a south course and was steaming at 16 knots. The indications both by sight and

9. It is not known what the target was, but *Daly* states that it was a different one from that which she fired at. This sub-section is based on the *Daly*'s Report, *Secret Information Bulletin, No. 22*, p. 78-21/25. No other reports from the group are forthcoming. Prisoner of war survivors state that the destroyer *Yamagumo* was hit by one torpedo about 0330 and was reported sunk at 0400. (Cinpac *Report*, p.77).

10. *Daly*'s Report, *Secret Information Bulletin, No. 22*. p.78-23.

radar were that the *Daly's* salvos were hitting, but at 0344 the *Hutchins*, which was apparently on her starboard bow, altered course to port and crossed her bows, and the *Daly* checked fire until 0347 when she had turned to port in the *Hutchins'* wake to course 050°. Radar indicated further hits, but the only results that could be seen visually were small flashes on the target, which the *Daly* thought were caused by projectile impact.

At the conclusion of the attacks by the destroyers of the Right Flank Force there remained only 15 torpedoes amongst the six ships. Gun ammunition also was very low, the *Hutchins* having no more than 50 rounds per gun.

32. Attack by Destroyers of Left Flank Force (Destroyer Squadron 56) 0333/25

By 0333 CTG 77.2 (Rear-Admiral Oldendorf) had co-ordinated the various enemy reports received from the light forces in the Strait and was able to form a picture of two columns of ships, comprising at least two battleships, four to six heavy or light cruisers with probably six to eight destroyers. He now launched the destroyers of his Left Flank Force to attack.

At 0333 when the order to attack was received, the nine destroyers of Destroyer Squadron 56 were disposed in three sections in line ahead, the rear section (No. 3) being approximately one mile north of the cruisers of the Left Flank Force (which were in line ahead on a course 90°, speed five knots, position 10° 30' 30" N., 125° 26' 30" E.). The senior officer in the USS *Newcomb* led the centre section (No. 1). The squadron had made radar contact with an enemy force, estimated to number three ships, at 0320, range 33,000 yards, bearing 165° course based north at 12 knots speed.

On receiving the order to attack, the squadron turned to a southerly course and manoeuvred to make a co-ordinated three-section attack from sectors ahead and on each bow of the enemy. Visibility was much reduced at this time, being 7,000 yards for ships of cruiser size, and the *Newcomb*, and probably other ships as well, conducted the attack entirely by radar control.

At 0353 ComDesRon 56 increased speed to 25 knots and commenced the attack on course 200°-210°. At this same time two targets were on the radar screen.

One large target was seen on SG radar at about 23,000 yards, whilst a target, believed to be other heavy ships, was seen on the same bearing at 33,000 yards, glowing dimly. The closer of the two was chosen by ComDes Ron 56 as his torpedo target; no screen of light forces was seen near it. The plot of the target indicated course north, speed 12 knots indicated, but about 0400, when the range was 8,300 yards, the target altered course eight points to port. At about 7,000 yards the *Newcomb* turned to 270°, the enemy plot indicating at the time a course 290°, speed nine knots. Four minutes later ComDesRon 56 fired a half salvo of five torpedoes set to six ft. depth, range 6,200 yards. About seven minutes after firing, the target, identified visually as a battleship of the *Fuso* class, again altered course about eight points to port, so that at the correct time for contact she was only in the area of the two torpedoes on the left. Two heavy explosions were seen at this time, and the target ship was seen to be burning fiercely as she proceeded south until radar contact was lost at 0440, it was presumed through the target sinking. At 0406, two minutes after firing torpedoes, the *Newcomb* altered course to north and increased speed to 32 knots. Zigzagging and making funnel smoke the section two minutes later bore round to a course about 060° for their post-attack rendezvous. Several splashes were seen close aboard. Smoke was stopped at 0410.

Meanwhile Sections 2 and 3 had struck from positions on each bow of the advancing Japanese force. The destroyers of Section 2 failed to observe in time the enemy's change of course to the westward, and most probably their torpedoes missed ahead, though the *Bryant's* torpedoes probably missed to port owing to an incorrect estimate of the enemy's course. The torpedoes of Section 3 also probably missed ahead through the enemy turning to port.

It is very probable that some hits were made by the torpedoes of the squadron on the *Fuso*, and it is possible that the destroyer *Asagumo* received a crippling hit at about the same time.[11]

Throughout the torpedo attack the *Newcomb's* section had been under fire from the enemy, as were also the other two sections towards the end of their approach to the firing position. Section 1 was also in the direct line of fire of American battleships and cruisers who were now engaging the enemy, but as soon as this information was passed to Rear-Admiral Oldendorf, the OTC, he immediately ordered all ships to cease fire and Destroyer Squadron 56 to clear the area. Meanwhile, salvoes from both sides fell near, and about 0406 the third ship in the line, the *Albert W. Grant*, was hit, both by the Japanese and by one of the American light cruisers. She slowed down and stopped at 0426. The *Newcomb* and the *Richard P. Leary* which had reached their post attack rendezvous three miles north of Hibuson Island, turned back at 0432 to assist her. The *Albert W. Grant* was severely damaged, and had several casualties, and she had to be towed clear of the battle area by the *Newcomb*.

---

11. The battleship target was thought at the time to be the *Yamashiro* but the Japanese accounts which have since become available make it clear that the *Fuso* was the ship fired at.

33. Results of the Destroyer Attacks. *Yamashiro* and *Ymagumo* sunk.[12]

The results of the various attacks by the Allied destroyers were disastrous to Vice-Admiral Nishimura's force. The battleship *Yamashiro* was hit by a torpedo which apparently caused her magazine to explode, and the ship broke in half and sank at 0349. The three leading destroyers, *Michisio*, *Asagumo* and *Yamagumo* were hit. The first named became unnavigable, fell out of the disposition and sank at 0335; the *Asagumo* sank about 1720 after cruisers and destroyers had pursued and shelled her at close range; and the *Yamagumo* sank at 0355. No torpedoes hit the *Mogami* but she was badly damaged by gunfire. Alone of the seven ships of 'C' Force the destroyer *Shigure* escaped unscathed. The torpedoes came from both west and east, but those which caused the damage to the Japanese force appear to have been fired in the attacks by the Right Flank Force destroyers (Special Attack Group) about 0330.

34. The Gun Action, 0350 25 October.

From the moment of first report at 2310/24th Rear-Admiral Weyler, Commander Battle Line, had been endeavouring to interpret the information he received from radar and the ships in contact with the enemy. At 0315 he regarded the situation as follows:

(a) A small destroyer screen about seven miles to the north-west of a group of two heavy units, exact type undetermined. [Nishimura's 'C' Force]

(b) The remainder of the force approaching but not yet visible on the plan presentation indicator or the radar plot. [Japanese Fifth Fleet]

By 0330 it seemed that the destroyer screen had either been eliminated or had joined the heavy units and taken station ahead, and that this group now consisted of two or three cruisers or destroyers in the van followed by two battleships in line ahead, the range of the battleships being about 3,000 yards, course north, speed 16 knots. The *Portland*, one of the cruisers of the Left Flank Force, who made initial radar contact at 0251 at a range of 54,000 yards, considered that the leading group was composed of four destroyers, two battleships, two heavy cruisers or light cruisers in line ahead in that order, with a second group composed of one heavy and four light units several miles astern. The inference was that the leading group comprised the two Japanese battleships, the heavy cruiser *Mogami* and four destroyers; and the rear group the Fifth Fleet. Apart from the last ship in the line which appeared to have

---

12. This section is based mainly on the *Interrogation* [of Commdr. Nishino, the only surviving Japanese commanding officer], *Nav. No.79*, U.S.S.B.S. No. 390.

stopped after the first or second destroyer torpedo attack[13] the *Portland* considered that the enemy ships continued to maintain their formation until they began to be hit by gunfire at 0352. The cruiser *Boise*, in the Right Flank Group, which had been tracking the enemy since she first made contact at 0252 at a range of 47,900 yards, thought that the course and speed of the two enemy battleships diverged from 0304 onwards, and that whilst both ships maintained a mean course north, the *Fuso* drew ahead and when the gun action commenced at 0351, she was some 4,000 yards to the northward of the *Yamashiro*. It seems probable, however, that the latter had fallen out and sunk by then and that the *Boise's* second battleship was actually the heavy cruiser *Mogami*.

(a) The Left Flank Force Cruisers

The cruisers of the Left Flank Force opened fire at 0351 whilst on course 090°. The *Portland*, second ship in the line, took as the target of her nine 8-in. guns the *Fuso* bearing 186°, range 15,500 yards; but after checking fire at 0356 for two minutes owing to the target being under fire from a number of ships and burning brightly she shifted target at 0358 to the second heavy ship (the *Mogami*) which had turned to southward some five minutes before the *Fuso* and was now retiring at high speed, the range on opening fire being 19,300, bearing 194°. This ship was soon out of range and, at 0406 O.T.C. ordered cease fire, the *Portland* shifted back to her first target, bearing 199°, range 14,200 yards. Some fire was directed at the Left Flank Force by the enemy, and at 0404 the *Denver* reported being straddled, but no ship was hit.

(b) The Right Flank Force Cruisers

The cruisers of the Right Flank Force opened fire by Rear-Admiral Berkey's orders immediately after the Left Flank Force. Their approximate position at the time was 10° 30′ 45″ N., 125° 19′ 25″ E., bearing about 250°, 15,000 yards from the Battle Line; and like the latter they were on course 090°, stationed on a line of bearing 050° from the cruiser guide in the order *Phoenix* (guide), *Boise*, *Shropshire*.

The light cruiser *Boise* opened fire with her main battery at 0351 on the *Fuso*, bearing 153°, range 18,100 yards. She maintained a steady rate of fire and reports that many hits were seen. The flagship *Phoenix*, sister ship to the *Boise*, opened fire half a minute later in full radar control at the same target estimated range 16,600 yards. After four spotting salvoes with high capacity

---

13. This may have been the enemy ship which was the subject of the following signal: "0048 – CTG 77.3 from ComDesRon 24 – 'We have one dead in the water – we are going to present him with five fish.'"

projectiles from the forward and after 6-in. groups alternately the range was found and full salvos were fired using armour-piercing shells from the tenth round onwards. The force and direction of the wind cleared the smoke between salvos and rendered optical spotting and observation possible. The *Shropshire*, equipped with a type of radar which was not designed for main armament fire control was unable to open fire until 0356, when she commenced firing eight 8-in. gun broadsides in full radar control, range 15,800 yards, her target also being the *Fuso*. The *Shropshire*'s turrets had been in service for 16 years, but the rate of fire exceeded any that had previously been attained.[14] Unlike the *Shropshire*, the American ships were all using a flashless propellant, and it is thought that the enemy, being unable to use radar control, fired at the *Shropshire*'s flashes, mistaking her for a capital ship, for at 0358 splashes were seen by the *Boise* near the *Shropshire*, though the ship was not hit.

At 0357 fire was checked and a 16-point turn to starboard was commenced to course 270°. Firing was resumed at 0401, but at 0409 Rear-Admiral Oldendorf ordered cease fire on account of the cruisers firing into Destroyer Squadron 56 further down the Strait. By this time the target was burning fiercely, rendering possible its optical identification as a battleship of the *Fuso* or *Ise* class. Her forward turrets were still firing. At 0421, after ComDesRon 56 had reported that except for the damaged *A. W. Grant* his destroyers were clear of the channel the OTC ordered the Right Flank Force to resume fire, but no target identifiable as hostile was within effective range, and as all the enemy ships appeared to be in full retreat down the Strait, the forces returned north at 0538 to resume the patrol of Leyte Gulf.

(c) The Battle Line

By about 0330 Rear-Admiral Weyler decided that the range was closing so rapidly that by waiting for it to close to 20,000 yards as originally intended he would lose some of the range advantage he possessed in having his guns and his shell hoists loaded with armour-piercing shell.[15] He, therefore, directed the Battle Line to open fire at 26,000 yards (0333),[16] in order to permit deliberate fire whilst the range was closing to the moderate range band.

---

14. *Shropshire* in her Battle Report states: 'A very high rate of fire was attained in rapid salvos. As many as eight broadsides in two minutes being fired.' Rear-Admiral Berkey's comment is: 'The overall performance was not fast.'
15. Battleships had been ordered to load projectile hoists with AP and to be prepared before to shift to HC or continue with AP. Each gun had thus five rounds of AP immediately available, (*Action Report, Battle of Surigao Strait*, pp. 2, 3.).
16. But *"Pennsylvania," Action Report*, p.6, states that the battleships were ordered to open fire by Com Task Group 77.2 (i.e. Rear-Admiral Oldendorf). The range 26,000 yards, was intended to be that of the leading enemy battleship, neglecting the destroyer screen.

No fire distribution signals were made since it was felt that the individual commanding officers had as clear, and in the case of ships equipped with modern radar, a much clearer, picture than the Commander of the Battle Line himself, for the radar equipment of Rear-Admiral Weyler's flagship, the *Mississippi* was of an inadequate type. At 0349 he informed Rear-Admiral Oldendorf of his intentions and was told that the OTC was himself about to open fire. When the range had closed to 24,000 yards and the Battle Line had not commenced firing Captain T.D. Ruddock of the *Maryland*, Commander of Battleship Division 4 (USS *Maryland* and *West Virginia*) directed the *West Virginia* to report that she was ready to open fire and then commence firing.

The Battle Line at this time was on an easterly course, steaming at standard speed,15 knots, to which they had increased at 0338. This course was taking them away from the Japanese ships, and to give a better turret training angle Rear-Admiral Weyler at 0354 altered course 30° towards the enemy. The order was *West Virginia, Maryland, Mississippi* (flagship), *Tennessee, California, Pennsylvania*.

Almost simultaneously with the alteration of course the Battle Line opened fire. The *West Virginia*, who had been plotting her target by radar from a range of 41,000–42,000 yards with clear target indications in range and bearing, had no hesitation in opening fire in full radar control. She was followed by the *Tennessee* and the *California*. These three ships were equipped with an up-to-date type of radar which gave them a great advantage over the *Maryland*, *Mississippi* and *Pennsylvania* in night firing.

The disposition of the Japanese ships at the moment of opening fire was apparently as follows. The *Yamashiro* had been sunk a few minutes earlier, The *Fuso* bore 192°, range 20,900 yards from the flagship *Mississippi*. A second large ship, presumably the heavy cruiser *Mogami*, bore 196°, range 23,800 yards. The three destroyers (one of the four, the *Yamagumo*, having been sunk by the same torpedo attack as sank the *Yamashiro*) were now apparently following astern of the heavy ships.[17] The enemy were steering an approximately north course, so that Rear-Admiral Oldendorf's ships, without necessity to manoeuvre, were in the classic position across their T. The *West Virginia* took as her target the leading heavy ship the *Fuso*, range 24,400 yards. The *Maryland*, after vainly attempting to find a target by means of the *West Virginia's* tracers finally found and opened fire on the second heavy ship just as the latter was altering course to port to retreat down the Strait and thus presenting to the *Maryland* a broadside target. The *Mississippi* received a message from her Flag Plot which she interpreted as instructions

---

17. *Report of Tennessee's Gunnery Officer* quoted in Cinepac, *Report*, p.82.

for her to take care of the rear enemy ships or groups. Since this was a logical fire distribution in the existing situation, she shifted to of the rear targets, but found her older-type radar inadequate at the greater distance. Before a solution could be obtained, the rear enemy group reversed course and opened the range still further. A shift back was made to one of the leading and closer targets, but there was time for only one full salvo before the order to cease fire.

By 0400 it was apparent that the leading American ships, the *West Virginia* and the *Maryland*, were getting under the lee of Hibuson Island and that the enemy had decreased speed. Moreover, the Battle Line of Oldendorf was beginning to overlap the Left Flank Force. At 0402, on the suggestion of Rear-Admiral Oldendorf, Rear-Admiral Weyler ordered his column to turn together to starboard to course 270°. The signal, 'Turn 15°' (i.e. alter course 150), was incorrectly reported to the commanding officer of the *California* as an alteration of 15°, and the ship there steadied on 135,°[18] and so for a time blanketed the *Tennessee*'s fire. Eventually she (0408) took up her proper station astern of the latter. The other ships continued to fire on the turn.

As the turn progressed it became apparent that the enemy had also altered course to the westward. The second heavy ship, the *Mogami*, had in fact turned some minutes earlier and was retreating down the Strait. The *Fuso* turned five minutes later, at 0400, and for some nine minutes steered a westerly course before turning south. At 0407 ComDesRon 56's report was received that the American ships were firing at the left flank destroyers in mid-channel, and at 0409 the OTC. ordered all ships to cease fire so as to permit the damaged *A. W. Grant* and the other destroyers to clear the area.

At 0415 the destroyer *Richard P. Leary* of the Left Flank Force, during her retirement northwards after carrying out torpedo attack reported seeing torpedo tracks.[19] Rear-Admiral Weyler assumed this to mean that the enemy had fired torpedoes to the northward, and he turned the Battle Line away in order clear the danger, a manoeuvre which took him too far north to resume the engagement. It was not Rear-Admiral Oldendorf's intention that the battleships would follow the enemy into the restricted waters of the Strait, and Rear-Admiral Weyler, for his part, was influenced by the consideration that although damage to the Battle Line at this juncture would not jeopardize its ability to defeat the Japanese Southern Force, the stronger enemy force in

---

18. *Comment by U.S.S. "California," Secret Information Bulletin, No. 22*, pp. 78-80.
19. ComBatLine Report, p. 9. Rear-Admiral Oldendorf's covering letter to the Action Reports of the destroyers of Squadron 56 (*CTG 77.2 Action Report*, p. 2) says: 'USS *Richard P. Leary* reported tracks of enemy torpedoes apparently headed for our Battle Line or Right Flank Forces. They did not reach their target.' No time is given, but the entry follows the statement of damage to the *A.W. Grant* at 0406. It is possible the torpedoes were fired by the cruisers of the Fifth Fleet (*see* Section 38).

the Sibuyan Sea was not yet completely eliminated from the picture.[20] This, then, completed the engagement as far as the battleships were concerned. None of them appear to have been under fire from the enemy, though some splashes of shots falling short were seen.[21] Although the Japanese used star shell and searchlights, no vessel of the main formation was illuminated.

The difference in the radar equipment of the battleships was reflected in the number of rounds fired respectively.

	Number of Salvos fired	Number of Rounds fired
FH radar equipped ships:		
West Virginia	16	93
Tennessee	13	69
California	9	63
FC radar equipped ships:		
Mississippi	1	12
Maryland	6	48
Pennsylvania	0	0

In a little over nine minutes firing the *West Virginia* expended half her outfit of ammunition suitable for heavy targets.[22] Firing in full radar control, her report states that every salvo was a straddle.[23]

35. Sinking of the *Fuso*

'The enemy', wrote the Gunnery Officer of the *Shropshire*,[24] 'must have been simply appalled by this drenching fire which was being most accurately poured on to them.' To the mighty 16-in. salvos of the battleships and the 8-in. broadsides of the heavy cruisers there was added the hosepipe shooting – for so it appeared – of light cruisers such as the *Phoenix* and *Boise* who could fire 200 or more 6-in. shells per minute. Such high expenditure evidently disquieted Rear-Admiral Berkey, for 3½ minutes after his light cruisers opened fire he ordered 'Fire slow and deliberately.' The tracers used by the American ships enabled their shells to be followed right on to the target. Almost from

---

20. *Endorsements to U.S.S. "Pennsylania" Action Report*, p. 29, and *ComBatDiv 3 Action Report*, pp. 4, 5.
21. Com at Div 4 *Action Report*, p. 2.
22. From the interrogations of Japanese officers, it appears that their ships had no special equipment for firing in radar control. The Americans used flashless propellant.
23. Comment by CTG 77.2, *Secret Information Bulletin, No. 22*, p. 78-50.
24. Lieut.-Commdr. W.S. Bracegirdle, DSC, RAN.

the time of commencing fire at 0350 the enemy ships appeared to observers to be a continual mass of flame and explosions, with the exception of two which appeared to Commander-in-Chief to turn round and escape at high speed to the southward, according to the Captain of the *Denver*. The leading battleship, the *Fuso*, which had turned to a westerly course at 0400, was sighted by the Japanese destroyer *Shigure*, on fire and apparently unnavigable; she bore round to the south just before Rear-Admiral Oldendorf gave the order to cease fire at 0409. About 10 minutes later she disappeared from the ships' radar screens, and though no eye saw her sink there is no doubt that this was her end.

It is difficult to link the reported incidents of the battle with the actual enemy losses as verified later. In the main, the Allied ships were firing by radar rather than at identifiable vessels; and it was not always certain whether the target on the screen was one enemy vessel, or two, or a group. The enemy ships twisted, turned and scattered under the devastating fire to which they were subjected; but the only movements definitely discernible were those of their advance up the Strait and the subsequent retirement of the survivors.

The comparative immunity of the Allied ships from loss or damage may be ascribed, in part, to the low efficiency of the Japanese radar, which was not suitable for fire control, and to the fact that the ships' installations were ineffective for search in this particular engagement. The Japanese were aware of the presence of a strong Allied supporting force in Leyte Gulf, but they did not know when or exactly where it would be met. Rear-Admiral Oldendorf, on the other hand, received sufficient warning by his patrols stationed in the approaches to the Surigao Strait. The column formation of the Japanese facilitated radar interception, and the majority of the American ships were able to plot the approaching enemy by radar from well outside gun range and to fire their torpedoes and guns in full radar control. It was perhaps a disadvantage that the *Yamashiro* and *Fuso* had not previously operated with the remainder of the force.

36. Sinking of the *Michisio* and *Asagumo*

Only one of the four Japanese destroyers which led Vice-Admiral Nishimur's force as it pushed into the Strait, came unscathed through the American destroyer attacks and the gunfire of the battleships and cruisers. This was the *Shigure*, which when the *Fuso* began to be hit, retired down the Straits, receiving as she turned a single shell which penetrated an oil tank and failed to explode. The concussion of near miss shell bursts eventually caused damage to her rudder, and at 0435 she lost steering control and stopped for half an hour to effect repairs. Whilst thus engaged, she sighted the Japanese Fifth Fleet coming up the Strait, but apart from identifying herself and reporting her steering difficulties she gave no information as to the situation Vice-Admiral Shima,[25] and it was not until 1018 that day, whilst retiring through the Mindanao Sea, that her commanding officer, Commander Nishino, reported to Admiral Toyoda and Vice-Admiral Kurita that Nishimura's force had been annihilated.

Meanwhile, the destroyers *Michisio* and *Asagumo*, which had been damaged by the American destroyer attacks about 0330, were lying crippled in the Strait. At 0427 Rear-Admiral Oldendorf ordered the Left Flank Force to resume fire and at 0434 the cruisers turned to a southerly course to 'pursue the retiring enemy'. The tactical situation and restricted waters compelled caution, and speed of 15 knots was ordered, which was increased to 20 knots at 0520. Three burning enemy vessels were in sight to the southward and fire was opened on one apparently undamaged enemy ship, thought to be either a large destroyer or a light cruiser (? the *Shigure*).

The Left Flank Force screen was joined about 0550 by the six destroyers of Division X under Commander M.G. Hubbard of the *Claxton*, which had been screening the Battle Line. The division had been ordered at 0432 to proceed south down the Strait to make a torpedo attack on the retiring enemy at 0513, at a range of 31,000 yards, but almost at once it became clear that it would be daylight before the destroyers could get into position for attack, and they were ordered accordingly to join the screen of the Left Flank cruisers. At 0543 Rear-Admiral Oldendorf ordered cease fire and returned with the Left Flank Force northward up the Strait in order to avoid possible enemy torpedo attacks.

Daybreak revealed some burning enemy ships on the horizon. About half an hour later Commander Cruiser Division 12, Rear-Admiral Hayler, was ordered to take the Left Flank Force light cruisers *Denver* and *Columbia*, screened by the *Robinson*, *Bryant* and *Halford*, on a sweep down the Strait to sink the cripples. The *Claxton*, which had remained behind when the Left Flank Force turned northward, to pick up survivors, of whom there were at least 150 within a radius of 2,000 yards, sank by gunfire one badly-damaged destroyer. This may have been the *Michisio*, which with the *Asagumo*, had been crippled earlier in the battle and sank about this time. The destroyer screen of the Left Flank Force also sank a destroyer, thought to be the *Asagumo*, at 0721

---

25. *Interrogation*, 'The reason I did not communicate directly with Admiral Shima and inform him of the situation was that I had no connection with him and was not under his command.'

in approximately 10° 5' 50" N., 125° 24' 20" E. Most of the survivors refused to take lifelines, but a few were picked up.

37. Sinking of the *Mogami*

The surface engagement was now at an end, and out of Vice-Admiral Nishimura's fleet there remained afloat only the heavy cruiser *Mogami*, and the destroyer *Shigure*; the latter was making good her escape, in default of orders, having appreciated that the remainder of the force had been destroyed.

The *Mogami* was in a bad way. She had come unscathed through the American destroyer attacks but had been badly hit later by gunfire. About 0410 the *Shigure*, retiring down the Strait at 30 knots, sighted her on a southerly course, on fire and apparently moving very slowly. The Fifth Fleet was now coming up the Strait towards the smoke screen which, extending across the Strait from east to west concealed the Allied ships. As the heavy ships of the Fifth Fleet turned to retire after firing torpedoes, the heavy cruiser *Nachi*, Vice-Admiral Shima's flagship, collided with the *Mogami*, which was not under control and was moving so slowly (about eight knots) that it was thought she was stopped. A destroyer – believed to be the *Akebono* – was detailed to escort her and she apparently reached a position in the Mindanao Sea, to the southward of Kamigin Island; but at 0500 that day she was hit by a bomb in the second of two air attacks directed at the surviving ships of the Japanese Southern Force. Damage to the ship was very severe and it was decided to abandon her, and she sank about an hour later.

38. The Japanese Fifth Fleet. Sinking of the *Abukuma*, 26 October

While these important events were occurring, Vice-Admiral Shima, commanding the Fifth Fleet, had been doing his best to carry out his mission, which apparently was to attack the invasion forces in Leyte Gulf during the confusion which it was hoped would result from the attacks by Kurita's and Nishimura's forces. His orders appear to have been vague, and he was neither responsible to Vice-Admirable Kurita, nor was Vice-Admiral Nishimura – his junior in the service – answerable to him although both his force and Nishimura's were due to arrive at the same place at approximately the same time and on identical missions. On his way south from Bako to Koron, when north-west of Lingayen he had sent an aircraft to Manila to get information of the movements of Kurita's and Nishimura's forces, but before its return he received information from Vice-Admiral Kurita's fleet by radio.

Vice-Admiral Shima received no further instructions after this radio message. He did, however, learn of the delay to the Centre Force caused by the fast carrier air attacks on the 24th, and consequently, whilst passing through the Sulu Sea he advanced his time of arrival at the objective by one hour in order to give more effective support to Nishimura. Later, he heard that Kurita had reversed his course about 1600 in face of the continuing air attacks; and Vice-Admiral Shima accordingly again advanced his time and increased speed to 22 knots, in order to make his entry at 0300 on the 25th in support of Nishimura. Faster than this he could not proceed on account of shortage of fuel. The fleet passed through the Sulu Sea and Mindanao Sea without any air attack being made on it. At midnight on the 24th–25th it bore 320° from Kamigin Island and was thus about 30 miles astern of Nishimura's force.

The gun flashes of Nishimura's ships repelling torpedo boat attacks were seen about 0100, and from the interception of inter-torpedo boat telephone communications it was judged that the main Allied force was waiting off Panaon Island; the Japanese had already received information as the result of air search on the 23rd, that torpedo boats were stationed at the entrance to Leyte Gulf. The Fifth Fleet proceeded however, without being attacked until 0300. The tide was running north, and the ships were set too close to the island and had to alter course to the eastward. When the original course was resumed, battle disposition was assumed with the fleet in column, the destroyers being stationed astern.

At 0300 this manoeuvre had just been completed, and the fleet had changed northerly course for the run up the Surigao Strait, when an attack was received from the MTBs. stationed off the south-east tip of Panaon Island. The light cruiser *Abukuma*, third ship in the line, was hit on the port side by a torpedo which reduced her speed to about ten knots and killed 30 men. Leaving her behind without escort, the fleet increased speed to 26 knots and continued on their course of 010° under frequent torpedo boat attacks from Panaon Island, though without suffering any further damage.

At 0330, shortly after altering course to 000°, burning ships were sighted ahead. They were apparently taken for two Japanese battleships, and it was not until the fleet returned to Manila, that it was known they were the battleship *Yamashiro* and three destroyers. Disregarding them, Vice-Admiral Shima pressed on. The rain had stopped, but visibility was poor and the Admiral did not know exactly where he was. A dense smoke screen lay ahead, the Japanese radar was not working effectively for search, and no American ship could be detected, though it was judged that they were behind the smoke attacking Nishimura's forces.

At length, at 0420 the *Nachi*'s radar picked up a group of American ships and though the indications were indefinite, it was decided to concentrate a torpedo attack on them. At 0425, just as they came in sight of another burning ship (the *Mogami*), the cruisers swung to starboard and fired their torpedoes. As the flagship, *Nachi*, turned away after delivering her attack, she collided with the *Mogami* on a converging course of about 10°.

This put an end to the attack. The *Nachi* could make no more than 20 knots. The destroyers, who had been ordered to deliver their attack after the cruisers, continued north at high speed until they could see Hibuson Island; but they could not see any American ships and they fired no torpedoes; and at about 0500 the Admiral recalled them and gave the order to retire. Off the north tip of Mindanao, about an hour later, the fleet was again attacked by torpedo boats which were successfully repelled with machine and AA guns. Meanwhile, despite torpedo damage, the *Abukuma* was still heading north following, though at reduced speed, the original instructions to attack. She was ordered to accompany the retreating fleet, and a destroyer was assigned to her, and also one to the *Mogami*, for escort. While the Admiral was assembling his ships, about 0730, an air attack was received. The attack was not severe, but at 0900 in a second air attack about 25 miles south of Limasawa Island, the *Mogami* received the bomb hit from which she sank. The *Nachi* and *Ashigara* continued westward with two destroyers, ordering the *Abukuma* to proceed to Butuan Bay, Mindanao, to effect repairs; an order which was later changed to Dapitan (8° 44′ N., 123° 03′ E) as the unsuitability of Butuan Bay was realised. However, a further air attack later damaged her so badly that she sank.[26] The crews of both the *Abukuma* and *Mogami* were taken off by the escorting destroyers, both of which made good their escape to Koron Bay.

39. Task Group 77.2 Prepares for Action Off Samar

Scarcely had Rear-Admiral Oldendorf's Task Group completed the sinking of the last of the Japanese destroyers, than he received orders from Vice-Admiral Kinkaid to send immediately one division of battleships, one division of cruisers and about half the destroyers in his group to the help of Rear-Admiral C.A.F. Sprague, who had just reported that his escort carrier Task Unit, 77.4.3, was in action with the Japanese Second Fleet east of Samar. Commander Task

---

26. Commander Mori stated in interrogation that the attack which sank the *Abukuma* occurred later on the 25th, but no details are known. Fleet Admiral E.I. King, *Final Official Report* states that the *Abukuma* was sunk on 26 October off Negros Island by B24s, and fleet units. The Naval Analysis Division, United States Bombing Survey states that carrier aircraft sank the *Mogami* and Army aircraft the *Abukuma*.

Group 77.2 at once ordered his ships back to Leyte Gulf where he formed a force consisting of the strongest of his three battleship divisions, the Second, comprising the *Tennessee*, *California* and *Pennsylvania*; his own Fourth Cruiser Division the *Louisville*, *Minneapolis* and *Portland*, reinforced by the *Shropshire* and nine destroyers. With the cruisers and destroyers deep in the southern part of the Surigao Strait, it took time to assemble the ships, which almost without exception were exceedingly short of ammunition and fuel. The light cruiser *Denver*, for example, which could fire her complete outfit of 1,200 rounds of 6-in. in 15 minutes had no more than 113 AP projectiles – less than ten rounds per gun – remaining after the action; whilst the destroyers had expended almost all their torpedoes and there were no replacements ashore or in the supply ships at Leyte. In the event, however, the Japanese Second Fleet broke off the engagement before the force could be made ready, and it remained at Leyte Gulf.

Chapter VII

The Battle off Samar, 25 October

40. Duties and Responsibilities of the Escort Carrier Force

Vice-Admiral Kurita with the Japanese Second Fleet had pursued his way to San Bernardino Strait undeterred by his losses during the day-long air attacks of the 24th by the Third Fleet fast carriers, and indeed, he had come through well considering his total lack of air cover.

His presence in the Sibuyan Sea on the 24th and possible approach to the San Bernardino Strait was known to the escort carriers of the Seventh Fleet operating under Rear-Admiral T. L. Sprague east of Samar in support of the landings on Leyte. These forces, which formed Task Group 77.4, belonged to the Pacific Fleet and had been temporarily transferred to the Seventh Fleet. They consisted of 18 escort carriers organized in three groups of six each with a screen of seven or eight destroyers or destroyer escorts.

In the northernmost station east of Samar was Task Unit 77.4.3 under Rear-Admiral C.A.F. Sprague,[1] consisting of the escort carriers *Fanshaw Bay* (flagship), *St. Lo*, *Kalinin Bay*, *White Plains*, *Kitkun Bay* (Rear-Admiral Ofstie); *Gambier Bay*, destroyers *Hoel*, *Johnston*, *Heerman*, and destroyer escorts *S.B. Roberts*, *Dennis*, *Butler* and *Raymond*. At daylight, some of their aircraft were already in the air carrying out the primary mission of the Task Unit to provide direct air support for the landing operations of the First Cavalry Division and the 24th Infantry Division on Northern Leyte. In addition, the unit was responsible for:-

(a) Providing Combat Air Patrol for the northern transport and objective areas.
(b) Providing a part of the Anti-submarine Patrol for the transport area.
(c) Providing their own Combat Air and Anti-submarine Patrols for the local defence of their own ships against submarine and air attacks.

---

1. The track chart in *Secret Information Bulletin, No. 22*, p. 78-27, shows him in approximately 11° 46' N., 126° 11' E., at 0645/25. '*Gambier Bay*' *Action Report*, p. 6 gives her position at 0500 and courses maintained until 0645, which place her at that time about 50 miles to the north-eastward of the position given on the track chart. All *Gambier Bay*'s records were, however, lost with the ship and her report was compiled from memory. Cincpac, *Report*, p. 90 says TU 77.4.3 was 60 miles north-north-east of Suluan Island.

Direct contact with units of the Japanese fleet was not expected.

In view of the possible approach of enemy forces to San Bernardino Strait Rear-Admiral C.A.F. Sprague, Commander Task Unit 77.4.3, who was in the northernmost position, on the night of 24–25 October had been enjoined to be ready to load torpedoes on short notice and to be prepared to attack enemy forces if directed. But he had been given no responsibility for covering the exit of San Bernardino Strait, and he assumed that his northern flank could not be exposed without ample warning.[2] His immediate superior, Rear-Admiral T.L. Sprague, had not been sent the Commander Third Fleet's signal 2024 stating that he was going north, nor the *Independence* aircraft sighting report of 2000 showing the Japanese Centre Force at a time and position which indicated that it had picked up considerable speed and intended to sortie through San Bernardino Strait nor, so far as is known, these messages were relayed to him by Vice-Admiral Kinkaid, consequently he made no changes in the night dispositions of his escort carriers, the northernmost group of which was close to the edge of the circle which the Centre Force could reach by dawn. Vice-Admiral Kinkaid, for his part, assumed that the Third Fleet was in position to intercept and destroy any enemy who might force the San Bernardino Strait.[3]

In his official report, the Commander Seventh Fleet states: 'At 1512 on 24 October Commander Third Fleet issued a despatch, which was intercepted by Commander Seventh Fleet, to all Third Fleet subordinate commands, stating that a force of battleships, cruisers, and destroyers was being formed as Task Force 34, presumably to engage the Japanese Central Force, Commander Task Force 38 reported at 1852 that planes had sighted another Japanese Force, hereafter referred to as the Northern Force, in position 18° 25′ N., 125° 28′ E., course 270°, speed 15. At 2024 Commander Third Fleet advised Commander Seventh Fleet that the enemy Centre Force (in position 12° 45′ N., 122° 40′ E. at 1925) was moving on a course of 120°, speed 12, in Sibuyan Sea towards the north-west tip of Masbate Island (in the direction of San Bernardino Strait). He further stated that he was "proceeding north with three groups to attack

2. *Secret Information Bulletin, No. 22*, p. 78-15. Comment ascribed to "CTG 74.4. (who was also CTU 74.4.3)'. *St. Lo* says that it was further believed that the Japanese Centre Force had been too badly damaged to be capable of an offensive sortie from San Bernardino Strait (*St. Lo Acion Report, Battle of Samar*, p. 4). *Gambier Bay Action Report*, p. 31, considers that the divided chains of command for the Naval forces in and near the Philippines for this operation may have been responsible for the situation which arose.
3. *Secret Information Bulletin, No. 22*, p. 78-25, Brief summary by Commander Task Force 77. *Gambier Bay* also states: 'Responsibility for the interception of any major surface attacks upon any of the Seventh Fleet engaged in the support of the landings was understood to be assigned to the Third Fleet.'

the enemy carrier force (Northern Force) at dawn.'[4] As the fast battleships had been removed from the carrier groups and organized as Task Force 34, it was assumed that Task Force 34 was still guarding San Bernardino Strait.'

Unfortunately, this assumption was due to a misinterpretation of Commander Third Fleet's despatch timed 1512 quoted above, for Task Force 34 was not actually formed until 0240 on 25th.

During the early hours of 25th it was borne in upon Vice-Admiral Kinkaid that there was no definite statement in Admiral Halsey's despatches that Task Force 34 was still guarding the San Bernardino Strait. The whole of his forces were now committed to the battle now in progress in the Surigao Strait. He decided to check definitely the position of Task Force 34. At 0312 on 25th he made a signal to Admiral Halsey asking if he was guarding the Strait. The latter apparently did not receive the signal until 0648, more than 24 hours later; and when the reply was received it was too late; the escort carriers were already fighting for their lives against the enemy which had fallen upon them from San Bernardino.

The movements of the Japanese Centre Force had remained unreported since 2145 on 24th, in the first place through the mischance of communication trouble, and secondly because, with the withdrawal of the *Independence* night search aircraft when this ship proceeded north with the Third Fleet at midnight 24th/25th, there remained in the southern area no aircraft equipped for night shadowing. There were as yet no air forces of any kind based on the captured Leyte airfields. The long-range searches by aircraft based on Morotai, which covered this general area, were daylight searches only, and hence of no help in the existing situation. The aircraft of the escort carriers of Task Force 77.4 were also being used for daylight missions only. Even had Vice-Admiral Kinkaid made a request for night searches from Morotai, it is uncertain whether the available aircraft could have responded adequately. Actually, the Commander Seventh Fleet made no such request, since the Third Fleet was assumed to be looking after the night searching.

Admiral Halsey had relayed to Vice-Admiral Kinkaid the *Independence* aircraft report of sighting the Centre Force at 2030 between Burias and

---

4. Between these two signals Admiral Halsey made another, at 2005 to C-in-C, US Pacific Fleet, which was sent to Vice-Admiral Kinkaid, though the time of receipt by Commander Seventh Fleet is not known. The signal summarized the air attacks on the Japanese Centre and Southern Forces, reported the new contact with the Northern Force, and stated: 'CTG 38.3 has scuttled *Princeton* and is closing 38.2 and 38.4 which are now concentrated off entrance to San Bernardino Strait. Night attack by enemy possible. More later.' Admiral Halsey was proceeding north (signal 2024) but failed to draw the conclusion that there were no Third Fleet battleships covering him, he also failed to draw the conclusion that there were no longer any Third Fleet aircraft tracking the enemy Centre Force. Cincpac Report, p. 124, considers that when Vice-Admiral Kinkaid learned that there were no longer any Third Fleet aircraft tracking the enemy Centre Force.

Masbate Islands;[5] but the sighting report of 2145, received by the Commander Third Fleet at 2320, giving the enemy position as 12° 45′ N., 123° 22′ E., the furthest to the eastward yet reported, was not retransmitted to the Commander Seventh Fleet as far as is known. Vice-Admiral Kinkaid apparently also knew nothing of the amplifying report of the last contact, made by the *Independence*'s reconnaissance aircraft at about 0010 on 25th, to the effect that the battleships, one of which was believed to be of the *Yamato* class, were in column on a north-easterly course between Burias and Tikao Islands when sighted, also that the course could be south-east as well as the north-east previously reported. The result was that neither Vice-Admiral Kinkaid nor Rear-Admiral C.A. Sprague was aware that the enemy main body, with its strength but little impaired by the day long air attacks of 24th, had passed through San Bernardino Strait during the night of 24th/25th and turned southward to attack the armada off the Leyte beaches, between whom and this powerful Japanese Fleet there stood no more than the 18 escort carriers of the Seventh Fleet, caught at a disadvantage, and totally unprepared for such an emergency, though 'this task unit (even though unsupported) could have raised havoc with the enemy if it had but an hour's warning of impending contact', stated Captain W.V.R. Vieweg of the *Gambier Bay*.

It is true that the escort carriers of Task Group 77.4 had considerable air power, nearly 450 aircraft in fact, though they would have found it difficult, with their slow speed, to evade Vice-Admiral Kurita's fast ships, even had they been moved further from the daylight circle of the latter. To have withdrawn them inside Leyte Gulf for protection, would have hampered them in working aircraft and rendered them more vulnerable to land-based air attack. In any case, their aircraft could not operate until daylight, and to have stationed adequate radar pickets to cover the necessary arc and distance in order to give warning of the approach of the Japanese Centre Force, would have seriously diminished Rear-Admiral Olendorf's available torpedo power in the more certain prospective action against the enemy Southern Force. Apart from this consideration, it would have been undesirable to employ all or part of the Seventh Fleet against the Japanese Centre Force for Kurita's battleships with their advantage in speed, could have fought at long range, outmanoeuvred the old American battleships until their limited stock of ammunition was exhausted.

---

5. Cincpac, *Report*, p.70, states that this contact when plotted, showed the enemy to be making good about 24 or 25 knots, radically greater than his previous rate of advance, and indicated that he was determined to get through San Bernardino Strait. This would appear to mean that Cincpac considered that Vice-Admiral Kinkaid should have been prepared for such an eventuality ... Since the *Nagato* could no more than 24 knots, the *Haruna* 25, and the damaged *Yamato* 26 it seems improbable that the Japanese Centre Force made good as much as 24 or 25 knots as estimated by Cincpac.

41. The Centre Force Transits San Bernardino Strait, Night, 24–25 October

Vice-Admiral Kurita was six hours behind schedule. It had been arranged that his force should come through San Bernardino Strait at 1800 on the 24th but owing to the delay caused by the Third Fleet air attacks in the Sibuyan Sea he was not at the exit until midnight. The distance to Leyte Gulf was about 180 miles, so that unless he abandoned all consideration of fuel economy he was bound to be behind time. Vice-Admiral Nishimura who was up to time, reported his estimated time of arrival at Leyte Gulf after midnight 24th/25th, whilst proceeding into Surigao Strait.[6] However, Vice-Admiral Kurita sent no order to him to delay his advance, nor did Admiral Toyoda order any change in the plan. It was a clear night, and the Second Fleet navigated the narrow places in the channel in column at 20 knots.[7] The ships were at action stations as they issued from the Straits, expecting to have to fight their way out against Admiral Halsey's Task Force. They found no enemy, and consequently turned south according to plan.

42. Contact with the Enemy, 0645 25 October

In both the fast and escort carrier task forces of the American fleet, the practice of conducting dawn and dusk short range air searches had gradually fallen into disuse, greater reliance being placed upon shore-based searches and intelligence from other sources to provide vital strategic information, and radar to prevent tactical surprise. On this particular morning, the Commander Seventh Fleet had ordered Task Group 77.4 to conduct a dawn search for enemy ships between 340° and 30° for135 miles from Suluan Island. This would have disclosed the Japanese Centre Force. But although sunrise was at 0627 and the search aircraft had been launched by the *Ommaney Bay* (Task Unit 7.4.2) they had not departed by 0645. The Leyte anti-submarine patrol of two torpedo aircraft, and the local combat air patrols and anti-submarine patrols had all been launched by Rear-Admiral C.A.F. Sprague's Task Unit (77.4.3); and to the southward, Task Units 77.4.2 and 77.4.1 had launched similar patrols and missions.

---

6. Vice-Admiral Kurita stated that he thought Vice-Admiral Nishimura reported he had been attacked by torpedo boats soon after midnight 24th/25th and this was followed by one or more reports giving his E.T.A. at the target and saying he would be delayed.
7. There were certain Japanese minefields in the Strait, but from the wording of Vice-Admiral Kurita's reply to the question regarding American mines it is not clear whether he disregarded the possibility or did not consider it likely that there were any.

The six escort carriers of Rear-Admiral C.A.F. Sprague's Task Unit 77.4.3 received their first warning of the enemy's approach a quarter of an hour after sunrise, about 0645 on 25 October, in various ways, all more or less simultaneous. Some intercepted voice transmissions in the Japanese language over the inter-fighter director net; some received reports of surface contact on the SG radar, the bearing and distance from the flagship, the *Fanshaw Bay*, being 292° 18½ miles, other ships picking up the contact at 47,000 yards. Anti-aircraft fire was also heard and seen; this came from the Japanese ships firing at aircraft of the escort carriers' anti-submarine patrol, which sighted and reported large groups of ships about 15 to 30 miles west to north-west of the carriers.

At this time, the northern carrier group, having completed the launching of scheduled air patrols about an hour earlier, was in approximately 11° 50' N. 126° 10' E. about 40 miles east of Samar, proceeding with the carriers in circular formation, diameter 5,000 yards, within a screen of destroyers and destroyer escorts 3,500 yards farther out, on a northerly course. This formation the carriers maintained as far as possible throughout the action.[8] The enemy, reported as four battleships, six to eight cruisers, and eight to 12 destroyers, was sighted astern a few minutes later, almost within gun range of the carrier group whose masts they sighted shortly after Rear-Admiral C.A.F. Sprague's aircraft made contact. Surprise was never more complete.

Directly the enemy were reported, Rear-Admiral C.A.F. Sprague ordered all available aircraft to be launched to attack, after which they were to proceed to the partially completed Tacloban airfield on Leyte, to rearm and refuel. He increased to full speed and turned his carriers to a course 90° (0655) which was sufficiently close to the light north-easterly wind to permit launching[9] whilst taking his ships directly away from the enemy, but their maximum speed of 17 to 19 knots[10] being much below that of the Japanese, the range at first closed rapidly.[11]

At 0705 the Rear-Admiral broadcast a contact report and asked for assistance. The news was received on board the Seventh Fleet flagship about 0724 and

---

8. Both *St Lo Action Report*, p.18 and *Gambier Bay Action Report*, p.3, state that they conformed throughout to the manoeuvring signals of CTU 77.4.3 apart from deviations to avoid enemy salvos. Eventually, however, the carriers undoubtedly became strung out. Both the above ships lost all their records of the battle.

9. *St. Lo Action Report*, p. 4, says the wind was of a force of about 10 knots from the east. "*Gambier Bay*" *Action Report*, p. 4, says about 10 knots from east-north-east. The exact direction of the wind was stated by CTU 77.4.2 to be from 049°, strength seven knots at 0935 (Report, *Secret Information Bulletin No. 22*, p. 78-31).

10. *Gambier Bay Action Report*, p.4, states that her maximum speed was slightly in excess of 19 knots.

11. The range was short enough for Vice-Admiral Kurita to be able to notice that the flight decks of the carriers were full of aircraft as they turned to starboard on the sighting of the Second Fleet.

was the first intimation Vice-Admiral Kinkaid had that the enemy Centre Force had succeeded in passing through the San Bernardino Strait. In addition to ordering all available surface forces to concentrate at the eastern entrance to Leyte Gulf, preparatory to moving to the support of the escort carriers, the Commander Seventh Fleet sent an urgent call for assistance to Admiral Halsey. All aircraft were recalled from support missions and sent to attack the Japanese Centre Force; and the remaining two groups of escort carriers, Task Units 77.4.1 and 77.4.2, moved northward to support their colleagues.

43. Disposition of the Japanese Fleet

The composition of the enemy force which passed through the San Bernardino Strait was as follows:

Battleships	*Yamato, Nagato, Haruna, Kongo*
Heavy cruisers	*Chokai, Haguro, Suzuya, Chikuma, Kumano, Tone*
Light cruisers	*Noshiro, Yahagi*
Eleven destroyers	

At the time of sighting, the Japanese Second Fleet was changing into circular formation after coming through the San Bernardino Strait in night formation.[12] The light forces had dropped back. In the centre were the 1st and 3rd Battle Squadrons. The former consisted only of Vice-Admiral Kurita's flagship, the *Yamato*, with the *Nagato*, for the *Musashi* had been sunk on the previous day. The 3rd Squadron also comprised two battleships, the *Kongo* (flagship) and the *Haruna*. On the right flank was the heavy cruiser *Chokai* from the 4th Cruiser Squadron, together with the *Haguro*, the only remaining ship of the 5th Cruiser Squadron since the *Myoko* was damaged on 24th. The 7th Cruiser Squadron on the left flank comprised the four heavy cruisers *Kumano* (flagship), *Suzuya*, *Chikuma* and *Tone*. On the starboard bow was the 2nd Destroyer Flotilla and, on the port bow, the 10th Flotilla. Owing to the necessity of assigning destroyers to escort the *Takao*, damaged on 23rd, and the *Myoko* next day, the 2nd Flotilla now contained only six or eight destroyers and the 10th Flotilla four. The distance between columns was about 4,300 yards.[13]

12. *Interrogation Nav. No.41*, pp.170–4 (*U.S.S. B.S. No.170*), states: It was before we had completed the execution of order to change from night formation to ring formation, that the sighting occurred. The order to change the formation had been given at 0630.
13. According to American reports the enemy were in three groups: the heavy cruisers to the northward; battleships in the centre directly astern of the American formation; and their light forces to the southward.

On sighting the masts of the American ships Vice-Admiral Kurita altered course from 200° to 110° in order to come up wind of the carriers and prevent launching and recovering their aircraft. All his ships increased to their individual full speeds. The slowest ship was the battleship *Nagato*, who could do no better than 24 knots. The *Haruna*'s top speed was 25, and the *Yamato* which was down by the bow as the result of bombing, could only make 26 knots. The course of the Japanese fleet tended to curve to the southward until the ships reached the windward position, when they altered course and bore down on the carriers.

44. The Enemy Open Fire, 0655

The enemy opened fire almost immediately after being sighted, the *Yamato* at 35,000 yards, the *Haruna* at 33,700 yards and the *Kongo* at 26,250 yards, whilst the cruisers are reported to have opened at the extreme range of 29,200 yards.[14] In the American formation at this time the *S. B. Roberts*, *White Plains* and *Fanshaw Bay* were the most exposed ships, and it was apparently at them that the enemy at first directed his fire. The carriers continued on their easterly course at full speed, arming and launching all available aircraft whilst under fire. The aircraft attacked at once, in small formations, causing the Japanese ships to scatter for better defence.

Meanwhile, the range was closing. At 0701 Rear-Admiral C.A.F. Sprague ordered the destroyers and escort vessels to lay a smoke screen astern of the carriers; the latter also made smoke. There was a 10-knot wind, with squalls and heavy rain showers which reduced visibility and, as the Americans believed, possibly contributed to prevent the enemy from appreciating the weakness of the force opposed to him – certainly he could not distinguish whether he was opposed by fast carriers or escort carriers, and his reconnaissance aircraft reports were inadequate. Instead of ploughing straight through the carriers, each ship of which mounted only a single 5-in. gun, he wasted time in encirclement.[15]

During the launching of aircraft, the range from the *St. Lo*, which now that the enemy heavy cruisers were drawing ahead was probably their nearest target, soon fell to 22,000 yards. Rear-Admiral C.A.F. Sprague had been awaiting a favourable opportunity to turn towards the Seventh Fleet battleships at

14. *Fanshaw Bay's Report, Secret Information Bulletin, No. 22*, p.78-36, but *Kalin Bay*, op. cit., p.78-87. Gives the opening range of the enemy heavy cruisers as 20,000 yards. The Japanese plan does not show the heavy cruisers opening fire.
15. Vice-Admiral Kurita states, however, that this was not due to caution. He did not expect more than one battleship, if any, to be with the carriers and he was unable to close the range any faster, op. cit., pp.47–10, 47–14.

Leyte. His chance came at 0720, in a rain squall which hid his ships; and a bold alteration of course from 080° to 170° opened the range a little.

45. Enemy Attempt at Envelopment

On this course, the relative wind was such that the smoke lay in an East-West line. In an apparent attempt to avoid the effects of the smoke which troubled him seriously, the enemy advanced first one and then a second and third of his heavy cruisers up the port quarter of the American formation, and under continuous pressure from these ships the carriers were slowly forced round to starboard, so that for a short time, between 0800 and 0815, they were on south-westerly course, and apart from one short period from 0815 to 0830 they were not again able to maintain a southerly course for more than a very few minutes. With all escort carriers making heavy black smoke and with escorts making both funnel and chemical smoke on the starboard quarter of the formation, the vision of both forces was largely obscured. This fact, with the failure of the Japanese to close the range more rapidly, was largely responsible for saving the task unit from complete destruction.

At 0738 the range of the nearest enemy cruiser was no more than 14,000 yards from the rearmost carrier, the *St. Lo*; and one heavy cruiser accompanied, it was thought, by a large destroyer moved up on the port beam of the formation at an initial range of 16,000 yards which later closed to 12,000 yards and fired very deliberately full broadsides at the ships in the Task Unit.[16] As the course was altered slowly to the westward, most of the firing was from the enemy cruisers, infrequent salvos being contributed by the battleships astern and by destroyers advancing on the starboard quarter of the task unit.

Throughout this period the bombing and torpedo aircraft of the Task Unit had been attacking the enemy desperately, for the most part with general purpose bombs of little use against armour,[17] whilst additional fighters were catapulted to aid by 'strafing'. Escort carriers had been increased for

---

16. *ST. Lo Action Report*, p.18, says: 'Flashes from all six [sic] of the cruiser's turrets were observed as salvos were fired.' None of the Japanese cruisers had six turrets, but the *Chokai*, *Chikuma* and *Tone*, all of whom were now on the port side of the escort carriers, might give the appearance of having six turrets when firing on the beam their main armament (8 × 7.87-in. twins) and four of their sided eight H.A. guns simultaneously.

17. '*Gambier Bay' Action Report*, pp. 6, 26, states that owing to the nature of the escort carriers' duties her aircraft armament consisted mainly of GP bombs. AP bombs had been landed and replaced by GP and only 24 SAP bombs and the normal allowance of nine aircraft torpedoes were carried. There was some difference of opinion in the fleets as to the relative effects of SAP, AP, and GP, bombs against armoured ships *Secret Information Bulletin, No. 22*, pp. 78-49 and 78-56), but none as to the relative superiority of torpedoes.

the Philippine operations from 21 to some 30.[18] Some had been launched on scheduled flights before the sighting of the enemy, but each carrier was able to launch perhaps 15 to 20 during the first half-hour or so of the battle,[19] others being brought up from the hangar decks and launched or jettisoned during the action. At 0745 the *Gambier Bay* launched a torpedo aircraft with full load of fuel and carrying a torpedo with only 15–17 knots of wind over the deck, though the catapult tables required 22 knots of apparent wind. The Japanese ships manoeuvred individually to avoid the attacks, which led to the gradual breaking up of their formation. The plan of operations on which they were working made no provision for protective air cover by land-based aircraft.

Up to now, no ship had been hit although salvos fell amongst the carriers. The Japanese ships opened fire visually when they could see anything and afterwards tried to work in radar control, but with their unsuitable installations the battleships were only intermittently able to find the range of the escort carriers screened as they were by the smoke which the Americans used with great efficiency. No targets were assigned, the ships being left to choose their own, and they continued to fire as long as they had a target. The enemy rate of fire was slow, over a minute between salvos, and full use was made by individual American ships of manoeuvers to avoid being hit. The carriers had been ordered at 0740 to open fire with their single 5-in, guns as soon as the enemy were within range (17,000 yards); the *Gambier Bay* and *St. Lo* opened fire at once and the other carriers as feasible, but although they reported some hits on the cruisers these had no appreciable effect on the enemy. During this period, the *White Plains* and the *Fanshaw Bay* were under concentrated fire, but the Japanese had not yet succeeded in making a single hit.

46. American Destroyers Launch Torpedo Attacks, 0740. The '*Kumano*' put out of action.

At 0740 Rear-Admiral C.A.F. Sprague ordered the screen commander in the destroyer *Hoel* to launch a torpedo attack.[20] Low visibility rendered coordinated attacks impossible. The destroyer *Johnston* apparently attacked first, firing a full salvo at a heavy cruiser. She received heavy damage but

18. *Gambier Bay Action Report*, p.25, gives 30–42 aircraft as the normal complement of this class.
19. *Gambier Bay* launched 17 by 0710, *Kalinin Bay* 20 by 0725, and *St. Lo* 19 by about 0730.
20. *Fanshaw Bay* (flagship), Report, *Secret Information Bulletin, No, 22*, p. 78-36. But *St. Lo, Action Report*, p. 19, says the screen was divided, one group ordered to make a torpedo attack, and one to continue smoke screen. *Raymond* says: "At 0743 CTU 77.4.3 ordered the destroyer escorts to make torpedo attack on enemy cruiser." (*Secret Information Bulletin, No. 22*, pp. 78-37). Cincpac, *Report*, p. 92, states that at the order of Commander Task Unit 77.4.3, the vessels of the screen undertook a series of torpedo attacks. No time is given but the *Johnston* is said to have made her attack at 0720 and the *Hoel* at 0727.

continued to fire her guns at ranges down to 5,000 yards. At 1010, after the crew had abandoned her, she sank.[21]

The *Hoel* launched a half salvo of torpedoes at a battleship at 9,000 yards. Almost immediately she was hit and her port engine and steering engine were put out of action; but steering by hand she continued to fire her guns at the battleships and cruisers which were now on either side of her. A few minutes later, she fired another half salvo of torpedoes and reports hits on a heavy cruiser at 6,000 yards. Riddled by some 40 hits by 5-in., 8-in. and 14-in. shells, she went down at 0855 whilst trying to repair battle damage.

About 0743, the destroyer escort *Raymond*, whose position in the formation whilst steaming on its present course was on the port quarter, made an independent attack[22] on an enemy cruiser coming up from astern. She was straddled by the fire of the latter during the run in but remained unhit, and at 0756, when the range was down to 10,000 yards she fired a spread of three torpedoes, apparently from a position almost dead ahead, and then re-joined her formation at 24 knots.

The third destroyer, the *Heerman* was more fortunate. No results were observed from her first seven torpedoes, fired at a heavy cruiser at 0754; but at 0800 she fired three at a battleship of the *Kongo* class and reported one hit. She was subsequently in a gun action with two heavy cruisers but escaped with comparatively light damage.

The destroyer escort *Samuel B. Roberts* approached to within 4,000 yards under cover of the smoke of the destroyers, before delivering her torpedo attack; one hit on a heavy cruiser at about 0800 is reported. She escaped out of this with her life, but between 0851 and 0907 she was hit 20 times, and sank at 1005 after her crew had abandoned her.

The destroyer escort *Dennis* fired three torpedoes at 8,000 yards with results which were not seen. The seventh vessel of the screen, the destroyer escort *John C. Butler*, made no torpedo attack.

Altogether three hits were reported, and it was no doubt in one of these attacks that the Japanese cruiser *Kumano* received the torpedo hit which reduced her speed to 16 knots. Vice-Admiral Shiraishi shifted his flag to the *Suzuya*, who for a time stood by her. Later the *Kumano* abandoned the operation and returned to Brunei.

In addition to the material damage to the *Kumano* the destroyer attacks caused dispersion of the Japanese ships through turning away and gained valuable time for the escort carriers, though the enemy quickly resumed the attack.

---

21. Of the original survivors when the *Johnston* went down, 45 died in the water.
22. 'Destroyer escorts have never, I believe, been trained in formation torpedo attack procedure.' (Comment by destroyer escort *John C. Butler*, Secret Information Bulletin, No. 22, p. 78-124.)

47. First hit obtained by the Enemy, 0750

In spite of the undiminished intensity of the enemy's fire, it was not until the action had been in progress for an hour that the first hit on any of the carriers was recorded. Early in the engagement the cruisers *Haguro* and *Chokai*, enabled no doubt to cut a corner when the Japanese battleships turned to a southerly course soon after 0800, moved across to the port side of the formation and took the lead, in rough line ahead, from the *Tone* and *Chikuma*, the only two cruisers left in the Seventh Squadron when the *Kumano* and *Suzuya* fell out. It was perhaps during this manoeuvre that shortly after 0800 the leading cruiser to port was seen to commence a turn away, only, however, to continue the turn through 360° and take station astern of her colleague. As the Japanese cruisers continued to gain, they shifted target to the leading ships, and from this time on, the *Kitkun Bay* and *Fanshaw Bay* were under heavy fire and were repeatedly straddled. The *Kitkun Bay* received no damage, but at 0750 the *Fanshaw Bay*, Rear-Admiral C.A.F. Sprague's flagship, was hit on the bow by an 8-in, shell, damaging her catapult. Only two other 8-in. shell hits were received, neither of them serious. The failure of the Japanese ships to inflict greater damage is remarkable. At one period, about 0844 a unit of the enemy force consisting of a light cruiser and eight destroyers closed to a range of 6,900 yards from the *St. Lo*, but the latter remained unhit. The slow rate of fire, more than a minute between salvos, and poor spotting enabled the ship under fire to manoeuvre to avoid the next salvo.[23] The general employment of salvos rather than broadsides and of AP shells, some of which apparently failed to detonate within the ships, saved the latter from more serious damage.[24]

48. The Enemy's First Destroyer Attack, 0754

At 0754 one of the vessels of the screen reported torpedoes approaching the carriers from the starboard quarter. These were considered to have been fired at very long range by the group of enemy destroyers (Tenth Flotilla) to

---

23. The Japanese used coloured dyes for spotting. *Gambier Bay* says that the Japanese apparently spotted in increments of about 100 yards. *St. Lo* says that in most instances they were over corrected. Both ships agree that spotting was poor. Some ships state that the small spread of salvos was a contributory factor to the failure of the Japanese to obtain more hits. CTG 77.4. comments (*Secret Information Bulletin, No. 22*, p. 78-97): 'Competent observers have stated and photographic evidence appears to verify the fact that the pattern size was in the neighbourhood of 200 to 300 yards. This pattern size proved, after a trial of 2½ hours, to be entirely too small to ensure hits.'
24. 'His AP went cleanly through our ships. There is no record of a single detonation.' *Secret Information Bulletin, No. 22*, p. 78-97. However, this does not agree with *Gambier Bay Action Report*, part IV Battle Damage, from which it appears that out of 15 hits of which details are recorded, 10 of the shells exploded within the ship or on impact, two failed to explode and the result of three is not stated. One of the latter was evidently blind.

starboard during the time the American destroyers made their attack. The timely warning enabled them to be avoided.

Two minutes later, three US destroyers of the *Fletcher* class were sighted on the horizon to southward. They responded correctly to the *Gambier Bay*'s searchlight challenge and acknowledged a signal informing them that the carriers were under attack. After first standing to the eastward towards the enemy they turned and disappeared to the southward without taking part in the battle. About 0805 there was a submarine alarm, culminating in a supposed sighting. No torpedoes were seen, and it is believed there was no submarine present, although about 0830 a torpedo aircraft from TU 77.4.2 reported attacking a submarine 20 miles north-west of TU 77.4 3.

49. Sinking of the *Gambier Bay*, 0810 to 0911

During all this time, the ships had been turning gradually to a south-westerly course, the effect of which, together with the differences of speed and the evasive manoeuvres practiced, was to string out the disposition with the *White Plains*, the Kitkun Bay and the *Fanshaw Bay* in the lead, the *St. Lo* only 10,000 yards from the enemy forces astern at 0810, and the *Kalinin Bay* and the *Gambier Bay* on the exposed windward flank, clear of the protection of the smoke which drifted to starboard and aft (i.e., to the north-westward). As a result, the latter three carriers became the principal targets. The *Kalinin Bay* was hit three or four times from, 0750 onwards, once apparently, by a battleship, for fragments of a heavy shell were found on board but was not seriously damaged. Not so, however, the *Gambier Bay*. Between her and the enemy heavy cruisers no screen remained to intervene, and she had been for some time under the 8-in. shell fire[25] of three heavy cruisers and occasional salvos from the enemy main body. For a long while she avoided one salvo after another by alterations of course; but at 0810 the ship received her first hit. From now onwards she was hit almost continuously in the flight deck and spaces above water. Few of these shells reached any vital part of the ship until at about 0820 a hit below water in the forward engine room caused the abandonment of the latter seven minutes later and the ship slowed to 11 knots and fell astern.

This was the beginning of the end for the *Gambier Bay*. By 0850 the ship, listing and on fire, was dead in the water, with three enemy cruisers firing at her at point blank ranges, and her Commanding Officer, Capt. W. V. R. Vieweg, gave the order to abandon ship. At 0911 she sank in 11° 31′ N.,

---

25. Actually, 7.87-inch.

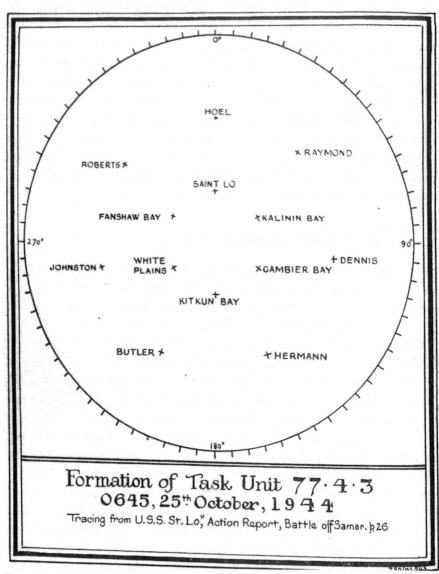

HOEL
+

× RAYMOND

ROBERTS ×

SAINT LO
+

FANSHAW BAY +   × KALININ BAY

270°   90°

JOHNSTON ×   WHITE   + DENNIS
              PLAINS ×   × GAMBIER BAY

KITKUN + BAY

BUTLER ×   + HERMANN

180°

Formation of Task Unit 77·4·3
0645, 25th October, 1944
Tracing from U.S.S. St. Lo, Action Report, Battle off Samar. p.26

Diagram IV. Formation of Task Unit 77.4.3, 0645, 25 October.

126° 12′ E., with an enemy cruiser firing into her at a range of less than 2,000 yards to the end. About 750 men left the ship, taking with them many seriously wounded. After some 40 hours in the sea without fresh water[26] most

---

26. Not a single water breaker on any raft retained potable fresh water notwithstanding the fact that all breakers had been refilled with fresh water only two days previously. The spigots were either knocked loose when the rafts were dropped to the water or accidentally kicked loose by personnel in the raft.

of them were saved by craft despatched from Leyte Gulf.[27] About 133 officers and men lost their lives.

50. Enemy Destroyers Again Approach, 0830

About 0830 the *Kalinin Bay*, one of the rearmost ships of the formation, sighted five destroyers on the starboard quarter, approaching head-on in column. They were at first thought to be friendly units coming to assist, until they opened fire at a range of approximately 14,500 yards. At the time, the enemy cruisers attacking from the port quarter were obscured from view by the smoke screen laid by the American escorts, and the *Kalinin Bay* shifted the fire of her single 5-in. gun to the destroyers, which when the range was down to 10,500 yards, were definitely recognized as of the *Terutsuki* class.

The enemy cruisers continued their attack. The *Kalinin Bay*, being between two fires was unable to use evasive courses and was hit by the Japanese cruisers several times at this period. Since, however, the five destroyers were closing the range rapidly she continued to direct her fire on them and never again during the action shifted back to the cruisers. Presently some of the American escorts closed the latter and apparently caused them to turn away somewhat, for the range from the *Kalinin Bay* began to open.

The firing of the Japanese destroyers appears to have been wild, and no hits are recorded. The *Kalinin Bay* made a direct hit on one of them about 0930, causing the vessel to be immediately enveloped in white smoke; and about the same time, they made some radical manoeuvers and commenced to withdraw, firing as they went. It was probably at this juncture that they fired the salvo of torpedoes which was seen a few minutes later.

51. Desperate Expedients Adopted

By 0826 the two cruisers to port had forged clear of the drift of smoke from the carriers, and Rear-Admiral C.A.F. Sprague ordered two destroyer escorts to cross from the starboard to the port side of the formation and lay their smoke on the port bow of the task unit. The destroyers and destroyer escorts had been rendering and continued to render valuable and devoted service by making smoke and distracting the enemy by their gunfire,[28] and

---

27. There seems to have been some hitch in the rescue of the survivors of the escort raft carriers and escorts sunk in the battle, 'They were "buzzed" by friendly planes, but there were no efforts at air-sea rescue, and they had to wait until craft were sent out from Leyte to pick them up.' (Cincpac, *Report*, p.96.).

28. The *Hoel*, for example, fired approximately 600 rounds of common and AA projectiles before being sunk.

this appears to have been one of the principal reasons why the Japanese ships were unable to close to the decisive range despite their utmost efforts. At 0902 the destroyer escort *Dennis* reported a hit below the waterline and her main battery out of action. The destroyer escort *Raymond*, which had survived the torpedo attack at 0740 was ordered at 0828 to intercept an enemy cruiser, later identified by the *Raymond* as of the *Nachi* class, approaching on the port quarter. The *Raymond* had no smoke or torpedoes left, but she closed the range from 12,600 to 5,700 yards, on which the cruiser, which during the approach, had shifted target from the carriers to the destroyer escort, straddling but failing to hit her, turned away, together with a battleship. About 0900, however, the enemy cruisers were threatening to turn the escort carriers to the northward, towards the main Japanese disposition, and the desperate expedient was adopted of ordering the TBM aircraft who had expended their bombs to make dummy torpedo runs on, the enemy. The effectiveness of the ruse is not known.

52. Task Unit 77-4-2 Enters the Battle, 0855

At last, however, welcome help was near for the hard-pressed escort carriers. At 0705, when Rear-Admiral C.A.F. Sprague broadcast his enemy report and asked for assistance, Rear-Admiral T.L. Sprague (TU 77-4-1) with the six ships of the Central Station Carrier Group was about 120 miles to the southward of the battle approaching Leyte on a north-westerly course and he sent off all available aircraft to support Rear-Admiral C.A.F. Sprague. At 0740, without warning, he was attacked by enemy aircraft when in approximately 09° 45′ N., 126° 35′ E., and the escort carrier *Santee* was hit by a suicider. At 0753 the same ship was hit amidships and further damaged by a torpedo fired by a Japanese submarine which was not located,[29] and six minutes later, another escort carrier the *Suwannnee*, was hit and damaged by a suicide aircraft, many casualties being caused.[30] Both carriers were soon back in operating condition, the *Santee* by 0900 and the *Swannee* an hour and a half later.

Two more air attacks were made on the Task Unit, both unsuccessful. At 1154 three enemy aircraft made a low local attack which was beaten off by

---

29. No mention is made of this torpedoing in the list of casualties suffered by TG 77.4. At 2240/25 USS *Coolbaugh* reported that she had sunk a submarine about 50 miles east of the position where *Santee* was hit, but the sinking was not confirmed. *Japanese Submarine Operations* states that submarines were used in concentration to the east of Leyte during the battle, and probably sank a transport on 24 October and an aircraft carrier and destroyer next day.
30. Cincpac, *Report*, p.95; but on p.100 it is stated that the ship was hit by two suicide aircraft, though no other mention of this attack has been found.

gunfire, and another attack was driven off at 1220, when an attempted suicide dive on the *Sandee* failed. Shortly before this latter attack Rear-Admiral T.L. Sprague quitted the area and steered to join the surviving ships of Rear-Admiral C.A.F. Sprague's Task Unit 77-43.

Nearly 100 miles to the northward of Task Unit 77.4.1, and consequently in a better position to render help, was the third escort carrier group, Task Unit 77.4.2, six carriers under Rear-Admiral F.B. Stump. The latter did not receive the news that Rear-Admiral C.A.F. Sprague was under heavy fire until more than an hour later, at 0814, for although one of his aircraft at 0643 had apparently sighted and reported the Japanese Fleet the message did not reach CTU 77.4.2. At the time, Task Unit 77.4.2 was about 20 to 25 miles to the south-eastward of the enemy, proceeding on a course 160° at 17 knots, except when headed to the north-eastward for launching aircraft. Placing his three destroyers, the *Haggard* (Captain Reynolds, ComDesDiv 94), *Hailey* and *Franks* about three miles astern of the carriers on a bearing towards the enemy, to intercept any attempt to attack by light forces, and his five destroyer escorts ahead for screening, Rear-Admiral Stump prepared to launch aircraft strikes. At 0817 shells, estimated to be 8-in., were falling short of the three destroyers. These were fired by the *Haruna*. The range, 35,300 yards by Japanese estimation, was closing 1,000 yards every ten minutes, and about 0841 the destroyers were straddled. They were unhit, but were ordered to close the formation.

At 0833 T.U. 77.4.2 altered course to 037° to launch a strike and land six of Rear-Admiral C.A.F. Sprague's aircraft who could not be taken on board their own carrier. This occupied until 0844, when course was altered to 140°.[31] As Rear-Admiral C.A.F. Sprague's aircraft completed their attacks they landed if and wherever they could, either at the partially serviceable Tacloban airfield on Leyte or on the carrier escorts of Admiral Stump's task unit. As his aircraft became exhausted, Rear-Admiral C.A.F. Sprague's attacks on the Japanese Second Fleet tapered off, until by 0830 they had partially ceased. In the belief that there would be a heavy air attack later, perhaps in an hour's time. Vice-Admiral Kurita at 0911 ordered his ships to close the formation. Rear-Admiral Stump's air attack struck him as he was passing the sinking *Gambier Bay* and destroyers and had just hoisted the signal for ring formation.

53. Sinking of the *Chikuma* and *Chokai*

Strike No. 1 began its attack at 0855. Part of the flight attacked two heavy cruisers and a light cruiser which had TU 77.4.3. under close fire. The

---

31. Strike No.2. It is not stated what time Strike No.1 was launched.

remainder, supported by eight fighter and 16 torpedo aircraft, the latter loaded with torpedoes, of Strike No. 2 attacked two heavy cruisers and one battleship directly astern of their own task unit. The main weight of the attack struck the enemy between 0910 and 0930 when the nearest enemy ship, visible on the horizon, had closed Rear-Admiral Stump's force to 16 miles and shell fire was coming closer to his escort carriers. The strikes reported considerable success, two torpedo hits being made on a heavy cruiser of the *Tone* class and one torpedo hit on a *Kongo* class battleship.

There can be little doubt that these strikes caused the damage to the cruisers *Chikuma* and *Chokai*, on account of which they had later to be sunk by the Japanese. At 0907 the *Chikuma* reported that she had been hit by one torpedo and was unable to navigate; later she reported being able to make 18 knots with one propeller, but was unable to steer. The precise manner in which the *Chokai* was damaged is uncertain, apart from a bomb hit on her forward aircraft; but three minutes after the *Chikuma* was hit, she too was out of action. The destroyer *Fujinami* took off the crew of the *Chokai*, whilst the *Nowake* was sent to assist the *Chikuma* and was sunk later in the day by carrier air attack, though the Japanese heard no more of her.

54. The Enemy fires torpedoes and breaks off the action, 0925

There now occurred something which, to the escort carriers, fighting with desperation but with small expectation of survival[32] must have seemed little short of a miracle. At 0925 the *Kitkun Bay*, who by reason of her position in the formation was now only 10,500 yards from the group of enemy cruisers to port, saw the latter turn 16 points to port in succession and retire to the northward. When steady on the opposite course they resumed firing at the *St. Lo* until their reverse course took them out of range.

At this time the three enemy groups bore from the *Fanshaw Bay* respectively 021° distant 21,000 yards, 152° distant 18,700 yards, and 088° distant 19,500 yards. All three enemy groups retired about the same time, and at 0952 they faded from the flagship's radar screen.

As the enemy broke off the action a dozen or more torpedoes were seen approaching, evidently fired at long range, for they were running very shallow and broaching to, and passed harmlessly astern, while the rearmost ships, the *St. Lo* and the *Kalinin Bay*, had no difficulty in combing the waters. Both ships fired at the torpedoes with 40-mm. and 20-mm. guns without success

---

32. Report of CTU 77.4.32 (*Kitkun Bay*), *Secret Information Bulletin, No. 22*, pp. 78–26, states: 'Until the moment when the enemy broke off and retired to the north there appeared only one possible outcome of the encounter – complete annihilation.'

though the explosion of a 5-in. shell, fired by the *Kalinin Bay* ahead of a torpedo astern, apparently caused it to alter course radically to port. One of the *St. Lo*'s aircraft also strafed them and apparently caused at least one to explode. There seems little doubt that the Japanese destroyers of the 10th Flotilla on the starboard quarter fired most of the salvo of torpedoes, despite their unfavourable position, but at least one torpedo approached the *St. Lo* from the port beam, indicating that the 2nd Destroyer Flotilla may also have launched an attack before retiring.[33]

Vice-Admiral Kurita had now given up hope of overtaking Rear-Admiral C.A.F. Sprague's ships. He was even now uncertain of their type, whether fast carriers or escort carriers, for Rear-Admiral C.A.F. Sprague's fighter aircraft had prevented the *Yamato*'s reconnaissance aircraft from obtaining any information; and he estimated their speed at about 30 knots. The evasive manoeuvres necessary to avoid the ceaseless American destroyer and air attacks, and the effective use of smoke not only prevented his ships from overtaking but in the prevailing low visibility had actually caused him to lose sight of his quarry though his light forces were in touch. He was drawing heavily on his fuel supply at these high speeds, and this he could not afford. About 0930 he recalled his cruisers, unaware that they were within 11,000 yards of Rear-Admiral C.A.F. Sprague's escort carriers, and set a course for Leyte Gulf to carry out the now badly overdue attack on the invasion forces.

55. Enemy Air Attack, 1050, *St. Lo* Sunk

By about 0940 all enemy gunfire had ceased and the retirement of all Japanese units was in progress. Task Unit 77.4.3 altered course to the southward for Leyte Gulf and for an hour the crews had a respite from attack, though enemy aircraft were about.

Battered though they were, Rear-Admiral C.A.F. Sprague's escort carriers lost no time in despatching their remaining aircraft to the attack. At 1000 the *St. Lo* and *Kitkun Bay* each launched a torpedo aircraft which had been loaded with torpedoes during the battle and despatched them in company. Aircraft

---

33. *Kitkun Bay* (second ship in the line) states: 'Heavy cruisers to port had obviously fired this torpedo salvo' (*Secret Information Bulletin, No. 22*, pp. 78–29). *Fanshaw Bay* (third ship in the line) merely states: "Enemy launched torpedo attack from extreme range.' op.cit. pp. 78–36. *Kalinin Bay* (rear ship) states that the torpedoes were fired by five *Terutsuki* class destroyers (op, cit., pp. 78–35 and 78–91). *St. Lo* believes they were fired the group of destroyers on the starboard quarter (*Action Report*, p. 7) but in addition to the many observed passing quite wide to starboard (op. cit., p. 19) one of her torpedo aircraft reported to her a torpedo approaching from the port beam. The only torpedoes shown on the Japanese Plan as fired by their ships were by the 10th DF about 0905.

from carriers whose flight decks were out of commission were landed by the rest and refuelling and re-arming commenced without delay.

At about 1050 an air attack developed on Task Unit 77.4.3, the first organized Kamikaze (suicide) attack of the war.[34] The attackers were land based. They came in below the effective altitude of the SK radar and climbed to the height necessary to launch their attacks when close enough to be able to ignore radar detection. Destroyer escorts on the starboard bow and beam opened up with AA fire as the enemy aircraft approached. The *Kitkun Bay* was hit first, but the aircraft merely dived through her catwalk and caused little damage. A second Japanese aircraft hit and damaged the *White Plains*. The *Kalinin Bay* hit one with her AA gunfire but failed to prevent it from crashing on board, where it caused fires which were, however, extinguished in a very few minutes. A third resulted in its diving into the sea close aboard.

At about 1053 an enemy suicider crashed on the *St. Lo*'s flight deck abreast the after funnel, some 15ft, to port of the centre line. At the time the ship was loading and servicing aircraft and an unusual condition existed due to the necessity of preparing these urgently needed machines for further action. The detonation of the enemy bomb caused an explosion which initiated a chain of events resulting in the self-destruction of the vessel within the space of half an hour. In quick succession a number of explosions occurred, causing a great fire amidships, putting out of action the fire-fighting equipment and communications. In a very few minutes it was clear to Captain F. J. McKenna of the *St. Lo* that his ship could not be saved, and as soon as she had lost sufficient headway he gave the order to abandon her. At 1125 the ship sank in approximately 11° 12′ N., 126° 30′ E. About 112 officers and men lost their lives and about 338 were injured.[35]

What remained of Rear-Admiral C.A.F. Sprague's force, the *Fanshaw Bay*, *White Plains*, *Kalinin Bay* and *Kitkun Bay*, all damaged except the last, retired south and south-east throughout the afternoon of 25th, recovering aircraft as practicable, and headed for an evening rendezvous some 75 miles east of Siargao Island which had been arranged with CTU 77.4.1. They sailed next day for Manus with a borrowed screen.

---

34. CTU 7742 criticizes the attack for poor timing in locating the escort carriers (*Secret Intelligence Bulletin, No. 22*, pp. 78–92). He states: 'In addition to poor timing a further error … was the poor selection of targets … instead of selecting a group of escort aircraft carriers already under fire of the Japanese Fleet, the Japanese flight leader should have attacked Task Unit 77.4.2 which was completely undamaged and was launching heavy air attacks against the Japanese Fleet.'

35. *St. Lo, Action Report*, p. 23, states: 'Four escort vessels were on hand, to pick up survivors.' It is not known who they were. The navigator, who was the last to leave the sinking ship before the Captain, carefully 'placed his binoculars on a convenient hook' before taking to the sea.

In the desperate air attacks of this battle the escort carriers lost 35 aircraft. Their total losses during the Battle for Leyte Gulf were approximately 105 aircraft, over a fifth of their total complement. In all, they made 252 torpedo and 201 fighter sorties, dropping 83 torpedoes and 191 tons of bombs. Out of 301 enemy aircraft encountered between 24–26 October, 138 were destroyed.

The escort carriers and their screen lost 994 officers and men killed and missing.

Chapter VIII

The Battle off Cape Engano, 25 October

56. Contact with the Japanese Northern Force 0205, 25 October

Whilst the Seventh Fleet escort carriers were fighting their gallant delaying action, the Covering Force – the Third Fleet, under Admiral Halsey – 250 miles to the northward was attacking the Japanese carriers.

It had not been possible to keep contact with the enemy Northern Force throughout the night. About 0030 on 25th the night carrier *Independence* launched a 10 sector, 350-mile night search, one aircraft per sector, between bearings 320° and 010°. Other searches to the northward were launched shortly after; at 0100 between the same bearings by the *Lexington* and at 0135 two night fighters by the *Enterprise*.

About 0205 a radar contact was made, by one of the search aircraft in 16° 42′ N., 125° 36′ E. Three large and three small ships were reported steering 110 at 15 knots, with a second group of six large ships 26 miles to the northward of the first. This put the closest enemy group almost due north (bearing 352°), at an estimated distance of 80 miles. Contact was lost soon. At 0300 engine trouble forced the night shadowing aircraft to return to base, the relief search aircraft had difficulties with radar equipment, and radar contact was never regained during darkness. When last seen the mean course of the two enemy groups was about NNE

It seems possible that the rearmost of these contacts may have referred to Rear-Admiral Matsuda's detached force in the process of re-joining the main body, for the Japanese carrier force normally cruised as a single group and only separated into two groups, which kept within visual signalling distance of one another, when air attack was expected.

57. Task Force 34 formed 0240 0430, 25 October

At 0226 Vice-Admiral Mitscher recommended to the Commander Third Fleet that course should be changed to north, and that Task Force 34 should be formed, to provide for co-ordinated surface and air attack on the enemy. This was approved by Admiral Halsey, who at 0240 directed Vice-Admiral Mitscher to form the force in position 10 miles north of the fleet guide, Commander Task Force 38 retaining tactical command of the fleet until otherwise ordered. Course was changed to 080° and speed increased to 25 knots, the carriers reducing to 10 knots to allow the heavy surface striking force (Task Force 34) to get clear ahead, for it was possible that a surface battle might develop by 0430. Task Force 34 as constituted comprised all the six battleships, two heavy cruisers, five light cruisers and 18 destroyers from Task Force 38, leaving in the latter the three groups of carriers with a total screen of 23 destroyers.

Formation in the darkness of so large a disposition as this heavy surface striking force occupied a long time. It was two hours or more before all ships from the various task groups of Task Force 38 gained their proper station. 'Had contact with enemy surface forces been made during this period', writes Rear-Admiral C.T. Joy, Commander Cruiser Division 6, USS *Wichita*, 'our forces would have been under a tremendous handicap.'

Course was set at 000. By about 0430 Task Force 34 was formed up[1] ahead of the carrier groups in Cruising Disposition 4N under Vice-Admiral W.A. Lee Jr., USS *Washington*. The six fast battleships were in three columns; the cruisers stationed as left flank, centre, and right flank; and the 20 destroyers formed an anti-submarine screen ahead. The disposition was altered from time to time,[2] but the course of the Task Force was only slightly modified throughout the morning. Speed was increased to 18 knots at 0724, 20 knots at 0801, and finally to 25 knots at 0835.

58. Dawn Searches Sight the Enemy, 25 October

It was considered certain that whatever course the enemy might have steered since contact was lost at 0300 he would be within easy range of air attack at dawn, and the first deckload strike was armed in the early hours, ready to take off directly there was sufficient light.

The weather at daybreak was excellent – clear with only a few clouds on the horizon and a 16-knot wind from 050°. Launching of patrols, searches and strike groups commenced at 0555, and soon afterwards the search

---

1. But *Santa Fe* (Left Flank) states she did not arrive on station until 0505. Admiral Halsey's Despatch (*Secret Information Bulletin, No. 22*. pp. 78–14) says: 'The force was formed up by daylight' (about 0600).

2. The light cruiser USS *Mobile* reports: 'The Heavy Surface Striking Force continued on ahead, first forming cruising disposition 4-S, in which the cruisers were spaced in the forward semi-circle on circle 6 and the battleships on circle 2, then forming the anti-aircraft disposition, Cruising Disposition 4-V. *Massachusetts* remained as guide in the formation centre, the remaining battleships and the cruisers were evenly spaced on circle 6. The destroyers remained as an anti-submarine screen on circle 13, then somewhat later formed sections.'

aircraft took departure from 16° 06′ N., 125° 55′ E. As there was no recent information of the enemy's position, the initial strike groups were stationed 50 miles to the north to await target data and further instructions. So many aircraft were employed on patrols, searches and communication relays, that Admiral Sherman could only muster one well-balanced strike group amongst the three carriers of his Task Group, 38.3.

In sector 290°-300° the two *Terutsuki* class destroyers seen the previous afternoon were again sighted, this time near Pamoctan Island. One was reported set afire by strafing. In sector 310°-320° a convoy of 14 ships, many of them transports, escorted by five destroyers was reported sighted in 19° 30′ N., 121° 30′ E., course 170°. The assigned search sectors did not extend east of 360°, but since it appeared likely that the enemy might be to the east ward of 000° one division of the *Essex*'s combat air patrol was vectored out on Vice-Admiral Mitscher's orders to conduct a high speed search to the north east. This was fortunate, for it was those pilots who first sighted the Japanese Northern Force at 0710° in 18° 37′ N., 126° 45′ E., bearing 020°, 135 miles, on a north-easterly course.[3] Enemy fighters forced the *Essex* CAP to climb steadily; nevertheless, for 50 minutes they circled over the enemy, reporting position, composition, and movements. The composition of the force, 17 ships in all, was reported, with considerable accuracy:-

Reported composition Actual composition

One *Zuikaku* class carrier *Zuikaku* (fleet flagship)
Two *Chitose* class light carriers *Chitose, Chiyoda*
One *Zuiho* class light carrier *Zuiho*
Two *Ise* class (battleships with flight deck aft) *Hyuga, Ise*
One unidentified heavy cruiser
One *Oyodo* or *Agano* class light cruiser *Oyodo*
Two *Natori* class light cruisers *Isudzu, Tama*
One unidentified light cruiser
Six or eight destroyers

---

3. *Lexington* gives time of sighting 0730 and her track chart shows the enemy steering 020° true. CTF 38 (*Secret Information Bulletin, No. 22*, pp. 78–38) gives the bearing of the enemy 020° true, course about 010°. Captain Ohmae, Chief of Staff to Vice-Admiral Ozawa, states that they 'knew' that they were 100 miles from the American carriers because the latter always took off on reconnaissance about half hour before sunrise. The Japanese carriers sent out search aircraft, but got no response. They did not really expect to be as close as 100 miles. Cinepac, *Report*, p. 102, states that the enemy was reported steering south when first sighted.

59. First Strikes by Third Fleet Carriers, 0840 and 1010, 25 October. Sinking of the *Chitose*

When the enemy were first sighted, the aircraft of the first strike were already orbiting 50 miles north of the Third Fleet and thus were only some 85 miles from the enemy. In half an hour they had the Japanese ships in sight, and at 0840 they struck. The *Essex* strike leader (Commander David McCampbell) was made target co-ordinator, and targets were assigned upon arriving. Anti-aircraft fire was heavy during all strikes, and the battleships were using their main batteries. Coloured tracers and bursts were employed. It was evident to the Americans that the enemy carriers had not yet flown on their aircraft, for only about 15 enemy fighters attempted opposition. These were quickly eliminated, and as a result it was possible to keep a target co-ordinator over the ships almost continuously throughout the entire day directing the attack, assigning targets, and reporting results. Vice-Admiral Mitscher had ordered the aircraft crews to sink the enemy carriers and cruisers before attacking the battleships, but this priority of targets was not strictly adhered to.[4]

In the ensuing chase the American carriers experienced great difficulty in closing the target, their aircraft launching and recovery courses being to eastward, whilst the enemy's retirement was to the northward. 'Every available minute of time was devoted to gaining distance to the north yet the necessity for getting off the maximum air effort required frequent launchings and recoveries, and many planes with battle damage had to be taken aboard with varying degrees of urgency', writes CTG 38.4, and he makes the point that retirement downwind (westward) instead of north would have taken the Japanese carriers towards their own shore-based aircraft in northern Luzon, and eventually into the comparative safety of the China Sea.

Vice-Admiral Mitscher gave his preliminary report of the first strike at 0850: Two carriers hit badly, one carrier hit, one light carrier untouched, one heavy ship (light carrier or light cruiser) sunk after tremendous explosion on fantail.[5] The *Zuikaku*, Vice-Admiral Ozawa's flagship, had her rudder damaged by a torpedo hit in the first attack and had to resort to hand steering though she could still steam at 20 knots. At 1100 her communication system broke down; accordingly, the Commander-in-Chief transferred to the light

---

4. CTF 38 comments: 'Normally in attacks on enemy combatant ships such as the carriers' engagement east of Luzon, carriers and cruisers should be bombed, torpedoed and sunk before attacking battleships. This priority of targets was specified by CTF 38 prior to the attack but was not strictly adhered to ... The battleship is almost impossible to stop except with another battleship. Many valuable ships, although heavily damaged, escaped being sunk by our air attacks because too much effort was expended on the battleships.' (*Secret Information Bulletin No. 22*, pp. 78–107.)
5. This ship may have been (a) the light carrier *Chitose* or (b) a destroyer which Captain Ohmae states was sunk in the first attack or (c) the *Zuikaku* which was damaged aft.

cruiser *Oyodo*. The destroyer *Akitsuki* is said to have been sunk instantly at 0857, and the carriers *Zuiho*, *Chitose* and *Chiyoda* were each hit and damaged by one bomb. When the second strike, furnished by Task Group 38.4, and joined by certain aircraft from *Lexington* and *Langley* (Task Group 38.3)[6] arrived over the Japanese force about 1010 only three carriers could be found – *Zuikaku*, *Zuiho* and one badly damaged *Chitose* class light carrier (the *Chiyoda*); the fourth one (the *Chitose*) had sunk at 0937. This strike, though smaller, apparently caused greater damage than the first, the three remaining carriers receiving hits which rendered them unmanageable.

60. The Battleships Return South, 1115, 25 October

Meanwhile, at 0705 the first of several urgent requests for assistance had been made by the Seventh Fleet escort carriers who were under attack east of Samar Island by the Japanese main body which had passed through the San Bernardino Strait about midnight. Vice-Admiral Kinkaid sent an urgent call for assistance to the Commander Third Fleet, and at the same time it was made clear that the nearest battleship force, the Seventh Fleet, could do little to help, being low on ammunition after its night action in the Surigao Straits.[7] In response to these calls Admiral Halsey at 0848 ordered Task Group 38.1 to proceed at high speed to assist Rear-Admiral C.A.F. Sprague.[8] In the confusion of the battle east of Samar it was not apparent until much later that the enemy had definitely broken off the action about 0930, after battering Rear-Admiral Sprague's ships for 2½ hours; and in fact, at 0940 another message came in from the Rear-Admiral, stating that his escort carriers were under attack by four battleships, eight cruisers and other ships and asking for battleships and a strike by fast carriers to be sent at top speed to cover Leyte. The Commander-in-Chief Pacific Fleet (Admiral Nimitz) was evidently uneasy, for at 1000 he inquired the position of Task Force 34. At 1055 Admiral Halsey, having reports that the Northern Force was already badly crippled, decided to take his battleships south to aid the Seventh Fleet. He, therefore, dissolved Task Force 34, which was about 42 miles from the enemy at the time, and ordered Task Group 38.2, consisting of the carriers *Intrepid*, *Cabot* and *Independence* with the greater part of Task Force 34, namely, all the six battleships, the light cruisers *Vincennes*, *Miami* and *Biloxi*, and the eight destroyers of Squadron

---

6. This was a small strike about 16 torpedo aircraft, six bombers, 14 fighters.
7 Cinepac, *Report*, p. 97 states that Admiral Halsey received the first call for help at 0822. Vice-Admiral McCain (Task Group 38.1) intercepted it at 0725, but ComBatDiv Nine says the escort carriers' calls for help were received about 0900.
8. Cinepac, *Report*, p. 98. But CTG 38.1 in his report does not mention the receipt of this order, and he makes it clear that he proceeded to help Rear-Admiral C. A. F. Sprague on his own initiative.

52 to reverse course at 1115 and proceed south. The remaining four cruisers and 10 destroyers in Task Force 34[9] were ordered to re-join their original task groups, 38.3 and 38.4 respectively, the commanders of which were directed to continue strikes against the enemy carrier force.

Admiral Halsey's decision to take his battleships south at this juncture left to the carriers of Task Groups 38.3 and 38.4 the task of dealing with the Japanese Northern Force. Brilliantly though the American aircraft performed that day in encompassing the destruction of all four of the enemy carriers it was beyond their powers to sink or stop the battleship carriers, *Ise* and *Hyuga*. The difficulty of stopping a battleship except with another battleship is now known; but at that date 'the practical difficulty of crippling by air strikes alone, a task force of heavy ships at sea and free to manoeuvre', was not universally recognized and was one of the lessons of the Battle for Leyte Gulf.

It is not known to what extent the Commander Third Fleet was hampered making his decision by the confused nature of the enemy intelligence available, which the Commander Seventh Fleet Battle Line represented. 'The outstanding feature of the operations of 24–25 October', wrote the Captain of the *Alabama*, one of Admiral Halsey's battleships, 'was the confusing and conflicting reports regarding the location, composition, formation, course and speed of the enemy groups, and of the damage inflicted upon enemy units."

At 1055, when Admiral Halsey decided to return south the air attacks on the Japanese Northern Force were reported to be going well; and Vice-Admiral Ozawa was in full flight. Already, two of the enemy carriers had been damaged and one stopped. The only danger to be feared from the Japanese carriers was their employment by any aircraft which might fly out to them from Luzon. One flight of aircraft, apparently intending to land on the carriers, had been reported approaching the force, but it turned back when the American attack developed. It must have seemed that the elimination of the potential threat from Vice-Admiral Ozawa's force could now be left to Vice-Admiral Mitscher's fast carriers alone.

It would appear that at this juncture the Commander Third Fleet was influenced by the necessity of coming to the help of the Seventh Fleet rather than by the hope of bringing Vice-Admiral Kurita to action though these two proceedings were one and the same, unless the Japanese Admiral retreated on his approach. It is true that the two fleets were then over 300 miles apart, which, taking into account the necessity of fuelling his destroyers, would prevent Admiral Halsey from saving daylight in his arrival in the south.

---

9. Light cruisers *Santa Fe*, *Mobile* and six destroyers (Task Group 38.3), heavy cruisers *Wichita*, *New Orleans* and four destroyers.

Having allowed himself to be decoyed to the northward on the previous evening he could do little to restore the situation. Nevertheless, the impact of Rear Admiral C.A.F. Sprague's calls for help eventually proved irresistible. The Commander Third Fleet set course south at 20 knots and in due course arrived too late to have any further effect on the course of the Battle for Leyte Gulf, other than to sink an enemy straggler – cruiser or destroyer – from the main body.

At this very moment, as coincidence would have it, his antagonist, Vice-Admiral Kurita, was also making a decision, which was to seal the fate of the Philippines and thereby in due course, of the Japanese Empire.

61. Sinking of the *Zuikaku* and *Zuiho*, pm, 25 October

After Admiral Halsey's departure, Vice-Admiral Mitscher continued to make what northing he could under the handicap of launching and recovering aircraft in a north-easterly wind. The third air strike, some 150 aircraft in all, took off at 1145, and shortly after the target co-ordinator, an aircraft from the *Belleau Wood*, reported that the enemy ships were then in two groups, one to the south, termed the 'Cripples', consisted of an *Ise* class battleship carrier, two light cruisers and three destroyers, some of them circling a *Chitose* class light carrier (the *Chiyoda*) which was dead in the water and burning as the result of the first air strike of the day. The other group was some 20 to 30 miles north-west of the cripples, and consisted of the carriers *Zuitkaku*, *Zuiho*, the second *Ise* class battleship carrier, three cruisers and two or three destroyers. The enemy ships were about 102 miles, 351° from the American carriers, and the aircraft from Task Group 38.3 were ordered to strike the northern group, which was apparently still steering due north at 15 to 20 knots' speed. Their attack at about 1310 resulted in the sinking about an hour later of the *Zuikaku* with nine direct 1,000 and 2,000 lb. bomb hits. Aircraft from Task Group 38.4 shortly after made a number of hits on the light carrier *Zuiho*, which was seen to sink at 1520, as the result of bombs delivered by the fourth strike.[10]

Judging by the number of attacking American aircraft and the direction from which they came Vice-Admiral Ozawa considered that he had succeeded in diverting two groups of enemy forces, distant from him about 150 to 200 miles and closing. To counter-attack was out of his power, for he had no aircraft and did not know the position of the enemy. He decided to draw the American carriers further north.

---

10. The Japanese times for the sinking of the *Zuikaku* and the *Zuiho* are 1414 and 1527 respectively.

At 1315 Rear-Admiral Sherman launched the available aircraft from Task Group 38.3 to join a strike from Task Group 38.4 on the northern battleship carrier. The attack at 1310 had reported one torpedo hit, and three more torpedo hits were now claimed; but after stopping for about ten minutes she got under way again. The first battleship carrier and the light cruiser and destroyers in the southern group were reported at 1410 by a division of *Lexington*'s Combat Air Patrol to be abandoning the carrier *Chiyoda* and heading north to join the main group.

To Rear-Admiral Sherman, the situation appeared most favourable. The Japanese air force had been destroyed on the previous day. The enemy was at the ideal striking range, between 80 and 100 miles away, with the carriers of two task groups closing him at 25 knots – he could not get away. A good fresh breeze for air operations was 45° on the carriers' starboard bow. But to the Rear-Admiral's dismay, at 1328 Vice-Admiral Mitscher ordered him to go no further north, and in accordance with these orders he headed west, which, with operations into the wind, kept him in the same general locality. However, at 1417 he requested permission to proceed northward once more, to ensure getting in his last strike of the day before dark. Permission was given, and Task Group 383 headed north again.

The final attack of the day – full deck-loads from the *Essex*, *Lexington* and *Langley* – took departure at 1615 when the enemy ships were bearing 327°, 92 miles. At this time only ten ships of the original 17 were afloat and under way, namely the light cruisers *Oyodo* (fleet flagship) and *Isudzu*, battleship carriers *Hyuga* and *Ise*, destroyers *Shimotsuki*, *Wakatsuki*, *Hatsutsuki*, *Kuwa*, *Sugi*, *Kiri*, with the *Chiyoda* stopped, afire, and abandoned by the remaining ships. Numerous, but certainly exaggerated claims were made by the crews of this strike. Two torpedo and six direct bomb hits were reported on the battleship carriers, but the only effect was to cause one of them to slow to eight knots temporarily, after which she steamed after her companions at 20 knots. One destroyer was (apparently incorrectly) confirmed as sunk and one 250-lb. bomb hit was said to have been obtained on the stern of a heavy cruiser. Ten US aircraft were destroyed by AA fire during the day.

62. Cruiser and Destroyer Sweep for 'Cripples', p.m., October 25. Sinking of the *Chiyoda*

In the course of the day's air attacks it became evident to Rear-Admiral Sherman that there might be several crippled Japanese ships which could best be finished off by ships' gunfire or torpedoes after dark, and at 1340 he asked Vice-Admiral Mitscher's permission to organize such a cruiser and destroyer attack. CTF 38 agreed, but warned him that he wanted to take the force out without having to tow damaged ships, and that faced with two enemy battleships this might be difficult. Rear-Admiral L. T. du Bose, Commander of Task Unit 38.3.3. and Com CruDiv 13, and temporarily in charge of the two light cruisers *Santa Fe* (flagship) and *Mobile* and two heavy cruisers *Wichita* (flagship of Rear-Admiral C. T. Joy) and *New Orleans* and the ten destroyers *Bagley*, *Knapp*, *Caperton*, *Cogswell*, *Ingersoll*, *Dortch*, *Healy*, *C. K. Bronson*, *Cotten* and *Patterson* of Task Group 38.3 and 38.4, which were all that remained from Task Force 34 after Admiral Halsey took the battleships south. Rear-Admiral du Bose, with his four cruisers in single line ahead and destroyers disposed as anti-submarine screen, had been ordered at 1253 to take station ahead of Task Group 38.3, the more northerly of the two carrier groups for his force was to form a special striking group. This proceeding had to await Rear-Admiral Sherman's next flight manoeuvre and in actual fact Rear-Admiral du Bose never reached his station or reported to CTG 38.3 for duty. He was now warned to be prepared if directed, to make a night torpedo attack on any worthwhile targets after dark. Rear-Admiral Sherman was instructed to reinforce him with two destroyers, and the *Essex* was to provide two reconnaissance aircraft.[11]

Orders to go in and attack the crippled group came at 1415, and accordingly the striking group proceeded on course 000° at 25 knots, Rear-Admiral Sherman providing a combat air patrol, whilst the cruisers' own aircraft were launched for search and possible rescue of ditched pilots. Vice-Admiral Mitscher had just received information, which he passed on at 1412, that an unconfirmed report stated the enemy battleship and one destroyer were quitting the southern group, which, if correct left one damaged carrier and two light cruisers in this group. The enemy were reported bearing 010°, 61 miles.

About 1510 the force reached the locality of the forenoon strikes, and the *Santa Fe* twice stopped to pick up airmen. The cruisers now launched aircraft to search the area for survivors and the destroyers were spread.

At 1610 a *Lexington* aircraft reported that a damaged light carrier (*Chiyoda*) was dead in the water 25 miles on the starboard bow. The destroyers were ordered to form two attack groups one on each quarter of the cruiser column which was apparently in the order *Santa Fe*, *Mobile*, *Wichita*, *New Orleans*. Visibility was 20 to 30 miles. There were scattered lower broken clouds, with light scattered showers.

---

11. Signal 1358. This says: 'CTU, 38.3.4 designate six destroyers to participate', but only *Callaghan* and *Porterfield* were the only destroyers which did so.

At 1612 the *Mobile* had radar contact bearing 028°, distant 31,000 yards, and three minutes later she sighted the *Chiyoda*, stopped, bearing 040°, at a range of 29,600 yards. The *Santa Fe* reported that the bearing and range were 041°, 23,000 yards when she in her turn sighted the enemy carrier at 1618.

Rear-Admiral du Bose at 1617 had ordered the heavy cruisers to open fire when ready. The *Wichita* and *New Orleans* opened at 1624. They were followed at 161 by the *Santa Fe* with her main armament, the range now being down to 14,460 yards. The *Mobile* opened fire with her main battery, using AP shell, at 1634 after requesting permission. The *Santa Fe* and *New Orleans* used no-dye-loaded projectiles, the *Mobile* orange, and the *Wichita* green. The light cruisers, at least, experienced no difficulty in spotting their own salvos, though assessment of damage inflicted by any one ship was not possible, since all four cruisers were firing simultaneously. The *Chiyoda* returned the fire, but her fall of shot, apparently of small calibre,[12] was very short, the *Mobile* observing no splash closer than 6,000 yards. At 1636, when the range was down to 12,800 yards the *Santa Fe* opened fire with her secondary battery, using AA common shell. The bearing of the enemy carrier was now 082°, and course was altered to 020°.

By 1639 the *Chiyoda* was being hit frequently and was heavily on fire, listing to port and down by the stern. ComCruDiv 13 ordered all cruisers except the *Wichita* to stop what was only target practice; his own ship had already expended no less than 281 rounds of 6-in./47 A.P. and 31 rounds of 5-in./38 AA common and the *Mobile* 294 rounds of 6-in. A.P. The destroyers on the starboard hand were ordered to close the target and torpedo her if necessary, but before they reached her, at 1655 she sank in 19° 08′ N., 126° 32′ E.

This was the only instance during the war in which surface craft participated in the sinking of a Japanese aircraft carrier.

63. The Night Action, p.m., 25 October

The next hour was occupied by the cruisers in recovering aircraft. This was completed at 1753, and the group then proceeded at 25 knots on course 345°; night fighters had reported the presence of enemy ships in that direction, and smoke had been sighted on the horizon on that general bearing. The destroyers *Porterfield* and *Callaghan*, sent by Rear-Admiral Sherman, had just joined and ComDesRon 55 – Captain C. R. Todd in the *Porterfield* – became

---

12. The *Santa Fe* said the splashes appeared to be 3-in. or 4-in., while the *Mobile* estimates one dual-purpose 5-in. gun.

officer of destroyers and formed four attack groups of three destroyers each, which were stationed astern of the cruiser column.

Just before sunset, which was at 1804, one of the aircraft sent in a report showing that the enemy were very strung out, no less than six or seven ships lagging astern of the main group. All were proceeding on a northerly course, at various speeds.

At 1813 two night fighter aircraft sent from the *Essex* reported on station and ready for duty. Sent on ahead by Rear-Admiral du Bose they reported at 1825 one enemy light cruiser or heavy cruiser and two destroyers bearing 335° distant 22 miles. At 1835 the *Santa Fe* made surface contact at 351°, 17 miles. The *Wichita* and *Mobile* reported the same contact two minutes later.

At 1811 ComCruDiv 13 altered course to 030° and after a short period of plotting, the enemy ships were identified as three in number, thought to be a light cruiser and two destroyers, stopped and engaged either in effecting repairs or picking up survivors. Probably they were the three destroyers *Hatsutsuki*, *Wakatsuki*, and *Kuwa*, engaged in rescuing the survivors of the *Zuikaku*.

Course was altered to 050° at 1851 and ships were ordered to open fire as soon as they were within range, the light cruisers on the near targets, the heavy cruisers on the far target. The *Mobile*, *Wichita* and *New Orleans* opened fire almost simultaneously at 1852. The *Mobile* took the nearest target, bearing 330°, range 18,870 yards. The *Wichita* and New Orleans opened up on the far target of the three. The *Santa Fe* opened fire at 1905 on the nearest target, bearing 348°, range 16,950 yards, target course 110°, speed 30 knots. All ships used full radar controlled blind fire up to the last four minutes of the engagement when the target was illuminated by starshells. The two smallest and most distant of the three targets (the *Wakatsuki* and *Kuwa*) made off to the northward shortly after fire was opened, and by 1905 were out of range.[13] At 1906 the *Wichita* obtained permission to shift to the nearest target, the *Hatutsuki*, whose range was 17,000 yards. The latter manoeuvred at varying speeds up to 26 knots, constantly and effectively, to throw off the gunfire. She returned the fire intermittently but none of the American ships was hit. Smoke was also employed for concealment and, apparently, to simulate damage. The spotting problem was complicated, on account of the great number of slashes near the target, particularly after the *Wichita* joined in until fire was checked at 1918. The *Mobile* changed from armour-piercing shell to high capacity and back to armour-piercing again between 1852 and 1907. The *Santa Fe* fired red

---

13. *Mobile's* track chart shows them falling from the screen at 1916 and 1919 respectively.

armour-piercing shell with her main battery and anti-aircraft common with her secondary battery, throughout the action.

It was, no doubt, as the result of Vice-Admiral Mitscher's warning to Rear-Admiral du Bose, against allowing any of his ships to become immobilized by battle damage, that the lone Japanese ship was able for a period to call the tune against her formidable antagonists. It must by then have been dark, and the American ships were still firing in full radar control. At 1904 the enemy commenced a turn towards them, the range being about 18,500 yards. The manoeuvre was apparently recognized on the plot two minutes later, for ComCruDiv 13 who had been steering 330° since 1902 altered course successively through 060° (1906) and 080° (1911) until at 1916 he was running directly from the enemy on course 120°, in order to avoid possible torpedo attack.

Meanwhile, despite the stupendous number of shells which had been fired (the *Santa Fe* alone expending 892 rounds of 6-in. and 5-in, between 1905 and 1918) the enemy, though on fire, was still steaming at 20 knots. At 1915 on the suggestion of ComCruDiv 13 ComDesDiv 100, Captain W. J. Miller in the *Cogswell*, with the two ships of his section, *Ingersoll* and *Caperton*, steamed out to make a torpedo attack. The enemy ship had made a radical turn to the northward two minutes before, and the impracticability of the destroyers attacking from the position in which they were soon recognized and ComDesRon 55, Captain C. R. Todd in the *Porterfield*, was permitted to recall them.

About 1918 both the American light cruisers checked fire, apparently without orders from ComCruDiv 13, who however, in general maintained a firm hold over his ships' gunfire. From now onwards firing was intermittent. Rear-Admiral du Bose turned back to course 030° at 1922. About this time the enemy, still steaming at 20 knots, made another short turn towards him, which was recognized at 1927, and he again steered to open the range. However, by 1930 the Japanese ship was on a northerly course once more, though with her speed a quarter of an hour later reduced to 17 knots.

At 1932 ComCruDiv 13 ordered the *Cogswell*'s section of destroyers to attempt another torpedo attack on the enemy, whilst the light cruisers covered them with slow fire. At 2012 the destroyers reached a position some 5,500 yards directly astern of the enemy ship, which after slowing until almost stopped had by now picked up speed and was once again proceeding about 20 knots. From this position the American destroyers fired half salvos of torpedoes and thereupon opened fire with their guns, which was returned.

At 2043, when the range was '6850 yards' the Santa Fe commenced firing starshells to illuminate the target which was still fighting back, though with the short range and flat trajectory it was obvious that the end was near. At 2047, with the range down to '4380 yards' Rear-Admiral du Bose ordered all ships to cease fire and a destroyer to finish off the enemy with a torpedo: but at 2056, before this could be done the Japanese vessel, burning furiously, sank to the accompaniment of six very heavy underwater explosions. She had been literally punched to pieces, and her type was not satisfactorily determined at the time, though she was thought to be a light cruiser or a *Terutsuki* class destroyer. She was the destroyer *Hatsutsuki*.

44. Sinking of the *Tama* by Submarine

At 2105 *Essex*'s night fighters reported that the nearest contact to the north bore 005°, 42 miles, on course 000° speed 20 knots and that there were no other contacts in the area 50 miles north-east to 50 miles north-west. Rear-Admiral du Bose considered the enemy were too far away to be caught. His ships were low on fuel, and he gave orders to form cruising disposition and set course at 25 knots to re-join the carrier groups. The force had fired 4,175 rounds of 5in., 6-in, and 8-in. ammunition in these two engagements.

Vice-Admiral Ozawa had meanwhile lost one more of his ships, the light cruiser *Tama*, sunk on the evening of 25th by submarine.

At 1509 on 25th, Commander Submarines Pacific had informed his submarines of the engagement in progress and ordered two 'wolf packs' of three submarines each to patrol on the probable line of retirement of the enemy. Of the first pack, composed of the *Haddock*, *Tuna* and *Halibut*, the first named at 1844 fired six electric torpedoes at a battleship screened on either side by a destroyer, at a range of 4,000 yards, the position of the attack being about 15 miles to the eastward of the ship sunk by Rear-Admiral du Bose at 2056. The attack apparently failed.

The second attack was delivered against the light cruiser *Tama* which had been damaged at 2301 early in the day and ordered to proceed to Okinawa unescorted. The *Jallao*, which was operating with the *Atule* and *Pintado*, fired three electric torpedoes at the *Tama* from the bow tubes at a range of about 1,200 yards. All three missed, but four stern tubes fired at a range of about 700 yards secured three hits, and the cruiser was seen to break up and sink by the *Pintado*, who had arrived on the scene. The position was about 60 miles to the northward of the *Haddock*'s attack.

Of the 17 ships of the Mobile Force that sailed from the Inland Sea on 20 October there remained with Vice-Admiral Ozawa only the light cruiser *Oyodo*, the two battleship carriers *Hyuga* and *Ise*, and the destroyer *Shimotsuki*. Nevertheless, he was still game: and when at 1915 he received a report from the destroyer *Hatsutsuki* and light cruiser *Isudzu*, who had been assigned to rescue the survivors of the *Zuikaku* and *Chiyoda*, that they were engaging enemy ships at 1905 and 1910, he turned 16 points (1930) and proceeded to their assistance at 16 knots. No reply was received to a request for the position of the *Hatsutsuki*; and after searching until about midnight without making contact with either friend or foe the Vice-Admiral turned northward once more. The *Wakatsuki* rejoined about this time and made her report of the attack by Rear-Admiral du Bose, who was credited with a force of two apparent battleships, two large cruisers and about one flotilla of destroyers. Of the *Hatsutsuki* nothing more was heard, and the fate of the *Tama* was also unknown to the Japanese. The destroyers *Sugi* and *Kiri* had also become separated from the main body during rescue work; failing to make communication and being short of fuel they proceeded to Takao, where they arrived at 0930 on 26th, and returned to Kure via Oshima on 30th.

This day's work had cost the Japanese four out of their existing total of seven carriers. Nevertheless, Vice-Admiral Ozawa had duly carried out his part of the complicated plan of operations and had enticed Admiral Halsey away to the north for sufficiently long to prevent interference with the Centre Force. But the carriers had been sacrificed in vain, for at the eleventh hour – literally – Vice-Admiral Kurita's heart failed him, he abandoned the plan, and the fate of the Philippines was decided.

Chapter IX

Pursuit of the Japanese Cenre Force, 25–27 October

65. Sinking of the *Suzuya*, 25 October

After abandoning the chase of the Seventh Fleet escort carriers off Samar Vice-Admiral Kurita spent some two hours in assembling his ships, appreciating the situation including fuel, and preparing for action in the Gulf. For the next two days he was to be subjected during daylight to constant air attacks by the Third and Seventh Fleets and Army aircraft, and to submarine attack, losing two heavy cruisers, two light cruisers and four destroyers, though his fleet was saved from complete destruction through the inability of Admiral Halsey's fast battleships to come up with it after their return south, on the morning of 25th, from supporting the Third Fleet carriers in their attacks on the enemy Northern Force.

Rear-Admiral Stump continued his attacks, launching his third strike at 0935. The *Haruna*, who had been ordered to attack him, was too close for him to risk turning into the wind which now was from 049°, 7 knots, but he successfully launched his strike, 12 torpedo aircraft, one with a torpedo, the remainder with tour 500-1b. SAP bombs each, and eight fighters, without casualty, whilst holding to his course of 120°. The strike immediately threw its weight against the enemy and reported three bomb hits on the previously twice-torpedoed heavy cruisers. One of these was sighted with destroyers attending her, by survivors of the *Gambier Bay* whilst in the water, and by an aircraft from the *Kitkun Bay*, which after being launched at 0700 landed about 1000 on board the Manila Bay and was launched again about an hour later after refuelling and reloading. At this time, the enemy cruiser had a bad list to port and her main deck was awash, and a destroyer was picking up survivors.

A fourth Japanese heavy cruiser, the *Suzuya*, was also now in trouble. Her movements from the time she left the formation at 0745, to stand by the torpedoed *Kumano*, are unknown, but she was damaged, apparently by air attack, and sank early in the afternoon when the fire aboard her got out of control and exploded her torpedoes.

Close by the sinking heavy cruiser was another large unidentified vessel, thought by some of the survivors and by aircraft pilots to be a battleship or smaller. She was stopped, but towards dark she got under way and made off to the northward. Her position was given by aircraft as approximately 40 miles 350° from Task Unit 77.4.2 at about 1130.

66. Communication Failure Wrecks the Japanese Plan

The skilful handling of Rear-Admiral C.A.F. Sprague's force, the selfless devotion of his aircraft and of his screening destroyers and destroyer escorts and the timely support of Rear-Admiral Stump had resulted in the sinking of three Japanese heavy cruisers and driving a fourth damaged from the scene. Apart, however, from one or more hits on the light cruiser *Yahagi*, which did not affect her speed and manoeuvrability, this was the extent of the damage to Vice-Admiral Kurita's force in the morning's fighting. On the credit side was the (quite unfounded) report from the Japanese 10th Destroyer Flotilla after the latter made its attack between 0900 and 0925, that three or four of the American carriers were seriously damaged or sinking: in all, the Japanese Second Fleet considered it had sunk these three or four carriers, two heavy cruisers, and some destroyers.

Nevertheless, the situation in which Vice-Admiral Kurita found himself called for resolution and clear judgment.

He had reason to believe that the American carrier aircraft, after attacking his fleet, were landing on Leyte to rearm and refuel. Whether, in addition, American land-based aircraft were also stationed on Leyte he did not know. He suspected the presence of another carrier force in the neighbourhood, for he had sighted the masts of one or more ships to the south-eastward and had despatched the *Haruna* to attack them at 0905. These were part of Rear-Admiral Stump's escort carrier Task Unit 77.4.2 though Kurita could not hazard a guess as to what they were, for he had not even identified the ships he had been chasing for over two hours this morning. His ignorance of the locations of the American forces in general was profound. He was dependent for enemy intelligence on the Combined Base Air Force at Manila, but the weather on the 23rd, 24th and 25th was bad, the Navy's land-based scouting force was at its lowest level at the time, and the aircraft were only able to cover small sections of the area. Although each task group of the American Third Fleet was reconnected by Japanese aircraft during the 24th the only intelligence which reached Vice-Admiral Kurita was that the American carriers were east of Luzon in about 17° 30′ N., 125° 30′ E. Since then, he had had no news of Admiral Halsey's force. He knew, however, from intercepted signals, that American forces, both surface and air, were concentrating to attack him off Leyte. He expected no assistance or cover from the Japanese naval land-based air fleet, most of which, he thought, was in Luzon, assigned for action in the north as circumstances might require, and he knew nothing of the air attack which had just been made by Japanese land-based aircraft on the survivors of the force with which he had been in action this morning, in fact, at 1150, an hour after the *St. Lo* was hit he made a signal to the Commanders-in-Chief of the First Air Fleet and Southwest Area Fleet, ordering them to attack. Altogether, he expected that his entry into Leyte Gulf would bring upon him heavy air attacks.

He was badly behind on his schedule. Under the revised plan, when Vice Admiral Nishimura advanced his time of arrival at Leyte by four hours, he should have been in the Gulf about 0700 (three or four hours earlier than 1100 of the original plan), whereas it was now well on in the forenoon and he was still some 50 or 60 miles from the entrance. On the other hand, Vice-Admiral Nishimura had reported that he was delayed: he had duly reported the air attack made upon him in the Sulu Sea on the morning of the 24th, the torpedo at attack in the early hours of the 25th in the approaches to Surigao Strait, and had sent a further message shortly after, saying that he would be delayed in entering the Gulf.[1]

It is not known at what time Vice-Admiral Kurita learned of the failure of the mission of the Southern Force, which he did through a brief message giving no details: it was clear that the Southern Force had suffered severely, but Vice-Admiral Kurita did not know where the disaster had occurred, and the news did not influence the important decision he was about to make.[2]

Of the Japanese carrier force in the north there had also been no news at all since the general report on the 24th that their aircraft had attacked and that some had landed in the water and others in Luzon; and Vice-Admiral Kurita was completely in the dark regarding the disastrous situation now developing in the north.

---

1. *Interrogation No. (U.S.S.B.S. No.47) Nav. No. 9*, pp. 47–24, of Kurita's Staff Officer, Operations (Commander T. Otano), states: 'We received a message from Admiral Nishimura that they were going to make their approach about 2 o'clock in the morning of the 25th although the plan was ... that they would approach one hour before daybreak on the 25th at the earliest ... We received this message late in the afternoon of the 24th at which time it was too late to order him to conform to the original plan.'
2. Vice-Admiral Kurita's Chief of Staff states the exact opposite to Kurita, namely, that one of the most important reasons for abandoning the plan to enter Leyte Gulf was that the 2nd Diversion Attack Force reported the almost complete destruction of Vice-Admiral Nishimura's force, though he could not remember at what time the message was received. His Staff Officer (Operations) says the news was received before 0400, and he reinforces his statement by saying that when they sighted Rear-Admiral C. A. F. Sprague's force off Samar, some of the men thought that it was a Japanese force; however, he knew that it could not be so, because he had received the report of the fate of Nishimura's force. This seems unlikely, however, since Kurita at 0702 ordered Nishimura to join him. The Japanese account gives as one of the reasons for abandoning the plan, the possibility, in view of what had happened to Nishimura's and Shima's forces, of falling into a trap if the intention to enter Leyte Gulf were persisted in (*The Campaigns of the Pacific War*, p. 304).

The *Yamato* sent up two reconnaissance aircraft, but neither of them brought any information: the aircraft which went north reported it had seen nothing; from the other, despatched over the Surigao Strait area, there came no word. Both aircraft landed ashore and neither returned to the flagship. This left Kurita without information as to the American forces in the Gulf. On leaving Brunei he had estimated that there were about 200 transports there together with a balanced fleet containing some seven battleships. Air coverage of the Leyte area was assigned to the seaplanes of the fleet which had been landed a day or two before the operation commenced and were based at San Jose, in south-west Mindoro. But the weather was bad, the range of the seaplanes was small, and they sent no information.

67. Vice-Admiral Kurita turns North, 1236, 25 October.

At 1236 Vice-Admiral Kurita took a "momentary" and far-reaching decision. On his own responsibility he abandoned the plan to enter Leyte Gulf and altered course to the north. By this time, the American landing at Leyte had been confirmed and to his mind it was now less important than before to attack the transports and invasion shipping moreover, it was thought that the transports would by now have heard of the battle and would have begun to disperse out of the danger zone. Ignorant as he was of the situation in the north Vice-Admiral Kurita could form no clear plan other than to bring Admiral Halsey's Task Force to action if he could happen upon them. 'The conclusion from our gunfire and anti-aircraft fire during the day', he states, 'had led me to believe in my uselessness, my ineffectual position, if I proceeded into Leyte Bay where I would come under even heavier aircraft attack. I therefore concluded to go north and join Admiral Ozawa for co-ordinated action against your Northern Task Forces ... It wasn't a question of destruction, that was neither here nor there. It was a question of what good I could do in the Bay [Leyte Gulf]. I concluded that under the heavy attack from ship and shore based planes, I could not be effective. Therefore, on my own decision I concluded it was best to go north and join Admiral Ozawa.'[3]

---

3. Vice-Admiral Kurita also stated: 'I sent a report to Admiral Ozawa that I had turned north and would be able to co-ordinate my attack with the night destroyer attack which I learned Admiral Ozawa was going to make, which I had learned from other sources ... sometime during the day – do not remember when ... I do not know the source.' Captain Ohmae, Chief of Staff to Vice-Admiral Ozawa, says that Vice-Admiral Kurita in his interrogation confused the times and that the message of which he spoke must have been that sent by Vice-Admiral Ozawa after [Rear-Admiral du Boses'] attack on a destroyer of the Northern Force at 1730 [actually at 1852, see Section 63] saying that he intended to attack Admiral Halsey's force by night, and that since Vice-Admiral Kurita could not have received this message until he was again approaching San Bernardino Strait, it could not have influenced his decisions.

And, almost in the same breath: 'My intention was not primarily to join Admiral Ozawa but to go north and seek out the enemy. I considered [it] my mission to go north and seek out your carrier task force and bring it under engagement with the assumption that Admiral Ozawa to the north would thereby be assisted by it. But it was not to join forces with Admiral Ozawa ... The immediate object was to hit the enemy.'

Somewhere to the north of him there was, or had been yesterday, an American task force. He hoped that it was now hurrying south to help the ships he had been engaging this morning and that he would meet it on the way in the open sea where his battleships would have liberty of manoeuvre under air attack.

Had Vice-Admiral Kurita but known, when on his own responsibility he abandoned the carefully prepared plan, he could have entered Leyte Gulf opposed by no more than battleships short of ammunition and destroyers short of torpedoes; and with immunity from air attack by Admiral Halsey's carriers other than the one group under Vice-Admiral McCain which, as yet of course, unknown to him, just half an hour ago had launched at his force from the great range of 300 miles, a strike whose effect would have been diminished by every mile of westing. For with the exception of Vice-Admiral McCain's Task Group, 38.1, all Admiral Halsey's fast carriers had been engaged since 0840 on this day in attacking the Japanese Northern Force, which had brilliantly fulfilled its function of drawing off the Third Fleet to the northward. But it was not until after he abandoned the attack on Leyte, that Kurita learned of the engagement, and even then he knew no more than that the *Zuikaku* had been damaged and the Admiral was shifting his flag. Vice-Admiral Ozawa's flagship, the *Zuikaku*, reported the attacks; the wireless station at Formosa got part of the messages; but neither Tokyo nor the Japanese Second Fleet heard anything, and it was not until later that it was discovered that the fault lay in the flagship's wireless transmitter. On this small mechanical failure, a great enterprise finally foundered.

68. Rear-Admiral Stump continues his Air Attacks

Vice-Admiral Kurita had not expected that by going north he would escape air attacks, but he considered his force would be better able to meet them in the open sea than in the narrow waters of Leyte Gulf, and he might, also, by co-ordination be of use to Vice-Admiral Ozawa.

Attack was not long in coming. At 1115 Rear-Admiral Stump launched his fourth strike, a large one consisting of 19 fighters and 37 torpedo aircraft, of which 11 carried torpedoes and the remainder SAP and GP bombs. The main body of the enemy's force was found in 11° 43′ N., 126° 13′ E., some 30 miles north-west of the crippled battleship and cruiser. Pilots reported its course to be 225° but CTU 77.4.2 thought it possible that it was engaged in evasive manoeuvres which prevented the air crews from estimating correctly the mean course. The attack was directed against the undamaged main body and one torpedo hit (on a battleship), several bomb hits, and strafing of destroyers were claimed. By the time the fifth strike, airborne at 1331, was over the enemy a destroyer (possibly the *Nowake*) in similar condition, was reported with the crippled battleship and heavy cruiser. Both this strike and the sixth and last, whose launch commenced at 1508, had no heavier loading than G.P. bombs and rockets, all available SAP bombs and torpedoes having been expended; and the last strike, which like No. 5 must have been primarily harassing, as directed against the light forces. Pilots of earlier strikes, including some of the returning aircraft of Vice-Admiral McCain's Task Group 38.1 which were taken aboard Task Unit 77.4.2, short of fuel, reported that at 1420 the main Japanese force was in 12° 05′ N., 125° 45′ E. on a northerly course. One cruiser (possibly the *Kumano*), was reported lagging astern, damaged, and from this time on, no more than three heavy cruisers were seen in company with the main body, though the battleship crippled by Rear-Admiral Stump's first two strikes in the morning, would appear to have joined by 1723/25 when his sixth and last strike of the day reported that the force appeared to consist of four battleships, three heavy cruisers, two light cruisers and seven destroyers, with two of the battleships trailing oil and seemingly in trouble, one of the light cruisers lagging astern, and one heavy cruiser apparently damaged.

69. An American Message Miscarries

Early in the afternoon the air attacks of the escort carriers were reinforced by massive strikes from Task Group 38.1 of the Third Fleet, though their possible effect was greatly reduced through an unfortunate failure of communication between the task group and the commander Seventh Fleet which necessitated arming the torpedo aircraft with the inferior weapon bombs.

When Vice-Admiral McCain, CTG 38.1 learned of the attack on Rear-Admiral C.A.F. Sprague's escort carriers off Samar on the morning of 25 October, through intercepting CTF 77's message to Commander Third Fleet at 0725, his five carriers, *Wasp* (flagship), *Hornet*, *Hancock*, *Cowpens*, and *Monterey* were fuelling in 15° N., 130° E., about 357 miles ENE of San Bernardino Strait. In accordance with Admiral Halsey's instructions he had launched searches at dawn covering a 400 miles area between 300° and 020°.

At 1900 he heard of the attack by aircraft of Groups 38.2 and 38.3 on the enemy Northern Force. By now, all but two of his ships, the carrier *Hancock* and heavy cruiser *Boston* had completed fuelling. Directing them to cast off from the tankers, he cancelled further searches to the north and ordered a strike to be prepared against the Northern Force.

It is said that at 0848 the Commander Third Fleet sent Vice-Admiral McCain orders to strike the enemy force attacking the Seventh Fleet escort carriers off Samar and to make best speed towards the Leyte area but these orders, if they ever reached CTG 38.1, had not been received by 0930[4] when the Commander Third Fleet reported the enemy carriers retiring to the northwards and ordered TG 38.1 to 'strike as practicable',[5] the intended target being these carriers. Ten minutes later, however, came Vice-Admiral Kinkaid's call for battleships to proceed at top speed to cover Leyte and asking for a fast carrier strike. 'There was an ominous tone in the frantic calls for assistance from the Seventh Fleet units under attack', writes the Captain of the *Hornet* and Vice-Admiral McCain reacted at once. Anticipating fresh instructions (which duly arrived at 1001) from CTG 38, his Task Group commander, Vice-Admiral Mitscher, ordering him to launch the earliest possible strike, he immediately altered course to 245° and increased speed to 30 knots to support the escort carriers under attack. This speed task group maintained for five hours. Computations showed that the distance to the target was too great for the torpedo aircraft to carry torpedoes and return without refuelling and CTG 30.1 therefore sent a message to Vice-Admiral Kinkaid, asking whether aircraft could land on Tacloban airfield on Leyte. No reply was received, consequently the torpedo aircraft had to be loaded with bombs. By this time the enemy was in full retreat, and the situation called for the maximum effort to be directed against his battleships, in an attempt to slow them until the Third Fleet could complete their destruction. But the bombs with which the torpedo aircraft had perforce to be armed, were of little effect against battleships. This was the more unfortunate because, had Vice-

---

4. There is no mention of the receipt of these orders in Vice-Admiral McCain's Report, nor in the report of his flagship, the *Wasp*. No reports are forthcoming from any other ships of the task group. The statement in Cincpac, *Report*, p. 18, viz: 'Task Group 38.1 was fuelling when the order to proceed to the support of Task Group 77.4 arrived, but when this was completed at 0940, the group headed on course 245° at 30 knots', is not borne out by Vice-Admiral McCain, who states that he stopped fuelling at 0900; his report makes it clear that he proceeded to help Task Group 77.4 on his own initiative, without orders from either Commander Third Fleet or his Task Force Commander (CTF 38). The only orders to proceed to assist Task Group 77.4 which are mentioned in Vice-Admiral McCain's Report are those received at 1001 from CTF 38. Admiral Haley's Despatch covering this period is not forthcoming.

5. It is not known why orders were sent to Vice-Admiral McCain at 0848 to assist the escort carriers off Samar and at 0930 to attack the Japanese Northern Force, although the situation had not changed in the meantime as far as Admiral Halsey could have known.

Admiral McCain but known, a portion of Tacloban airfield was serviceable and was actually used by many both of his own distressed aircraft and those of the escort carriers, after completing their strikes.

70. Task Group 38.1 Strikes 1300, 25 October

A hundred aircraft – 48 fighters, 33 bombers and 19 torpedo aircraft – composed the first strike, launched at 1030 at a range of 300 miles, the limit of the torpedo and bomber aircraft range with bomb load, with a small chance of survival unless the target could be located promptly and conditions were favourable for recovery. The flight was picked up by Rear-Admiral Stump's (CTU 77.4.2) radar and at 1255 was vectored by his flagship, the *Natoma Bay*, until the flight leader 'tallyhoed' the main enemy force at 1302. The main force at this time was reported by aircraft to be in approximate latitude 12° N. some 15 miles off Samar Island, heading on a course 330°, speed 25 knots, towards San Bernardino Strait.

At 1255 Vice-Admiral McCain launched his second and last strike of the day. As there was still no indication whether aircraft could land at Tacloban he was led to assume that the Japanese had control of the air over the airfield or else that it was not operational, and accordingly he instructed his carriers to rig wing tanks on all bomber and torpedo aircraft of this strike also and to load with bombs instead of torpedoes. The returning aircraft landed aboard the carriers between 1530 and 1600. In all, the air groups of Task Group 38.1 placed 177 aircraft over the Japanese Centre Force in these two strikes, the only two undertaken. An aggregate of 65 tons of bombs was dropped and 64 rockets fired; several hits were recorded.[6] The Americans lost eight aircraft – two bombers on take-off, one fighter missing, three bombers shot down, two torpedo aircraft landed in the water short of fuel; but some of the air crews were saved.

71. The Centre Force retreats through San Bernardino Strait, Sunset, 25 October.

None of the many air attacks on the Japanese Centre Force as it steered north – the *Yamato* sustained 11 – caused serious damage. Ships' bulges were perforated and all the heavy ships were trailing oil, but all of them could

---

6. 4 ½-ton bomb hits on *Yamato* (battleship), 4 ¼-ton on a *Kongo* battleship, 1½-ton and 1¼-ton on *Nagato* (battleship), as well as 3 rocket hits, 4¼-ton and 1½-ton on unidentified battleships, 2¼-ton on one *Nachi* (heavy cruiser) and 1½-ton on the other *Nachi*, 1¼-ton on a *Tone* heavy cruiser, 1½-ton and 4¼-ton on an unidentified heavy cruiser, 3¼-ton on the *Noshiro* (light cruiser), 1¼-ton on each of four destroyers; one Zeke was shot down. Cincpac, *Report*, p. 98 gives only one bomb hit on a *Nagato*.

maintain 20 knots, increasing to 24 when aircraft appeared; and all were battleworthy.

Although he was proceeding north, Vice-Admiral Kurita was not prepared to prejudice his chances of retreat. One thought was clearly over-riding – that he must be at San Bernardino at sunset so as to get through the Strait and as far west as possible during the night. Two tankers awaited him in the Sulu Sea and a third was stationed at Koron in the Mindanao Strait. Now that he had abandoned the decision to enter Leyte Gulf with its line of retirement through Surigao Strait, the necessity for replenishing his fuel supply before returning to Brunei chained him to the San Bernardino Strait. Had he been able to attack the invasion forces the question of fuel would have been disregarded but matters now were different.[7]

His situation had not improved. During his run north he had received information that Vice-Admiral Nishimura had met with disaster. The messages were very short and gave no details; the source, apparently a destroyer, had not actually seen the battle but had sighted fires.[8]

Admiral Toyoda sent no orders.

From some source, though not from Vice-Admiral Ozawa himself, he had heard that the latter had become heavily engaged and the flagship was damaged, and the flag was going to be shifted to another ship;[9] though information of the extent of the damage to the Northern Force was not vouchsafed to him. He hoped that as the result of this engagement and the calls for help from the force he had been chasing this morning he would find an American force in his path before he reached 13° 20′ N., the critical latitude from which he did not wish to stray too far northward and prejudice his passage of the San Bernardino Strait at dark, unless he could before sunset find and attack the enemy, when he would cease to consider his own retreat.

As regards fighting trim he was fairly well placed, though his losses had been severe. His ships were low on fuel but had sufficient ammunition left to fight a fleet action.[10] Of his five battleships he had lost one of the two most

---

7. With regard to entering Leyte Gulf he said: 'There was no consideration for fuel. There was no consideration for how to get home.'

8. Vice-Admiral Kurita stated that he did not hear the result of the Battle of Surigan Strait until about 11 o'clock of the following day, but it seems clear that 'the following day' refers to the 25th and that he must have received the news very soon after his turn north on 25th.

9. The time of receipt of this message is not given. Captain Ohmae, Chief of Staff to Vice-Admiral Ozawa, stated that they changed flagships from the *Zuikaku* to the *Oyodo* about 1000, after the first attack, but it seems clear that Vice-Admiral Kurita did not receive the message until he was proceeding north although he could not remember at what time he received it. He makes some observations on time lag in the passage of messages. The defect in the *Zuikaku*'s wireless, which was not discovered until 'later', must also be borne in mind.

10. N.L.D., pp. 47–17.

powerful, the *Musashi*, sunk by air attack on the 24th, but of the nine heavy cruisers which left Brunei Bay with his fleet there remained with him only one, the *Haguro*.

His hopes of meeting an American force were raised by sighting, in latitude about 12° 30' N., a Japanese aircraft flying over; but they were not fulfilled, and consequently he rounded Cape Espiritu Santo and entered San Bernardino Strait.[11] He passed through the Strait at 2130.

72. Two Fast Battleships Sent in Pursuit

Vice-Admiral MeCain launched no more strikes on 25th. At 11357 Admiral Halsey ordered him to rendezvous at 0600 next day in 12° N. 126° E. with Task Group 38.2, consisting of the three carriers and eight destroyers,[12] under Rear-Admiral Bogan which had come south with the bulk of the Heavy Striking Force when Admiral Halsey, influenced either by the calls for help of the escort carriers off Samar or having decided that he could leave the destruction of the enemy Northern Force to the carriers and light forces of Task Groups 38.3 and 38.4, turned south at 1115 on the 25th.

After the turn south, Admiral Halsey proceeded at 20 knots until 1345 when the destroyers commenced fuelling from the battleships and carries, completing at 1621.[13] His two fastest battleships, the *New Jersey* (his own flagship) and the *Iowa*, three light cruisers, the *Vincennes*, *Miami* and *Biloxi*, and Destroyer Squadron 52 he now (1620/25) formed into a special Task

---

11. *Secret Information Bulletin, No. 22*. Composite Plot, pp. 78–28. It was stated by Captain Fuchida, Air Staff Officer to the C-in-C Combined Fleet that 'Kurita's retreat was on orders from Toyoda' (N.I.D., p. 113-10). There is no support whatever for this statement in Vice-Admiral Kurita's interrogation, though Captain Ohmae, Chief of Staff to Vice-Admiral Ozawa, states that Admiral Toyoda 'gave the general orders to attack and return' *in an operation like this*, but he does not specify that he did so in the present operation and the weight of evidence is against it (N.I.D., p. 36–9). Commander Otano, Staff Officer (Operations) in the Second Fleet stated that Vice-Admiral Kurita's decision to turn west through San Bernardino Strait was determined by a despatch received from Vice-Admiral Ozawa about 1700 for assistance against the Third Fleet in the north but Kurita decided to retreat because his fuel was running low and he did not consider his force to be ready for a night action on account of damage received during the day (N.I.D., pp. 170–7). Ozawa denied ever asking Kurita for help, but he stated that at about dusk on the 25th he informed the Second Fleet he was turning back to support of his destroyers which was being attacked by gunfire by American forces. When he came to the scene he did not see any American forces, though the destroyer was there carrying out rescue work: accordingly he reversed his course and went north again. It seems probable that this message was indeed the determining factor in Kurita's decision: since he knew nothing of Admiral Haley's return south he would now believe himself to be faced, at this late hour of day, with a run of over 400 miles before meeting the American Third Fleet.
12. *Intrepid*, carrier (flagship), *Cabot*, light carrier, *Independence*, light carrier, Destroyer Squadron 53 less *Benham*.
13. Viz. Task Force 34 less the *Wichita* and *New Orleans*, light cruisers *Santa Fe* and *Mobile*, and Destroyer Squadron 50.

Group 34.5 under Rear-Admiral Badger (USS *Iowa* flagship) which increased speed to 28 knots[14] in an attempt to catch and destroy the retreating enemy before they reached the San Bernardino Strait, since it was doubtful whether Task Group 38.2 could arrive in time. His doubts were all too well founded, for it was not until 1825, half an hour after sunset, that the night carrier *Independence* was able to launch a long range search and attack.

Unfortunately, the Japanese Centre Force had re-entered San Bernardino Strait before Admiral Halsey's arrival. A sweep of the approaches was made, and thence along the coast of Samar. At 0026 on 26th an enemy straggler, on fire, was encountered and was reported to have been sunk at 0146 by destroyer and cruiser gunfire and a half salvo of torpedoes from the destroyer *Miller*, being identified as either a large destroyer or a cruiser.[15]

73. Third Fleet Air Strikes, 26 October

As instructed by the Commander Third Fleet, Vice-Admiral McCain steered during the night for the appointed rendezvous with Task Group 38.2, which was sighted at 0450 on 26th. At dawn, about an hour later, launching of Combat Air Patrol, search, and the first strike commenced, for the triple purpose of a fighter sweep of the Visayas, a search of the Philippines to the west and south-west, and a composite strike of aircraft carrying torpedoes and bombs[16] against the enemy main body, which was expected to be found near the east coast of Mindoro. Each carrier was instructed to expedite the departure of its strike, each air group moving out separately as soon as it had made rendezvous.

At 0810 the strike leader reported the enemy, consisting of four battleships, two heavy cruisers, two light cruisers and 10 destroyers[17] in Tablas Straits, 10 miles north-west of the north tip of Panay Island. The second strike was launched immediately, and a third strike of 25 aircraft was sent out at 1245. This strike, composed of B.24 aircraft armed with heavy bombs made no hits nor any appreciable damaging near misses.[18]

---

14. *USS Massachusetts, Action Report*, p. 3. *CTF 34 Action Report*, p. 11, states that Task Group 34.5 proceeded at 24 knots for San Bernardino Strait, course 195°.
15. This ship cannot be identified. The list in the Final Official Report by Fleet Admiral E.J. King, C.-in-C., U.S. Pacific Fleet and CNO makes no mention of any ship sunk by Task Group 34.5.
16. *Wasp Action Report*, p. 7. But CTG 38.1 in his *Action Report* p. 25 merely says 'the first strike with torpedo aircraft carrying torpedoes'.
17. Report of CTG 38.1 p. 25.
18. Interrogation No. *(U.S.S. B.S. No. 47) Nav. No.9* pp. 47–22.

Task Group 38.2 also launched strikes throughout the day.[19] In all, 174 aircraft reached the targets, dropping 58 tons of bombs, 45 torpedoes, and 82 rockets.[20] The light cruiser *Noshiro* was hit and immobilized by two torpedoes in the first attack and was sunk by bombs in the second attack at 0810 near Maniguin Island, off north-west Panay, in 11° 35′ N., 121° 45′ E. A few miles to the north-west, in 11° 40 'N., 121° 30′ E a destroyer was hit at 1050 with two torpedoes and a quarter ton SAP bomb, and her bows were blown off. This may have been the *Hayashimo*, which is reported to have been sunk by aircraft on this date off south-east Mindoro. Further east, the light cruiser *Kinu* and the destroyer *Uranami* was sunk on this date by carrier air attack south-west of Masbate Island, both perhaps being engaged in the reinforcement of Leyte.

Photographs showed the battleship *Yamato* hit by bombs, 10 miles off the north-west tip of Panay, and it is reported that the ship was also hit by a torpedo from one of the *Wasp*'s aircraft, but the depth setting was only 10 feet and no effect was seen. Many other hits by torpedo and bomb were reported but none of them had the effect of stopping any ship permanently.[21] The survivors scattered.

Twelve Japanese aircraft were destroyed in the air during the day's operations, in addition to others destroyed on Legaspi Airfield in the south-east of Luzon. The American aircraft losses were four fighters, two bombers and two torpedo aircraft shot down by AA and one torpedo aircraft lost operationally.

74. Air Strikes, 27 October

At dawn on 27th the *Essex* and *Lexington* of Task Group 38.3 which had now returned south launched air patrols and a search to the westward. The

---

19. The only authority for this statement is the *Action Report* of the *Massachusetts* p. 2. This report gives a good concise account of the actions in which the Third Fleet was engaged, but naturally, not all of them came under her personal observation. No reports are available from any of the carriers of Task Group 38.2.

20. These details and those of damage inflicted are based mainly on Vice-Admiral McCain's *Action Report*. He does not state, though it is presumed, that as Senior Officer he took charge of both task groups after making rendezvous at 0450/25, and that the details he gives cover the operations of both groups and not only of his own.

21. The following additional claims are also made: One seaplane tender blown up after being bombed by *Hancock* in 11° 05′ N., 123° 05′ E. (north entrance to Guimaras Strait) – this ship cannot be identified; a *Kumano* heavy cruiser seen exploding and burning fiercely after two torpedo and five half-ton bomb hits at 1030; an unidentified heavy cruiser dead in the water, hit by two torpedoes on the starboard side; the *Nagato* hit by one torpedo at the same place and time as *Yamato*; group of five destroyers attacked in 12° N, 120° 45′ E. (Mindoro Strait) at 1515 and three hit with bombs. There are also the following undated claims: 'One heavy cruiser or battleship went on alone (presumably after the first attack off North-West Panay) and was hit at 12° N., 121° E. One heavy cruiser was hit and left at 11° 55 N., 121° 40 E. and later believed sunk.' A destroyer sunk at 1100/26 in 11° 309 N., 124° E. This vessel cannot be identified, and the claim is considered to be incorrect.

search aircraft reported a damaged Japanese cruiser and two destroyers off the south tip of Mindoro, and at 0840 the *Essex* and *Lexington* launched a minor strike to sink them. The strike aircraft could not find the cruiser but bombed the destroyers and reported damaging one of them. This was perhaps the *Fujinami*, which was sunk in this position as the result of Third Fleet air attacks on 27th or the *Shiranuhi*, one of Vice-Admiral Shima's (Fifth Fleet) destroyers, which was sunk on the same day by carrier aircraft off Panay where she had gone to assist in the rescue of the crew of the light cruiser *Kinu* sunk on the previous day.

The remaining survivors of the Japanese Second Fleet, many of them damaged, made their way to Brunei Bay. The heavy ships proceeded direct; the destroyers *Isokaze* and *Yukikaze* were re-fuelled at Dangerous Ground from the *Nagato* and *Haruna* whilst the *Hamanami*, *Kishinami*, *Akishimo*, *Shimakaze* and *Urakaze* fuelled at Koron en route.

About noon Rear-Admiral Sherman sent a fighter bomber sweep over Manila to sink damaged ships reported there. Two Japanese heavy cruisers, one light cruiser and four destroyers were visually sighted in Manila on 29 October though some of these may have been the damaged ships sighted in Manila Bay on 23rd and 24th; and one damaged *Tone* class heavy cruiser was seen on November 3rd in Bacuit Bay, Palawan.

One of the three tankers which took part in the operation, that stationed at Koron escaped to the north-west after sustaining one hit in air attack. One of the two in the Sulu Sea was sunk in Balabac Strait by submarine torpedo: the other, though also damaged by submarine torpedo escaped in Paitan Bay, North Borneo (06° 45 'N., 117° 20 E.).

75. Losses of the Centre Force

Of the five battleships, 10 heavy cruisers, two light cruisers, and 15 destroyers which constituted the Japanese Centre Force when it sailed from Brunei Bay, only four battleships, five heavy cruisers and 13 destroyers succeeded in escaping from the scene of battle, most of the important units considerably damaged. Losses included the *Musashi*, one of the two most modern battleships, possibly the two greatest and most heavily armed ships afloat[22] whilst the five heavy cruisers sunk and three out of action with major damage represented more than half the enemy strength in a type of which no additional ones had been added to the fleet since the commencement of hostilities.

---

22. Displacement at full load 72,800 tons, main armament 9 3 18.1-in. guns.

Chapter X

Results Of The Battle

76. Victory – but not annihilation

Five days of co-ordinated fighting by American submarines, Allied surface vessels and American aircraft had ended in a decisive defeat of the Japanese Fleet, though not its destruction. Apart from its losses, three battleships, four carriers, 10 cruisers and eight or nine destroyers, almost every important unit was damaged to a greater or less degree, so that the fleet was crippled and henceforth became strictly auxiliary. For the Japanese naval air force, the battle spelt disaster and the beginning of the end: it became a purely defensive force relying upon a weapon of despair, the suicide bomber, which had been tried out and achieved by surprise a single initial success in sinking the escort carrier *St. Lo* on 25 October. This, with the light carrier *Princeton*, a second escort carrier (the *Gambier Bay*) two destroyers, a destroyer escort, a motor torpedo boat and a submarine, constituted the total and comparatively insignificant Allied losses in the five days' fighting.

The battle sealed the fate of the Philippines. For a few weeks their land-based aircraft continued to give the Japanese control of the air over Leyte Gulf. Under this cover they ran in a number of convoys of reinforcements which enabled resistance to be prolonged. But any serious interruption of the Allied operations was henceforth out of the question.

Nevertheless, the failure to destroy completely the Japanese fleet was to cost the Allies a vast effort in the months to come, and it was not until July of the following year that the final seal was set upon the work begun at the Battle for Leyte Gulf.

Index

INDEX OF PERSONS

INDEX OF VESSELS